RICHELIEU
AND HIS AGE
POWER POLITICS AND THE
CARDINAL'S DEATH

by Carl J. Burckhardt

RICHELIEU AND HIS AGE
I. *His Rise to Power*
II. *Assertion of Power and the Cold War*

1. Philip IV of Spain, by Velasquez

CARL J. BURCKHARDT

RICHELIEU
AND HIS AGE

VOLUME III
POWER POLITICS AND THE
CARDINAL'S DEATH

TRANSLATED FROM THE GERMAN
BY BERNARD HOY

A HELEN AND KURT WOLFF BOOK
HARCOURT BRACE JOVANOVICH, INC.
NEW YORK

Translated from the German
RICHELIEU, GROSSMACHTPOLITIK UND TOD
DES KARDINALS
© Georg D. W. Callwey, München, 1965

ISBN 0–15–177158–8

NOTE

A minimum of notes is given in this English translation.
Greater detail and a complete list of references for the quota-
tions may be found in Carl J. Burckhardt: *Richelieu*, Vol. IV
(Registerband), Munich 1967.

CONTENTS

A*

ILLUSTRATIONS

LORRAINE

Charles IV of Lorraine

The territories which originally were designated as Lotharingia, a small portion of which later became known as Lorraine, had a fateful influence in countless quarrels arising from dynastic marriages and claims of succession, and above all in the rivalry that developed between France and Germany from their very beginnings and continued throughout the centuries. In the age of Louis XIII this perpetual crisis was to reach its climax.

Charles III of Lorraine, a forceful prince, had transformed his country in many respects into a modern state. We can distinguish three periods in his long reign. During the first, which reaches to the year 1584, Lorraine kept the peace with both its powerful neighbour France and with Spain, avoiding involvement in the religious wars which tore France apart. From 1584 to 1596, Charles III took sides with the Catholic League, that is, with his cousins the Guises. In the third phase, between 1596 and 1608, he not only made peace with his opponent Henry IV, the former Huguenot, but became his personal friend, at the same time keeping on good terms with Spain.

Henry II, Charles' son and successor, was much more volatile and less sure of himself than his father. However, in his day France's paralysis caused by her civil wars still made itself felt. In his favour it may also be said that perhaps because of a certain weakness he had an undeniable intuitive gift. Of his nephew, who was forced on him as son-in-law and

13

successor, he said with an outspokenness in marked contrast to his irresolute nature: "You'll see, this blockhead will lose everything."

The prediction proved true, but it did less than justice to the latecomer on the throne of Lorraine. All the evidence we possess confirms that Charles IV was a quick-witted and intelligent prince, extremely accomplished in all physical skills, and a man of bold temperament. Observers are agreed, however, that he lacked political acumen, was inclined to hasty decisions and was unable to see any of his undertakings through to the end. His groundless confidence in his own powers as a negotiator appears curious: he never doubted his complete mastery of the art of persuasion, which in his case amounted to no more than a propensity for agreeing with every proposal advanced by the other side, with the inevitable result that he suddenly found himself in their power.

In the early years of his reign, his amiability and his fun-loving character created an atmosphere of irresistible good cheer. The members of his entourage mention his lean, aristocratic face, his perpetually raised eyebrows and the look of surprise that this lent it. He was admired for his eloquence and for his ability of assuming occasionally the role of listener. But all commentators were agreed on one point: he was always strangely excitable. He had been brought up in France among his cousins, the Guises, and had often stayed with the Duke of Chevreuse in Dampierre; his memories of his years in France were particularly dear to him.

He has been made responsible for many things, but calamity first struck long before his time, in the fourteenth year of Henry II's reign. Even then Lorraine had been unable to stem the invasion of the Thirty Years' War and prevent Mansfeld from crossing the borders of its flourishing territories. In 1621, when he was fighting for the Count Palatine, Mansfeld had invaded Alsace with the object of establishing a principality centred on Hagenau. His starving hordes, intent on plunder, wrought havoc with fire and sword wherever they passed, and introduced the plague. Although Charles III had created a regular army, Henry II had been unable to check the mercenary leader.

At the beginning of the Thirty Years' War the Duke of Lorraine had not been invited to join the German Catholic League. In 1619 and again in 1623 he himself forbade his subjects to take any part in the German war. But by the early twenties it was already clear that both he and his successors would be drawn into the maelstrom.

Henry II, Charles IV's uncle, had modelled his politics on the flexible policies of his great-grandfather, Duke Anthony; by steering a middle course he had avoided any major calamities and compensated for losses sustained by his duchy; he had even extended his borders by buying land from the Duke of Mercoeur in the west and from the Count Palatine in the east. But Charles was unskilled in the art of evasion; whenever he tried to apply it the result was a blatant and unsuccessful attempt at deception—a highly perilous undertaking *vis-à-vis* a Richelieu.

In 1626 Charles entered Nancy in state. He swore the traditional oaths and ratified the ancient liberties. He then failed to keep the oaths, disregarded the liberties and, in contrast to his predecessors but in keeping with the spirit of his times, strove to establish absolutist methods. In 1627 he dissolved the Courts of Assize in the province of Vosges, and in 1629 the Estates General were convened for the last time.

Meanwhile, in the three bishoprics of Metz, Toul and Verdun, which it regarded as its protectorates, the French government was striving to dissolve the last remaining links with the Holy Roman Empire, that is, the last remaining liberties. Although the Bishop of Metz, Henri de Bourbon-Verneuil, an illegitimate son of Henry IV of France, had sworn solemn allegiance to the Holy Roman Emperor, France had not reduced his income, which makes it obvious that he was a willing tool of French policy from the outset. France met with some initial resistance in Verdun, from Bishop François de Lorraine-

Chaligny. But the French line had hardened and Paris acted with great despatch and force. Richelieu was in power and the citadel of Verdun, on which work had first been started under the French King Henry II, and again under Henry IV, was completed. The new structure was erected on ecclesiastical territory; the bishop fought back and threatened the workmen and Gillet, the King's representative in Verdun, with excommunication. But Chaligny was far too weak to keep up the struggle and was forced to flee, first to the Court of Nancy, then to Cologne. In 1629, after the Emperor had refused him all help, Chaligny climbed down, whereupon Louis XIII, after first defeating the French Huguenots, returned his benefices to him; from then onwards he too was simply an instrument of French policy. In 1632 the Prince of Condé took over Verdun, after which even the most tenuous links with the Empire were effaced.

In the following year Louis XIII closed the old courts of justice by edict and the House of Bourbon set up a parlement, identical to the parlements in the provinces of France, to dispense justice in the cities and bishoprics of Metz, Toul and Verdun, much to the discontent of citizens and clergy, who, however, were powerless.

It was about then that Charles IV of Lorraine's grave errors in foreign policy started.

Charles was under the delusion that he might escape the ever-growing French threat by establishing contacts with the French opposition, that is, with the party of the Queen-Mother and Gaston d'Orléans. By so doing he crossed Richelieu's path in a most provocative fashion. Flashing back briefly to the period immediately preceding the fall of La Rochelle, we again meet the Duchess of Chevreuse, now a member of the House of Lorraine by marriage; she had figured in every crisis throughout western Europe along the borders of the Empire, and also played her part in this affair. Following the execution of the Count of Chalais in 1629 (cf. Vol. I, p. 207), Charles IV of Lorraine had offered asylum to his cousin, the Duchess of Chevreuse. But, even though she had fled the country, Richelieu was kept fully informed of all her activities.

The garrisons in Metz, Toul and Verdun were reinforced; Charles IV's protests, needless to say, went unheeded.

The misgivings that Henry IV of France had felt about Lorraine as a source of potential danger proved more than ever justified. No sooner had she arrived in Nancy than Marie de Rohan-Chevreuse set up a network of political intrigue that had far-reaching implications. The scene in which she was then appearing, the Court of Lorraine in Nancy, was far too provincial for her liking; if she could not breathe the air of the French Court, she could live only in London. Nancy she regarded as exile. She kept in close and constant touch with the Queen of France, Anne of Austria, and in her early days in Nancy she never missed an opportunity of asking her to intercede with Louis XIII and his Prime Minister and to obtain permission for her to return to Paris.

At the time Richelieu wrote to Bouthillier:

"I believe that the Queen will have to content herself with telling those who speak on Madame de Chevreuse's behalf that all she can do for this lady is to cease to importune the King with the question of her return. . . ."

From time to time Marie de Rohan also appealed to her husband, who, good-natured as always, advised her to withdraw to Auvergne or Bourbonnais; if the King gave his permission he would accompany her. And in fact, although only by way of an experiment, she set her foot on French soil again briefly; but somehow she felt uncomfortable and returned post-haste to Lorraine.

And so she stayed on in Nancy and tried to strengthen her hold on Duke Charles; this was not difficult, for he too had become completely infatuated with her. In France preparations were under way for the final campaign against the Huguenots. Marie persuaded Charles to exploit the internal

17

difficulties that had recently risen in France, to lodge complaints, start diplomatic warfare, increase tension with France and again seek support from the Emperor. No sooner had the game begun than an English envoy, Lord Montagu, appeared in Nancy (cf. Vol. 1, pp. 222 ff.).

By then Madame de Chevreuse was living in Bar-le-Duc; Montagu called on her. He unfolded Buckingham's plans and told her that three fleets were to be equipped, each with a complement of ten thousand men; the first would attack in support of La Rochelle, the second would defend Guyenne, while the third was intended for Normandy; troops would be landed and the estuaries of the Seine, Loire and Garonne blockaded. London wished the Duke of Lorraine to join with the Holy Roman Emperor in an offensive war against France; the Duke of Savoy was to occupy the Dauphiné and Provence, while Henri de Rohan must unleash a great Huguenot rising.

We have already encountered Walter Montagu, son of Lord Manchester, on his many journeys across the continent of Europe, which took him to Venice, Turin, Nancy and Brussels.

On this occasion Marie de Chevreuse succeeded in persuading Charles IV of Lorraine to back the English plans, and she herself put Montagu in touch with the Duke. Commenting on this episode, Richelieu said: "She will destroy this young Prince." Charles had enough prudence to say that he would reserve judgement until English troops had actually landed in France.

When Richelieu wrote his Memoirs he made special mention of the connections that Marie maintained at that time, not only with the leaders of the French opposition but also with the Emperor, with Spain, England and many other parties. It was she who advised Gaston d'Orléans to flee from France in all haste.

Montagu went on to Savoy, where he conducted successful negotiations. He also visited Switzerland; he achieved nothing with the shrewd Venetians and finally he met Henri de Rohan.

Richelieu's secret police followed his every move. After reporting back to London, this extremely able negotiator was told to return to the Continent at once. He travelled through the Netherlands along the French border, heading for Nancy; two of Richelieu's agents, disguised as Basques, shadowed him. When he arrived in Barrois and stopped for a short rest one of the agents informed the commandant of a French frontier post. The commandant crossed the border, accompanied by twelve of his officers, and seized the English diplomat together with his servant and a case full of documents. Montagu was taken to the Bastille. While Charles IV protested in vain against this violation of international law and demanded the immediate release of the English representative and the punishment of the commandant of the frontier post, the Englishman's papers were being examined in Paris at leisure. They proved, to quote Richelieu, "that England, Savoy, Lorraine, Soissons, Rohan and La Rochelle were in shameful league against the State [France] . . . and all this had been brought about by Madame de Chevreuse with the approval of the reigning Queen."

Following these events Anne of Austria found herself in a very difficult position. And yet her name was not mentioned in any of the confiscated documents. Montagu tried to put everything in as harmless a light as possible. From the Bastille he wrote to Louis XIII, explaining that the King of England had taken to arms because he had felt that the King of France did not bear him the same respect and affection which he himself had shown towards Louis. Savoy and Lorraine had joined in the coalition because Louis had treated them with such contempt. Once this impression had been dispelled the will to peace, which was present in all of these lands, would reassert itself.

For as long as the siege of La Rochelle continued Louis was obliged to negotiate. And only one thing stood in the way of successful negotiation: the tireless activities of the Duchess. Montagu said in the Bastille that it was she who had spurred Buckingham on in all his ventures. Richelieu confirmed this and mentioned that after the English defeat a report had been found in Buckingham's quarters, in which he himself had described the Duchess as the prime mover. But the strongest indication of the high assessment the Cardinal placed on Marie's political skill lies in the fact that, despite everything, he continued to treat her with the greatest forbearance.

While Louis XIII sojourned in Saintonge, Marie de' Medici was receiving Monsieur de Bréval, the envoy from Lorraine. She informed him that the King had learned of all his master's plots from Montagu's papers, but she quickly added that the best way of coming to terms with Louis would be for Duke Charles to travel to Paris himself.

Bouthillier spoke with Bréval about Madame de Chevreuse. He mentioned the Court's satisfaction with the propriety of her husband's conduct, and remarked that it was the King's intention to show the benevolence he felt towards Monsieur de Chevreuse by dealing charitably with his wife. All that was needed to rectify the confusion she had caused was for her to mend her ways and use her influence in future on behalf of the French State. If she did so, she would be at liberty to return. Bouthillier even hinted at the possibility that Buckingham might be invited to Paris. Meanwhile Claude de Chevreuse was tireless in his attempts to persuade his wife to return.

Charles IV of Lorraine—prompted of course by Marie de Chevreuse—then announced that he was prepared to meet the King of France. But Charles made conditions, one of them to the effect that his cousin, Marie de Chevreuse, should again be permitted to live in Dampierre or in Jouarre. One of Henry IV's former mistresses was put forward as mediatrix and Richelieu subsequently wrote to Marie de' Medici:

"Whether Madame de Chevreuse stayed in Jouarre or Dampierre seemed to me of no consequence and, although Madame des Essarts was a bad woman, it was not advisable in the first instance to refuse her services, since . . . a thief is better able to deal with one of his own kind than a Capuchin. . . ."

A little later, when there was more room to manoeuvre, there was a change of tone. To save face the forbearance shown to Marie was explained on the grounds that the King wished to reward the Duke of Chevreuse for his loyal services. At first, however, his wife had not responded to this act of grace. In her letters to the Queen she wrote that she felt perfectly safe, for she had the backing of Buckingham, the King of England, the Holy Roman Emperor, the King of Spain and the Duke of Lorraine. This feeling of security was suddenly to be shattered when, on August 23, 1628, Felton murdered Buckingham in the entrance hall of his house in Portsmouth, where the Duke had appeared to supervise the embarkation of the auxiliaries intended for the support of La Rochelle (cf. Vol. I, pp. 268 ff.).

Two months later La Rochelle capitulated. From then onwards Louis XIII was in a position to employ his power abroad; the whole coalition collapsed at once.

On April 30, 1629, Richelieu wrote a coded letter to Monsieur de Rancé, Marie de' Medici's secretary:

"England is demanding [that we recall] Madame de Chevreuse; we have refrained from this for reasons well known to the Queen-Mother."

And on July 7th he wrote again to Rancé:

"The King would be well pleased if the Duchess of Chevreuse were to be seized near the border and conducted to the Bois de Vincennes, although it would be essential that no outsider should be allowed to see her. The cabals instigated by the Duchess . . . between Lorraine and Spain are intolerable."

In 1629–30 there came Gaston d' Orléans' decision to marry Princess Maria of Gonzaga. We have already seen how his intentions were thwarted (cf. Vol. I, p. 312). At that time Gaston also left France for Lorraine. Charles IV committed the great indiscretion of receiving the "heir to the throne" with royal honours, first on the streets of Toul and subsequently in Nancy. Every person who was in disfavour with the French government and acted against French interests seemed to be welcome in the neighbouring state of Lorraine. At the Court of Nancy Orléans appeared to be highly impressed by Charles IV's fourteen-year-old sister, Marguerite de Vaudémont; this too was to have far-reaching consequences. Then in 1630, after Gaston had been reconciled yet again with Louis XIII, he was given what he had always wanted, a high command in Champagne. But no sooner was he at the head of an army than he renewed his secret contacts with Charles IV and continued his old intrigues.

Following this new rebellion, which coincided with the final phase of Louis' conflict with his mother, Gaston again appeared in Nancy.

Even at this stage, though with extreme difficulty, it might have been possible to preserve Lorraine's neutrality. The guaranty of independence given by Emperor Charles V had been designed with this end in view. On the other hand, of course, it was not so easy in the 1620s to give Lorraine an isolated status.

As early as 1622 Ernst von Mansfeld had offered the French control of the strongholds on the Rhine. This was two years before Richelieu's appointment, and La Vieuville did not accept the offer. But even prior to 1617 it was apparent that the fate of Lorraine was inextricably bound up with the future of Alsace. At that time an event took place which, as we have seen, might well have proved calamitous for France: in the Prague agreement Archduke Ferdinand undertook to cede to Spain the Austrian possessions in Alsace in return for Spanish support at the Imperial election. The Valtelline, Alsace and the Palatinate in Spanish hands—the recurring French nightmare!

Two-thirds of Upper Alsace, Breisgau and the Four Forest Cantons actually were Hapsburg dominions. In Lower Alsace things were different. The lands there were either free Imperial territories or dependencies of free Imperial cities. The Bishop of Strassburg on the other hand was one of the Austrian Archdukes. For France it was essential to prevent the Spanish from penetrating into Alsace and establishing themselves in the Palatinate.

Emperor Ferdinand II did not stand idly by when France took possession of the three bishoprics. In 1630 he sent troops to occupy the two important strongholds of Vic and Moyenvic in the Bishopric of Metz. Louis XIII retaliated by establishing an army in Champagne and Richelieu sent appropriate instructions to his two representatives, who were then negotiating in Regensburg.

On August 24, 1630, he wrote to Father Joseph:

"If the projected peace treaty is brought to a successful conclusion you must try to ensure that the Germans withdraw from Vic and Moyenvic by impressing on them that this would be the best guaranty of good relations, which could never be entirely satisfactory if, while settling our differences in one sphere, we left other problems unsolved in another."

To the French Ambassador, Brûlart de Léon, he wrote on September 5th of the same year:

"It is altogether relevant and necessary to ensure, through the intercession of the Electors, that the Emperor withdraws his troops from Vic and Moyenvic and that these places be restored to their former condition; if possible an article should be inserted [to this effect] in the special treaty between the Emperor and France, which would then form a natural extension to the provision that stipulates that their Majesties will not attack or harass those territories that they held prior to 1628. The insertion of this article would compensate for the advantage the Emperor would appear to have derived from the fact that the treaty was concluded within the Empire."

It was primarily because of the guarantees given to Lorraine (cf. Vol. I, pp. 375 ff.) that Richelieu, despite the apparently hopeless personal situation in which he then found himself in Lyon, tore up the treaty that had been signed by the Emperor and the French representatives in Regensburg on October 13, 1630.

But following Regensburg and the dismissal of Wallenstein, which the French had pressed for with all available means, the Emperor was no longer in a position to attack in force on his western front. As for the evacuation of Vic and Moyenvic, no agreement was reached. But in 1631, following the Armistice of Cherasco on April 6th and the end of the War of the Mantaun Succession on June 19th, Louis mounted an offensive against both of these fortresses.

The Duke of Lorraine, alarmed by the French troop movements, was received in Château Thierry on October 23rd. The discussions produced no positive results.

Moyenvic was taken by the French on December 27, 1631. As a result Charles IV was obliged to sign the Treaty of Vic on January 6, 1632. One of the conditions he had to accept was the cession of the town of Marsal to the King of France for a period of three years. This pledge was handed over on January 13. On January 10, 1632, Richelieu had written:

"Acting on the advice of his father and all those whom he had consulted in this affair, Monsieur de Lorraine has signed the treaty drawn up in Metz. . . . He has chosen to transfer Marsal to the King rather than Stenay."

As soon as the Duchess of Chevreuse had returned to France Richelieu had acquired her services for the implementation of his plans only to discover that, while working for him, she was also continuing to promote his opponents' interests. Nonetheless, it was she who advised Charles IV to sign this treaty. The concessions that she obtained from her cousin of Lorraine at that time were very considerable. He had to allow French troops transit rights through his Duchy and to refrain from any form of contact with any state hostile to France (a secret article referred specifically to the House of Hapsburg). Charles IV further promised to conduct no negotations and to conclude no alliances with other states without first informing the King of France. Charles forfeited his military independence and was forbidden to extend his territories. France was authorized to pursue her rebellious subjects on the soil of Lorraine. Louis XIII, for his part, undertook to protect Lorraine from all future aggression.

Even before circumstances forced him to seek the support of the German Catholic princes and despite the fascination that France and all things French held for him, Charles IV had always maintained links with the Bavarian Court. These were prompted by family considerations, for the Elector Maximilian's first wife had been a princess of the House of Lorraine.

After the battle of Breitenfeld Charles IV had hastened to the aid of Maximilian I, but he was recalled by his father only two months later. Louis XIII had marched into Metz. Gustavus Adolphus had sent a sharp protest to the French King, censuring him for not having prevented his "vassal," Lorraine, from interfering in the German theatre of war. This Swedish protest provided Richelieu with a pretext for mounting a punitive expedition against Lorraine.

Charles' crucial mistake was his failure to realize that initially Richelieu would not have been disinclined to incorporate him into his system of alliances, although ultimately this would not have saved the Duchy from the measures that had always formed part of the Cardinal's plans.

Soon after Vic had capitulated, Gaston d'Orléans suddenly joined forces with the army led by González de Cordova and advanced into Burgundy; instead of marching against him, Richelieu launched a second preventive action against Lorraine, which was of course made possible only by Gustavus Adolphus' great victories and the Swedish occupation of Munich.

When, in terror of the Swedes, the Elector of Treves (or Trier, in German) had asked for French protection, Richelieu, exploiting the element of surprise, without a declaration of war mounted a double offensive from Thionville and Metz via Pont-à-Mousson and from Champagne via Bar-le-Duc. An unsuspecting Lothringian regiment was massacred in its encampment. Once again Charles IV was forced to accept a dictated peace, which he signed in Liverdum on June 26, 1632, albeit with the same inner reservation as at Vic, that, since he had been forced to sign the treaty, he would not hestitate to break it.

To justify his invasion of the Duchy Richelieu produced many legal arguments. Chief among these was the inexcusable failure of the Duchy of Bar to pay homage to the King of France. But underlying the legal argument there was the very real event, which was to set the seal on the rupture between Paris and Nancy: the secret marriage of Gaston d'Orléans to Marguerite de Vaudémont, which took place on January 3, 1632, just three days before the Treaty of Vic was signed. The French heir-apparent had married with the collusion of a foreign Prince and without obtaining permission from the head of his house. The Paris parlement preferred an action against Charles IV for having lent his support to this contract.

Under the terms of Liverdum, Charles was forced to cede Clermont-en-Argonne, Dun, Stenay and Jametz to the French and to ratify anew all the provisions of the Treaty of Vic.

On July 8th Louis XIII met the Duke of Lorraine at Sechepré, where the Duke craved his pardon and Louis again declared that the past should be forgotten. But in August news reached France that Charles was rearming and negotiating with Orléans, the Spanish, the Emperor and Wallenstein. In fact, although Wallenstein promised help, he did nothing. The French troops, who had marched into Lorraine immediately the treaty had been signed and had occupied positions on the Rhine with the approval of the Elector of Treves, were commanded by Marshal d'Effiat.

It will be recalled that at the end of 1632 Philip von Sötern had placed himself under French protection and that as a result French and Spanish troops faced one another across the Rhine.

Following the French successes in Lorraine, Richelieu's attention was directed, primarily for tactical reasons, to Alsace, for he was expecting an attack of the Imperial forces on the west bank of the Rhine. However, this brought him into conflict with the Swedes; the consequences might have been unpredictably far-reaching, but France was rescued from this extremely hazardous position by the death of Gustavus Adolphus at Lützen—one more of the amazing coincidences in Richelieu's career which transformed perilous situations at the last moment. In Alsace, as in the Rhenish territories, fear of the Swedes was greater than fear of a French hegemony, and a Professor of History in Strassburg by the name of Bernegger, as spokesman for the magistrature of Strassburg, praised Louis XIII as the protector of the German Liberties.

When the great King of Sweden died the lands of Treves were in French hands, those of Mainz in Swedish hands, while one half of Alsace was also occupied by Swedish or French troops. The Franconian Circle, as we have seen, was bound to Sweden under the terms of Oxenstierna's Treaty of Heilbronn. Lorraine was completely encircled. In despair Charles IV continued his secret negotiations with the Spanish. With mounting impatience, he waited from day to day for the Cardinal-Infante to intervene.

Irresistibly, Richelieu completed the annexation of the western part of Bar. Although outnumbered, Charles IV attacked the Swedes, who, at Richelieu's instigation, had laid siege to Hagenau, the stronghold given to the Lothringians by the Emperor to protect their eastern frontier. On August 10, 1633, Charles' cavalry was defeated at Pfaffenhofen. Without any formal declaration of war, Louis XIII then suddenly marched at the head of a powerful army against Nancy. François de Vaudémont immediately recalled his son, but armed resistance on two fronts—against the Swedes and the French—was out of the question. From then Charles was no longer recognized as the sovereign Duke of Lorraine; he had conspired with all the external enemies of the Bourbon kingdom and aided and abetted Richelieu's enemies at home, especially Gaston d'Orléans and Marie de' Medici; he had been responsible for Gaston's secret marriage to Marguerite de Vaudémont and during one of his meetings with Louis had been forced to admit that the marriage had in fact taken place. At this point Richelieu invoked the great historical arguments:

Going back to Carolingian times, he declared that the supreme sovereignty exercised by the Holy Roman Empire over Lorraine was an arrogation of power. The King of France was the true sovereign of this territory, whose illegal association with the Imperial Crown he had been obliged to tolerate out of weakness. But statutes of limitation did not apply to kings, and now that the French Crown was in a position of strength it was reasserting its hereditary sovereignty in full.

Every stronghold from Epinal to Mars-la-Tour and Charmes fell, with the exception of Remiremont and the redoubtable fortress of Nancy. The Duke, meanwhile, had retired to the south-eastern corner of his realm. Still he waited for Spain. He had placed great hopes in Wallenstein, but to no avail. It was Wallenstein's reaction which had enabled the Swedes to march for west Germany and invade Alsace. After defeating Charles IV at Pfaffenhofen they had then advanced into Lorraine. On July 30, 1635, the parlement of Paris, acting on Louis' instructions, had proclaimed the confiscation of the *Barrois mouvant* for alleged *défault d'hommage*. Charles sent his brother, the Bishop of Toul, François-Nicolas, to Louis to make soothing protestations. Richelieu was inexorable and insisted that Charles surrender his capital and deliver up Princess Marguerite.

A second interview, which François-Nicolas had with King Louis, was also ineffectual. But this Prince of the Church did succeed in another venture: he managed to smuggle the young Duchess of Orléans out of Nancy disguised as a pageboy, when the city was already surrounded by French troops. She reached Thionville and then continued her journey to Brussels, where she was reunited with her husband.

Nancy was "the strongest fortress in Europe at that time." How did it come to capitulate? The principal reason was the lack of Imperialist support. This too was Wallenstein's doing. When Lorraine was most sorely pressed and Aldringer was marching to the defence of Nancy, Wallenstein tied his general's hands with the result that he led his troops back to Bavaria without accomplishing his mission; this in turn caused the Spanish to withdraw. In Alsace, too, town after town opened its gates to the French; the Duke of Württemberg allowed Louis XIII's forces to occupy Mömpelgard, and the Archbishop of Cologne recognized the French King as his patron. It was at this point that Richelieu said of Charles IV: "He is only a skeleton and a ghost of a Prince."

From then onwards it was clear that Richelieu was determined to eliminate the ducal House of Lorraine, with which France had had such an intimate connection for centuries. He acted in accordance with Machiavelli's motto: "*E a possederli sicuramente basta avere spenta la linea del principe che li dominava* (In order to annex other territories all that is needed is to wipe out the ruling house)."

Charles IV, imprudent as ever, had meanwhile accepted an invitation from Louis XIII to visit him in Lunéville, near Nancy. He was received with full honours. After dinner, when he prepared to leave, he was pressed to stay awhile longer, and when he finally decided that it was time to go, the guards barred his way; he then realized that he was Louis' prisoner. He had, finally, no choice but to sign a document commanding the Marquis of Mouy, the governor of his capital city, to open the gates of Nancy to French troops and surrender the famed fortress without a blow being struck. On September 25th, Louis and his Queen entered Nancy in state, to the accompaniment of great military pomp and the embittered silence of the populace.

On September 20, 1633, the Duke of Lorraine was forced, under the terms of the Treaty of Charmes, to accept French occupation of Nancy for a period of thirty years, that is, until August 1663.

Then, on January 19, 1634, Charles IV abdicated in favour of his brother, Bishop François-Nicolas, and immediately left his territories with the intention of fighting on the Catholic side in Germany and returning to Lorraine at some future date as a conqueror. But he left his wife Nicole behind. Richelieu decided at once that Nicole and her younger sister, Claudia, must be brought to Paris, where he would have them in his power and could insist on the principle of female succession for Bar and Lorraine. The idea of marrying Claudia to a French prince was revived. Since Nicole was childless, Lorraine and Bar would pass to her sister and consequently to the French Crown, just as Henry IV had envisaged. François-Nicolas and Claudia meanwhile were in Lunéville. Richelieu immediately dispatched Marshal de La Force with a powerful contingent. But the Cardinal and Bishop of Toul was not an ordained priest. As La Force approached Lunéville, François-Nicolas determined, as the representative of his brother Charles IV, to save the hereditary territories for his dynasty and to this end to take Claudia as his wife. She was a first cousin; consequently he needed a papal dispensation and, in order to obtain it, he would have to relinquish his ecclesiastical offices. But he had no time to wait for a papal decision; he therefore sought the advice of the official canons, the *chanoines réguliers de Notre-Sauveur*, and on February 18th he married Claudia. The ceremony was carried out by the Prior of Saint-Rémy and was valid in ecclesiastical law provided a papal dispensation was subsequently granted. When Marshal de La Force entered the castle of Lunéville early in the morning of February 19th he surprised the newly-weds in their nuptial bed. Together with Nicole, they were taken to Nancy and handed over to the Count of Brassac for safe-keeping. The news of all this moved Richelieu to the most violent rage. It was only out of deference to the Curia that he refrained from taking extreme measures against François-Nicolas. He ordered the couple to be brought to Paris with all speed. But despite their strict guard the newly-weds succeeded in escaping from the palace disguised as peasants and fleeing, first to the Duchess of Tuscany and then, three years later, to Vienna. Nicole had remained behind in Nancy; from there she was brought to Paris, where she was to live out her days in solitude.

The Paris newssheets proclaimed to "the capital city of France and to the world" that, thanks to their King's glorious feats of arms, a new province had been added to their great kingdom. All Lothringian officials were commanded to swear an oath of allegiance to Louis XIII.

While the western part of Bar was brought under the jurisdiction of the Paris parlement and the members of the court of justice in St-Mihiel, the "Cour des Grands Jours," who had meanwhile sworn allegiance to Louis XIII, were also kept under direct control, the King of France set up a council with sovereign powers in Nancy, which was the ultimate authority for the administration of the territory and to which all government officials were accountable. All other courts of justice were suppressed, as was the Court of Assize, and all the ancient rights of the Estates were revoked. In order to gain the support of part of the nobility and to reconcile them to the suppression of the Court of Assize, the King offered several members of the hereditary nobility offices in the new judicial and executive council, whose jurisdiction was subsequently transferred to the parlements of Metz.

After François-Nicolas had escaped abroad in April 1634, Charles IV had again assumed the title of sovereign Duke of Lorraine, and in a manifesto he declared that none of the decrees promulgated by the King of France in respect of his territories were binding. From Besançon he issued manifestos against "the thief" who had stolen his lands; he urged his former subjects to deny their allegiance and to refuse to pay taxes. During this time most of the Lothringian strongholds fell to the French. The major part of the populace remained loyal to their Duke, for which they were later to pay a terrible price.

At the battle of Nördlingen, Charles fought as a General of the Catholic League.

By then, as has been demonstrated from various points of view, the situation had been totally transformed. France could escape its threatening consequences only by taking the extreme decision of active participation in the war. But before this, before the French declaration of war on Spain, we again encounter Henri de Rohan, this time in connection with events in Lorraine.

Henri de Rohan

From 1629 onwards Richelieu had built up his system of Protestant alliances with absolute consistency and strengthened it in a number of ways. But the cornerstone of this policy remained the peace of Alais, the "act of grace" that brought the civil war to an end on June 28, 1629, following the final fierce campaigns in southern France, and which was accepted unconditionally—even with gratitude—by the conquered Huguenots (cf. Vol. I, p. 330).

It is precisely in this act of grace, whose complexity can scarcely have been fully appreciated by Richelieu's contemporaries, that later observers have been able to recognize his great statesmanship. To have shown such a sense of proportion, such a sure hand, after a victory which could not have been more final was truly astounding.

As for the French Huguenots, once they had overcome their initial feeling of astonished relief, they soon began to wonder whether the Cardinal's restraint was not in fact simply a necessary concomitant of his short-term plans and whether the amazing tolerance extended by the monarch to his Protestant subjects was not merely a prelude to his preparations for the grand alliance against Spain. But such assessments also failed to do full justice to the exact nature of Richelieu's motives. His long-term political aims and his short-term decisions always interacted contrapuntally.

Of course the reconciliation with the Huguenots fitted in, at precisely the right moment, with his general concept of foreign policy; it was a calculated attempt to influence the Protestant world in Germany, Holland and England. France had to have internal unity at all costs. The extent to which this unity was achieved, at least temporarily, as a result of harsh coercion followed by the completely unexpected offer of religious tolerance was clearly demonstrated both during the rebellion staged by Montmorency and Orléans and during the peasants' and artisans' riots. The Protestants did not intervene on either occasion.

After the capitulation Rohan had asked Louis XIII to grant him safe conduct to Venice. Bernard de La Valette was delegated to escort him.

And so we encounter Rohan again, the Breton dynast, who had been regarded as the probable heir to the French throne prior to the birth of Henry IV's legitimate children. In 1629 this man of small physical stature was fifty. From early youth he had spent the greater part of his life exposed to extreme danger: behind the walls of beleaguered towns, on the battlefields of the civil war, in partisan engagements. He had travelled widely, always pursuing his one great passion, the study of strategy and of fortification technique.

The famous general's arrival in Italy caused quite a sensation. In Genoa he was received with the highest honours. His appearance in the Republic was taken as a sure sign that the Huguenots of France had been definitively eliminated as a power group and that their conquered leader was being conducted from city to city as ostentatiously as possible.

Rohan's situation upon his arrival in Venice is revealed in

a letter he sent to the King of England on August 2, 1629, in which he wrote:

"Sire, After concluding this peace in accordance with your Majesty's wishes . . . I asked my master, the King, to give me permission to come to this country [Venice], which he has freely granted. . . . I am totally ruined, the whole of my property having been confiscated [and transferred] to the Prince [of Condé] . . . the properties belonging to my mother, brother and sister have fared no better. . . ."

He then reminded Charles I of his former promises. He pointed out in precise terms how painstakingly he had respected the King's wishes throughout the whole campaign in France, and he expressed surprise that the peace of Alais should have been celebrated in England. He also pointed out that he had been forced to capitulate, once the King of France had returned from his victorious Italian campaigns with very powerful forces and attacked the last remaining Huguenot armies at five different points.

It is understandable that Rohan should have been treated with great mistrust, not only in the Republic of Venice but also by the French, the Spanish and the Imperialists. The fact that he corresponded with the King of England, that he maintained relations through a middleman with the Duke of Savoy and above all with the Spanish, that he was in touch with Bernhard of Saxe-Weimar and was trying to establish contact with Gustavus Adolphus, that he had even entered into relations with Wallenstein, is enough to explain the watch kept on him, not only by Richelieu's agents but also by the Signorie with their tried and trustworthy methods. There were ample grounds for suspicion. The collection of treaty texts edited by Jacques Bernard, published in Amsterdam in 1700, contains one surprising document dated May 3, 1629. Its substance is as follows:

His Catholic Majesty undertakes to pay high subsidies to the Huguenots and to supply them with auxiliaries. He will also grant pensions to Duke Henri and his brother, Soubise. In return Rohan is to conclude no peace treaty without the approval of the King of Spain but is to continue to wage war in Provence, Languedoc, the Dauphiné and any other place where conditions appear favourable. But if the Huguenots should be forced to conclude a peace, Rohan should not hesitate to break it at the first opportunity, even though it should have been approved of by the King of Spain.

And so, after Spain had supported the French Holy League in every possible way throughout the entire course of the religious wars, Philip IV entered into such a far-reaching agreement with the French Huguenots at the very end of the civil war!

In the fourth volume of his Memoirs Rohan writes at length about a certain Michel du Clausel. He recalls that Clausel had left Spain and, travelling via Piedmont, had brought him proposals of Spanish support and opened up the prospect of massive help, if this should be requested. Clausel, Rohan reported, had spoken with the Spanish ambassador in Piedmont, who had made a number of far-reaching statements; in the course of their conversation it had been made abundantly clear just how important it was to Spanish interests that the civil war in France should not cease; the success of the Spanish undertakings in Italy depended on its being continued. At that time the Abbé Scaglia was in Madrid as the representative of the House of Savoy; he was prepared to do everything within his power to bring about an agreement between Philip IV and Rohan. Scaglia had already been to England, where he had said that, because of his hatred for Richelieu's régime, he would do anything for the French reformers. At that time Rohan himself was without funds of any kind; the ravaged countryside was no longer able to sustain his fighting troops, the towns had refused to contribute, nothing could be expected of England, while the Duke of Savoy had simply fed him on empty phrases; in other words, if they were to hold out any longer the Huguenots would have to give serious consideration to the Spanish offer made by Clausel. But Rohan had not cared to accept Philip IV's proposals without the approval of the King of England. Consequently, although he had not rebuffed Clausel, he had avoided an early meeting with him; once he had Charles I's approval for this extremely hazardous engagement with Madrid, he would have room to manoeuvre and could then negotiate with Clausel. The English reaction was positive, and Rohan received Clausel, whom he sent back to the Spanish Court—and this is important, for it fixes the date for this whole sequence of events—at the precise moment when the second English fleet returned to port without having accomplished its mission. This second English failure to supply La Rochelle by naval action fell in May 1628.

The Duke went on to say that he had authorized Clausel to inform His Catholic Majesty that, if the continuance of the civil war in France was likely to further the plans of the Spanish monarchy, then, provided His Majesty helped the Huguenots in time, he would undertake to prolong the war for as long as possible. If no help was forthcoming he would be forced to make peace; he still had the whole winter ahead of him and so could afford to wait, and he undertook to accept instructions even as late as March of the following year. Shortly after Clausel's departure news came that La Rochelle had fallen. Rohan immediately informed his agents that he had not been surprised by this grave turn of events and that he still stood by his original undertaking. And so the agreement outlined above was signed.

During the period between the fall of La Rochelle and Gustavus Adolphus' landing in Pomerania in July, which also saw the fall of Pinerolo and the lightning campaign in Savoy, Richelieu had been kept informed of Rohan's dealings with Spain. His knowledge of these events had a dual effect: it led to the terrible severity with which the Huguenots were treated during the actual campaign, but it also brought about the "Act of Grace , . . ." the peace of Alais, whose moderation imposed a diplomatic defeat on the Spanish because of its effect on the Protestant camp. Meanwhile the Cardinal had waited before intervening in Savoy and northern Italy until he had made certain of English neutrality by secret negotiations.

But despite everything, instead of suffering the fate that was to befall Montmorency, Rohan was permitted to go to Venice, where he was received with full honours, though he had at first to contend with material difficulties. His wife, Sully's daughter, who had stayed in Geneva and subsequently in Berne during the civil war, had already gone to Venice in August 1627. She had been treated with great consideration and had even been allowed to have divine service in her house, a privilege usually accorded only to Protestant diplomats. She too was without means and was obliged to live on the sale of her jewels.

The Duke's military reputation was so widespread and secure that within a short time the Venetians appointed him Commander-in-Chief of their military forces. Here, too, the driving force of "opportunity" merely brushed the Duke's sleeve. He did not see action in Venice—the Republic was at peace—and, despite his appointment, the mistrust lingered.

It was not only the Venetians who employed him; his own King commissioned him to carry out an extensive recruiting campaign. In every part of the world Huguenot refugees were trying to establish themselves in the economic life of their new communities. Rohan had even thought of launching a collection on a grand scale. His latifundia in France, which had been confiscated and conferred on the Prince of Condé, had been graciously returned to him by Louis XIII, and Rohan had authorized his wife to sell part of these properties. With the proceeds of the collection and the income from the sale of his lands he intended to buy the island of Cyprus. He entered into negotiations with Cyril, the Patriarch of Constantinople, to effect the purchase and arrange for the payment of an annual tribute to the Porte. But this project, which would have enabled Rohan to settle his French co-religionists on a new territory, his own sovereign Duchy, foundered on the death of the Patriarch.

Rohan corresponded regularly with his mother, to whom he was deeply devoted and who had lived through the siege of La Rochelle and suffered all the privations that this involved (cf. Vol. I, pp. 244 ff.). He wrote to her every week and told her of the levies he was raising, not only for the Venetian Republic but also for the King of France. If they were to reach their objective speedily, he said, they must concentrate on Languedoc and the Mediterranean area. He intended to enlist the aid of his old comrades in arms to this end. The fact that Marillac, the Keeper of the Seal and "his greatest political opponent," was now a "lost man" he regarded as a favourable circumstance for his undertaking, whereas his successor, Châteauneuf, he was persuaded, would adopt a positive attitude, since he was related to his wife. And again he insisted on the need for speed, so that the enlisted men might soon be concentrated beyond the French border. He then added: ". . . if I turn my thoughts northwards, it will be when I have greater control over my friends. . . ."

This can only mean that Rohan was thinking of taking his loyal followers to join forces with Gustavus Adolphus. But he bided his time, for he had lost a great deal of his former influence over his fellow Huguenots. There were occasions when he fell into apathy, as is evident from another letter to his mother:

"As for peace or war in Italy . . . , peace is made and then broken again; as for my levies, when the King gives permission for some project the Venetian Ambassador impedes its execution; as for myself, I have become enough of a philosopher as far as these matters are concerned to remain unmoved by any of them; I have the feeling that since the capture of La Rochelle and the waning of the religious wars in France all other theatres of war no longer concern me. . . ."

The Duke nonetheless followed the course of the war in

38

Germany with the utmost attention. It seemed as if the great objective that he himself had striven in vain to achieve in his own country was about to be realized by Gustavus Adolphus as the providentially appointed champion of the Protestant cause. Rohan wrote that he wished to be nearer to the German frontiers. He was hoping for a decisive confrontation between Sweden and France. Although he could have gone over to the Swedes, the French successfully prevented him from doing so by threatening to make final the confiscation of his properties or, alternatively, by promising their restitution. Time and again he expressed the wish for a personal meeting with the King of Sweden. In his letters to his mother he wrote of the "Battle of the Rhine," which was bound to break out between the nordic hero and Catholic France once the tension between them had reached its peak.

By this time, however, a general peace had been concluded in Italy. Rohan commented on it as follows:

"The Spanish have little liking for this peace, which was made against their will, and they are doing all they can to disturb it."

In 1631, when the Armistice of Cherasco was signed, Rohan's recruiting was not yet complete. His wife, who had since returned to Paris, had been granted permission to raise ten companies for Venice in France; but meanwhile it had become difficult to find soldiers.

And so Rohan waited. He kept himself occupied by translating Boccaccio. He also began to write his Memoirs. His comments on the German Princes, who had failed to join forces in support of Gustavus Adolphus, were bitter.

When the plague broke out in Venice he moved to Padua. There he wrote *Le parfait Capitaine* (The Perfect Captain), which he dedicated to Louis XIII. At the same time he continued to work on his Memoirs. During these years of military inactivity he was constantly productive.

On October 26, 1631, he suffered a severe personal blow when his seventy-seven-year-old mother died.

Rohan was a man of action; extremely lively by nature, when he was not on active service he was totally absorbed in other activities. Richelieu feared his meeting with Gustavus Adolphus and so he decided to tie him down to a specific task; he needed a negotiator with political experience who could tackle the Valtelline question, and in choosing Rohan he would also have been thinking of the great Alpine tactician who could, if need be, secure the outcome of the negotiations by force of arms.

The following memorandum, which was composed as early as 1616 and deals with the Valtelline question, shows the extent to which Richelieu prepared his actions in advance and the great detail of his planning:

"To march with an army from France to the Valtelline, starting from Bresse, you have to go to Geneva, from Geneva to Lausanne, from Lausanne to Sion. From Sion . . . [to] Bellinzona, from Bellinzona via Mesocco . . . to Chiavenna . . .

"Following the same route from Valais to Bellinzona you also gain access to the Grisons, approaching via the Urseren and Mt Chimoult [Oberalp Pass] before descending into the valley of Disentis.

"On the other route starting from Dijon you proceed via Dôle, Neuchâtel, Soleure, Schwyz, Uri, the Urseren, Bellinzona, etc. But on this route you have to fight."

(Richelieu listed thirteen different routes that could be used by armies marching from France to Italy.)

We have already dealt with the Valtelline question in Volume I (cf. pp. 160 ff.), and we have also demonstrated later just how important this Alpine valley was, not only in objective terms but also as a constant factor in Richelieu's thinking. It should not surprise us to find, therefore, that Richelieu persuaded the King to employ Rohan, first in a diplomatic and subsequently in a military capacity, for this purpose. From Rohan's correspondence it is clear that he reacted to this opportunity with pleasure and placed great hopes in it. He immediately put aside all other plans. As soon as he was approached by the French he went to the Venetian Senate and asked for permission to carry out a commission on his King's behalf while still retaining the office vested in him by the Venetian Republic. Meanwhile Richelieu asked him to proceed to the Grisons.

On December 4th the Duke arrived in Chur, and on the 7th he wrote a letter to the Venetian Resident in Switzerland, in which he referred to Venice as *"mia buona padrona"* and asked if he might continue to exchange confidential information with him. He went on corresponding with the Venetian representatives in the Confederation until 1635.

Immediately upon arrival in Chur, Rohan asked Richelieu for Swiss and French troops. He guaranteed that he would hold all approaches to the Grisons and occupy the Valtelline, on condition that he was provided with six thousand French and four thousand Swiss troops in addition to the Grisons contingent already under arms. But Richelieu did not consider the time ripe for an attack on the Valtelline. His principal concern was to prevent the Swedes from becoming too powerful. He wrote: "My object is to prevent the Catholic religion in Germany from being destroyed."

Initially Rohan's employment in the King's service was to suffer as a result of the uprising staged by Montmorency and Orléans. Although it was owing to Rohan's influence that no Huguenots joined in this venture, he was again suspected, and all the more so since Clausel, his intermediary, whose loyalty he had personally vouched for in a letter to the Cardinal, had compromised himself by further contacts with Spain; and then there were the treaty negotiations with Philip IV in the year 1629, which had never been fully clarified.

The French needed Rohan and they feared him. Richelieu was censured by the Catholics for employing him, and he

B*

replied by asserting that it was neither dishonourable nor imprudent to make use of the "enemy" against the enemy.

Nonetheless, when Rohan left the Grisons in 1632 for a lengthy stay in Zurich and to take the cure in Baden in the Aargau, the French Court was again disturbed. Was he conspiring with the Swedes? It had been learned in Paris that Rohan had again established contact with Bernhard of Saxe-Weimar, although he had received no instructions to do so. At that point the King suddenly ordered Rohan to return immediately to Venice, and on February 10th a letter from Louis XIII to the Protestant cantons in the Confederation, to whom Rohan had been accredited as special representative, put a sudden end to his mission there. On June 2, 1632, Rohan sent a detailed memorandum on the Grisons question to Paris. He stated that no help could be expected from the small Catholic cantons, for they were Spanish to the core. He suggested that Chiavenna and Poschiavo should be defended. He then requested the King yet again to allow him to occupy the Valtelline and to use this and Casale as bases to take the Duchy of Milan. His proposals were not badly received. On June 23, 1633, Bouthilier sent Rohan a document authorizing him to recruit three thousand men, and on July 2nd his appointment as Lieutenant-General commanding the army in the Grisons was ratified. He corresponded with Father Joseph and asked him to use his influence so that he might at least be permitted to recruit two thousand Swiss troops. He was back again in Chur on August 2nd, he asked for two hundred thousand livres, which would be put to good use in the Confederation.

Ceaselessly Rohan urged Paris to authorize him to attack the Valtelline. Time and again he begged them not to leave him in the lurch with his work half done.

In that phase of his career he did all he could to gratify Richelieu and Father Joseph. Rohan, the Huguenot, even went so far as to reintroduce the Capuchin Order in Lower Engadine. And for as long as he considered himself a servant of the King of France he continued to adopt this strictly non-partisan attitude.

In the Cardinal's opinion the only army commander then available who could successfully conduct mountain warfare and block the Alpine passes was Henri de Rohan. And so, still vacillating between the high assessment placed on his talents and suspicions as to his aims, the King's Council invited him to appear at Court in person to conduct negotatiations and obtain new instructions. Although, understandably enough, Rohan felt uneasy as to the real motives underlying this invitation from the all-powerful Cardinal, he nonetheless complied. He arrived in June and was received with courtesy. But then, after having been urged to come with all speed, he was kept waiting for four months before being told what was wanted of him. His presence in France went almost unnoticed. During this period of waiting he wrote his book, *In the Interests of the Princes and States of Christendom*, which he dedicated to Richelieu. The dedication is dated Paris, August 1, 1634.

As to the Valtelline, the Cardinal had still not made up his mind. He wanted to see the territory restored to the Grisons—in this his attitude had remained unchanged since 1617—but on condition that the Catholic Church was given specific guarantees. He told Oxenstierna that the King of France was prepared to undertake the Valtelline action provided Sweden played an energetic part, for French intervention must inevitably lead to an open rupture with Spain.

On October 17, 1634, Rohan—still in Paris—wrote to the French Resident in Switzerland, informing him that, at the very moment when he had been about to set out for the Grisons, he had suddenly been instructed to assume command of the newly formed army in Picardy.

But even this was reconsidered, for it was felt that to place such great power in his hands and so near to the French capital was far too risky. And so alternative employment was found for him and he was entrusted with another diplomatic mission to the Swiss Confederation. This project was then cancelled in its turn and to his complete surprise Rohan was ordered to intervene in Lorraine.

He was only supposed to keep watch over the movements of Charles IV, who was approaching from Germany with powerful contingents to reconquer his Duchy, and also any troop movements between Franche-Comté and Alsace. But Rohan immediately mounted an offensive. He took Altkirch and laid siege to Belfort. He raised the siege when he heard that Duke Charles had built a pontoon bridge north of Breisach and that an advance guard led by General Mercy had crossed it and marched through the Hardt the same night; they had launched a surprise attack on a French encampment and taken prisoners; Charles IV was following hard on Mercy's heels. Rohan acted at once. He threw in his cavalry against Mercy, four hundred mounted musketeers. When the Duke of Lorraine discovered that the French army had crossed the Ill, he hurriedly withdrew across the Rhine. He made no attempt to cross the river again until the following March, this time at Neuenburg. Rohan was ready for him; he defeated Mercy at Ottmarsheim, took Ruffach and again forced the Duke to return to the east bank of the river.

During the brief period that Rohan had at his disposal for his operations in Alsace-Lorraine, his tactical achievements were astonishing and he did much to promote the great task that Bernhard of Saxe-Weimar, whom he loved and admired, was soon to undertake for France. But suddenly Rohan was given quite a different commission. In March 1635—that is, before the outbreak of warfare—he was ordered to take seven regiments and four squadrons from the army operating on France's eastern border and to lead them south to join up with the small force under the command of Monsieur du Landé, whch was stationed in the Grisons, whose people were allies of Louis XIII. Once there, he was to block the Alpine passes between Lombardy, the Tyrol and the upper reaches of the Rhine, thus denying their use to the Spanish and Imperialists alike. We shall encounter him again when we consider the way in which he accomplished this task.

The further course of the Lothringian tragedy will also be considered within the general context of the open war which was shortly to break out.

CHAPTER II

BEFORE THE DECLARATION OF WAR

Bernhard of Saxe-Weimar

In his essay on the concept *"vaste,"* which he dedicated to the members of the French Academy, Saint-Evremond, who was one of the most percipient observers and judges of French foreign policy, wrote:

"Richelieu was a genius; in terms of scope, he brought our State astonishing benefits; but his 'boundlessness' brought us to the very brink of ruin." We are told that Turenne, Louis XIV's Army Commander, admired "a hundred qualities" in the Cardinal but that he condemned his recklessness and stated that Cardinal Mazarin was wiser than Richelieu, his measures were more considered and more appropriate than those taken by his predecessor, whose plans could never really have been brought into line with one another because they stemmed from a "boundless" imagination.

As early as 1635 the Duke of Aumale, author of the history of the Princes of Condé, reported that this same Turenne, who was then twenty-four years old, had said:

"Gustavus Adolphus is dead, all the good men are dead: Montmorency, Schomberg, d'Effiat; and he asked: 'How are we to fight against commanders like Gallas, Johann von Werth and Charles of Lorraine?'"

But in 1653 France had two important army commanders who are not mentioned here: Henri de Rohan and Bernhard of Saxe-Weimar, whom Turenne, the man destined to lead

French arms to their highest achievements under Louis XIV, was soon to admire and regard as a model military leader.

Bernhard of Saxe-Weimar was the eleventh son of Duke John III of Saxe-Weimar and Princess Christine of Anhalt. From earliest youth he had spent his life on the battlefields of Europe. He had fought against Tilly under both Mansfeld and Frederick of Baden. Together with his brother William, who had been planning a new league of Protestant Princes, he was embroiled in the defeats imposed on Christian of Halberstadt by Tilly in 1622 and 1623. Shortly afterwards we find him in the Danish army, where he also met with nothing but military reversals. He then established contact with Wallenstein and through him obtained the Emperor's grace and pardon. But when Gustavus Adolphus began his triumphant progress Bernhard was quick to recognize him as the saviour of the Protestant cause, and together with the Landgrave of Hesse he approached the King of Sweden and entered his service, where he distinguished himself fighting against Tilly and was appointed Commander of the Swedish Body Guards. In the course of the general defections which followed Lützen he temporarily accepted a subordinate position under the Swedish Lieutenant-General, William of Saxe-Weimar, his own brother, who had taken over the supreme command. But a relationship of this kind did not accord with his ambitions and desires.

Bernhard was intolerant. Even his relationship with Gustavus Adolphus was difficult. On October 23, 1632, when they met in Arnstadt, he told the King quite openly that he was no longer in his service, he was his ally. At Lützen it was he who held the field when the King had fallen.

Following Gustavus Adolphus' death Saxe-Weimar's relations with Oxenstierna's son-in-law, Marshal Horn, were distinctly strained. But then his earlier relations with the Landgrave of Hesse, the Count Palatine and the Margrave of Baden had not been good either. And there was always tension between him and the Swedish Chancellor. Oxenstierna claimed that Saxe-Weimar had no sense of solidarity and always placed his personal interests above those of the army or the requirements of the general situation. Nonetheless, Oxenstierna always made allowances for him and let him have his way; he counted on his powerful personality and on his skill and treated him as an independent ally at all times.

Throughout the whole of his life Bernhard had stood in the very midst of a fluctuating war, entering into one short-lived alliance after the other against the Emperor until eventually he was seized by a hand which would not let him go and which was to be his ruin. In the course of his many defeats and victories he perfected his knowledge of strategy. His ambition, in the last analysis, was for territorial gain, the acquisition of a sovereign territory of his own within an integrated Empire, which he envisaged as a predominantly Protestant confederation of states, with a very powerful position for himself.

After the catastrophe of September 6, 1634, when he was forced to retreat with the shattered remnants of his army as far back as Cannstatt on the Rhine, he persevered in a desperate situation and under the most trying circumstances in a truly remarkable way. Prior to the battle of Nördlingen, the fortress of Ehrenbreitstein and the strongholds of Treves were in French hands. Following the surrender of Nancy and Louis XIII's entry into the Lothringian capital on September 25, 1633, the conquest of the Duchy of Lorraine appeared to be complete. France controlled the Moselle, and Richelieu was determined to extend that control to the Palatinate and Alsace so as to dominate the Rhine. Olivares saw the full implications of this situation at once. While the combined Swedish and Protestant forces had established themselves, first in southern Germany and subsequently in Franche-Comté, in Lorraine and on both banks of the Rhine, a large number of towns in Alsace had put themselves under French protection.

We know that in the closing months of the year 1633 work had been progressing in Vienna and Madrid on the preparation of the grand coalition, which was to embrace both the Austrian and the Spanish lines of the House of Hapsburg, the German Catholic Princes, the majority of the Italian Princes, the Duke of Lorraine and also the opposition party in Louis XIII's own realm, which was led by his brother, Orléans. The object of the coalition was to launch a general offensive from Germany and the Spanish Netherlands against France, which would be accompanied by a Spanish naval attack on the French coast. This project had strengthened Richelieu in his resolve to make France so powerful on the Rhine that the Spanish would no longer be able to march southwards along its course and the Imperialists would be unable to force a Rhine crossing. His object was to acquire bridgeheads, fortresses such as Philippsburg and, ultimately, Breisach. The fact that the Swedes, after conquering Philippsburg early in 1634, had been in no hurry to cede this crucial position to the French had clouded Franco–Swedish relations for a while. In order to gain time Oxenstierna had asked the Protestant Estates to settle the question at their forthcoming convention. It was only after Regensburg had fallen that the convention decided to give Philippsburg to the French as the price, so to speak, of her open rupture with Spain, whereupon the fortress was occupied by a French garrison.

For the time being all earlier victories won by the Swedes and their Protestant allies and also by the French were cancelled out by the defeat at Nördlingen. But when, following this defeat, the victors failed to pursue the vanquished army with all the forces at their disposal, the tangible rewards of their unique military success were soon dissipated. Emperor Ferdinand II and his son were not to blame for this. Their intention was the total destruction of the remnants of the enemy army and their object the separation of the Swedes from the French. They wanted to attack, not only on the Rhine but on the Elbe and the Oder as well. The Cardinal-Infante was asked to advance into the Lower Palatinate, to go into winter quarters there and not to proceed to the

Netherlands until the following spring. But Don Fernando could not agree to this. Slowly but surely he marched with his army for the country where he was Stadtholder. He reckoned with the possibility, not only of a French attack between Lille and Sedan but also—and rightly so—with a new Dutch offensive. The Netherlands had to be prepared.

Generals Piccolomini, Isolani and Götz were ordered to put an end to Duke Bernhard's reign in Franconia; the Bavarians were to take Augsburg and keep the Lech open. King Ferdinand himself, accompanied by Charles of Lorraine, intended to advance with his main force towards Württemberg, where the defeated Swedes had massed, bringing calamity to the entire province. The young Duke of Württemberg, whose only hope lay in France, had fled to Strassburg.

Bernhard of Saxe-Weimar had written to Oxenstierna from Cannstatt: "I am collecting as many troops as I can, but I must take them a long way from here, otherwise they may well defect."

He moved to Heilbronn. His troops were indeed unreliable. Men deserted daily. He placed garrisons in the most important towns: Schorndorf, Hohenasperg, Urach and the Hohentwiel. Meanwhile, in mid-September 1634, King Ferdinand, the Emperor's son, entered Stuttgart and took possession of Bernhard's Duchy. Bernhard then made for Frankfurt. He did all he could for the defence of Franconia, but his main forces were centred on the Main; as always, he lacked the necessary money with which to reorganize his army and which the Protestant Estates, who were concerned only with their own special interests, refused to give him. Only the Palatinate tried to raise a contribution. By then Bernhard had given up all idea of holding the line of the Danube; instead, he had decided to make his stand on the Main and the Rhine. But in his own mind he had already allocated the defence of the Rhine to the French. He intended to reorganize the army of the North German Protestant League beneath the walls of Frankfurt. At that point the Cardinal-Infante also reached the

Main en route for the Spanish Netherlands. He occupied both Miltenberg and Aschaffenburg and approached to within a few miles of Frankfurt. With his army in a disorganized state, Bernhard could not risk an engagement. How could he stake everything on a battle with the Spanish while at the same time defending his Duchy of Franconia and his homeland of Weimar? Meanwhile, with Don Fernando, equally intent on avoiding an encounter, slowly proceeding on his way to get his army intact to its destination, Bernhard conceived the plan of leading his own forces to Saxony and Thuringia in order to join up with the Swedish troops and the Hessian and Lüneburg contingents. By removing his army from the Rhine he hoped to create a situation in which the French would at last be forced, in self-defence, to go into action. But Oxenstierna was opposed to this idea. For the time being he wished to remain in close touch with the King of France and establish binding agreements with him. He said of Bernhard that it was not the enemy but this German Prince who caused him the greatest anxiety, for since Horn's capture he no longer had any means of opposing him. On another occasion he said: "Bernhard is striving for absolute power over everything directly or indirectly connected with the war."

In the end these vacillations and disputes were settled, as so often in that phase of the war, by the urgent need to find food for the army. With Bernhard's consent but without Oxenstierna's knowledge the troops crossed over the pontoon bridge at Mainz on to the west bank of the Rhine, where, it was hoped, they would be able to forage for adequate supplies.

Otto Ludwig of Hesse, the Rhinegrave, had accompanied Bernhard from Cannstatt to Heilbronn but, upon hearing that the Duke of Lorraine and Johann von Werth were marching for the Upper Rhine, had immediately broken camp, lest he be cut off from the west bank of the river. But he soon found himself threatened by Duke Charles, whose troops were reinforced by Bavarians; fearing for Strassburg, he made for Kehl but at the river Kinzig was forced into a perilous situation by Johann von Werth's troops and was even captured, although not recognized, and subsequently made his escape by diving into the river. Marshal de La Force had refused to come to his aid. Driven to extreme measures, he tried to obtain support from the French, to whom, in his panic, he was prepared to pay any price and to pay it in advance. In order to retain the command of an army, which would be reinforced by the occupation troops from Colmar and Schlettstadt, he decided to surrender these towns to France together with a large number of the neighbouring villages and their dependencies, that is, practically the whole of Upper Alsace.

Under the terms of the relevant agreement the French received not only the towns then threatened by the Imperial troops under Generals Reinach and Mercy but also nearly all the other strongholds in Upper Alsace. In the initial discussions there was talk of "French protection", of the preservation of Imperial rights and the Liberties of the Estates and also of consideration for the interests of the Heilbronn League. As to Colmar, it was stipulated that the French protectorate should last only until the conclusion of peace, whereupon the town's legal position would revert to that obtaining in 1618. King Louis XIII and eventually, albeit unwillingly, Oxenstierna ratified the agreement; four days later, on October 10, 1634, Colmar was occupied by French troops. On September 18th—the very day on which Otto Ludwig had agreed to hand over Upper Alsace to France—Jakob Löffler, the Chancellor of Württemberg, and Philipp Streiff, the minister from Zweibrücken, had appeared at the French Court. When they offered the entire province of Alsace, except for Benfeld, and asked for massive financial aid in return, they were coolly informed that the territory was already in French hands thanks to the Rhinegrave, who had been obliged by the force of circumstances to transfer it to France.

There then followed Richelieu's masterly achievement, the draft treaty of October 22nd: France, Sweden and the Heilbronn League agreed to join together to "bring about a good peace in Germany" by every means at their disposal and to guarantee that peace for a period of twenty years. The Electors of Saxony and Brandenburg were to be invited to participate, and—the most important point as far as Richelieu was concerned—none of the signatories to the agreement was to conduct independent peace negotiations with the enemy and none was to conclude an armistice for more than two to three weeks either in Germany or in Lorraine. All who wished to leave the Emperor and place themselves under French protection were to be offered the incentive of neutrality, and Richelieu succeeded in obtaining the reinstitution of the Catholic religion in the territories conquered by the Swedish and allied armies. For his part, the King of France undertook to keep a powerful army on the west bank of the Rhine and to use it, both offensively and defensively, whenever necessary. He did not undertake to make an open declaration of war.

Oxenstierna was extremely loath to put his signature to these agreements. He was embittered by the Rhinegrave's conduct and the haste with which these measures had been carried through. It had always been his intention to surrender Alsace only in the very last resort as the price of French entry into the war. Now this province had actually been handed over to Louis XIII without any worthwhile undertakings in return. The Swedish Chancellor commanded the Rhinegrave—who, after having disregarded Horn's instructions prior to the battle of Nördlingen, had now perpetrated another capital error in Alsace—to proceed to Worms and appear before him. Otto Ludwig was forced to comply. But shortly after his arrival, aged only thirty-seven years, he died from exhaustion.

France now found herself in possession of the whole of the Upper Rhine from Basle to Mainz. But the presence of Protestant troops on the west bank of the Rhine at that time was something which Richelieu found highly undesirable, for it meant that Alsace would remain a theatre of war for a long time to come and consequently many of the future battles in the German civil war were likely to be enacted on the French side of the river.

After taking Schweinfurt and Würzburg, the major part of the Imperialist army had been used to garrison these cities and only cavalry units had advanced to Heilbronn to strengthen the new force then being assembled in Württemberg by the Duke of Lorraine. From this Saxe-Weimar assumed that the Imperialists had made no plans for an offensive for the time being and that everyone was intent on finding reasonably tolerable winter quarters. Given Saxe-Weimar's character, this thought was enough for him to go over to the offensive. His principal object was to obtain supreme command of the entire Protestant army and also of the French auxiliaries. The internal difficulties that beset the League of Protestant Princes, which had made themselves felt frequently during the negotiations in Mainz, could only serve to further Bernhard's aims. At their convention in Worms he informed the Estates of the League in unmistakable terms that he was intent on acquiring the generalship. He exploited the discord between them and Oxensterna and considered trying to supplant the Swedish Chancellor. He also tried to exploit the threat that Johann von Werth then offered to Heidelberg.

Although Werth had been obliged to withdraw his forces for a while, by the beginning of December powerful units of the Imperial army had again appeared before the walls of the Palatinate capital. This might even have endangered the League's convention in Worms.

In order to defer France's definitive break with the Emperor, Richelieu decided that Saxe-Weimar and not the French army should relieve the capital. But Saxe-Weimar made conditions; as on previous occasions he demanded massive military support. At this point Oxenstierna reversed his earlier policy and tried to persuade Bernhard to follow him with his army to northern Germany, which, he explained, would force the French to conduct the battle on the Rhine themselves. It may

54

also be assumed that he had begun to fear that Bernhard might enter into closer contact with France, for by then Feuquières had arrived on the scene as Richelieu's special representative and was using all his skill to prevent Saxe-Weimar from agreeing to Oxenstierna's request; he even tried to persuade Bernhard's troops to defect. Later he was to admit that, for a moment, he had thought of seizing both the Swedish Chancellor and the Duke of Saxe-Weimar. At this point the Emperor also made Bernhard a tempting offer: he undertook to guarantee him his Duchy of Franconia.

But Saxe-Weimar could not consider Imperialist offers, although he did exploit them as a means of bringing pressure to bear on the French. Even at that early stage the French Marshals wanted to relieve Heidelberg themselves, but Richelieu warned of the consequences of such direct action against the Emperor. Bernhard of Saxe-Weimar's co-operation appeared indispensable. To the surprise of everyone save Richelieu, who had instigated the move, Feuquières then received the support of Henri de Rohan, a man whom Bernhard greatly admired, and whose deeper designs were of course well known to the Cardinal. But the fact that up to Gustavus Adolphus' death Duke Henri had ardently longed for a Franco–Swedish war to bring about the downfall of Richelieu's régime did not prevent the Cardinal from employing him in a calculated attempt to persuade Duke Bernhard, a fellow-Protestant, to agree to the French proposals. The Cardinal felt quite certain of the effect of his influence.

Initially Saxe-Weimar was offered six thousand French troops, but he insisted that a whole army must be placed at his disposal if he was to drive the enemy from the territories between the Neckar and the Main and to free both Hanau and Frankfurt from the threat of attack. At the same time Bernhard was negotiating with the Protestant Estates. Their representatives came to him and were prepared to offer him the generalship on condition that he march to the defence of Heidelberg and Württemberg. The French, however, were too quick for them. Forgetting their earlier qualms, they moved into Heidelberg on December 4th and took possession of the town. The "last-ditchers" in Vienna were already hoping for a declaration of war. In Paris a treaty was drawn up between the Duke of Württemberg and other German princes, which was hastily ratified on November 1st by a number of the Estates then convened in Worms, the Administrator of the Palatinate, the Palsgrave of Zweibrücken, the Duke of Württemberg, the Margrave of Baden, Landgrave William of Hesse and various others. The Imperial cities did not sign, on the grounds that they lacked the authority. This treaty split the League, and some of its members, acting on the assumption that Sweden was no longer in a position to help them, entered into contractual agreements with France. Oxenstierna, for his part, declared that the terms of the treaty rendered the Franco-Swedish alliance null and void.

Feuquières quickly arranged to provide the half million livres needed to pay the troops of the Protestant Princes. Oxenstierna hoped that he himself would be able to control the distribution of this money, but the French informed him that it had been promised to the German Estates and would be paid out to Bernhard of Saxe-Weimar, the General commanding the Protestant army, on the condition of his not moving out of the four northern Circles; Bernhard accepted this condition.

There then followed the hard winter campaign of 1634–5. After Richelieu and the cabinet had insisted on the amalgamation of the Protestant forces and the French contingents, pressure was brought on the German army leaders to follow France's protégé, Duke Eberhard III of Württemberg, into his Duchy in order to reconquer it. But Bernhard of Saxe-Weimar was reluctant to move away from Mainz, which was increasingly beset by the Imperial General, Philipp von Mansfeld. In order to be free to execute the Württemberg project, Bernhard advanced towards Mansfeld, with the aim of defeating him or at least cutting off his supply routes. But the roads were wretched, there was sharp frost and the march proceeded very slowly. This gave Mansfeld time to mass troops at Aschaffenburg, to reinforce the earthworks on both banks of the Main and to secure the river line with Croats; he avoided open battle.

Meanwhile the Imperialists had made speedy progress in their occupation of Bernhard's Duchy, Franconia. After Würzburg had fallen together with its citadel, and those of Saxe-Weimar's troops still left in the Duchy had been decimated by the cold as they marched and counter-marched in bitter frost, Bernhard tried to give all his units a period of rest at Hanau. Meanwhile Philippsburg, too, had fallen. While French units had been encamped on the mountain road the Imperialists had succeeded in crossing the frozen moats surrounding the fortress and storming the walls on scaling ladders. They found large stores of money, corn and war materials. Almost simultaneously Johann von Werth crossed the Rhine and forced the fortress of Speier to capitulate.

In Paris the Court was alarmed to find that the enemy had taken the initiative in opening hostilities. The fact that French troops had undertaken the second relief of Heidelberg was not regarded in France as a hostile act but as a necessity imposed by treaty obligations. When Johann von Werth and the Duke of Lorraine appeared on the west bank of the Rhine and Werth announced that within two or three weeks he hoped to be standing before the walls of Paris, when he had coins minted on which a sword was depicted descending from the clouds and piercing the French lily, when the rumour began to circulate that the Duke of Lorraine was to be placed on the French throne and Imperial officers even began to speak of the French provinces to be given to them in reward for their services, the French became alarmed. Then came reports that Ferdinand's troops had been ordered "to show no quarter to the French", news filtered through of the failure of the French garrison to hold the fortress of Philippsburg and of the May treaty concluded between Orléans and the Spanish, and all this, combined with other rumours, many of them quite ridiculous, created a warlike spirit, especially in Paris. Richelieu calmly took note of it and decided that on no account should this fire be allowed to die out.

Bernhard of Saxe-Weimar was a disciple of Gustavus Adolphus, and a kindred spirit. Like him, he went for all-out victory. Contrary to the military practices of his time and with no regard for the seasons, he always tried to force a military decision. In critical situations, however, when he was faced with superior forces, he was also a master of the art of disengagement. He was to demonstrate this mastery when, within the framework of the general offensive launched by the Imperial forces on the eastern borders of France, the army under General Gallas advanced across the Rhine and completely wore itself out with its marches and counter-marches. It had been clear since 1634 that the French armies would not themselves be in a position to repel the invasion and that only Saxe-Weimar could help them. The French Marshals, also aware of this, pressed Richelieu to win the Duke's services for France. Not that he needed pressing, for Richelieu had long been determined to pay a very high price in order to bind Duke Bernhard of Saxe-Weimar to the French cause. Throughout the whole of 1634, at Richelieu's orders, relations between Feuquières and the supreme commander of the German Protestant armies were particularly close, although this had not prevented the French negotiator from being sharply critical of the Duke right up to 1635. On numerous occasions he expressed the view that they could expect more unpleasant surprises than benefits from Saxe-Weimar.

In the new situation, Bernhard rejected the proposal that he lead his tired troops to Luxemburg and quarter them there. Although the curse of the century, the plague, had broken out in his ranks, he was determined to retake Philippsburg. For, although his position on the east bank of the Rhine had been so endangered by the latest Imperialist successes that he had no option but to cross over to the west bank, he wanted his Rhine crossing to appear, not as a retreat but as the prerequisite of a glorious feat of arms. And just as he had insisted that Philippsburg must be stormed on the east bank, so too he insisted on the capture of Speyer (Spires) on the west bank. The Estates, convened in Worms, must not be allowed to conclude their negotiations in an atmosphere of continuous military failure.

Speyer was besieged at the beginning of March, and on March 11th the town surrendered. The French Field Marshal, Hébron, and Saxe-Weimar's Colonel, Taupadel, first disarmed the members of the garrison and then immediately recruited them for their own regiments. By paying a high indemnity the town escaped plunder.

CHAPTER III

FRANCE'S ENTRY INTO THE WAR

Though the Prague peace negotiations were still tentative and hampered by a series of hedging provisions, they provided the basis for a general peace settlement in Germany and harboured at the worst the following dangers for France: a combined assault on the part of all the Hapsburg states, following the elimination of their Scandinavian and German opponents in consequence of a Spanish-Dutch armistice or peace; collaboration between the Spanish and the Imperialists in Italy, on the Rhine, in Alsace and in the Netherlands; attacks across the Spanish border and on the Mediterranean coasts.

But the situation was not yet so extreme. The countries that might have combined to oppose France were divided among themselves because of their vested interests and total lack of mutual trust. One thing was certain, however: if France wished her Protestant allies, who were abhorred by the opponents of the French régime, to stick together, if she wished to preserve the coalition, which had been formed to oppose the Emperor and the great might of the Counter-Reformation, she could no longer hope to do so by the mere mention of a parade-ground army of forty-thousand men on the Rhine and by desperately trying to hand out subsidies in all directions; she must take action, and the only action that would suffice was a declaration of war.

In the first chapter of his *Political Testament*, that is, in the *Succincte Narration* (Short Report), Richelieu wrote to his King:

"If it is a sign of singular prudence to have held down the forces opposed to your state for a period of ten years with the forces of your allies, by putting your hand in your pocket and not on your sword, then to engage in open warfare when your allies can no longer exist without you is a sign of courage and great wisdom; which shows that, in husbanding the peace of your kingdom, you have behaved like those economists who, having taken great care to amass money, also know how to spend it in order to safeguard themselves against greater loss."

No doubt about it, it had taken great courage to win time in this way, but above all it had taken an exceptional degree of skill. Richelieu had always regarded open warfare as a necessity that might suddenly descend upon him. In the most difficult circumstances and in the face of well-nigh insuperable obstacles he had been re-arming ever since 1624, and that despite the constant and disproportionate demands made on the nation's finances. We have already discussed Richelieu's endeavours to rebuild the navy (cf. Vol. II, pp. 17 ff.); we must now turn our attention to the army. Memories of the religious wars were far too fresh for the Cardinal not to have realized that a state that was surrounded by the power of Spain and the Hapsburgs could not afford to tolerate the existence within its borders of powerful independent groups, who might form alliances at any time with the country's external enemies. While conducting a "masked" war abroad Richelieu strove increasingly to establish positions that would afford him the greatest possible advantages, should France suddenly find herself embroiled in a fight to the death. He carried out troop movements on the frontiers and local campaigns beyond them in order to help his allies and confuse the enemy.

In 1625, as we have seen, he intervened in the Valtelline. In 1629, in connection with Mantua's War of Succession, he established, partly by force of arms but more especially by negotiation, assault points from which he could advance into northern Italy. In 1630 these gains were consolidated by the occupation of Pinerolo. In 1632 the feasibility of invading Alsace was discussed in the King's Council. In 1633, in The Hague, Charnacé prevented the conclusion of an armistice between Spain and the Netherlands. Between 1633 and 1634 Lorraine was occupied. Even before the severe defeat imposed on the Swedish army at Nördlingen the French armies had advanced into Alsace in order to safeguard the Rhine: February 1635 saw the conclusion of the Franco–Dutch offensive alliance, which was negotiated by Charnacé.

On April 5, 1634, the States General had accepted French subsidies and undertaken not to negotiate with the Spanish before May 1st of the following year. Then, on February 8, 1635, Henry IV's old alliance with the Dutch was formally renewed. Both sides undertook to conduct only bilateral negotiations with the common enemy; their objective was the division of the Spanish Netherlands between France and the States General.

Without this system of military safeguards France could never have undertaken offensive action. A second system, which was equally important and in the event was to have much more far-reaching consequences, was incorporated into the Treaty of Compiègne, which was concluded on April 28, between France and Sweden. Twenty-two days before the French declaration of war Louis XIII and Queen Christina solemnly undertook never to agree to a peace or an armistice or to cede strongholds without first consulting one another. Thus was created the pernicious condition that chains two States together for better or worse, deprives them of freedom of action and obliges the war-weary partner to fight for as long as the other party to the treaty is able to obtain even minor, ephemeral advantages. This treaty also guaranteed religious freedom in Germany, or rather the *status quo ante* of 1618. France promised the Swedes the Archbishopric of Mainz and the Bishopric of Worms. In fact, Oxenstierna, who was at first reluctant to negotiate with the French from the position of weakness in which he found himself following Nördlingen, finished up by obtaining considerable concessions. He retained Benfeld and the sovereignty of various Rhenish territories and also forced Richelieu openly to condemn Ferdinand II's work for the restoration of Catholicism in Bohemia. At that point in time, when France might well have lost her allies, the Cardinal was forced to yield to this chain of binding alliances.

Sweden, for her part, had taken measures to try to cover her eastern flank as early as 1634. On May 27, 1634, following the conclusion of the Russo–Polish Peace of Polyankowa, the Swedes and the French had tried to draw Russia, the great unknown factor at that time, into the European conflict. The attempt failed. Impressed by the reversals suffered by the Catholic coalition, of which Poland was a member, those responsible for Russian foreign policy had ordered an army to advance against Smolensk in 1632. This was the sign for Sweden and France to try to draw Russia into the alliance against the Emperor. But the Smolensk garrison held out, and after the beleaguered town had been relieved the Russian army was forced to capitulate. In granting the Russians peace terms the victors were motivated primarily by the threat of a renewed Turkish attack but also by the fact that as the war continued in Germany, Poland had constantly to face new problems. And so this political stratagem devised by Richelieu and his allies, which is reminiscent of the Turkish policy pursued by Francis I, did not succeed.

But Richelieu could not and did not accept full responsibility for the declaration of war on Spain. That he was wrongly blamed for having done so in the hard times to come was due to circumstances that we shall discuss later. The King had to make the decision, he had to be prevailed upon to do so—and he did so, not because Richelieu forced him into it but because over a considerable period he had been warning him against it.

The Cardinal was completely vindicated by a letter he received from his sovereign from Chantilly dated August 4, 1634, that is, one month before Nördlingen. The text reads:

"My Cousin,

Since you have asked me to enumerate the reasons about which I spoke to you a few days ago and which might make it necessary for us to break with Spain, I have set them down for you in my own hand. Nobody has seen them; I enclose them in this packet. Pray excuse me if they are not well composed, but I acquired my eloquence in the army and among soldiers. I shall not write at length but merely assure you of my affection, which will endure unto death and shall continue to pray to God that He may always keep you under His blessed protection.

Louis."

The arguments then follow, set out, clumsily but pertinently, under ten headings. We have already indicated their contents. But to recapitulate: The declaration of war is an act of necessity; without it the Protestant coalition will collapse, we shall lose all our allies and be isolated and exposed to the combined power of Austria and Spain. On the other hand, if we nail our colours to the mast and act, we will strengthen and encourage our allies and so retain them; we could scarcely find a better time to strike than at this moment. In the Spanish Netherlands a new revolt is threatening and the Dutch are great fighters; but if we disappoint them now, then the party that is intent on promoting an armistice with Spain will gain the upper hand, and this must be avoided. Italy has been denuded of Spanish troops; without the Germans the Spanish can achieve nothing in Italy, and at present the Emperor is unable to deploy effective fighting forces in the north Italian theatre of war. Spanish army organization is bad. Philip IV's kingdom is at present faced with difficult undertakings on all sides, ergo: the King of France is unreservedly in favour of entering the war.

In considering this memorandum of August 4th it is important to bear in mind the document that Richelieu submitted to his sovereign after September 6th, that is, in the completely different circumstances obtaining subsequent to the decisive battle at Nördlingen. There, for the first time, he gave his full approval to the persuasive reasoning of the royal memorandum. The Cardinal, as a rule given to presenting the pros and cons of a matter in rhetorical counterpoint, was unusually unambivalent this time. He begins his sentences with locutions such as "It is certain . . ." and "there can be no doubt . . .", and he fully concurs with the King's arguments.

Unlike Louis, however, the Prime Minister still wrote with circumspection:

"In order to make the right decision in such an important and difficult question we have to be extremely well informed; we have to listen to our defeated allies, we have to call on them, hear what they have to offer, encourage them and assure them of His Majesty's good intentions and even of his readiness to help; but only if they are really able to prove that, given such help, they will then be able to resist Imperial power. We ourselves must arm with great energy and all possible speed so as to be able to make such decisions as are called for by both prudence and necessity."

Richelieu knew how uncertain the outcome of such a weighty venture could be. The military position that he had slowly built up in Germany was at the moment not unfavourable: French units or units under French control held Lorraine, the southern part of Alsace and the County of Mömpelgard (Montbéliard), from which troops advancing against Burgundy through the gap between the Jura and the Vosges could be kept under observation. In Lower Alsace, Hagenau, Buchsweiler, Bischweiler and Zabern had been taken. On the Rhine a French garrison was established in Philippsburg up to January 1635; Ehrenbreitstein and Coblenz were still in French hands, which meant that France controlled the line of the Moselle from Treves and Sierck. Richelieu could reasonably assume that the Swedes would agree to the replacement of their own garrisons in Alsace by French units.

The French line of defence stretched from occupied Lorraine as far as Breisach, where the Imperialists were still holding out. The Cardinal regarded Strassburg as a possible danger point; at any time, he said, this Imperial city might allow a hostile army to cross the bridge at Kehl on to the west bank.

But there were other, far more critical considerations; the French army contingents were much too small; there had been talk of a hundred thousand men, but they existed only on paper; the army's military experience of recent years had been limited to civil wars. The French government was headed by two men of uncertain health: the King and his Prime Minister.

At this point we have to ask ourselves: To what extent were the foreign policy considerations, which were the mainspring of Richelieu's policies, based on an objective assessment of actual conditions?

In the first volume of this study on the Cardinal and the influence he exercised on present and future times, on his immediate environment and the world at large, it was seen that the France of the Bourbons, first utterly exhausted by religious warfare, then initially rescued by Henry IV, found itself as late as the third decade of the seventeenth century still encircled on all its frontiers by the combined powers of Spain and Austria. This is the basic premise for the thesis of one school of French historians, which explains all of Richelieu's policies in terms of defensive actions essential to the survival of the State. Richelieu himself also constantly referred to his policies as rescue and defensive actions.

But those of the Cardinal's contemporaries, both at home and abroad, who were his political opponents insisted that even during Philip III's reign the Spanish threat to France no longer existed. They also asked how the Holy Roman Emperor, who was constantly pushed into extremely precarious situations by both the Turks and the Protestants, could possibly have constituted a serious threat to France.

Let us recapitulate a few of the relevant facts. During the religious wars the French Holy League, which was supported and financed by the Guises, was an instrument of Spanish power. Time and again Spanish troops had been garrisoned in Paris. The members of Richelieu's generation still had vivid memories of these events; towards the end of his life Henry IV considered a preventive war against Spain to be inevitable. After his reign, even after the Franco–Spanish marriages of 1613, relations between the two neighbouring countries remained tense, and this despite the decidedly pro-Spanish line adopted by Marie de' Medici during her regency. This tension was clearly manifested during the struggle between the French Crown and the Huguenots right up to the moment when Spain, suspicious and ineffectual, made a pretence of helping the King of France before La Rochelle, only to conclude a secret treaty with Henri de Rohan, the Huguenot leader, immediately afterwards. At this point we notice the influence of the Duke of Olivares, Richelieu's opponent, who immediately exploited every French weakness, in all parts of the world, and who, despite the Counter-Reformation programme adopted by the Kings of Spain, not only incited Huguenot resistance but also gave support to all the other revolutionary groups in France, especially the Princes and the great nobles. Just how much Richelieu's policies were prompted by the conviction that he was under threat of attack will be brought out in the further course of our inquiry.

As for the Viennese Hapsburgs, they had first constituted a potential and unpredictable source of danger for French foreign policy following the Battle of the White Hill, then throughout the period of Wallenstein's victories and finally—and most unequivocally—following the Battle of Nördlingen and the conclusion of the Peace of Prague. For a considerable time Richelieu was most certainly convinced that the combined forces of Spain, the Emperor and the German Catholic League were still able to deal a mortal blow to France. This is shown by the proposals submitted to Ferdinand II in 1635 by the Imperial Resident in Paris. Seen in this light, it seems obvious that the man responsible for the political destinies of France should consider it incumbent upon him, not only to form alliances with the Protestant Estates of the Holy Roman Empire but also to promote in every possible way, first the Danish and then the Swedish invasion in Germany and, further, to do all within his power to separate the Catholic Estates, especially Bavaria, from Austria, to eliminate Wallenstein and to create assault points on his own frontiers. We should also remember that in 1635, when Richelieu was forced to declare war on Spain for fear of losing every one of his allies, it looked as if all of these preparatory measures, which he had planned with such consistency, were going to fail him, so that in 1636 he found himself facing a combined Austro–Spanish offensive in an almost desperate situation, from which he was rescued only by a series of astonishing military feats on the part of Bernhard of Saxe-Weimar and by the lack of co-ordination between the enemy commands.

Ever since the great Swedish defeat France's allies had pressed and threatened her from Frankfurt, asserting that the only way to salvage the situation was for Louis XIII to break with the House of Hapsburg. But Richelieu kept them waiting; month after month he played for time. When it was finally no longer possible to avoid the rupture, he was faced with deteriorated rather than improved conditions, owing to fresh Imperial victories.

And so, while still officially at peace with both Spain and the Emperor, France was actually threatened by all the dangers of war. Although the terms of the Peace of Vervins and subsequently the Treaty of the Pyrenees had fixed the borders of their respective kingdoms and had also satisfied the claims of their allies, by that time France and Spain had gone a long way to inflict harm and injustice on one another by unacknowledged warfare; they had already clashed unofficially on many a battlefield in Germany, the Netherlands and Italy. In Madrid it was said that, under pressure from Richelieu, Louis XIII was about to repudiate his Queen. Philip IV communicated

on this matter with Christoph de Benavente, one of his representatives in Paris:

"I was surprised to learn from the despatches which you
sent to Señor Conde-Duque [Olivares] what is happening in
France with regard to the Queen, Our sister. It is reported that
Monsieur de Créqui has been sent to Rome with instructions
to negotiate the dissolution of her marriage."

In the same letter Philip instructed his representative to
call on Cardinal Richelieu in order to convince him that Madrid
still believed his intentions to be honourable; his projects, it
was known, were far-reaching, his mind of the first magnitude,
he was cut out for fame; let him therefore recognize that
nobody could offer him more effective help in realizing his
high-flung intentions than the King of Spain. At the same time,
however, the King advised his representative to exercise the
utmost discretion so as not to spoil Spain's relations with the
Queen-Mother and Gaston d'Orléans by these advances to the
Cardinal. We possess a further letter of Philip's, written only a
little later to his Ambassador, the Marqués de Mirabel, instructing him to distribute immediate subsidies to further the revolt
then being staged by the Dukes of Guise and Epernon. (The
underlying causes of these revolts will be explained later.)
By this time France's preparations for war had reached a
pitch which made it clear to Madrid that further negotiations
and political manoeuvres were pointless. The Spanish regretted
that neither the welfare of Christendom nor the close family
ties that linked the two dynasties were any longer being considered.

The time had come for the Spanish diplomats to leave Paris.
The Duc de Montbazon had already called on the special
envoy, Fabian de Coutreras, and informed him that he would
be given safe conduct on his journey. The Spanish diplomat
ordered post horses. Then suddenly, as he himself reported,
close to a hundred armed men forced their way into his house.
They were led by the chief of police in the suburb of Saint-

Germain, who had issued a proclamation calling upon all able-bodied men in his district to take up arms. He arrested the diplomat in the name of the King, accused him of harbouring various high-ranking Spaniards and asserted that incriminating documents had been taken from four couriers. Coutreras was threatened with execution, but shortly afterwards the French authorities apologized and released him.

A year later Sebastian Lustrier, Canon of Olmütz, the last Imperial Resident in France, was to receive much the same treatment. His first report was sent on December 28, 1633, and his final letter from Paris was dated August 10, 1635.

With the departure of the Spanish representative from Paris the inevitable step had been taken and the official French declaration of war, which was made in Brussels on May 19, 1635, following the conclusion on April 28th of the new alliance with Sweden in which the major provisions of the Treaty of Bärwalde were renewed, was a purely formal act performed in traditional style when a herald in medieval costume, bearing the arms of France and accompanied by a trumpeter, presented himself to the Cardinal-Infante. This grave step was taken on the grounds that the Spanish Stadtholder in the Netherlands had not returned his lands to the Archbishop of Trèves, who enjoyed French protection. For a while Don Fernando considered whether he would even receive the herald, but then he granted him an audience. And so the pretext for France's entry into this war, which continued long after the death of Richelieu and Louis XIII and even after the Peace of Westphalia, was furnished by the fact that, following the fall of Philippsburg, the Spanish had advanced into the Electorate of Trèves and compelled the French army under Duke de La Force to withdraw. On March 26, 1635, Spanish troops had seized the Elector of Trèves, Archbishop Philip von Sötern, although he enjoyed the explicit protection of His Most Christian Majesty. They conducted him as their prisoner to Ghent. Since, as ally of Sweden, Louis XIII had undertaken to guarantee the safety and possessions of the ecclesiastical princes along the

Rhine, this constituted an open act of aggression, a provocation from one sovereign to another to which there was only one response.

A special meeting of the Royal Council was convened on April 1st in Rueil and presided over by the King; the ministers unanimously agreed that Louis must retaliate immediately by force of arms.

But before giving an account of the outbreak of open warfare and of the forces at the disposal of the belligerent powers, we must consider the nature and condition, the main historical premises of the Spanish Hapsburg monarchy.

CHAPTER IV

SPAIN

Philip II

Under Philip II the Spanish dominions were twenty times the size of the Roman Empire at the peak of its expansion under Trajan. And yet, in the mid-eighteenth century, the Scottish historian David Hume called the Spanish Empire a "gigantic bluff" based solely on its prestige, and much earlier Sully, in his Memoirs, pointed to the disproportion between Spanish claims and Spanish might. Though Richelieu constantly used the oppressive power of Spain in his argumentations, we shall see later what he really thought of it. *Prestigium* implies magical delusion. But is not the incalculable power of appearance one of the strongest elements in the shaping of history? And further, behind that appearance were the tangible factors that had created it. These were the superhuman achievements of the explorers, the accomplishments of Castilians going to the very limits of self-sacrifice, their heroic endurance—in brief, the Spanish character, exerting itself to the utmost over a period of two hundred years.

Philip II, son of Charles V and Isabella of Portugal, did not become Emperor. As King of Spain he administered all his domains from Castile. These different territories stood in marked contrast to one another and strategically were extremely difficult to defend. Philip always remained a stranger to the Flemish. The first time Charles V took him to Burgundy and Germany the heir-apparent proved a disappointment.

Members of the Prince's entourage, especially his aunt, Queen Maria of Hungary, the regent of the Netherlands, tried to loosen up his rigid nature and make him adapt to the happy spontaneity of the Dutch way of life. But it was not in Philip's nature to adapt; his was an uncompromising personality, destined to find its essential expression in the ceremonial of the Escorial.

Unlike his father, when Philip mounted the throne he did not move from residence to residence in the tradition of the great medieval Emperors. He gave his unreserved allegiance to Castile, the very heart of Spain, and his capital and residence was Madrid. This monarch, who was so un-Spanish in appearance, identified himself with Spain; he looked upon all disturbances, even in the most distant provinces, as revolts against Spanish power. The remaining territories of the Spanish world, over which he ruled, were foreign countries and completely alien to him.

Emperor Charles V, as King Charles I of Spain, had always preferred a representative administration. His Council contained delegates from every territory in the realm. Philip II's Council of State, conversely, consisted almost entirely of members of the Castilian aristocracy; it included the Duke of Alba, the Prince of Éboli, the Duke of Feria and Antonio of Toledo. Granvelle, who had been Charles V's most important adviser during the latter part of his reign and who had once said of himself: "I come from all parts", was only a nominal member of Philip's Council and spent most of his time in Brussels. The Italian Princes were admitted only to the Council of War, which the monarch referred to as "The Plebeian Council".

The army of State officials was greatly increased under Philip. The wasteful practices of a proliferating bureaucracy were established; the inevitable consequences were to be seen on all sides. Recourse was had to a type of institution created by Ferdinand and Isabella, that is, to the juntas or Provincial Councils: the Council of Castile, the Council of Aragon, the Council of the Orders, the Council of the Inquisition, the Council of the Indies. But this consultative system concealed a centralizing trend. Charles V had hardly ever interfered in the internal affairs of Castile and Aragon, and in his time the Spanish and German Chancelleries had dealt with foreign affairs under the supervision of Granvelle and Los Cobos.

Under Philip the Council of State became less important, while the Secretaries of State acquired greater influence. But this latter development did not please the King. He had no use for a German Chancellery, and he reduced the Chancellery of Aragon to a mere administrative department. Philip himself took control of Milanese and Neapolitan affairs. The Italian Council simply provided him with information. The same was true of the Netherlands Council and subsequently of the Portuguese Council. All in all there were thirteen Council organizations with widely differing administrative spheres. The so-called "Council of the Crusade", which Charles V had founded at the beginning of his reign, still survived. There was also a Finance Council, which was attached to the Council of Castile and dealt with benefices and acts of grace. The Council of War came under the Council of State. The Councils of Castile and Aragon had overall jurisdiction on a nation-wide scale; the Council of State had general jurisdiction; the Council of the Inquisition, against which the Flemish and the Italians had never ceased their opposition, had mixed jurisdiction. One of the King's principal advisers was his confessor. The monarch could convene juntas whenever he saw fit. They were composed either of outside advisers or of the members of other Councils.

Philip was provided with detailed information and respectful advice, but he himself made all decisions. He also had his favourites, some of whom were faithful servants of the State. Both Éboli and Alba were merely advisers. Éboli was regarded as Philip's creature while Alba was the foremost member of the Castilian nobility; but both were certainly no more than officials, although undoubtedly they were rivals. Éboli, who always strove for reconciliation and tried to incline his master to clemency, waited on Philip with calm devotion and sought to win him over by his modesty. By contrast, Alba pressed for decisions, for action, for speedy and often brutal intervention.

When Alba was sent to Flanders Diego de Espinosa entered the scene. Within a few years this priest became a Cardinal, President of the Council of Castile and Grand Inquisitor. The King soon came to distrust him. One day, when Espinosa was reporting on Flemish questions, he interrupted him with the words: "So that is your way of lying."

Since 1484 the Inquisition had been one of the royal organizations in Aragon and since 1489 in Castile; but in Castile its jurisdiction had always been limited and subject to the control of the Council. The *inquisitio haereticae pravitatis* had developed out of the Church's struggle against the Cathari and Waldenses. Its origin goes back to a Jewish institution, the religious tribunal. Coercive measures against heresy, albeit without torture and without the death penalty, had been practised by the Early Church ever since the fourteenth century. The papal decree sanctioning the tracking down of heretics was promulgated at the Synod of Verona in 1184 by Pope Lucius III. This was the beginning of the pontifical Inquisition. The provisions of Verona were subsequently endorsed by Innocent III at the Lateran Council of 1215. But it was the percipient and in many ways enlightened Emperor, Frederick II of Hohenstaufen, who first introduced the death penalty and the burning of heretics. The papal Inquisition was founded between 1231 and 1232 by Gregory IX. It was administered primarily by Franciscans and Dominicans. All believers were placed under an obligation to denounce heretics, all heretics were required to come forward. Then came summonses, to be followed shortly afterwards by arrests. The identity of informers and witnesses was not revealed to the accused. If the prosecuting counsel was a personal enemy of the accused he could be excluded, but defence counsel was not allowed. The use of torture was permitted by Innocent IV.

In France the Inquisition was deprived of its powers as

early as the fourteenth century, although it continued to exist as a formal institution until 1772.

In Spain, this ancient organization was revived in 1478, as a tool for the State to proceed against baptized Jews and Moors accused of sham conversion. In the same year it was centralized under a Grand Inquisitor; the King's influence was the crucial factor in determining its reinstitution.

Protestantism had already found its way into Spain during Charles V's reign. The largest group among its adherents was that of the baptized Jews. Church and State joined forces to oppose both them and the converted Moors, who were accused of secretly adhering to the Prophet. A papal bull issued by Paul IV required that all heretics be handed over to the secular arm. Jews who had become Catholic under duress were referred to as Marranos. The two hundred thousand emigrants who left Spain in 1492 included many Marranos; they settled on all the Mediterranean coasts and also in Antwerp, Amsterdam, London and Hamburg, where many of them reverted to the religion of their fathers.

On May 21, 1599, the first *auto-da-fé* took place in Valladolid. We possess a description of such an event from the reign of Philip II: over two hundred thousand spectators were gathered, the majority of the condemned were women, including nuns from the convent of Belém and a Poor Clare from Valladolid. When they had been led up to the green cross of the Inquisition, which stood in front of the stake, the Grand Inquisitor, Valdés, turned to Philip II with the words *"Domine, adjuva nos!"* The King rose and drew his sword as a sign that heresy must be extirpated. Valdés then read out the oath, whereby the King pledged himself to protect the Inquisition from all enemies and to promote the extirpation of atheism and of all deviation from orthodoxy. Philip replied: "I swear".

The punishment for deviations was particularly severe and and most severe of all for any divergence, however slight, towards the Protestant doctrine. Charles V's confessor,

Bartolomé Carranza, Spain's distinguished envoy to the Council of Trent, was thrown into prison because, when Charles V lay dying, he had pointed to the crucifix and said: "He will take your part, there is no sin now, all is forgiven." This was interpreted as a statement of the doctrine of justification by faith and consequently as Lutheran. Carranza remained in prison for nine years; to save him from execution the Pope had to threaten King Philip with the interdict. Political motives also played a part in this case. But Carranza was not the only high prelate to suffer in this way; the Archbishop of Granada and Santiago, the Bishops of León, Almería and Lugo, were subjected to searching interrogations. The Inquisition trials in Valladolid and Seville uncovered numerous links between the Protestants in Spain, Germany and Geneva. It was then that the authorities began to isolate Spain from the intellectual life of the rest of Europe. Even converted Moors were treated with the utmost mistrust. But this oppression should be regarded as a continuation of the centuries-old struggle against the Arabs. Under Philip II an attempt was made to force those Moors still living in Spain to give up their language and customs. For the last time they took to arms. Don Juan of Austria, the son of Charles V and Barbara Blomberg of Regensburg, suppressed the rising and eradicated further resistance.

All this is as dismal as the dispute between the King and the severely tainted heir-apparent, Don Carlos, and Philip's relationship to his half-brother, Don Juan of Austria, whose successes as a military commander both on land and at sea were galling to the King, for no man was allowed to excel the monarch in personal prestige. But there were also a number of objective factors which counted heavily against the great Bastard. Don Juan was pursuing fantastic plans. He intended to invade England from the Netherlands in order to free Mary Stuart, marry her and thus gain sovereign power over England, Scotland and the Netherlands. It was inevitable that Queen Elizabeth should request his recall. Rumours proliferated concerning his death and that of his nephew, Don Carlos, and the interest that the world has taken in the fate of these two Princes found its reflection in literature.

Don Juan of Austria's meteoric rise to fame is linked to one of the crucial events in Spanish history. Attempts have been made to belittle the consequences of the naval battle of Lepanto, which was fought under his command on October 7, 1571; but this victory over the Turks undoubtedly called a temporary halt to the Turkish advance in the Mediterranean. The Turks were also mighty opponents at sea; they organized fleets of up to two hundred ships. Their great assault was mounted in 1565, when they blockaded Malta. Garcia of Toledo, the Spanish Viceroy in Sicily, succeeded in relieving the strategically immensely important island. Following Lepanto, the Turks were driven back to the Aegean, Italy was saved from an Islamic invasion and the Italians were spared the fate that had befallen the Greeks.

Don Juan was acclaimed as a saviour throughout the entire Western world—one of the reasons why Philip II felt over-shadowed by his half-brother, even though this victory had enhanced his own prestige. In the following summer, 1572, when all was prepared to exploit the Lepanto victory, it was Philip who halted all action, referring to a memorandum from the Duke of Alba, which, even in those days, stressed a potential threat from France if Spain were to venture a hazardous long-range action against Constantinople; Alba insisted that the fleet should not be risked again. It was argued against this objection that Catherine de' Medici and her son, Charles IX, had just committed the Massacre of St Bartholomew's Eve and that consequently France would have to depend on Spanish support. But if we consider that French aid to the States General, who were then rising against Philip II, was not in the least affected by the massacre and that Franco–Dutch collaboration against Spain continued unabated despite the murder of the leading French Protestants, it is obvious that Catherine's action was prompted by purely personal and domestic considerations, and had no bearing on France's relations to her Protestant allies. Philip saw the issues clearly: seven years earlier he had made an attempt to promote a Franco–Spanish alliance for the common defence of the Roman Church; a meeting between his beloved wife, Isabella (Elizabeth) of Valois, twenty years old at the time, and her mother, Catherine, had been arranged in Bayonne. Catherine had made considerable promises, which, however, she subsequently failed to honour. The St Bartholomew's massacre of 1572, the eradication of the foremost French Huguenots, was to the King of Spain an incident of no great political moment. On the contrary, when he was informed of this wholesale assassination, he is said to have startled his entourage by laughing out loud for the first and only time in their experience. But this laughter probably expressed his contempt for the Florentine queen.

After Lepanto, the sea was again safe for the Christians inhabiting the Mediterranean shores. But Turkish power had been repulsed only for a time; it had not suffered a mortal blow.

The harsh suppression of the Morisco revolt in Granada, the reversal at Malta and finally the naval catastrophe of Lepanto acted as a challenge on the entire Moslem world and stimulated further Turkish military preparations. As in the days of Charles V, Spain found herself the lone defender of the West against the new Turkish naval power. Despite the most urgent exhortation from the Pope, the offensive against the Sultan was not revived and the Christian League which had triumphed at Lepanto broke up. The Emperor and France refused to take part in the Crusade. The Venetian Republic, concerned only with the threat to its Levantine trade, also withdrew and so paved the way for its decline.

Italy

Once the immediate danger had disappeared, the Italians were no longer inclined to sacrifices. The great alliance, brought about by Pope Pius V, was relinquished in parochial disputes between the individual Italian states. The mortal danger which had threatened the Apennine peninsula was forgotten and soon the Mediterranean again became the scene of maritime guerrilla warfare and ceaseless piracy.

The Spanish satirist Quevedo y Villegas, who was later to fall a victim to Olivares under Philip IV, wrote with astonishing foresight in his highly intelligent work, *Fortuna con seso* (Fortune with Reason), on the Italian situation at that time:

"Since there is no ground on which to walk Italy is practising tightrope-walking, the tightrope being stretched between Rome and Savoy. The Kings of France and Spain form the audience. Both watch with avid interest to see which way the ropewalker is leaning, so as to catch him should he fall. Italy is off-balance and uses Venice as a balancing pole; with the help of this pole she performs such feats as are a joy to behold. At one moment it seems as if the ropewalker must fall to the right, then to the left, but he stays on his high rope and mocks the covetousness with which the two onlookers stretch out their hands in order to seize him when the moment comes."

The situation could not have been described more vividly. But in this connection the relations between the Spanish kings and the popes is of particular interest. Of the European monarchs Philip II was the only completely uncompromising representative of the Counter-Reformation. He regarded himself as the guardian of the Curia but also to a considerable extent as its master; at the same time, however, he treated the Pope with even greater respect than his father had done. Nonetheless, his reign had started with a war against Pope Paul IV. Acting in concert with France, the Pope, who was also a territorial Prince, had prepared to invade Naples. The Commander in Chief of the Spanish army, the Duke of Alba, had reproached him bluntly, stating that he was defiling his own name and would be unable to vindicate himself in the eyes of posterity. If the Pope were to continue with his preparations and betray the King of Spain, to whom he should act as a father, then he, Alba, would make him bitterly regret it. The Prince of the Vatican State feared nothing so much as the power of Spain, especially at a time when the Bourbons had been deprived to a very considerable extent of their freedom of action by the French religious wars.

When Philip II, in the second half of the 1550s, discovered that the Pope was about to excommunicate him he wrote from London to his sister, who was acting as regent during his absence, saying that he would continue to enjoy the blessings of the sacraments and that he commanded his subjects to do likewise and to take no notice of edicts from Rome. He gave orders that a strict watch should be kept on the passes leading into his kingdom and that any person attempting to enter with the interdict should be severely punished. But when Paul IV was defeated and at the mercy of the Spanish Philip did not humble him; and later he was to write to Pope Pius V: "I trust that in future the welfare of Christianity and the repulsion of the evils which threaten today will be the only issues between us. . . ."

But Rome always remained on the defensive *vis-à-vis* this most Catholic of all Kings. Sixtus V also opposed him and, although both his predecessor Gregory XIII and subsequently Clement VIII showed themselves more compliant under military pressure, the basic trend of curial policy remained unchanged.

When Henry IV of France underwent his politically inspired conversion the principal reason for the sense of relief felt in Rome was that the Vatican once again possessed a Continental counterpoise to Spain. But because of this curial attitude there is a marked tendency to forget how greatly Spain's Italian policy was determined by the need to repel the Sublime Porte and the Berbers, which, ever since the days of Charles V, she had regarded as a solemn duty.

Portugal

Between the two extremes of the naval victory of Lepanto in 1571 and the defeat of the Armada in 1588 the last of the independent states in the Pyrenean peninsula, Portugal, was incorporated into Philip's domain. Here too the decisive factor was the principle of family. Sebastian, King of Portugal, was Philip II's nephew. He too seems to have been tainted by the psychic disturbances carried over into the maternal line of the Spanish Hapsburgs from the House of Portugal. His teachers, the Jesuits, had imbued him with an exalted crusading zeal. He received a Spartan training, was drilled to the peak of his physical powers by ascetic methods and overtaxed in the process. All his actions and all his aspirations were alienated from reality and determined solely by the desire to fight the "heathen". With feverish impatience he waited for a pretext to strike, and he was presented with this when a Moroccan pretender appealed to the Christian peoples for help against the ruling Sherif. The last descendant of the so-called false Burgundian line, the son of Don Pedro, who was himself the illegitimate son of John I, was not driven into this venture by the King of Spain. On the contrary, Philip warned him against it, for he knew the dangers of African wars. The view, often advanced, that the King of Spain had refused to help the Portuguese so as to prevent them from extending their sphere of interest is not convincing; given the political constellation obtaining at that time, the subjugation of Morocco by Portugal would have benefited Spain. It seems that from the outset Philip considered the whole enterprise as hopeless; even the Portuguese viewed their monarch's plans with reserve. It was only with great difficulty that Sebastian and his retinue of nobles succeeded in raising an army of seventeen thousand men consisting of peasants and unemployed recruited from the lowest levels of city life; in addition, as always, there were German mercenaries.

On August 4, 1578, Sebastian was defeated by the superior forces of the Sherif; he himself fell and his corpse was never found. A large proportion of the Portuguese nobles who had followed him also lost their lives; but the troops failed in their duty.

At first the regency was headed by Sebastian's uncle, Cardinal Henry, an old and tired man; but he died on January 31, 1580. Among the claimants to the throne, the principal contender was Philip II. He tried to win over Portuguese public opinion, which was opposed to a union with Spain. He ransomed those of Sebastian's comrades who had survived the battle and were being held prisoner and sent one of his favourites, Cristóbal de Mura, who was of Portuguese descent, to Lisbon. Once there, de Mura spread the idea that what was envisaged was a condominium; he also distributed large sums of money, above all to the great nobles and the jurists, who would be called upon to state their views on the question of the succession.

Shortly before his death Cardinal Henry had done his utmost to persuade the Cortes to recognize Philip II. Philip had the majority of the great nobles and priests, the late Prince of the Church and even the right of succession on his side. Only the towns were opposed to a Spanish King. The protagonists of independence gathered behind Antonio de Crato, a man with no powers of leadership. Philip gave orders for his veteran regiments from Italy to be deployed on the frontier, while he continued to negotiate in Lisbon; he gave the army command to Alba, who, after having fallen temporarily from favour, again stood in the forefront of affairs. Crato tried to oppose the Spanish with undisciplined companies; on August 25, 1580, he was defeated at Alcántara and shortly afterwards the capital city of Lisbon was taken. Philip had waited for news of the victory at the frontier, where he almost died of smallpox. His fourth wife, the Archduchess Anne, who was pregnant at the time but had nonetheless accompanied her husband, also caught the disease and, like Isabella before her, soon lost her life, largely as a result of excessive bloodletting. The King nonetheless continued his journey. He travelled as a sovereign with indisputable rights; on April 16, 1581, he accepted the homage of his new subjects and swore to respect their laws and customs. The conquest had been easy, but Philip failed to overcome the aversion felt by the Portuguese. Fifty-nine years later this was to be made palpably obvious.

The incorporation of Portugal into the Spanish dominions was bound to have powerful repercussions on Anglo–Spanish relations. We are often told that the growing tension between Philip II's realm and Elizabethan England, a country whose development had been determined by the popular reaction against Mary Stuart, should be regarded in terms of the antithesis between "Reformation" and "Counter-Reformation". Undoubtedly the English would have sympathized with the sufferings of their Flemish co-religionists. Similar sympathy was felt by both the Spanish and the French Catholic majority, when news reached the Continent of the persecution of the English Catholics. But the real reason for the growing opposition between England and Spain was that, following the Hundred Years' War, England had embarked on her great maritime mission, while Spain was intent on defending her trading monopoly both in her colonies and at home against England's growing power as a trading nation. The English Ambassador in Madrid lodged strong protests when the Inquisition burnt English merchants as heretics and when he himself was illegally spied upon by the police; but he protested far more vehemently against the interdict that forbade English ships to carry Spanish cargoes, and against the fact that the English fleet was denied access to the harbours of the gold- and silver-producing countries.

As for the part played by religious motives, this was to be defined in glacial terms by Richelieu when he commented on his policy of alliances:

"A religious peace cannot be enduring because it is never concluded in order to establish settled relations but in order

that the adversaries may seek to gain some advantage over one
another by deceit and subterfuge."

Spain and England

Just as England was not prepared to tolerate Spanish or
subsequently French or, in the first half of the twentieth
century, German control of the Netherlands, so too she opposed
Spanish control of Portugal. For England Portugal was a
Continental foreland and an Atlantic bridgehead. And in this
connection we should remember that Sully had predicted a
decisive Anglo–Spanish naval battle in the Indian Ocean (cf.
Vol. II, p. 248).

The mad daring of English naval raids, the enterprises of
a Francis Drake, of a Sir Walter Raleigh, were the prelude,
as it were, to the great maritime mission of the island people.

Whenever his transports, harbours and colonies were
subjected to sudden attack, Queen Elizabeth always assured
her Spanish brother-in-law that the guilty parties would be
severely punished and then proceeded, with a characteristic
display of independence, pride and humour, to bestow recognition and favour on the adventurers. Despite all prohibitions,
John Hawkins ran a successful and lucrative trade in negro
slaves from the colonies. Drake, one of England's great
navigators, harassed the Spanish, not only in their own harbours but as far afield as Chile and Peru. The Queen received
part of the profits from such enterprises. And if she suffered a
loss she recouped it from the Spanish ships that carried the pay
to Philip's army in Flanders.

At first the Queen of England attacked Spain at her weakest
point—namely the Netherlands. The intervention of an army
of six thousand men under Leicester's command on behalf
of the rebellious Dutch Protestants and then the great provocation, the execution of Mary Stuart, prompted Philip to go over
to an all-out offensive against England. This King, who was
constantly concerned with the "art of waiting", "that art of the

favourable moment", was suddenly filled with burning impatience; his cup was full; action was called for, instantaneous and annihilating.

Meanwhile Spain's great old naval hero and expert on naval warfare, Santa Cruz, engaged in preparing with meagre resources an invincible fleet in Lisbon, exasperated his monarch by countering his urgent warnings and orders with requests for more time and by stressing the tremendous difficulties attendant on a precipitate operation in the Atlantic, the Bay of Biscay and the Channel. He considered the ships then available inapt for the enterprise, especially in the winter months. Even the most powerful of them were undergunned to an alarming degree, and also undermanned. Of the fifty galleons on order, only thirteen had been delivered and they were unseaworthy. Additionally he had insisted on a further hundred large ships, six galleasses, forty galleons and seven or eight fast boats. But knowing that he would be forced to sail in any case, he exerted himself to the utmost. Cannon were brought in from every quarter. Crews were recruited from the prisons and hospitals, from the merchant ships in the harbour and from the plains around Lisbon; the men were pressed into service. Then, when the order to sail had been given and there was only a week to go before the ships were due to leave harbour, the old Marques suddenly died. But Philip had a successor in readiness, Don Alonso Pérez de Guzmán el Bueno, the Duke of Medina Sidonia and "Captain General of Andalusia and Admiral of the Ocean". This Castilian duke was of such high birth that, in Philip's opinion, nobody could possibly take offence at being asked to serve under him.

This hierarchical premise had to make up for the Duke's total lack of professional qualifications. The unfortunate Medina Sidonia wrote a letter at the time to the King's Secretary, Idiáquez, which could not have been less Castilian in spirit but presented the situation most clearly:

"My health is not equal to such a journey. I recall that on

the few occasions when I was at sea I was always seasick and constantly caught cold. My family is encumbered with a debt of 900,000 livres and I shall not be able to spend a single *real* in the King's service. Since I have not the slightest experience of either seafaring or naval war it is impossible for me to take command of such an important enterprise. I know nothing of the disposition made by the Marques of Santa Cruz nor of the information he had regarding England. Consequently I feel that I am duty bound to submit a negative assessment of my suitability for this post. If I were to command the fleet without knowledge I would have to rely on the opinions of others, in which case I would be unable to distinguish between good and bad advice and would not know which of my advisers were misleading me. The Adalentado Mayor of Castile is far better suited for this post than I. He is a man of extensive knowledge of military and nautical affairs and is moreover a good Christian."

The impracticability of this commission, which imposed such a marked and concentrated degree of responsibility, could not have been stated in more pertinent, forthright and natural terms; but Philip had made his decision. On this occasion he was absolutely convinced that God would reward the great enterprise undertaken for His sake and would send favourable winds.

Long before his death Santa Cruz had fallen from favour because of his independent views. But, contrary to the strictures passed on him when the great attack on England had failed, the findings of subsequent research prove that he was guilty of no personal errors and of no negligence.

Philip II's orders to his fleet were that it should set course for the coast of Flanders to embark the army of Alessandro Farnese. The improvised English fleet, which had been brought up to strength of 180 ships by the last-minute acquisition of a number of small craft, could have been bottled up in Plymouth harbour; but Medina Sidonia failed to take this offensive action, with the result that his cumbersome floating fortresses were subjected to a night attack by the fast English sailing ships. As early as August 6th he was forced to seek refuge in the harbour of Calais, where he dropped anchor. But Francis Drake, acting under Lord High Admiral Howard of Effingham, sent fire-ships among the closely packed Spanish vessels. In the ensuing conflagration the Spanish cut their anchor ropes. To gain room to manoeuvre they took to the open sea, where they were exposed to the elements. By daybreak the strong south-easter had turned into a hurricane; the English returned to their harbours and the Duke, despairing of the outcome of his enterprise, decided to sail for home. In an attempt to evade the enemy he tried to circumnavigate the British Isles. On the reefs of the Orkneys and Hebrides he lost more of his ships. Wherever Spanish crews managed to get ashore they were murdered by the coastal dwellers. The most savage of all were the Catholic Irish. More than seventy-two big ships sank, over ten thousand sailors and soldiers were drowned. The English pursued the fleeing enemy; Drake even tried to force an entry into the Tagus and attack Lisbon.

Queen Elizabeth had a special coin minted bearing the inscription: *Afflavit Deus et dissipati sunt*. The issue of the great event was regarded as a divine judgement. It was the first seed of English supremacy at sea, which at the time was no more than an idea in the mind of the nation, but an idea backed by a sense of self-assurance, whose influence was to make itself felt in the distant future.

In this calamity Philip showed his real stature. His only comment was that he deeply regretted "not having been able to render this great service" to God.

From then onwards the coasts of Spain and Portugal were exposed to naval attack. In the summer of 1596 an English fleet under Lord Howard appeared before Cadiz and landed ten thousand Englishmen and five thousand Dutchmen. Cadiz was the richest city in Spain, the warehouse for all the goods flowing back to the mother country from the colonies.

This town was sacked and burnt. Howard then tacked off Lisbon and subsequently, during the whole month of June, off Cap San Vincente. He cut the lines of communication between Spain and the West Indies. Henceforth Spain was unable to recover her absolute supremacy at sea, although for a long time she remained a dangerous opponent, especially for France, who had been forced to abandon the seas entirely.

Spain and France

Philip II and his advisers had counted on what they took to be the pro-Spanish tendencies of Catherine de' Medici, the first of the French rulers of Florentine descent. Then came disenchantment. The Valois pursued a sophisticated and decidedly insidious policy *vis-à-vis* Spain. This was particularly true with regard to the Netherlands. The French Huguenots had always kept in close contact with the Flemish insurgents. Calvinism, from which resistance in the Netherlands drew its inspiration, had crossed the French borders and penetrated into Holland and Zealand. The Huguenots and the Gueux felt a common bond. There is no doubt but that the Court of the Valois constantly strengthened this bond or that Philip II and the Duke of Alba failed to notice French propaganda in the Netherlands until it was too late, when, however, they kept an extremely anxious watch on it.

France never ceased to intrigue against Spain in the Netherlands, and the House of Nassau continued to accept all possible aid from Charles IX of France, even though he was responsible for the massacre of St Bartholomew's Eve.

Spain for her part carefully plotted her counter-moves; one of these, of particular importance to us, was the diplomatic activity begun in Lorraine in 1580. The princes of the House of Lorraine, the Guises, were the leaders of the French Counter-Reformation. Philip II had gone to great lengths to make King Henry III the captive of the French Holy League. The Duke of Guise stated to the Spanish Duke of Mendoza that he believed that he had done enough for the League to guarantee it majority support in France. After the two Guises had been assassinated in December 1588 in Blois, Philip II showed his hand quite openly. At the time the kingdom was split by civil war, the followers of the League would have nothing to do with the Protestant heir-presumptive, Henry of Navarre, and Paris, which was in the hands of the League, was offering fierce resistance to the King's army. In the capital the "Council of Sixteen", which was composed primarily of ecclesiastics, bought weapons and succeeded in raising an army of thirty thousand men. It was a simple matter for the Commander of the Spanish forces in France, Alessandro Farnese, to lend help to the capital. It appeared possible that the civil war would end with the dissolution of the monarchy and that the King of Spain would then reap a rich harvest, for the daughter of his third marriage, to Isabella of France, had a claim to the French throne. Meanwhile, however, the French jurists were hard at work trying to invalidate this claim by invoking Salic law. The Spanish, for their part, considered the legal position to be as clear-cut as in Portugal and were already toying with the idea of Hapsburg sovereignty over France, the most powerful state on the Continent along with Austria and Spain. The legal arguments in favour of Spanish succession were certainly strong, but here too the really crucial factor was the French national consciousness, already well developed at that time. Even the Estates General, which had been elected with the support of the League, would have nothing to do with a daughter of the King of Spain or with a King who enjoyed Philip's favour.

In 1598, nine years after Henry of Navarre had ascended the French throne as Henry IV, Philip was obliged to write off the long years of unproductive strife and the enormous sums he had spent in France trying to strengthen the Catholic party, and to sign the Peace of Vervins, thus renouncing his dynastic ambitions. But his policy in Lorraine, as we shall see later on, transferred the Franco–Spanish dispute to Imperial territory.

This, an important point to remember, explains why France entered into her alliance with the German Protestant Princes.

The Spanish Liberties

In order to assess Richelieu's struggle with Spain correctly one has to realize to what degree the innumerable privileges enjoyed by the ancient Spanish territories inhibited any attempt to concentrate the forces of the State in times of need and danger, when unity was vital.

This is most graphically illustrated by an event that concerned Philip II himself and the only close human contact—one might say the only friendship—which this lonely monarch ever formed. The person in question was Antonio Pérez, who, furthered by royal patronage, had developed into an ostentatious Renaissance prince. The metamorphosis from trust to love and then from love to fear and mistrust which developed between the sovereign and his favourite recalls the bond between Louis XIII and Cinq-Mars.

The final drama between Philip and Antonio Pérez equally concerned crucial political events. Cinq-Mars, whom we shall come to later, was speedily dealt with; in the case of Pérez, we see the insuperable legal barriers with which the King of Spain had to contend.

The cause of the dissension between master and servant was the murder of Escobedo, Secretary to King Philip's half-brother, Don Juan of Austria. He knew too much about everything, even about the King's private life. Philip is alleged to have ordered his murder after studying incriminating documents of Escobedo's which were submitted to him by Pérez. It was immediately rumoured that Pérez was the murderer. The many who envied him and who were his enemies spread the tale that he had eliminated Escobedo because he had been a troublesome witness to his own relations with the Princess of Éboli, the widow of Ruy Gómez, in whom the King also was interested. When the monarch heard this, he fell prey to one of the crises of conscience to which he was prone. It would seem that he had ordered Escobedo executed without observing due process of the law. Now he grew fearful that the papers presented to him might have been forged, that Pérez might have tricked him in order to prevent the disclosure of his own personal relationship to the Princess. The King became obsessively preoccupied with his responsibility in the matter. Had he ordered the death of an innocent man?

At the first opportunity, Philip had the Princess of Éboli and Pérez arrested. The Princess was thrown into prison, where she was soon to die; but Pérez served only a brief term of imprisonment, after which he was placed under house arrest and very soon he was allowed to move about freely in Madrid. Quite simply, he knew too much.

Meanwhile a secret enquiry was set up. The men hired to murder Escobedo were interrogated in the customary manner. Not so Pérez. Where he was concerned the King proceeded strictly according to the law. It was only after he had been denounced for extorting bribes that it was possible to confiscate his property and papers. At first he denied all knowledge of the murder. Later he claimed to have lied in order to cover up for the King, for he had acted on the monarch's behalf.

As was only to be expected, Pérez took advantage of the leniency accorded to him by escaping from the prison to which he had been returned because of the blackmailing charge. His flight gave rise to a complex legal situation involving state jurisdiction. For he went to the kingdom of Aragon, a territory with chartered rights and freedoms. In Castile the King's wishes carried great force, but in Aragon no special commissions were allowed to sit, no special courts allowed to pass judgement. Aragon was still separated from Castile by customs barriers, and the territory had its own regional Estates to represent it in all its dealings with the King; if the King wished to convene these Estates he had to journey to Monzón. Aragon had a Chief Justice, who bore the title of *Justicia mayor*. This *Justicia* embodied the forces of law.

Those who appealed to him for protection received protection. He was even authorized to grant the accused the right to choose his own place of detention.

In Aragon the authorities immediately sided with Pérez, whom they regarded as an innocent victim of oppression. But Madrid also pressed its case. The King's State Prosecutor was instructed to arrest Pérez regardless of the Chief Justice and to charge him with treason. But when Pérez openly reaffirmed that he had had Escobedo murdered on instructions from the King, public indignation reached such a pitch that the charge had to be withdrawn.

After further unsuccessful attempts to seize Pérez by lawful means, it appeared as if all legal resources had been exhausted. Would the King use force? Philip chose another solution. No legal objections could be raised against a judgement issuing from the Inquisition; even in Aragon protective legislation did not apply to this institution. Under a flimsy pretext Philip had Pérez arrested by the Inquisition and incarcerated in Saragossa. A further veto was impossible. But at that point the population gave vent to its bitterness at Philip's increasingly absolutist methods and to their hatred of the Inquisition, particularly marked in Aragon, as well. The citizens, artisans and great nobles joined forces quite spontaneously in revolt against what appeared to be a boundless injustice cloaked by legal formalities. Under pressure from an enraged mob the Inquisitors were forced to release Pérez.

Only then did Philip deploy his troops on the frontier of Aragon; but he still hesitated to give the order to intervene. He promised to forgive the insurgents if Pérez returned to captivity. The troop movements had had a sobering effect. The *Justicia* himself and even Pérez' closest friends urged compliance.

But on September 24, 1590, when, in view of the King's threatened intervention, the *Justicia*, together with a number of delegates and counsellors, attempted to conduct Pérez back to prison, their solemn procession was attacked and dispersed by the artisans and the servants of the great nobles. Pérez was taken to a safe retreat until he was able to flee abroad. He first crossed into France, taking compromising documents with him. Upon his arrival Henry IV granted the Spaniard a large subsidy. Pérez then went on to England but was unable to obtain a permanent post at Queen Elizabeth's Court and soon returned to France, where, however, the provision made for him was far more modest than on his first visit. Nobody was interested in him. In 1611 he died in Paris in poverty.

The importance which Richelieu attached to the Pérez affair is demonstrated by the fact that he mentioned him not only in his Memoirs but also in his *Political Testament*, where he wrote:

"One of the three pieces of advice which Antonio Pérez gave to Henry the Great was to make himself powerful in the [Papal] Court; and there was good reason for this, for the ambassadors who are accredited there and who represent all the Princes of Christendom are of the opinion that those who enjoy the greatest credit and authority in that Court hold the greatest power at home."

Richelieu, however, added:

"Nor is this opinion ill-founded, for, although it is quite certain that there is nobody in this world who should esteem reason as greatly as the Pope, it is equally certain that there is no place on earth where power is more highly regarded than in the papal Court, this being most clearly demonstrated by the respect paid to the ambassadors of the various Princes, which grows or diminishes and daily changes in appearance according to whether their masters' affairs are going well or badly, with the result that these ministers are not infrequently shown two different faces on the same day, if a courier should arrive in the evening with news which differs from that received in the morning."

And in point of fact the rivalry between Spanish and French

prestige was nowhere more pronounced than in Rome. Not only was Spain the mainstay and champion of the Counter-Reformation, in its most exalted spirit; it furthered the renewal of Catholic thinking in all directions and to unparalleled depths. But for non-religious, purely political reasons, gallic, sceptical France, which was soon to enter into diplomatic alliances with Protestant Europe, was more favoured by the Curia in the diplomatic sphere than Spain.

The Golden Age

As far as religious and intellectual life, art, politics and customs are concerned the early Baroque period from the Sack of Rome to the Peace of Westphalia may be regarded as the Spanish century, as the *siglo de oro*. But this "Golden Age" of Spanish art and literature above all gives us a hint of what Spain might have been if, once *reconquista* was established, she concentrated on internal reforms, thus giving tangible shape to her lofty ideals.

In 1607 Francisco de Medrano wrote:

Spain grows in sorrow
At the very peak of fortune;
For the dead weight of her great majesty
Overpowers and oppresses her;
And constellations, which heaven
Does not support, are toppled by this weight of hers.

But if we are to understand the character of the Spanish nation, whose reduction to a state of weakness and paralysis was to become one of the aims of Richelieu's life, we must not forget the tremendous achievements of this great period; it fashioned a whole era of European history and its influence is felt to this day.

Philip IV

In his portrait of Philip IV, Velásquez has depicted the

95

chivalry, distinction and sensitivity of a kindly man, who was capable of sympathy and gifted with the sagacity of the genuine connoisseur. And it is perfectly true that all these qualities were discerned by Philip's friend, Count Lemos, in the youthful aspirant to the throne and carefully nurtured. Nonetheless, the decisive character trait in Charles V's heir was his morbid will, about whose nature and development we are better and more accurately informed than is usually the case with historical personages. A series of completely uninhibited confessions, which the King made over a period of many years, tells us more than all the guarded statements furnished by diaries, memoirs or correspondences; they reveal Philip's weaknesses, his helplessness and his needs, which he confided in stammering tones and with the effeminacy of a child to a nun, Maria de Agreda, who served him as a mother-substitute.

Periods of decay are characterized among other things by the fact that the sexual urge and all its perversions not only gain the ascendancy but become the focal point of interest, of expert enquiry and representation. This condition had reached its peak in Spain following the ascetic strivings of the sixteenth century. All chroniclers of the period report a kind of erotic frenzy ranging from sadistic blood-lust to a passive thirsting after sensuality; the serious social consequences resulting from the suppression of these conditions, the massive practice of abortion, the organized and lucrative trade in procuring and the emergence of homosexual unions, which carried the death penalty, were intensified, not by analytic enquiries as in our own day but by the tremendous force of the concepts of sin, punishment and repentance.

In his unstable reports to the nun, whom he considered to be endowed with second sight, Philip went on and on about the same temptations, to which he constantly succumbed. He implored the heavens for help to combat such enticements and the holy sister for her advice and intercession, for her fasting and penance on his behalf. He tried to unload the burden of his adventures, which oppressed him as sinful acts, on to the shoulders of intermediaries. The idea of mediating authorities between God and the King of Spain offered comfort. He once wrote: "I fear nothing so much as myself", and on another occasion, "although we mortals know what is good [i.e. abstinence] our passion constantly drives us into the arms of evil. . . . I am resolved to follow your advice and teachings, honourable Mother Maria, but if I am to do so I shall need your active support.—Oh! Mother Maria, my weakness is great and I have reason to fear that it will frustrate the outcome which you desire."

These laments were unending, and it is therefore not surprising that the pious and, to judge by her patient replies, clever and energetic woman should have eventually written to Cardinal Borja:

"My correspondence with His Majesty continues but it is less and less to my liking. Shall I tell you why? Firstly, because it is rumoured that the King has still not given up his youthful follies. Please tell me if this is true. If this is really the case, then who could find the courage to continue writing to him? The other reason: I see that the monarchy is in extreme danger, that half of Europe is allied against it and that everybody here is shutting his eyes; and all I can do is give way to my sorrow and shed secret tears, for any serious attempt to warn His Majesty is a waste of breath."

On one occasion, when Philip was so preoccupied with the unbridled pursuit of pleasure that he expected divine retribution to strike at any moment, it happened that his son was about to engage in a battle, which the King automatically regarded as lost; and so when, instead of sustaining a defeat, the Spanish were victorious, he wrote to his counsellor:

"I am more than a little confounded to find that God should show me such kindness when I have offended Him so sorely. Help me with comforting words and good advice, so that I may recognize my unworthiness and act accordingly. Help me with comforting words!"

Along with innumerable other documents, this correspondence shows the extent to which the Spanish monarch, who should have guided the destiny of his great nation with a firm hand through one of the most difficult periods in its history, suffered from a paralysing weakness of character.

This Hapsburg King of Spain, who was both an amiable and a gifted person, lacked the qualities which his chief adviser possessed to such a high degree: self-assurance and the ability to concentrate. But his favourite was also possessed by an exaggerated sense of his own superiority and motivated by a rigid conception of duty and over-ambitious aims; obsessed with the desire for Spanish supremacy, he spent his life trying to crush all opposition until in the end, driven by his own impetus into catastrophes and débâcles, he ended his days in mental derangement.

This adviser, who controlled the King, was Don Gaspar de Guzmán y Pimental Rivera y Velasco y de Tovar, Count and Duke of Olivares, Richelieu's greatest and ill-starred opponent (cf. Vol. I, p. 172 ff.). But whereas the Spaniard's actions were dictated by powerful emotions, in the Frenchman even the most violent impulses were subject to the control of a shrewd intellect, which was Richelieu's dominant faculty. However, to explain the tragic outcome of the heroic endeavours of the great scion of the House of Guzmán, it is not enough to point to the oscillation in him between states of pathological excitement and nervous exhaustion. The forces at work in Spain at that time were the decisive factor. Like Richelieu, like Wallenstein, Olivares was intent on concentrating the power of the State which had been entrusted to him, and strengthening the absolute monarchy in order to save his country's world-wide possessions. Olivares was to outlive Richelieu. In return for the constant threats and the chronic infirmity to which he was subject throughout his life Richelieu was granted a lasting success, which he was able to predict but whose triumphs he was not destined to enjoy. Olivares, conversely, was to drink the cup of failure to the dregs.

He was the last Spaniard of stature from the era of Charles V and his brief moment of international glory. His political views were in many respects adapted to the new times, but his methods belonged to the past. He did not give way to the forces pressing in on him; he opposed them and was broken by them. He was unable to save the greatness of Spain, precisely because he was too conscious of her past glory.

In the thirteenth century one of his ancestors, faced with the choice between evacuating Tarifa, which had just been conquered, and leaving his son, who had been captured by the Moors, to die at the hands of the executioner, acted like Colonel Moscardo, who was defending the Alcázar in Toledo some seven hundred years later, in 1936; he sacrificed his son and considered him fortunate to be able to die for his country so young.

In the seventeenth century the House of Guzmán, prolific in men of vigorous action, again produced powerful personalities. The most successful opponents of Olivares' policies were members of his own family, among them the wife of the Portuguese pretender, Doña Luisa, a close relative, and the Duke of Medina Sidonia, his great-uncle, who tried to found an independent kingdom in Andalusia. In the defensive battles on the home front Philip IV's "master" faced powerful men and women of his own blood.

The pressures and exigencies of internal politics and the fortunes of Spanish foreign policy were inseparable under both Philip III and his successor, Philip IV. Philip II had been able to conduct his foreign policy irrespective of difficulties at home, something that was no longer possible under his grandson. But our principal concern is with the foreign policy pursued by the Duke of Olivares. Olivares came to power in 1621. From then until 1624, when Richelieu took control of French affairs, the Duke showed time and time again that he wanted peaceful relations with France. For as long as France was faced with her Huguenot problem this objective was fairly easy to achieve; but Olivares continued to pursue it for some time after that, although he always had his reservations, which, in view of France's attitude, were always justified.

Immediately the Duke entered the political scene the Valtelline massacres took place (cf. Vol. I, pp. 162 ff.). By recognizing the population of the Grisons as her charges and affording them support France took the first extremely tentative and barely perceptible step towards re-establishing herself in northern Italy. Olivares proceeded with great caution and under the terms of the Treaty of Madrid of April 25th appeared to be accommodating Louis XIII and his allies, Venice and Savoy, by undertaking to return the Valtelline to the Grisons and by granting a general amnesty and guarantees of religious tolerance. But at the same time he tried to influence the Catholic Swiss Estates, while Feria repulsed the attack mounted on Bormio by the men of the Grisons and deprived them of Chiavenna and Poschiavo; meanwhile Archduke Leopold marched into the Engadine.

As we have already seen, two years later France, Venice and Savoy insisted on the implementation of the Treaty of Madrid, which had given rise to a tripartite alliance, and the problem was eventually solved by sending in papal troops to occupy the Valtelline. It was at this time that Prince Charles of England undertook his unsuccessful journey to Madrid in search of a Spanish bride and shortly afterwards the Anglo–French marriage was brought about as a result of the policy which du Fargis, the French Ambassador, had consistently promoted in Madrid. The provisions of the Treaty of Madrid, which was signed in Monzón on March 5, 1626, in its revised form, constituted a diplomatic success for Olivares. The Valtelline remained exposed to attack by the Spanish forces stationed in Milanese territory. Meanwhile Richelieu, angered and determined, wrote in July of the same year to his King:

"If God is so gracious as to permit me to live for another six months, as I hope He will . . . , I shall die content, having seen the pride of Spain humbled, Your allies sustained, the

Huguenots tamed, all factions dispersed, peace established within the realm and close harmony within Your royal household. . . ."

This letter was drafted at a time when Orléans was conspiring, Marie de Chevreuse was hatching her plots, Ornano was arrested and Bérulle's policies were gaining an ascendancy that gave Olivares good reason to hope for further successes. It was in that year that Bérulle received his Cardinal's hat; the defeat of the so-called "bons français", the "politicians", seemed imminent. Fancan, whom Richelieu was soon to lay low as an adherent of the pro-Spanish party, wrote at the time that the only reason why France found herself at such a low ebb was that too much trust had been placed in those who, in affecting piety, had equated religion with the welfare of the State.

We have already pursued the course of the *condottiere* war in the Palatine. Although, ever since the time of Alba and Spinola, war had lived off war, the interest taken by the Spanish monarchy in these often seemingly unrelated incidents was in fact prompted by a clear-cut and extremely ambitious plan evolved by Olivares. He had advised Onate, his envoy in Vienna, that the Rhenish Palatinate must be united with Alsace for the Infante, Don Carlos. Under Philip III the Spanish had still intended to restore the Palatinate to the son of Frederick IV, provided he converted to Catholicism. But subsequently Maximilian I of Bavaria was supported in his claim by Pope Gregory XV, and the Capuchin diplomacy pursued by Father Joseph had also been directed to this end.

The strategic assessments, which Olivares had formed at an early stage, were quite as clear-cut as Richelieu's. He had realized that, despite the crucial importance for Spanish interests of the Lower Rhine as a theatre of war, the Valtelline and the Grisons were the real key positions for Spain and Austria. For him and his opponent alike, what mattered was the route between Milan and Brussels. Charles the Bold's original vision of Lorraine as a Spanish State and a European buffer State was familiar to Philip II also. It was at the basis of the Hapsburg family contract as it evolved following the engagement of Ferdinand II's second son to Philip III's daughter. Yet Olivares and Richelieu tried to preserve the peace over a long period and continued to do so even when Toiras was defending Casale against the ageing Spinola.

One of the most surprising features of this cold war was the fact that the French succeeded in persuading the Spanish that it was their duty as promoters of the Counter-Reformation to afford naval support against England during the siege of La Rochelle, although Olivares restricted this support to a mere demonstration. This appears all the more astonishing since the Duke never doubted that, once the Huguenot stronghold had fallen, France would have an entirely free hand where Spain was concerned and, for the very first time since the death of Henry IV, would be in a position to re-instigate an active foreign policy in Europe, which is exactly what she did when Richelieu intervened in the Mantuan War of Succession.

The naval action in support of the French took place in 1628 and within the year, on May 3, 1629, Olivares concluded the treaty with Rohan which we have already discussed in some detail.

To recapitulate: in the light of this last circumstance the haste and harshness with which Louis XIII and Richelieu conducted their final campaign against the Huguenots becomes understandable, as does the great statesmanship underlying the "grace" of Alais (cf. Vol. I, pp. 320 ff.), the peace treaty inspired by Richelieu and granted to the Huguenots following their defeat.

The fact that Richelieu, acting against the advice of his closest collaborators and in the face of virtually the whole of French public opinion, successfully outmanoeuvred the Spanish diplomats in Regensburg, getting his way in the Mantuan question, put Olivares in a very awkward initial position.

As early as 1631 Spain's external enemies and her internal difficulties increased to an alarming degree. Olivares was obliged to appeal to the good will of private individuals in order to cover the cost of his arms programme. Cardinal Borja transferred his own subsidies and benefices—a considerable sum—to the King. Various grandees raised armies at their own expense. Olivares equipped three fleets with which to fight the Dutch in Brazil and the East Indies. But these forces were wiped out almost at once; the crews of the first fleet were annihilated by the plague and the second and third fleets were defeated by the rebels. Spain found herself obliged to conclude the Peace of Cherasco, which brought the Italian war to a temporary halt but proved highly detrimental to Spain's interests. At that very juncture Gustavus Adolphus intervened in Germany; Wallenstein was recalled. At the same time the Spanish provinces began to resist the Crown. Don Carlos, Philip IV's talented brother, whose successes were unbearable to the King, died at the age of twenty-six. A tempest destroyed his Catholic Majesty's Mexican fleet. Olivares raised funds, which he was unable to repay, in order to support Ferdinand II and finance Gaston d'Orléans' revolt. The Netherlands nobles under Count von Bergen rose against Spanish rule, the Prince of Orange conquered Geldern, the Stadtholder Don Fernando took Venlo and Roermond, Maastricht was forced to capitulate. The Imperial General Pappenheim was defeated, Limburg fell, Tilly succumbed to his wounds and Cardinal Borja accused the Pope before a whole consistory of having betrayed the cause of religion. Meanwhile the Portuguese had lost nearly all of their Indian territories. A welter of events, whose effects tended to cancel one another out.

In Spain Gustavus Adolphus' death was celebrated as a great victory. Philip had the bad taste to appear in person at a performance of a burlesque tragedy entitled *The Death of the King of Sweden*. Soon Spain found herself obliged to offer peace terms to the Netherlanders, but, contrary to the wishes of the powerful peace party in Brussels, they were rejected. Following the death of the Archduchess Isabella Clara Eugenia, the Stadtholder in the Netherlands, Don Fernando, continued the war. The only tangible Spanish success at that time was the reconquest of Ceylon by the great Portuguese Almeida. In 1634 Olivares harshly put down the ringleaders of the Netherlands revolt. Once again a treaty was concluded with Gaston d'Orléans, and even before the arrival of the Cardinal-Infante in Brussels the Spanish succeeded in relieving Breda, which had been besieged by the Prince of Orange. It seemed that the turning point had been reached. On September 5th the battle of Nördlingen was won by the Imperial forces.

When Richelieu persuaded his King that the time had come for open warfare the great monarchy on the Pyrenean peninsula was already considerably weakened, for reasons we have already enumerated. Richelieu, who had always opposed the unremitting and extremely energetic internal resistance to his Spanish policy with the argument that France was encircled and thus in mortal danger from Spain, was fully aware of Spanish weakness.

Power as Reality and Appearance

The ideas that dominate a given age are more easily recognized than the collective emotional dispositions of its successive generations, the passions that lead to the re-emergence or resuscitation of general propositions and philosophical notions or the revival of submerged doctrines. The varying states of exaltation and excitation in the mental life of a group, their creative and their destructive effects, are determined by laws that have yet to be adequately investigated. But amongst their many causes one fundamental feeling common to all creatures predominates: fear. Although subject to wide variation, fear is a constant. Collective fear is released both by objective factors and by ideas and fantasies; it can have either a material or a metaphysical source, it can be transmitted as a result of severe traumatic incidents and thus take renewed effect long after the original motivation has ceased to operate. One particularly powerful trigger mechanism frequently encountered in human groups is the idea that they are encircled by hostile forces. The fear of suffocation threatens. The result is a pathogenic condition of absolute mistrust.

The group then tries to defend itself, often simply by lashing out in a blind panic. Many tragic examples of such reactions could be cited.

Since the religious wars the French people had felt encircled by a singularly impressive power. This power was furthermore in league with a French minority which, in the interests of the Estates and their Liberties and heir to the spirit of international solidarity of medieval Christianity, was working against the nation's aspirations—born of fear and the will to resist— toward a central authority that would afford protection. For this minority the preservation of Church unity within the Counter-Reformation was more important than the consolidation of a segregated collective organization which was gradually coming to maturity and which presented itself to the outside world as the French nation. The differences between the representatives of growing French nationalist feeling and the French "Europeans", the reactionaries of those days, created two hostile camps. There were Catholics and Protestants in both camps even during the religious and civil wars, which began in 1562, four years after the death of Emperor Charles V and seven years after the accession of Philip II, and did not die out for sixty-seven years despite the edict of tolerance promulgated by Henry IV, i.e., the Edict of Nantes. To recapitulate: The French people were bled white by the demands made on them during the religious wars and large areas of the countryside were completely devastated. Spain was the ally of the French Counter-Reformation factions, which joined together to form the Holy League. But this Spanish alliance unleashed a great wave of resistance, which carried the first Bourbon, the Huguenot Henry of Navarre, on to the throne; his conversion to the Roman Church, which followed soon after, demonstrated the triumph of political ambition. For years to come the French were saying: "The real victor in our wars was the King of Spain." It was this realization that led to the formation of a third party, consisting of both Huguenots and Catholics, which was promptly dubbed the "party of the politicians". At the start it took tolerance as its motto, not on humanitarian grounds, however, but for purely practical reasons. Once the redistribution of power had been effected, tolerance could again be dispensed with. This became immediately obvious when the "offspring of danger", as he was called, Louis XIII's Prime Minister, Cardinal Richelieu, entered the scene as the all-powerful exponent of the aims of this party.

On the domestic scene the Cardinal took energetic action against anything that threatened the monarchy as the embodiment of state authority; he broke the power of the Huguenots; he fought the great feudal nobles, who sought foreign aid wherever they could in defence of their privileges. He restricted the rights of the parlements because they refused to recognize the primacy of foreign policy; but his fiercest disputes were with the heirs to the Holy League, the so-called "devotees". During the regency of Marie de' Medici, Henry IV's widow, these elements opposed to centralization were treated with consideration and even pampered. Richelieu proceeded to use terrorist methods against them, although moving with immense caution; he never acted until he had manipulated the groups or individuals concerned into a position which allowed him safely to deliver the final blow.

In his foreign policy, the Cardinal pursued with the utmost consistency and with every means in his power the objective formulated by Henry IV, Louis XIII's father, towards the end of his life: "Spanish power must be broken." He took extreme measures but—and this was still a legacy of the religious wars—he did not resort to armed force. He laid the foundations for his life's work within an economy that had been destroyed by the civil war and in the face of a confused financial situation which this supreme politician was never quite able to master; he carried out his work during a period of great social change, without an army, powerless at sea, with his coasts constantly threatened, unable for long years to participate in the colonial rivalry of the age and hard pressed on all seas by the Berbers, the Spanish, the English and the Dutch. Everything had to be created from nothing.

Forced to gain time by every conceivable method, Richelieu, from 1625 to 1635, conducted what he himself called a "masked" war, a "cold war", "simply by placing his hand in his pocket and not on his sword". This last statement should not be taken too literally. There were French troop movements on the frontiers; local operations were conducted here and there; but by the terms of seventeenth-century international law help accorded to allies did not constitute an open act of war. Temporary alliances were easily concluded and pretenders, whose cause one might espouse, easily found.

What really mattered was to ensure that Spain was constantly harassed by every possible military means short of a French declaration of war; above all, her virtual ally, the Viennese Hapsburg and Emperor, had to be kept under pressure; that was why the great German war, begun in 1618, had to be constantly supplied with fuel.

As for French attempts to influence Anglo–Spanish relations, the following instructions, which the Cardinal sent to his Ambassador in London on August 28, 1629, provide an interesting comment:

"It is hoped that peace will not be made between Spain and England; but since the English always do the opposite of what is asked of them, you would, I think, do well to advise the King of Great Britain and his leading ministers to make peace with Spain on condition that the Palatinate is restored [to its legitimate owner] . . . this Spain will never do, which will prevent the conclusion of a peace, or, failing this, ensure that it is soon broken again . . ."

Richelieu worked with a fully organized intelligence service, which covered the entire seventeenth-century world; his informers also acted as his political agents. Through them he not only exploited every possible chance of bribery, he also tried to provoke foreign leaders into bringing influence to bear on his own sovereign, when he himself had failed to get his way. For example, he once offered to make a private contribution to William of Orange of two to three hundred thousand livres, of which the French finance department would know nothing. But then the Prince could have one and a half million if he succeeded in persuading the King of France to besiege Dunkirk and Gravelines, in which case, however, the Prince would not have to lend naval support. Any number of such cases could be cited from the available source material. We are able to follow Richelieu's method—his other-directed psychology, his knowledge of men, his consummate skill in dealing with men—in the day-by-day account of his activities. In doing so we note his rational thought, the attention he paid to even the most trivial circumstances, whether favourable or unfavourable, his thorough and untiring analysis of all available data, from the military strength and the economic situation to the internal opposition of the particular State under consideration of all relevant persons. The principal enemy was chance, and in so far as it was humanly possible this had to be eliminated. Richelieu fulfilled Clausewitz's requirement that policy and strategy should be interlinked. With him all initiative rested with the director of policy; his collaborators had to content themselves with executive posts as experts, as diplomatic, military or economic specialists; above all he wanted dedicated people, for it was only with people who did not question that his method could be made to work. These disciplined men could delegate their tasks to others; a man out of the ordinary could not; Richelieu knew himself to be exceptional; irreplaceable. In the service of his politico-strategic conception he demanded blind allegiance; in practice he ruled by martial law, even in times of peace.

What, in the last analysis, was Richelieu's motivation? He himself always insisted that it was "to save the world from the tyranny of Spain and to free his country from her murderous encirclement"; he repeated this time and again in the strongest terms.

Did Richelieu himself believe in the Spanish threat? The majority of his influential contemporaries did. It was precisely because the danger seemed to them to be so great that they opposed the Cardinal's policy, which they censured as fool-hardy and provocative.

The great territories united under the Spanish Crown did indeed appear overwhelming; but was this not a deceptive impression? Despite her many internal tensions France was already a homogeneous bloc during the struggle between Charles V and Francis I. Her population was by far the largest in the whole of Europe. The Spanish territories were peripheral to France. Spanish encirclement was the encirclement of the strong by the weak; as has already been pointed out, it was only the French civil war that enabled Spain to threaten her neighbour.

But Richelieu went on issuing warnings against the Spanish menace until the day of his death. He also appealed to a new idea, which he linked up with the old conception of the *gesta Dei per Francos*; he appealed to the sense of mission felt by so many of his French contemporaries.

As early as December 15, 1625, he received a letter from Jean-Louis Guez de Balzac, the important political publicist, who had been schooled in the diplomatic methods of the Curia and was one of the chief originators of rhetorical prose. In this letter we read:

"Your Eminence will live to see the day when the oppressed peoples will come from the ends of the world to seek the protection of the French Crown. The Spanish will cease to be conquerors and oppressors and we shall stand as the liberators of the whole world."

And now one final consideration: what did Richelieu think of the Spanish threat when he was communing with himself or with an agent who possessed his full confidence? In 1632 he wrote to his representative in Madrid :

"The Spanish forces are dispersed over a number of provinces which are widely separated from one another. Nowhere is Spain in a position to resist a concentrated power such as France over a long period, and in the final analysis the outcome of a general war must necessarily be calamitous for our Iberian neighbour."

Richelieu unveiled such secret thoughts only on very rare occasions, perhaps only when he was intent on bringing a specific influence to bear on a diplomatic opponent.

But his personal opponents, including the two Marillacs, the Keeper of the Great Seal and the Marshal, asked time and again: If the Spanish threat is no more than a pretext, if the profound disquiet and fear felt by the people of France is largely inspired by Richelieu's propaganda, then what is the reason for the alarming measures employed in the masked war, which are calculated to infect every wound suffered by our opponent, to deepen every conflict, increase every discontent and constantly create new tensions, all of which must eventually lead to the outbreak of an endless hot war? Both Marillacs were made to pay for asking such questions, the Keeper of the Great Seal in prison, the Marshal on the scaffold. But the Spanish problem, which Richelieu equated with the European problem as such, appeared to him in a far more complex light than his contemporaries and many later critics were able to recognize. Of course he was fully aware of the weaknesses with which Madrid and his personal adversary, Olivares, had to contend; but he also knew that, owing above all to the importance attached to the concept of the Holy Roman Empire, the Spanish system could call on incalculable forces in Central Europe. This explains Richelieu's Central European policy. He was dealing with an unknown quantity, which his logical mind could not easily assess. He did not regard Germany as an entity; to assume that he did would be an anachronism. Napoleon was the first to see the problem clearly. He said:

"Faced with the great mass of Germany, I was obliged to proceed slowly; I merely tried to simplify her enormous complexity to some extent. Not that Germany was unprepared for centralization; on the contrary, she was all too prepared and might easily have effected her union without circumspection and to our detriment, before having learned how to understand us."

Richelieu, conversely, did not for one moment consider simplifying German conditions; the Liberties, which he abolished in France, he defended in the German territories, but only because of the Hapsburg hegemony based on the Madrid and Vienna axis, which he had to break.

Against this background it is easy enough to see why Olivares and Richelieu should have addressed their monarchs in much the same terms. Olivares said:

"Your Majesty's principal goal should be to make Yourself the real King of Spain. In other words, not to be content with Your present position as King of Portugal, Aragon, Valencia, Count of Barcelona, etc., but rather to strive to harness the multiple and isolated forces which together form the total concept of 'Spain' into a united and uniform whole within the framework afforded by the laws and customs of the public life of Castile. After this goal has been reached, but not before, Your Majesty will be the most powerful ruler in the whole world."

Time and time again the Duke urged the King to travel from province to province, holding his court in each in turn, to draw the leading members of the various provinces into his immediate circle and appoint them to important government offices. For a long time Olivares moved with care, trying to respect the special rights of the different territories and to ease the King's subjects gradually into a centralist system. It was only when events abroad had created a state of emergency which could not be handled by traditional methods that he recommended the consolidation of absolutist rule by means that could not be justified by the end. Thus he made the following proposal to the King:

"Another way of reaching our goal, more irregular perhaps but on the other hand more certain, would be for Your Majesty to pay a seemingly friendly visit at the head of an appropriate force to the province to be overrun. In the course of this visit carefully prepared, large-scale disturbances would have to break out, in order to justify the use of troops. Under the pretext of restoring law and order and preventing any possible recurrence of such incidents the work of 'peaceful' conquest could then be initiated, which means that the province in question would be completely incorporated into the mother country of Castile in both the legislative and administrative spheres. The same process could then be applied with equal ease and certainty to the remaining provinces and principalities."

Richelieu used all manner of expedients, but a passage such as this could never have come from his pen, save perhaps as a grim joke. But, after all, if we consider the mercurial facility and the endless capacity for dissimulation that enabled Richelieu to correct the course of events, we see at once that the Spanish Duke's mental processes were more clumsy, especially when he tried his hand at deception, for which he had no real natural gift. Later historians have censured him for having failed to realize that in his day a Counter-Reformation policy based on the hegemony of the twin Hapsburg dynasties was no longer tenable and have argued that he should have pursued a policy of consistent non-interference in order to preserve as much of Spain's possessions as was possible. In the later years of his reign Philip II, the son of Emperor Charles, obviously recognized that the time had come to consolidate

Spanish power and to discontinue the policy of overseas conquest. But both Philip's son and his grandson were to prove insensitive to the changes in the international situation and, although the instruments of power at his disposal were dwindling away, Olivares continued to devote his energies and ingenuity to the preservation, in its full grandeur, of the political system which he represented. In the process he not only disregarded the impoverishment of the country, the untenable level of the national debt and the constant decrease in the population, he also underestimated the strength of the resistance triggered off by his attacks on the surviving mediaeval Liberties; it was to prove a stumbling block for him wherever he turned; for in Spain feudal rights were defended far more vigorously than in France, where, despite the religious wars and the nobles' revolts, despite some opposition on the part of the towns and the recalcitrance of the parlements, the great majority of the population was moving towards the concept of a centralized state, thus supporting Richelieu's plans.

In such circumstances Spain could not prevail in a protracted war. If her armies, despite many reversals, continued to be victorious, these were victories on the road to an inevitable decline.

CHAPTER V

DECLARATION OF WAR ON SPAIN

Even before the declaration of war between the Holy Roman Emperor and France, Ferdinand II, whose army was covered in the rear as a result of the Peace of Prague, launched a three-pronged attack on France from the Lower, Mid and Upper Rhine and forced the French armies on to the defensive on all fronts.

This war, which began officially on June 18, 1645, continued until six years after Richelieu's death. With insufficient forces at its disposal and a lack of capable army commanders, the Royal Council made the following military dispositions at the outbreak of hostilities:

The army deployed on the eastern frontier against the Imperialists was to be commanded by Cardinal de La Valette, with Feuquières serving under him. Bernhard of Saxe-Weimar, who was then still serving the Swedes, was also to fight on this front and maintain close contact with La Valette. The operations in Lorraine were to be conducted by the Duke of Angoulême, the ageing Marshal de La Force and, as we have already seen, by Henri de Rohan and Condé. In Italy Marshal de Créqui was to share the command with the Duke of Parma and Savoy.

As for Flanders, the Dutch had insisted that the command be transferred to Châtillon, since Coligny had previously recommended that the Netherlands be divided between France and Holland. And so the grandfather's plan came down to the grandson for implementation.

Before we concern ourselves with the first military engagement, which took place in Flanders, let us consider the armies of the two opposing powers.

The Spanish Army

The Spanish army had far greater experience of actual warfare than the French. Its organization was much tighter and its troops were subject to the kind of discipline once imposed on the Roman legions. They came from every corner of the Spanish dominions. Walloon guardsmen were often stationed in Naples and Sicily, while Neapolitans and Catalonians served on the Zuyder Zee. New recruits received a strict and thorough training. Nearly all the officers had studied tactics for many years. The Spanish infantry, the *tercios*, were said to be unbeatable. Spanish armies were deployed with great care in order to avoid heavy casualties; in retreats especially they displayed exemplary discipline. No soldier left his post without orders. These troops fought on land and sea, in India and in Europe and in the forests of America. Always and everywhere the Castilians were in the van. The Spanish navy was, however, manned by Catalonians, Andalusians from Cadiz, by the men of Valencia and Galicia, by Sicilians, Neapolitans and Portuguese, whose forefathers had discovered the world. The Spanish army was a renowned instrument of great power that was held together by its ancient traditions. In France, by contrast, practically everything had to be created from scratch.

The French Army

Nowhere is the transition from a feudal state to a centralized and authoritarian state, the tremendous social regrouping that took place under Louis XIII, more obvious than in the sphere of army organization.

The basis of the modern army was laid in the Thirty Years' War. In medieval society the fighting nobles had formed the nucleus of the army, but as early as the sixteenth century the warrior had become a mercenary—in other words, a professional soldier. He no longer received privileges for risking his life, but money. From then onwards, general conscription was gradually introduced as a concomitant of equality.

The peoples of Europe have suffered the ravages of war throughout history. They have submitted passively to the consequences of military action. If certain districts were affected by warfare, others escaped and from the areas which had been spared new, fresh life flowed into the places where war had been waged. Civil wars hit the population harder than foreign wars, and the greatest suffering of all was caused by wars of religion.

It is difficult for the contemporary mind to imagine how disruptive and far-reaching were the changes effected by the infiltration of central authority into every sphere of human life, at the expense of particularist and individual authorities and their rights.

At first the State mercenary was held in low esteem. He simply represented a material asset. But as such he was handled with care. He was war material. In the early years of Louis XIII's reign, a soldier was wryly defined as "a man who, although not a criminal, kills and risks being killed at any time." Surely a more objective evaluation than an earlier definition found in one of Francis I's edicts:

"Soldiers are idle vagabonds, lost souls, who are given over to every vice, highwaymen, murderers, who rape women and children, deny God and blaspheme against Him, who destroy everything they come across, misuse their fellow-men, drive them from their homes and do greater injury to our subjects than any enemy, even the Turk."

Only gradually, as a result of punishments, which were often extremely harsh, and discipline, which in the course of time was to become rigid, did the soldiery change.

In the seventeenth century recruiting was usually carried

out in the following way: a private entrepreneur engaged soldiers much as a tradesman hired apprentices. The entrepreneur then sold his troops to the highest bidder. Such entrepreneurs would undertake to deliver a specified number of armed and soon after also uniformed soldiers. This trade in human material between contractor and customer was called a "commission".

Raising a regiment was costly. A Colonel, who placed a regiment at the King's disposal, also had to supply its equipment. He himself did business with recruiting officers, whom he then placed in command of companies.

In these undertakings certain formalities were observed, for if all comers were accepted there was a risk of engaging deserters, who wandered from country to country, regiment to regiment, drawing their pay in advance wherever possible and then disappearing again. Of all the tradeable raw materials the soldier was the one whose price rose most rapidly. A Bassompierre was still able to supply men for a thaler; but people were soon complaining that the Duke of Lorraine was ruining the market price. Gaston d'Orléans, whose resources were limited, engaged his notorious "juveniles", children of fifteen and sixteen, for only two pistoles. The average cost of a regiment was about 8,000 livres. Prices were determined by the quality of the troops; a twenty-year-old was worth more than a veteran.

The cavalry was more expensive. A nag cost between fifty and sixty livres. But prices of up to 3,000 livres were paid for good horses for the use of officers.

Even in those days the State was already requisitioning horses, although sometimes it hired them instead. A soldier was usually given six months' rest after six months in the field.

In the long-drawn-out wars of that century losses among troops were always high, especially from epidemics, although by then the artillery was claiming heavy casualties as well. This also led to an increase in the soldiers' pay.

As yet the various armies had no specifically national character.

In the 1630s, for example, the Generals serving the Emperor included a Frenchman, the Count of Dampierre, a Fleming, the Count of Bouquoi, and the Italians Piccolomini and Monte-cucculi. Henri de Rohan, as we have seen, served the Republic of Venice. Hauterive and the famous Marshal Châtillon were in the service of the Dutch. German, Scottish and Irish commanders fought for the King of France, leading their own countrymen, whom they had recruited themselves. Schomberg and Bernhard of Saxe-Weimar also served under the French Crown. Foreign commanders were not allowed to recruit Frenchmen. The troops all served the flag, to which they swore allegiance. At that time the more senior officers were nearly all noblemen.

For a long time the French found the best-stocked markets for soldiery were in Germany and Switzerland, although they also recruited in Scotland, Ireland and, primarily for the light cavalry, in Hungary and Poland.

Italy was inundated with German mercenaries. Philip II had defended his position in the Netherlands and suppressed the Dutch revolt with German troops stiffened with Spanish *tercios*. The French thought very highly of the German cannoneers, although their experiences with German cavalry, whom they called *"les reitres"*,[1] were bad.

The army that Venice employed to defend her interests consisted entirely of mercenaries. Since the Republic paid well it managed to recruit up to 2,000 French infantrymen. Once, when the German *condottiere* Mansfeld was operating in Holland, 13,000 Englishmen, 1,000 Germans and 1,000 Frenchmen fought under his command. The King of England, for his part, recruited 2,000 French cavalrymen with the consent of the French Crown. The Duke of Parma gave Louis XIII permission to raise troops in the Dauphiné and allowed the Dutch to do likewise in Normandy. Gustavus Adolphus

[1] *Reîtres*: adaptation of German *Reiter* = rider (Tr.).

recruited 3,000 Englishmen and 3,000 Scots. Whole armies of fifteen to twenty thousand men passed from hand to hand among the warring Princes. As a general rule prisoners were recruited on the spot and proceeded without ado to fight against their former comrades.

It was also important to have the wives of recruited men join them as quickly as possible. Otherwise, it was said, the mercenaries always ran off again. As a result every army was followed by an enormous train. In districts where a scorched-earth policy was pursued the surviving peasants and farmers, who had been rendered destitute, also joined the troops, so that every army unit was followed from one end of Europe to the other by a horde of marauders, highwaymen and gypsies, who maintained themselves by robbery and plunder.

The Swiss mercenaries drove the hardest and most minutely specified bargains. In the 1630s they were considered somewhat less martial than before, but still the best available soldiers. According to the terms of the old contracts, called capitulations, the commander of the Swiss troops in France had to be a Prince of the blood royal. Consequently, when Bassompierre was given this command, protests were immediately raised. It was only by appearing in Soleure in person and distributing rich gifts that he was able to overcome this resistance.

The recruited soldiers gave up their homeland and soon became stateless. After a while nobody knew where they had come from. They lost their original names and were all given *noms de guerre*, an expression used to this day in France. In the registry of deaths in Bourges for the year 1637 a sergeant is listed under the name of "La Violette" (the violet). In a Breton parish the following entry was made in the parochial register: "Nobody died this month, only a few soldiers, who cut one another's throats. Their names are not known."

The men in charge of the baggage train were referred to as "Goujats", a word originally denoting a soldier's servant but subsequently having the meaning of blackguard or ruffian. Most of these servants had been born in camp and they did all the dirty work. No musketeer would perform the menial tasks required of every private in the modern army. Honourable soldierly duties included the preparation of earth-works, trench systems and communications trenches. The baggage servants were forbidden to take part in these operations.

The fighting strength of the various military units was subject to enormous variations. There were companies of 15 men and others of 200 men. Most of Louis XIII's newly formed regiments had a paper strength of 1,200 men. The army commanded by Marshal de La Force was made up of seventeen regiments, whose effective strength varied from 600 to 1,700 men. The officers' ranks did not correspond to those of today and their authority was not necessarily commensurate with their rank. The Colonel of one regiment was sometimes subordinate to the Captain or even the Lieutenant of another.

According to d'Avenel:

"The Marquis of Créqui was in charge of a small army, in which the young nobles were trained as in a military academy. A Captain of Horse, who had 250 soldiers under his command, every one of them well built and well turned out, retained his command on full pay even in times of peace. He was not to be compared with an officer in one of the 'little regiments'. The regiment of Guards was the principal French regiment."

Even under Louis XIII this regiment comprised 30 companies of 200 men apiece. Next to the Guards in prestige were the regiments of Picardy, Piedmont, Champagne and Navarre, the so-called old regiments, dating back a hundred years. They were commanded by leading personalities such as Béthune, Saulx, Tavannes, Schomberg, d'Andelote tc. Every one of these regiments was brought up to an effective strength of 2,000 men; each of the officers was personally known to the King, who himself supervised their replacement, if any fell in battle or resigned his commission. The preferential treatment accorded these regiments was shared by a number of others, which subsequently came to be known as *les petits vieux* (the little old ones). Their command changed frequently but they had priority over the provincial regiments, in which Turenne was to serve as Colonel. Last of all came the newly created regiments—in 1640 they numbered 100—which grew or dwindled according to the state of the nation's finances. In these regiments the Colonels had sovereign powers. They appointed their own Captains, who in turn appointed the subalterns.

Within the period of seventeen years in which Richelieu had held office the French army was built up along these lines. From his time onwards France possessed the rudiments of a standing army. But since the Cardinal's diplomatic measures had successfully prevented open warfare for a great many years, the army at the disposal of the monarchy was not in peak condition when hostilities finally broke out.

For the implementation of his foreign policy, Henry IV had never had more than 30,000 infantry and 4,000 cavalrymen at his disposal. During the regency Marie de' Medici was content with a force of 10,000 foot and 1,500 horse. Even during the civil war of 1617 to 1620 the strength of the royal army had never exceeded 12,000 men, which elicited from Richelieu the scornful remark that, prior to his appointment as Minister, the King's military expeditions from Paris had been more like "a hunting party than a triumphal procession".

In the course of the "masked" war the French army was brought up to a strength of 60,000 men. The invariably critical Marillac once wrote: "How are we to maintain 60,000 men over any length of time?" But when France declared war on Spain in 1635—an act that astounded contemporary observers—six French armies appeared in July of that year in the various continental theatres of war, whose total strength was estimated at 134,000 foot and 26,000 horse, and from then on these army groups constantly grew right up to the Peace of Westphalia and even beyond that great event.

In his *Political Testament* Richelieu wrote:

"Logic requires that the thing that is to be supported and the force that is to support it should stand in geometrical proportion to each other. It is certain that a body as immense as this kingdom cannot be maintained by mediocre forces."

And again:

"The most powerful State in the world could never rest assured unless it were in a position to defend itself at all times against unexpected attack."

The Cardinal considered wars unavoidable:

"States need war from time to time to expel their base humours, to win back what is lawfully theirs, to requite affronts which, if they went unpunished, would provoke further affronts, to preserve their allies from oppression, to humble the arrogance of the conqueror."

He went on to say that wars must be just and that if one took up arms one must be moved by moral motives. One should never act affectively, never like a goaded animal but as a rational human being.

Although open warfare constituted a tremendous risk for France in the years following 1635, it was thanks above all to Richelieu that the groundwork had been done when Louis XIV came to create his armies and Louvois to organize them. In the Cardinal's day army administration was in the hands of civilians, whom he carefully selected and constantly instructed in every detail of their work. Throughout 1635 Servien, one of the four Secretaries of State, was "Minister of War"; in February 1636 he was succeeded by de Noyers, who was succeeded in turn by Michel Le Tellier. An intendant was attached to each army to supervise the distribution of pay and to punish any offences committed by the soldiers. These "commissaries" even took part in military conferences.

When there were serious military reversals Richelieu passed harsh judgement on his countrymen's qualities as soldiers;

but he took the part of the provincial nobility, of whom he said:

". . . the poor gentry, whose wealth is in their land, will never augment their income . . . since agricultural products nearly always fetch the same price . . . and if there is a seasonal rise the excess product results in a drop in sales so that at the end of the year the poor noble finds that his income has not increased although his expenses have . . . with the result that he is no longer able to send his children to serve their King and country as would befit their social standing."

These sober statements stand in marked contrast to the general dissatisfaction he expressed on the subject of military failures. There were times when he lost all sense of proportion, as when he wrote:

"There is no other people so ill-suited to war as ours. The frivolity and impatience that they display in the most minor tasks . . . only serve to demonstrate, I regret to say, the truth of this proposition."

And he continued:

"Although Caesar is said to have observed that the Franks understood two things, the art of war and the art of conversation, I must confess that I have yet to discover on what grounds he attributed the first of these qualities to them, since stamina and endurance, which are so necessary in war, are so rarely found in their ranks.

"If their courage were enhanced by these two qualities the world would not be large enough to encompass their conquests. But, although the great heart which God has given them enables them to conquer all who try to oppose them with force, their frivolity and lack of stamina render them incapable of overcoming even the most minor difficulties which the delaying tactics employed by a cunning enemy may impose on their ardour. . . . Quite apart from this, however, they are also

123

accused of being discontented with this present epoch and of bearing their country little affection; and this accusation is indeed so justified that it would be difficult to deny that [in France] there are more who fail in the duty imposed on them by their birth than in any other country in the world . . . no offensive is conducted against France in which Frenchmen do not participate, and, when they do fight for their country, her interests mean so little to them that they make no attempt to overcome their natural deficiencies for her sake . . . they are so lacking in phlegm that they cannot wait even a single moment for a favourable opportunity; . . . when they prosper they lose all sense of proportion, more than any other nation, and in adversity and hardship they lose heart and all sense of judgement. . . . Whenever [France] has been attacked her enemies have always found factionists in her bosom who, like vipers . . . eat their mother's entrails."

The Cardinal later tried to soften the impact of these sentences surely written in wrath, by praising his countrymen's courage and *élan*:

"I know that the French compensate for these imperfections with many good qualities. They are valiant . . . their courage and impetuosity often enable them to accomplish in one fell swoop what others accomplish only after repeated attempts."

He then placed his views in perspective by dealing with the national characteristics of other peoples:

"It is certain that the Spanish are superior to us in stamina, perseverance, zeal and loyalty towards King and country. But on the other hand this barren and in parts almost denuded kingdom is so short of manpower that, were it not for the hardihood of its soldiers, it would be lost. . . . Moreover, although certain individuals in France stage revolts against their master, in the Spanish army the men sometimes revolt and mutiny *en masse*."

He then turned his attention to the Germans:

"Although the Emperor enjoys the advantage of ruling a nation that is a breeding ground for soldiers, he also suffers the disadvantage that this nation is prone to change sides and even its religion. . . . To sum up, all nations have their faults and the wisest are those that try to acquire by art what nature was unable to endow them with."

Richelieu's complaints about the French High Command at the beginning of the war were well founded.

The archives of the Bibliothèque Nationale in Paris preserve a document from the hands of a copyist with corrections by Le Masle which contains Richelieu's merciless censure of the High Command, in the form of character sketches of various Generals, brief notes dashed off in a hurry: their fragmentary nature is supplemented by passages in Richelieu's correspondence. There is scarcely any other instance in the history of warfare in which the leader of a national government speaks so scathingly of his High Command. Most of the Army Commanders are severely criticized—Châtillon, for example, and also Richelieu's own brother-in-law, Maillé, to whom the Cardinal once wrote: "I regret the kindnesses that I have done you." Vitry also had a hard time of it. Richelieu did not like him. His notes on the Army Commanders were for the most part tense, passionate pronouncements; of Montmorency he said: "A strong heart, a weak head, in the final analysis disloyal"; of Marillac: "Unreliable, disloyal" and of Rohan: "Businessman with little heart and no loyalty whatever".

He was also capable of praise. Marshal d'Effiat received recognition, and Schomberg was singled out for special commendation. Of the Duke of Orléans, however, Richelieu wrote: "A person of such high rank and with so little zeal that, although he is extremely intelligent and knowledgeable, he is loth to stoop to military labours."

Quite apart from the state of the French army and its High Command, Richelieu was also faced with the extremely serious problem of how to finance the war, and we shall have to consider this problem if we are to assess accurately the difficulties under which the Cardinal played his historical role.

State Finances

Under Louis XIII the French State found itself in a parlous financial situation. Its regular income covered scarcely a quarter of its expenditure, an emergency that called for dangerous measures in order to wipe out the deficit. The tax farmers and the money lenders got rich, the people poor. Money was hoarded. In trying to create a centralized State by disposing of the last vestiges of the former feudal rule, while at the same time initiating a foreign policy with far-reaching aims, distributing enormous subsidies abroad and conducting a general war that was likely to last for a number of years, Richelieu had created insoluble financial problems. There was no effective national budget. All attempts to introduce one broke down in the face of local traditions and coercion. Most of Richelieu's contemporaries and the majority of later historians maintain that he had no aptitude for financial affairs. He himself not only admitted to this deficiency but constantly proclaimed it. This prompts the question whether he was not in fact dissembling in order to rid himself of a responsibility that has led to the downfall of so many of his predecessors.

Hanotaux has given an impressive survey of the fate of most of the French Superintendents of Finance since the reign of Philip Augustus. From him we learn that under this great King it had proved possible, thanks to an early wave of national enthusiasm, to persuade the people of France to make a war contribution. At that time the States General had approved the measure because they felt it had the support of public opinion. The Crown had then seized the property of the Knights Templar, using extreme measures in the process, and subsequently made Enguerrand de Marigny, whom we may regard as a "Superintendent of Finance", responsible for this grave act. When the King died Marigny was instantly hanged. At that time the Jews were either killed or banished and their property was confiscated. Subsequently, however, those who had been driven out were allowed to return and were even given the means with which to revive trade, which had slumped following their removal.

Under John II, surnamed Le Bon, when there was yet another English invasion, the French followed the example set by the Doge Vitale Michiel at the siege of Constantinople and minted money from leather. Charles V of France introduced direct taxation, four livres for each hearth in the towns and thirty sols in the villages. He also imposed a salt and wine tax.

Under Charles VI there were violent riots in Paris and again the Finance Minister, Jean de Lagrange, was executed. His successor, des Essarts, met a similar end. It took a Constable of Armagnac to master the position of Superintendent of Finance. After his courageous action the political parties then took charge of the State's financial resources.

Charles VIII was called Charles the Victorious because he drove the English out of France. But the cost of that triumph was high. He arraigned Pierre de Brézé and Jacques Coeur, wholesale merchants and bankers, in order to lay his hands on their wealth. His Superintendent of Finance was condemned to death but was spared on payment of a very high ransom. To maintain the economy after the war direct taxation was increased, with the proceeds going to the King. Originally this form of taxation, first imposed under Philip IV to help meet the cost of the war, had been envisaged as an exceptional contribution. But following the Hundred Years' War it became a permanent feature and was handled as follows: each year the King would stipulate the total sum to be raised and apportion specific amounts to the various territories, districts and parishes, and also to individual persons. Those liable for taxation were assessed on the basis either of their total income or of their landed property by so-called *"asséeurs"*.

It was Louis XI who introduced the profitable and pernicious system of selling offices. His Superintendents of Finance fared no better than so many of their predecessors; although he was a Cardinal, the unfortunate La Balue, for example, was imprisoned in an iron cage and kept there until he died. When Charles VIII needed money for his Italian enterprises he convened the States General; they gave him the subsidies he asked for on condition that a board of control be set up. The King accepted the condition, after which no more was heard of it. Louis XII solved many pressing problems by stepping up the sale of offices still further. Under Francis I this practice then became general. He made the greatest profit from the bestowal of judicial offices. His Superintendent of Finance, Semblençay, also ended up on the scaffold, as if this were a traditional consequence of his office. Henry II's reign was steeped in murder; riots were constantly breaking out because of the *"gabelle"*, the salt tax. Conditions had become intolerable and everywhere people were taking the law into their own hands.

Then, under Charles IX and Henry III, that is, between 1561 and 1576, it seemed as if things were about to improve. The Edict of Saint-Germain of January 3, 1562, gave hope of prolonged civil peace. But this hope was quickly dashed by the outbreak of the religious wars. There was total devastation and unspeakable misery set in.

Both before and after the Massacre of St Bartholomew's Eve the Huguenots persistently demanded the convocation of the States General. But it was their very persistence which prevented any development towards a representative form of government in France, for any suggestions emanating from the Huguenots at that time were inevitably dragged into the religious maelstrom. The States General nonetheless met. The Assembly was opened by the King on December 6, 1576. He lamented the general misery, stressed the need for peace and promised to furnish the delegates with detailed accounts of income and expenditure.

2. Olivares, detail from a portrait by Velasquez

3. Bernhard of Saxe-Weimar, contemporary engraving

The legist, Jean Bodin, a powerful and original thinker, was the only one of the assembled delegates who had the courage to speak his mind. Though a Catholic he dissociated himself from the objectives pursued by the Holy League.

Towards the end of the sixteenth century the journals began to concern themselves with questions of finance and taxation. This was something new. Bodin's *République* had popularized concepts that had been unknown before. People began to think about the structure of the State, its functions and its methods of administration. In various parts of the country demands were made, critical ideas formulated, motions of censure introduced. But in 1588–9, when the Estates of Blois were convened at the instigation of the Holy League, practically no progress was made in the sphere of reform; fanatical patriotism and sectarian passions held sway. In his closing report the chairman of the Third Estate was able to write: "The delegates took leave of one another with tears in their eyes and all anticipating dismal events."

Then came the great turning point, the restoration of internal peace under Henry IV and the reforms introduced by the Duke of Sully, an outstanding organizer.

Sully had been Secretary of State since 1594; he kept the closest personal contact with his sovereign. From 1593 onwards he had drawn his master's attention to the general state of the finances and undertaken to determine the country's real resources, to establish the exact amount of the national debt and to put a stop to the mischief caused by the constant increase in the number of offices.

When Sully joined the Finance Committee he proved his ability at once. The King had given him far-reaching powers, which he applied by visiting the *généralités*, that is, the financial districts in the vicinity of Paris. But, as was to be expected, the finance officials had received advance warning. The "auditor" came too late; some were away on journeys, others had prepared plausible stories and arranged for their records to disappear. But Sully held his ground. He declared that he intended to retain only two treasurers in each office and two *"élus"*. This frightened the officials, and those who had left home quickly returned lest they lose their positions; the missing records reappeared, the accounts were examined, abuses and embezzlements were discoverd. Since the Crown was in urgent need of money, Sully had all bills of exchange, which were drawn at sight but were normally settled quarterly, paid out to him on the spot. In this way he brought back with him from his tour the sum of 1,500,000 livres. Everyone complained bitterly to the King, who allowed himself to be impressed and demanded an explanation. But when seventy cartloads of gold arrived, Henry, who had never before known what it was to have a surplus, was placated.

That was the beginning. For as long as Sully was allowed and able to operate he always created order.

In April 1597 Henry gave his friend and First Servant full responsibility for financial affairs, and in 1599 he made him Superintendent of Finance. For eleven years, until the King was assassinated, the Duke had a completely free hand in the administration of his functions and his power constantly grew.

Sully confronted the great nobles, the courtiers, the King's successive mistresses, who were a considerable drain on the treasury money, and also the Provincial Governors, who had been accustomed to levying taxes on their own initiative for forty years, with rigid austerity, promulgating ordinances and supervising their implementation; this was his most significant achievement. But even under this extraordinary man abuses proved resilient and it seemed that they could not be entirely eradicated.

Sully made few important innovations. He too was obliged to continue the practice of selling offices, and he failed to reduce the number of officials significantly. But what mattered chiefly was the way Sully administered his office under prevailing conditions; he was a man of absolute integrity. The personal wealth that he acquired came entirely from gifts openly bestowed on him by the King. Sully was incorruptible;

what is more, he himself kept a constant watch for fraudulent practices. He tirelessly checked the returns, which he demanded from every state department, especially the tax offices.

By these methods and by resolutely confronting even the most powerful in the land Sully made the present secure. Not even he could undo the past. It was not easy to pay off the royal debt. The pensions granted to the former leaders of the Holy League alone swallowed up enormous sums of money. Throughout his life he fought to eradicate the tremendous corruption which was the principal legacy of the religious wars, and his achievement was essentially of a moral order.

The tragic period of Sully's life began when his King died and he himself, after a brief and fruitless attempt to assert himself, was deprived of his powers, ridiculed, held suspect and obliged to stand idly by and witness the destruction of all his work and the heedless way in which the great reserves he had accumulated were squandered.

Marie de' Medici's regency introduced a time of weakness; it was as if a dam had burst, releasing every conceivable form of greed. This regency, in which the most unjustifiable desires were gratified, especially those conceived by the Queen-Mother herself, was followed by the period of rule with which we are concerned and in which everything was subordinated to the actual or assumed requirements of an international policy, which Cardinal Richelieu served to the limits of what was bearable. Rearmament now had priority over all other considerations.

It was inevitable that the appalling burdens imposed on the Third Estate should eventually lead to the breakdown of social barriers. While the country was making the most arduous preparations for war and was exposed to extreme danger from enemies abroad, an early and alarming form of class struggle arose which combined in a curious union with the assassination attempts directed against the leading representatives of the great families, who were fighting their rear-guard action against

the monarchy and the authority of the State before making
their exit from the stage of history.

But in the seventeenth century—which, far from being the
static and majestically proportioned period of popular belief,
was positively teeming with revolts—the real social dynamite
was supplied by the additional fiscal burdens imposed by the
requirements of power politics. In 1610, the year in which
Henry IV died, the *taille* had yielded 17,000,000 livres; in the
year after Richelieu's death, when France was still in the midst
of war, it brought in 44,000,000.

In the light of this account it is not difficult to see why the
Cardinal should have done all within his power throughout
the whole period of his office to prove the truth of his own
assertion: "I understand nothing of finance."

To this end he quite intentionally made naïve or provocative
remarks on the subject, saying for instance to Schomberg:
"Money is unimportant. What matters is the realization of our
policies". Or he took recourse, obviously intentionally, to
such platitudes as: "A balance must be struck . . . between
what a Prince takes from his subjects and what they are able to
give, not only without being ruined but without being notably
inconvenienced."

But upon closer examination the Cardinal's lack of interest
and alleged incompetence appear specious. He is known to
have said in the presence of Louis XIII that, though the King
was sufficiently provisioned with money and so, for the moment,
were the army treasuries, nobody could guarantee that France
would be able to keep up such an astronomical level of
expenditure. For in estimating the cost of a war one had to
consider that, although everybody knew when a war began,
nobody could predict when or *how* it would end, especially
in view of the fact that appetites often increased in the course of
a meal and the needs of the armies were subject to fluctuation.

Richelieu was also capable of precise evaluations. He was
not above making calculations. Once he tried to reduce expenditure by two-thirds. On that occasion he estimated annual

naval expenses at 2,600,000 livres and those for the artillery at 600,000; by contrast, the assessment for the royal household, the Queen's household and "Monsieur's"[1] household was 3,600,000 livres. He calculated the subsidies for the *Schweizer*, who had to be retained for reasons of prestige, at 400,000, the building costs at 300,000, the envoys' expenditure at 250,000 and the fortresses at 600,000. He added that all other subsidies could in fact be cancelled (4,000,000 livres per annum) but that since it was not possible to go from one extreme to the other he considered it desirable to tread a middle path and start by making economies at Court. This was all the more desirable since it would have a beneficial effect on public opinion; instead of rewarding the idle life of the Court, the parasites would be obliged to participate in the trials and tribulations of war. Consequently the pensions and salaries of the courtiers should not exceed 2,000,000 livres, the King's personal expenses should be limited to 50,000 and the *acquits patents*[2] to no more than 400,000. Over and above this Richelieu allowed 2,000,000 livres for Court journeys, 150,000 for emergencies, and 300,000 for the King's *comptants* (ready money). He estimated total expenditure at 25,000,000 livres; the actual figures given by Richelieu add up to precisely 13,250,000. By comparison, income at that time amounted to 35,000,000 livres, which meant that the *taille* could be reduced. The Cardinal added that the only real way of creating order was by reducing the burden on both the people and the state; by cutting back on state expenditure the *taille* could be lowered, and this should be the chief objective.

The techniques of a credit economy had not yet been developed. No war loans could be raised and there was no flow of capital into France. In our modern financial systems those who administer public money are free to make quite considerable miscalculations without fear of retribution, and

---

[1] Monsieur = Gaston d' Orleans, the King's brother (Tr.).

[2] *Acquis patents*—the King's instructions for payment to his accountants, in contrast to *acquis de comptants*, the King's ready cash (Tr.).

in the event of a lost war those responsible for issuing loans have usually long since disappeared from the scene.

But under the *ancien régime* everything had to be paid for out of state income, which meant that the brunt of the burden was borne by the Third Estate, whose members (especially the farmers), despite sudden acts of desperation, by and large accepted and endured with unbelievable patience a standard of living that was constantly sinking. This was a very impressive fact and one to which Richelieu gave a great deal of thought.

He always remembered the assembly of the States General of 1614 and the words of a representative of the Third Estate: "Sire, every province in Your Majesty's realm is indissolubly linked with the Crown to form a single body under the rule of the one sovereign. All Your Majesty's subjects are united by a common allegiance."

Following the religious wars the people were fired by a genuinely passionate desire for a simplified and united State, and despite local revolts the Crown felt that it was able to rely on the devotion of the popular majority.

Among the ideas that Richelieu sketched out immediately following his appointment to office and which Miron, the Bishop of Angers, then drew up in the form of ordinances, the need for financial reforms was considered to be of the utmost urgency. The aim of these reforms was to eliminate the existing discrepancies in taxation between classes and material possessions. Richelieu always subscribed to this general principle. At the Assembly of Notables of 1626 he described the major financial needs of the country, while at the same time enumerating and elaborating on all the dangers that had threatened France in the course of the preceding twenty-five years. He went on developing a programme for the nation's security, and asserted that beginning with Henry IV all good Frenchmen had been in accord with his basic ideas. He called upon the property-owning class—the only class represented at that Assembly—to meet the financial needs of the State, pleading that they should not make the lot of the poor even worse than it already was.

"Gentlemen, the King has called you together here so that we may seek and find the necessary means and join together in solving this problem." But the Assembly was not prepared to accept far-reaching reforms. Those that reappeared in the ordinances of 1629 were rejected by the parlement. Richelieu was to say later that the reforms project would have to wait until times of peace. But he was not to live to see them. All he could do was to incorporate his ideas in his *Political Testament* and in all other respects keep himself at a safe distance from financial responsibilities. His desire for an equitable distribution of the tax burden, however, remained unabated. Thus we read:

"It is only for true enemies of the State to tell their Prince that he should take nothing from his people and that his entire wealth should lie in the hearts of those subject to his rule. Similarly, it is only for the flatterers and the true pests of the Court to whisper in the ears of Princes that they are at liberty to demand whatever they think fit and that in this respect their royal will is the criterion of power."

And again:

"Provided the absolutely essential expenses of the State have been ensured, the less one raises from the people the better."

And finally:

"The real way of enriching the State is by relieving the people of their burdens."

We sense Richelieu's anger when he writes:

"By taking extreme measures [against profiteers] the people could be greatly relieved."

And he continued:

"We would do well to dismiss over a hundred thousand officials. After their dismissal they would be obliged to do something useful, either in the forces, in trade or in agriculture."

Resignedly he adds:

"I know that it is easy to make the kind of plans that are found in Plato's *Republic*. This work contains wonderful ideas, but they are utopian. If God should be so gracious as to grant Your Majesty an early peace and sustain it for this kingdom and its servants, among whom I count myself one of the least, then I trust that, instead of setting down these ideas in my *Testament*, I shall be able to put them into practice."

He did not put them into practice, and he did everything in his power to prevent an end of the war before a truly final victory had been attained. But even in the turmoil of war his thoughts continued to be preoccupied with the abuses of the fiscal system. He anticipated many measures that were put into effect a full century later.

Richelieu, in whose own conduct of affairs personality counted for everything, constantly pressed for the depersonalization of offices, for objectification, and he was trying to wipe out the innumerable privileges usurped from the State.

In this connection he wrote:

"We must reform the finances by removing the principal means whereby it has been possible to obtain money from the King's coffers by illicit practices. There is no greater evil than the *comptants*, which have been subjected to such abuse that we must either find a remedy or let the State go to ruin. . . . I am well aware that there is a certain amount of expenditure abroad, which by its very nature must be kept secret and which brings great advantages to the State [subsidies and pensions] . . . but under this pretext so much is stolen that it would be better to give up some of the advantages rather than permit such abuse."

The Cardinal wanted to restrict the uncontrolled distribution of money from accounts that we today would call "secret funds". But he himself distributed bribes in Germany and the Scandinavian states. Two years after his death the sums intended for use abroad in this way amounted to 59,000,000 livres.

The King accepted Richelieu's advice that he should discontinue the practice of entrusting the finances to a single person, that is, a Superintendent of Finance. In his Memoirs Richelieu gives an account of the arguments he advanced:

". . . it seems desirable that the King should name three persons whose social condition would be neither too high nor too low, who would be called heads or administrators of finance and would perform the duties previously discharged by the Superintendent, who would, moreover, have no powers to pass decrees that had not previously been approved by the Council, who would not be 'nobles of the sword', for such men are too ambitious and arrogant and demand offices and positions to an excessive degree and to the detriment of the State, for which reasons it would be preferable to appoint *gens de robe*. . . ."

But then he had second thoughts and suggested that perhaps such men would not have the courage to hold their ground when faced with the wrath of those whose applications they had to refuse. In the end he advised the King to give the system a trial.

Putting this plan into practice was not easy. The King asked Richelieu to name three men. But after Louis had rejected his initial proposal that Schomberg should return to the Ministry of Finance (cf. Vol. I, p. 160) the Cardinal—still intent on avoiding all personal responsibility—declined to submit any names. The King insisted on having his own way, and eventually he himself proposed Monsieur de Champigny, the Comptroller General, and, interestingly enough, Marillac, who "is so capable", and finally the Procurator General of the parlements, Molé, whose "innocent hands" had "greatly contributed" to the establishment of a sound financial administration. The King's proposals were duly considered, but only Champigny was elected unanimously, Molé of the innocent hands was rejected, while Marillac, who was the Queen-Mother's *protégé*, was elected with a large majority.

On August 15, 1624, Richelieu said to the Venetian envoy:

"These members of the new department will be capable and correct. They will divide the work among themselves in order to simplify the management of affairs but will act jointly and will pass joint resolutions."

It is quite evident that, although Richelieu wished to remain in the background, he intended to keep the ultimate control of financial affairs in his own hands. Eventually this cumbersome mechanism broke down. Champigny belonged to another generation. He was soon swallowed up in the Department of Foreign Affairs. For Marillac the position was simply a springboard to more important functions, and as early as 1626 he left Finance to become Keeper of the Great Seal. And so they were back again to the old system with a single departmental head; the office of Superintendent of Finance was revived. But by then Richelieu had found a man who was totally loyal to him, the sort of person he always liked to take into his service, the son of a noble of the Paris parlement, whose family had little influence. He belonged to no group and was easily led; his name was d'Effiat. He had already distinguished himself as an Ambassador to England and as a soldier. In the Department of Finance he and Richelieu shared a completely impenetrable secretiveness: this imperturbable confidant formed a perfect complement to Father Joseph. Some fairly cynical comments of Richelieu's on d'Effiat are reported. By controlling the purse strings through him, he said, one controlled everything. And when people began to talk about the rapid growth of d'Effiat's fortune the Cardinal, despite his fundamental aversion to irregularities, said: "Who does not enrich himself in public office?" Subsequently, after d'Effiat's death, the collective system was reintroduced. We shall deal with it later. As for d'Effiat, he was the father of Cinq-Mars; if Richelieu had not promoted the father, he would not have founded the short-lived fortunes of the son, who was to prove so dangerous.

In 1632, after Châteauneuf's brief spell, Bullion and Claude

Bouthillier, Chavigny's father, were appointed as joint Super-intendents of Finance. These two followers of Richelieu's took no bold or constructive measure in their period of office. They simply carried on routinely, selling offices whenever money was needed. The two famous B's had equal powers. But Bullion had the stronger nerves and was also the more intelligent. He remained in office until 1640. From 1635 onwards, however, despite his natural joviality and great optimism, he fell prey to occasional fits of despair. A few years after the declaration of war he drew up a memorandum on the chaotic state of the nation's finances. He did not always inform the King and Richelieu of the measures he took in order to procure money. The Cardinal was always dissatisfied and even resorted to threats if, on the one hand, his demands for money were not complied with and if, on the other, the Superinten-dents found themselves obliged to increase the pressure of taxation. In this connection Richelieu went in constant dread of revolts, for which he did not want to be held personally responsible. And so he always passed responsibility on to Bullion and Sublet de Noyers, as is clearly demonstrated by a letter he wrote the King on March 29, 1637. And in a letter to Bullion of March 28th of the same year he put the blame for the defeat suffered in the Valtelline on them, because of their failure to send the money needed to complete the construction of the fortresses.

An attempt was then made to restrict Bullion's powers. But it would seem that no valid decree was promulgated to give official force to this move.

Whatever the rights and wrongs of the matter, a permanent and steadily growing deficit was carried forward from one year to the next. Richelieu's unpopularity increased in propor-tion to the growth in the national debt; before his far-reaching foreign policies had been put into effect he was all but brought down by domestic affairs. By and large the movement of money was not subject to the control of the *cour de comptes* (audit office). In 1626–7 d'Effiat had submitted a report on the nation's finances to the Assembly of Notables, in which he stated:

"When it pleased the King to appoint me to this office I found there was not even enough money to meet the requirements of the coming months. When I had enquired about the estimates of income and expenditure for the rest of the year I discovered that no further income was to be expected and that the income for the year 1627 had already been heavily mortgaged."

The Superintendent complained that it was quite impossible to keep accurate records. He explained that it was not easy to check the accounts of ten different *trésoreries*, all of whom enjoyed equal powers, while at the same time trying to settle with a hundred tax commissioners and over a hundred and twenty collectors and *traitants*, who for the past five years had kept no records of the moneys they should have handed over to the State.

In the memorandum that d'Effiat drew up for the year 1629 we read:

"When the Marquis d'Effiat took office on June 7, 1626, the garrisons were due thirty months [in back pay]. Those who had been paid most regularly were owed two years and the armies in the field two months of the preceding year and all of the current year; the nobles of the Court [had received] no bounties during either the past or the current year, the army that had returned from Italy had received no pay at all, likewise the armies in the Valtelline, Montpellier and the fortress of La Rochelle . . .

"All income from the fifth month of the [current] year onwards had been spent, as had the income for the first quarter of 1627; the income for April and even the revenue from the *gabelle* and the five large estates had been partially mortgaged."

It was under such conditions that France was pursuing a most ambitious policy of expansion. The moneylenders had been receiving 30 per cent from the King on all loans, which d'Effiat promptly reduced to 20 per cent, while introducing economies in every sphere. But he was still obliged to borrow money, both in the form of government credits and also through personal contacts. He even helped the State from his own personal means. We are told:

"In order to meet current obligations he raised 6,000,000 livres on his own account over and above the assignats which he issued and which themselves amount to more than 6,000,000 livres."

D'Effiat's achievements were remarkable. He had always wanted to remove the *paulette* tax, which imposed an excessive burden on the farmers. But by doing so he would have prejudiced too many vested interests and so had to give up the idea. (We have already discussed d'Effiat's successors in the chapter dealing with Richelieu's collaborators; Vol. II, p. 150 ff.).

To sum up: the French needed ready money—money for pensions, money for the Court and the courtiers, money for Orléans and money to buy the people in Orléans' and the Queen-Mother's entourage. They needed large sums for subsidies, first for Mansfeld, then for the Danes and always for the Dutch; above all they needed money for their German allies and for the Swedes.

To obtain it they used every possible means. For a time Richelieu had in his service a Spanish Jew by the name of López, who dealt in troops and antiques and acted as go-between, occasional diplomat and spy. The following passage from their correspondence is typical:

"The linen from Haarlem [he wrote Richelieu on October 15, 1640] is clean and white in my hand. I will bring it to you; I am waiting for my pass. I have been asked to buy a large quantity of vases, carpets, agates, porcelain, crystal, Gobelins and pictures *en masse* from Rubens' collection [Rubens had just died]. The Duchess of Chevreuse has presented me with a pearl necklace, but I have no money. There are some very beautiful tapestries of great value, some of them modern, but I have no money."

Why did he have no money? By the terms of a treaty concluded on August 22, 1639, France had undertaken to pay the widow of the Landgrave of Hesse-Cassel the sum of 150,000 livres and to write off certain debts that she had incurred. In partial settlement of the first of these provisions Lopez advanced her 50,000 livres from his own pocket; since he had not been reimbursed he had no means with which to pay the subsequent instalments. In his accounts he also listed the personal sums that the Cardinal owed him for the purchase of powder and ships in Holland and also the amounts he had advanced on his behalf in the form of loans to various people. Hence his bitter lament: "After having served you, after having done all that I was commanded to do, I cannot even obtain enough money to leave the country." Lopez was being held in detention for the debts of the French nation.

But there were also accomplices of quite a different order. In a report dated December 4, 1636, Richelieu informed his sovereign about the alchemist, Dubois, who had undertaken to manufacture gold and had been conducted to Vincennes to carry out his experiments there. Louis XIII wrote in the margin of this letter: "It will be good news for M. de Bullion if this enterprise proves successful."

Richelieu proposed that kilns should be built in the forest of Vincennes and in Rueil to give Dubois the impression that he was not being held captive there but was pursuing his art as a free man. Once the alchemist succeeded in smuggling in a small lump of gold, but when he was unable to repeat this stratagem he was soon incarcerated.

We have already seen that Richelieu himself cost the State enormous amounts of money. Even his confidants complained about this, for it was not only the Cardinal who kept on asking for more but his family as well.

In our account of Richelieu's close associates (Vol. II, p. 159) we quoted Bullion's maxim: "If you will satisfy two appetites, that of His Eminence's household and that of the Artillery, I'll guarantee the rest." But it should not be forgotten that once Richelieu had grown rich he sometimes advanced large sums to the State that had made him rich.

We have now reached a point in the first phase of France's entry into the war where this commitment might appear altogether too hazardous. Insuperable difficulties of rearmament, of the military command and of finance increased the risk alarmingly. But our appreciation of Richelieu's politics would be inadequate if we failed to consider the broad historical perspectives underlying the relations and the tensions between the European States in the first half of the seventeenth century. Under Richelieu everything assumed a particularly dramatic character, and after a decade of cold war this led to a life-and-death struggle, from which France was to emerge as the leading power on the Continent of Europe for a long time to come.

De Paris ce 4e Debre 1636

Ce sera une bonne nouuelle pour Mr de Bullion

ci ce comancement vient a efect

il ne se peut rien adjouter a cette proposition la quelle je trouue tres bonne

L'affaire de Du Bois sera un peu de peine estant un effect fascheux, mais i'espere que le Roy y trouuera son compte; Et en effect Mr de Noyers a trouué chez luy selon que nous enuions de quoy faire Deux Montres D'Armée

Pourueu qu'on puisse faire paruenir ce que cet honnoste homme a comancé

Pour cet effect on estime qu'il faut faire dresser des fourneaux au Bois de Vincennes et a Ruel pour luy donner esperance de uenir quelquefois comme non prisonnier, qui est un nom qui luy fasche autant que la chose

Ou cet homme se resoudra a trauailler, ce que le Roy qu'il fera de gré ou de force, quand il se verra sans esperance autrement, Ou il faudra tascher de faire acheuer ce qu'il a comancé selon les Memoirs qu'on a trouué dans son laboratoire. Ie tascheray pour cet effect de m'asseurer dès auiourd'huy de deux hommes qui ont trauaillé louent auec luy sans sçauoir le fonds disons secrets et ie les meneray demain a Ruel auec moy pour y faire faire un laboratoire.

J'asseure sa Maté que ie le feray en ceste affaire comme

A report from Richelieu to the King, with handwritten marginal note by Louis XIII

CHAPTER VI

FOLLOWING THE DECLARATION OF WAR

Open warfare began with a French attack on the Spanish Netherlands. It should be remembered that the French army operating in this sector was commanded by a Protestant, Marshal Châtillon, the grandson of Admiral Coligny, in conjunction with Richelieu's brother-in-law, the Marquis of Brézé. In placing the most important army group under Protestant command at the beginning of the war France was undoubtedly thinking of her Protestant allies and also of England. On May 22, 1635, Châtillon and Brézé defeated an army led by Prince Thomas of Savoy at Avesnes. Unlike his brother, Prince Thomas had espoused the Spanish cause and placed himself at the disposal of Duke Victor Amadeus; in this way the ruling dynasty of Savoy would be ensured, whatever the outcome of the conflict. At that point it seemed that nothing could stop the French army from joining up with the forces of Frederick Henry of Orange, and on May 30th the two armies were in fact united between Maastricht and Loo. Following the victory of Avesnes, Orange took Tirlemont; but, although strictly forbidden to do so, his troops plundered the town in the most brutal fashion whereupon the population immediately switched their allegiance to the Spanish régime. At that time the Spanish Stadtholder, the Cardinal-Infante Don Fernando, was waiting on the far side of the river Nethe with the army he had led to the Netherlands from the battlefield of Nördlingen. The two French Marshals, meanwhile, were arguing over the question of precedence. Charnacé, who was attached to the High Command as Richelieu's representative, furnished a detailed account of their dispute: the Cardinal's reply revealed both his anxiety and his anger.

After a month of dissension between the two commanders, during which time the army remained inactive, the Spanish landed powerful fighting units by night on the island of Wal from eight hundred small boats. These units occupied Fort Schenck, which was then in a bad state of repair, and put its Dutch garrison to the sword as rebels. Until then the fortress of Schenck had protected the frontier of the United Netherlands. On hearing that it had fallen, the Prince of Orange instantly left his French allies and proceeded by forced marches to the defence of his homeland. Brézé was convinced that Orange was conducting secret negotiations with the Spanish.

Meanwhile the victory of Avesnes, which had cost five thousand lives, had been cancelled out. The siege of Louvain undertaken by Frederick Henry had to be given up with all speed, as had the attempt to encircle Brussels, for the French lines of communication had been cut by the Imperialist forces under General Piccolomini, hurrying to the aid of their Spanish allies after having crossed the Rhine at Mainz.

The French offensive had collapsed. France herself was threatened with invasion from Flanders. The Cardinal-Infante had good grounds for arguing that France would be unable to resist a combined attack by the Spanish and Imperialist forces.

At that time Madrid and Vienna were co-operating more closely than Paris and Stockholm.

The suggestion made by the Stadtholder of the Netherlands that France might be invaded successfully from Picardy rather than from Flanders could easily have been realized in the course of 1636. Maximilian I of Bavaria, bitterly disappointed by Richelieu's policies, placed Johann von Werth's light cavalry at Don Fernando's disposal. What a change there had been in Franco-Bavarian relations since the Treaty of Fontainebleau! Thanks above all to the achievements of Bernhard of Saxe-Weimar, France escaped catastrophe in 1636. In 1635, however,

Bernhard was still a General in the army of the Heilbronn League and an ally of the Queen of Sweden; Sweden was fighting the Emperor and was already defending herself against the full power of Spain before a formal Franco–Swedish agreement to oppose the Spanish was concluded in Compiègne.

The Netherlands

The Forest of Ardennes, in which the French language had survived and the feudal practices of the Middle Ages continued to hold sway for much longer than in other parts of the country, formed France's northern border. Between this forest and the North Sea lay the broad, fertile and thickly populated plain which was completely exposed to invasion by both the English and the Spanish and also to constant incursions from the German territories beyond the Rhine. The rich cities of Flanders, such as Ghent and Bruges, were a tempting goal to the conqueror.

As early as the thirteenth century the cloth and linen industry had undergone a great expansion thanks to the ease with which raw materials could be brought to the Netherlands. The cloth-makers of Brussels and Louvain supplied the whole of France. They exported their products via Bruges, which was also one of the principal centres of commerce for the Hanseatic cities. Antwerp had become the most important harbour on the North Sea. The rivers and canals afforded excellent means of communication. In his description of the Netherlands Guicciardini wrote: "It is the most impressive thing to be in Antwerp and see the countless ships and the great wealth of merchandise and foodstuffs and hear men from every country in the world speaking in every tongue." The strong position of the burghers and the emergence of powerful municipalities was due to the prosperity of such towns. "*Flandriam continuam urbem*", people once wrote.

Ever since the Treaty of Verdun the territory on the south

bank of the river Scheldt had been a French dependency. But the King of France soon discovered that it was not at all easy for his knights to impose his royal will on the merchant classes who lived there. These burghers were the natural allies of the English for as long as England remained a purely agricultural state and continued to send her rich supplies of wool for them to manufacture into cloth.

Michelet wrote: "In the midst of the warring Princes the English butchers and the French weavers maintained close bonds. When France tried to break these bonds it cost her one hundred years of war."

In the course of the Hundred Years' War this splendid province passed into the hands of the House of Burgundy. If Louis XI's successors had not undertaken their disenchanting policy of conquest in Italy, then—as we have repeatedly pointed out—they could have won back the Netherlands. But in 1529, after exhausting themselves in their Italian campaigns, they were obliged to grant the Duke of Burgundy, their most powerful vassal, rights of sovereignty which ultimately passed to the King of Spain, who was the heir and successor of the last of the Burgundian Dukes.

In fact, ever since the days of Charles V, the Île de France, cradle of the French nation, had been under constant threat from the Netherlands. In the sixteenth century Spanish armies advanced as far as Château-Thierry, Saint-Quentin and Amiens and during the religious wars Alessandro Farnese occupied Paris. The forces invading from the Netherlands were drawn from Burgundy, Spain, Franche-Comté, from the banks of the Rhine, from Naples and Sicily. They were reinforced via Savoy, Franche-Comté, the Valtelline, Lake Constance and Alsace.

But then occurred the great event that was to bring relief to France: Philip II of Spain was unable to prevent the seven northern provinces, which were Calvinist, from forming a separate federation and founding the Republic of the United Netherlands. In the face of Spanish religious persecution the skilled workers fled from Flanders, and soon the textile industry had shifted to the separatist provinces. Antwerp, in whose harbours twenty-five thousand ships had dropped and weighed anchor every year, thus providing the city with a very high income from tariffs, was replaced by Amsterdam. The moment the United Provinces reached the estuary of the Scheldt and began to raise import tariffs and road and bridge tolls Antwerp was ruined. Amsterdam became the most important deep-sea harbour and the leading financial centre of Europe. Thanks to their sudden wealth the Netherlanders were able to conduct wars as far afield as Brazil and the East Indies, and from the very beginning they showed great nautical skill.

This revolt imposed an immense burden on the Spanish Netherlands. Even under the Valois, even at times when Paris and Madrid enjoyed friendly relations, France had often supported the Netherlands' revolt surreptitiously and sometimes openly.

In 1625 the hardened and disciplined Spanish veterans had taken the allegedly impregnable fortress of Breda under Spinola's command. But immediately afterwards Spain suffered severe reversals, especially at sea. In 1629 the Dutch East India Company seized the Spanish silver fleet, which was carrying eleven and a half million florins. With these resources at his disposal Frederick Henry, Prince of Orange, raised what was for those times a tremendous army: 120,000 men. He took Herzogenbusch, and in the following year the Amsterdam West India Company captured the Brazilian paradise of Pernambuco. But the heaviest blow for Spain was the loss of Maastricht, for the whole valley of the Meuse and Brussels were then endangered, and the provinces that were later to form the State of Belgium were soon impoverished.

In 1598 Philip II had united his possessions in the Netherlands with Franche-Comté and transformed the combined territories into a dependent principality, which he then placed under the rule of his daughter Isabella, who was married to her cousin, the Austrian Archduke Albert. The King's interests

were represented in Brussels by Spanish ministers, by the
Commandant of the King's army, the head of the Spanish
Secretariat of State and the Archduke's confessor. But after
Albert's death in 1621 the Spanish envoy, Moncada, took over
all these functions. In order to provide some measure of
protection for her subjects Isabella sought the advice of her
Flemish Secretaries of State, the most influential of whom
were the *Audienciat* and the Secretaries of Foreign and Northern Affairs. There were three advisory bodies: 1. The Privy
Council, which was composed of seven administrators versed
in law, who were required to deal with all legal matters and
benefices; the President of this body had influence in the
Finance Committee, and he was also President of the Council
of State and Keeper of the Great Seal. 2. The Council of State.
This was composed of great nobles, who long played a
dominant part in the affairs of the country until their patriotism
rendered them suspect in the eyes of the Spanish, whereupon,
in 1628, this body was abolished and replaced by two juntas;
the first of these was all-Spanish and met every Monday to
discuss military matters, while the second, the "Subsidiary
Council", which also included a number of Netherlanders
and met on Tuesdays and Fridays to deal with foreign affairs,
was directed by the King's representative in Brussels. 3. The
Flemish Council in Madrid, which was renewed by Philip IV
in 1628. In this Council the majority group, which was Spanish,
was composed of men who had never been to the Netherlands;
they passed laws and made decisions, which took priority
over those arrived at by the Council in Brussels. Moncada
reported that there was some danger that the King's Flemish
subjects might be tempted to enter into an alliance with the
Dutch and set up a confederation after the manner of the
Swiss cantons. Three years later Jansen was to make this very
proposal to the Netherlands nobility. It is clear that Richelieu
would be very favourably disposed towards such a project,
especially since the Brussels government had granted asylum
to Marie de' Medici, Gaston d'Orléans and all the leading

malcontents in France and had also afforded help to Lorraine.

Holland was the centre of the anti-Spanish resistance movement. Parts of the country lay below sea-level. In 1421, seventy-two villages were inundated in a single night and there were 100,000 dead. The land was not very fertile; approximately 700,000 people lived from fishing and maritime trade. Wicquefort said that the Dutch were accustomed to drawing the sap from other countries: from the forests of Norway, the vineyards of the Rhine, the Garonne and the Dordogne, from the sheep pastures of England, Ireland, Scotland and Germany, from the Polish and Prussian wheat granaries and from the gardens of India and Arabia.

The astounding assets of the Bank of Amsterdam, which was founded in 1609, offer the best indication of the country's prosperity. For the United Provinces, which were an extremely modern State, supremacy at sea was indispensable. The overseas colonies, which were rapidly increasing in number, were managed and exploited by the East and West India Companies. The first of these was founded in 1602 with capital assets of six-and-a-half million florins, while the second was set up in 1621 and given a monopoly in Atlantic trade. Their dividends were never less than 20 per cent, they possessed 800 ships and they needed war in order to extend their sphere of influence and garner prize money by plundering Spanish ships. They were always in close contact with French diplomats.

The East India Company, which was created on Oldenbarneveldt's initiative, was a real power organization administered by a board of seventeen directors, who were elected by the shareholders and supervised by a Governor General, who also took all decisions on the Company's military operations. It minted coins, made peace and declared war. From the Cape of Good Hope to Japan it exercised a monopoly in the colonies it had seized from the Spanish. Once or twice a year it sent cargo in convoy to Batavia. From there the European merchandise was carried to the various Asian harbours by a fleet of coasters, which then returned to Batavia laden with local products for shipment to Amsterdam. The Company's shares were quoted at five times their face value and showed dividends of up to 63 per cent. The Company paid the State an annuity of 8,000,000 florins and a further 400,000 florins a year in duties.

The United Provinces enjoyed two freedoms that were virtually unknown elsewhere in the seventeenth-century: freedom of religion, which attracted a large number of emigrants, and freedom of the press, which created an international public for Dutch newspapers. As far as its political constitution was concerned, the territory was really a confederation of cities. The Dutch had succeeded in developing the colonial principle while remaining independent of the Pope and the King of Spain. There were feudal nobles in only a few of the northern provinces, the clergy no longer existed as a class and the farmers were excluded from the government. All power rested in the hands of the burghers. As in the days of antiquity, as in the Middle Ages, this Republic was governed by patriciates, whose representatives determined the level of taxation, the size of the standing army and all issues of war and peace. No resolution could be passed without a vote of at least 1,200 persons; every city was responsible for its internal affairs. The Stadtholder and the members of the States-General were obliged to journey from city to city to overcome opposition on the part of the patrician regents. Foreign envoys had to keep a representative in every city and distribute money on all sides. The cities divided the country up into provinces, which were governed by the States General; these usually met four times a year and were represented by delegations between sessions. The Provincial Directory, which had between six and twelve members, was responsible for convening the States General, implementing their ordinances and dealing with day-to-day business. The Republic also had a military and a civil head, who led the resistance against Spain.

As Stadtholder of Holland and Commander-in-Chief of the

Army Prince Frederick Henry of Orange was nonetheless required to submit his military plans to the States General and the Council of State. He was also Lord Chief Admiral, although the effective command of the fleet was in the hands of a Vice-Admiral. But despite this restriction Frederick Henry became the virtual President of the Republic and seemed to have acquired permanent tenure of office of Stadtholder for his family. As the youngest son of William the Silent he had succeeded his brother, Prince Maurice of Orange, the Count of Nassau-Dillenburg. His principal advisers were: Constantin Huygens, the father of the famous scholar, and Jan van Knuyt, who incurred Richelieu's enmity when he suppressed the Falkenberg conspiracy. In 1627 Falkenberg, who had been bought by Richelieu, had tried to deliver up the castle of Oranienstein, but he was thwarted in this attempt by Knuyt's intervention.

England's Reaction

England did not react to Richelieu's Netherlands policy in the way in which the Cardinal had hoped and expected. He had counted on the anti-Spanish and anti-Catholic feelings of the English people and on their sympathy for the Dutch Calvinists; this pragmatic politician had thus failed to appreciate one of the constant features of English foreign policy, which transcended all sympathies, all likes and dislikes. Informed of the contents of the Franco–Dutch Treaty of 1635, Charles I of England realized that the Netherlands were to be divided up between the States General and France and that by the terms of the agreement France's share of the territory would extend as far as the line of the Scheldt. He also knew that, if the objectives specified in the treaty were attained, France would gain possession, not only of the harbour of Dunkirk but of Ostende and Antwerp as well. That England could not tolerate. For some time London had been paying very close attention to French expansionist moves from the

Bay of Biscay to the Scheldt estuary. Admiral Coligny's advance towards Flanders had already elicited an energetic reaction from Elizabeth I. Because of the difficult conditions with which he was obliged to contend at home Charles first sent a whole series of warnings to his brother-in-law, Louis XIII, before officially informing him through his ambassador, Lord Germain, that, whilst the King of England was prepared to negotiate an agreement between France and Spain, if the proposed division of the Netherlands between France and the States General were put into effect a powerful English army would immediately occupy the Spanish Netherlands.

The significance of a string of harbours under French control stretching from Brest to Zeebrugge and facing England across the Channel is quite obvious.

Richelieu had left nothing undone in his attempts to ensure the full support of England before declaring war on Spain. But then came the British threat, and the Cardinal realized at once that even an Anglo–Spanish alliance was not impossible. Charles I was rigidly adhering to traditional foreign policies. But there was a further factor at work here, for at that time, because of the internal situation which threatened to topple him from the throne, Charles was obliged to seek the aid of the moribund English Catholic party. In this connection he had also entertained the idea of Spanish support. Parliament had been dissolved and the King was soon to take up arms against the Scots Presbyterians who, in 1638, renewed the covenant which they had first set up in 1581 in defence of their faith.

We have now anticipated the early events of the Franco–Spanish war, which are the object of our enquiry, in order to demonstrate the extent to which France was subject to the constant threat of English intervention on the side of Spain. We shall also see how, because of the weakness of the British monarchy at that time, Richelieu, after vainly seeking its support, was afforded an opportunity of eliminating it from European politics. He tried to win England and he was disappointed.

Queen Henrietta of England's close relations with her mother, who lived in exile in Brussels, and also with Marie de Chevreuse, were a source of considerable annoyance to him. When these two ladies were offered an honourable refuge in England he regarded this as a personal affront. At that time he had not yet recognized the full extent of Charles I's isolation. He realized too late that in the years preceding Cromwell's seizure of power the King's Puritan opponents, on whose influence he was then counting, had failed to appreciate the traditional needs of English foreign policy; subsequently, following the Puritans' victory but before their foreign policy had had time to take effect, he also failed to realize that an Anglo–Spanish alliance was temporarily excluded by the very fact of their victory. Richelieu, however, did not wait for these developments. Immediately the English made their threat, he prepared to hit back. Although his representatives in London were still under instructions to seek an alliance with Charles I and to bring him to break with Spain, Richelieu also began to woo the leaders of the Scots rebellion. This is clearly demonstrated by his correspondence. He successfully established contact with the Presbyterian preacher, Mobel, and also with Gordon, the Scottish noble delegated to present Scottish complaints to Parliament. The Cardinal's instructions to his envoy, d'Estrades, read as follows:

"The confidence inspired in me by the ability, loyalty and affection of M. le Comte d'Estrades had prompted me to suggest to the King that he should be sent to England as His Majesty's representative in order to persuade the King of England not to give help to the strongholds on the coast of Flanders in the event of their being attacked by the Prince of Orange in the course of this campaign. And in order that M. le Comte should be fully informed, so that he may be better able to carry out His Majesty's proposals, he should know that, since Madame de Chevreuse, with her customary malice, has turned the Queen of England against me by misrepresenting

me to her, it would be desirable to establish Her Majesty's
[present] attitude towards me before making any disclosures to
her; should the Comte d'Estrades find her attitude favourable
he will hand her my letter, from which she will learn of my
desire to re-establish myself in her favour and to do anything
she may care to ask of me. But if the Comte d'Estrades does
not find her well disposed he will hand her the King's letter
only."

In a despatch which d'Estrades drafted immediately upon
arrival in England we read: "I await Your Eminence's commands. The present moment seems a favourable one in which
to create difficulties for the King of England."

Richelieu replied immediately from Rueil on December 2,
1637:

". . . in a few days' time I shall send my chaplain, the Abbé
Chambré, who is a Scot, to Edinburgh to wait for the two
persons whom you have named, and enter into negotiations
with them. Before the year is out the King and Queen of
England will be sorry that they did not accept the offers which
you made to them on the King's behalf. . . . If your two
Scottish friends should still be in London tell them that they
may rely on what the Abbé Chambré tells them; and give
them a letter for the Abbé, so that he will be able to identify
them. You have rendered the King a great service by dis-
covering these two men."

In such circumstances there was little likelihood of English
mediation in the Franco–Spanish conflict.

Colonial Affairs

The keen interest that Richelieu had always taken in Anglo–
French relations, his constant efforts to establish friendly
relations with the island kingdom and set up a united front
vis-à-vis Spain, his attempts to persuade the two peoples to

resolve, virtually by an act of will, their memories of the centuries-old feuds that marked their turbulent past, were unsuccessful. Not only had the marriage of Charles I and Henrietta of France not led to a *rapprochement*, it had constantly disrupted the relations between the two nations. Henrietta's links with her mother and her policies and consequently with the heirs to the French Holy League complicated matters, and Richelieu was never able to dissociate himself from the protection she required for her religious needs and which Louis XIII wished to extend to his sister. In this sphere he too constantly provoked tension and irritation. He made numerous comments on England that became tinged with irony and subsequently with impatience. He once wrote of the English that, if you wished to get anything out of them, you had to ask them to do the opposite of what you really wanted, and he mentions the envy of French successes felt by the English.

We have already considered (Vol. II) French colonial policy in the chapter dealing with the development of the French navy. In this sphere above all Anglo–French rivalry was to prove keen, and certain events, notably in Canada, were stored in the Cardinal's infallible memory with unforgiving bitterness.

Long after the promulgation of Alexander VI's papal bull in 1493 and the conclusion of the Treaty of Tordesillas in 1494, Spain and Portugal had continued to divide any newly discovered territories in the New World between them. Although, understandably enough, this treaty had not been formally recognized by other States, its validity had never been seriously questioned, not even after the union of the two Iberian States, because of the advantage they enjoyed in that sphere in terms of actual power.

England, France and Holland tried in their own way to claim their share of the newly discovered riches, especially precious metals and spices; to this end they searched for gold and silver, while the Dutch and English also mounted expeditions and sent out privateers to capture Spanish ships and attack Spanish harbours. From the end of the sixteenth century onwards Spain lost considerable quantities of precious metals in this way.

Despite their lack of geographical knowledge, the English, Dutch and French started at a very early date to seek new routes to the East Indies which would circumvent the areas of Spanish power. There was much talk of the famous North-West Passage along the coast of North America.

The fishing grounds off the coast of Greenland and New-foundland had been known to the intrepid French and English fishermen since the late Middle Ages. At that time there was a great abundance of fish (cod, whale, herring). But since the location of these fishing grounds and their exact yield were regarded as a trade secret we possess few documents relating to the early period of this fishing industry.

Francis I had shown a keen interest in the possibilities of overseas trade; he strongly opposed the "papal division of the world", the "monopolization of Adam's legacy", and he already spoke of the freedom of the seas. He gave his support to Jean Ango, a ship-owner who established a centre for the study of navigation in Dieppe. When Ango's ships sailed round Africa in search of a route to the Indies and reached the coast of North America, they carried letters of marque. Ango was a Florentine. In both France and England Italian seamen were the first to undertake voyages of discovery. In 1544, after the Treaty of Crépy, Francis I, who wished to preserve the peace with Spain, gave orders that no French discovery ships were to be armed. But this did not lessen his interest in seafaring. He helped Jacques Cartier to undertake his voyages to the coast of Canada and the Gulf of St Lawrence (also in search of a passage to the Indies), and it was in his reign that the French first took possession of lands within the territory subsequently to become the province of Quebec. At that time, however, no permanent bases were established. Francis I's alliance with the Ottoman Empire also helped to promote French seafaring. And then there were the two expeditions under Admiral Coligny to the coasts of Brazil and Florida in the 1550s and 1560s. These were probably undertaken with a view to securing refuge for the Huguenots, who were already sorely pressed. No tangible successes were achieved at that time.

But then the religious wars eradicated every spark of enterprise and led to the total paralysis of French seafaring. Ships grew obsolete and decayed; many sailors, including a large number of Huguenots, left their homeland and entered into foreign service, especially in Holland.

As France recovered, Henry IV tried to revive trade and seafaring; this he did in spite of Sully's warnings. He concluded trading agreements with the Hanse and also with England; and this, together with the renewal of the capitulations with the Porte, helped to increase French prestige at sea. By contrast, the founding of the first State-aided companies for the East Indies trade produced no immediate results. But the King's interest in his overseas projects did not diminish. He was determined to enforce recognition of France's claim to Canada. To this end he granted territorial concessions, allowed the nobility to organize their own shipping concerns and appointed a Viceroy for Canada. Because of his untimely death, Henry IV's endeavours produced very few concrete results; but then he was more concerned with the planning than with the implementation of a colonial policy, and it was during his reign that the colonialization programme subsequently pursued by the French in Canada was first formulated. Its principal objectives were to take possession of the territory in the King's name and to establish a French colony, which would then collaborate with the indigenous tribes.

The great champion of all Canadian expeditions both under Henry IV and during the regency, and even in the early years of Richelieu's era, was Champlain. He undertook nine voyages and devoted thirty-five years of his life to the Canadian venture. In 1605 a small settlement was established in Port Royal, followed a little later by a settlement in Tadoussac on the St

Lawrence and finally, in 1608, by the settlement in Quebec. Champlain's journeys into the interior, which, strange as it may seem, were also undertaken in the hope of finding a route to the East Indies, appear particularly daring, for they brought him to what is now Lake Champlain and, further west, to Lakes Huron and Ontario. At that time the approximate boundaries of the French colonial empire were first mapped out.

But the practical results of colonialization were still modest. Those involved were primarily interested in short-term profits; to an ever greater extent they turned from fishing to fur-trading.

The activities of the French missions had a dubious effect. Owing to the immigration of large numbers of Huguenots, both confessions were represented and by the beginning of the seventeenth century they were already quarrelling violently. The indigenous population was utterly confused by these conflicts. Besides the confessional disputes there was also wrangling between the Catholic Orders: the Franciscans and Jesuits were at loggerheads. Although the missionaries had some success in the St Lawrence valley, the Jesuit practice of founding Indian settlements in isolation from the French community led to their involvement in a succession of bloody feuds with the warlike Iroquois, which culminated in a fearful massacre.

In the course of the 1620s Duke Henry of Montmorency had made ambitious attempts to revive French seafaring and to found two trading companies. After he had been deprived of his powers Richelieu took the whole project in hand.

Following the catastrophe of the Armada, Spain's hegemony at sea entered into a decline. One of the crucial factors at work here was the rupture with the States General.

Ever since the late Middle Ages the great economic prosperity of these territories had been one of the essential ingredients of the Hapsburgs' rise to pre-eminence; following their revolt it had to be realized that the Iberian Peninsula alone provided too weak a basis for such a mighty overseas

4. Breisach, from Merian's *Topographia*

5. The Cardinal's Palace in the rue St. Honoré

empire, although, because of her early advantage and also of her staying power, Spain retained possession of enormous territories all over the world. The English, fortunately for Spain, failed to exploit their victory over the Armada to the ·full. In the closing years of Elizabeth's reign, and especially under the Stuarts, their spirit of adventure and enterprise went into a temporary decline. But in England's case periods of inertia were always the prelude to some new impetus, a time in which to gather strength and consolidate her forces. For the time being, however, Raleigh's cruel death and James I's attempt to promote a policy of peaceful relations with Spain had put an end to the privateering previously tolerated by the State. On the other hand, it was under the early Stuarts that the great African trading companies and above all the India Company, which was subsequently reorganized on such a large scale, first began their operations. Although the India Company received concessions and was granted special privileges and monopolies by the State, its management and financial backing, which was what really mattered, remained in private hands. Both were provided by a consortium of London merchants and bankers. Even in the early days of Stuart rule it was readily apparent that the Company's activities were to have far-reaching consequences. These began with the emigration to the East coast of North America of small, homogeneous groups of settlers. In 1607 Raleigh had founded Jamestown in Virginia. But the Dutch base of New Amsterdam at the Hudson and the Puritan settlements to the north were to become more important. There the settlers were not looking for easy profits nor were they motivated simply by the spirit of adventure; they were extremely hard-working and capable people, determined to create a new and lasting home for themselves, in which they would be free to practise their outlawed faith. From small beginnings, aided more by the weakness and indifference of the early Stuarts than by their protection, these men and women created something great and full of promise. The stretch of land which then came to be known as New England soon entered into its first phase of prosperity. By 1640 it supported some twenty-five thousand settlers.

In the first half of the seventeenth century, supremacy at sea and the major share in overseas trade had passed to Holland. Following the decline of both the Hanse and Flanders, Holland also took over most of the European carrying trade. Among other things, this meant that the Dutch then had control of the timber trade with the Baltic, which was a factor of prime importance for shipbuilding. This, together with a number of important technical innovations, formed the basis of the new boom in Dutch shipbuilding. Thanks to her low prices (nearly a third less than England's) Holland built a great number of ships for export, especially to France. Ever since the armistice concluded with Spain in 1609 there was an unwritten law whereby any country was allowed to trade in those areas not immediately subject to Spanish rule, which meant that Spain had in fact rescinded the monopoly she had claimed in 1494. The resulting boom in Dutch trade in the Atlantic, Indian and Pacific Oceans was a phenomenon almost without parallel. From the very outset Holland had concentrated on trade. She established no important settlements, just bases and agencies. One of these bases, New Amsterdam, was extremely well placed at the mouth of the Hudson to serve as a launching point for the conquest of the weak French Canadian possessions. The French would have been no match for the Dutch fleet. That this opportunity was never exploited was due to the friendly relations that existed between Holland and France because of their anti-Spanish interests. This too was a further aspect of Richelieu's Spanish policy.

Contacts between France and England in the colonial sphere at that time were episodic. Nonetheless, they do give a hint of certain future developments.

In 1613 an English captain, Samuel Argall, at the request of the government of Virginia mounted an attack on Acadia, between the St Lawrence River and Gulf and the Atlantic, which the French regarded as theirs. Argall destroyed the French base of Port Royal (now Annapolis Royal). James I ignored French protests and eight years later renamed this territory Nova Scotia and New Brunswick and made it over to one of his favourites, Sir William Alexander. The first voyage undertaken in order to seize the provinces was unsuccessful, but Charles I subsequently renewed the charter and encouraged emigration, especially among Puritans, by the grant of titles and lands. The venture was financed by London bankers, the most important of whom was Gervase Kirke. It was no accident that three ships set out from England under the command of Kirke's son David and his brothers in 1628, during the siege of La Rochelle. They carried letters of marque authorizing them to halt or sink French vessels and destroy the French bases in Canada and establish a monopoly of trade in Nova Scotia.

In 1627 Richelieu founded the "Compagnie des Cents Associés" to promote the systematic colonialization of Canada and to provide Champlain with sorely needed supplies of men, stores and weapons. In the spring of 1628 the new company sent out its first expedition. Twenty ships carried food, guns and ammunition together with carefully selected emigrants of both sexes and "unimpeachable character", including skilled craftsmen and a number of priests; the command of this flotilla was given to Admiral Roquemont. Kirke had a lead and held it; he reached Tadoussac, then Quebec, which he destroyed and where he lay in wait for the unsuspecting French emigrants. The French had stored all their guns deep in the hold, but Roquemont refused to surrender. Kirke gave orders to open fire. His men boarded three of the French ships, including the Admiral's. The booty was enormous— so great that Kirke was forced to burn a number of the French vessels. Those that he kept he sent to Newfoundland, and then he set course for home. In the following year a larger expedition was commissioned by Sir William Alexander, whose father had originally been granted the tenure of Nova Scotia, and this too was placed under the command of David Kirke and his brothers. Kirke sailed up the St Lawrence to attack Champlain in Quebec province. On the way he captured a French supply ship laden with sorely needed stores and powder. Champlain was left with just a handful of men, including missionaries, to defend his tumbledown fort. The remaining French were women and children. The town was forced to capitulate. On July 20, 1629, the Cross of St George was hoisted above the citadel. Meanwhile, however, and before the fall of Quebec a provisional peace was arranged between France and England. Consequently, the French refused to recognize the subsequent surrender of Quebec. Under the terms of the final peace treaty, which was concluded in Saint-Germain-en-Laye on March 29, 1632, after long-drawn-out negotiations, the province of Acadia, Port Royal, all the fishing harbours on the St Lawrence and Quebec were restored to France. No clear frontiers were established; at that time they were scarcely possible. But the important thing was that France and England had recognized each other's colonial territories on the North American continent. Here too Richelieu showed great skill as a negotiator, although Charles I's difficult position at home also worked in France's favour. The King of England was faced with a hostile and restrictive Parliament and he was in urgent need of money. This, together with a few English ships captured by the French and the remaining half of Queen Henrietta's dowry, which had yet to be paid, enabled Richelieu to conclude a favourable treaty.

Unlike Colbert, whose policies were to be based primarily on commercial considerations, Richelieu placed the main stress on political objectives in every sphere of his activity; his over-riding aim was the consolidation of France's position as a great power. This, as we have already seen, was made particularly clear by his endeavours to build up the French navy.

In the economic and colonial sectors the Cardinal adopted the ideas of Henry IV and Henri de Montmorency. What was new was that all his plans and measures were permeated by what might be called a "directional" trend. This is especially noticeable with regard to the trading companies that he planned and created and which were typical of the great private enterprises of the age. It was only in Spain that the State acquired a virtual monopoly of the nation's trade; from the very beginning the Spanish colonial empire had been under the direct control of the mother country. Richelieu also was of the opinion that the exploration and long-term exploitation of the potential wealth of the New World could not be encompassed by private enterprise alone, even when firms joined together to form syndicates. Louis XIII's principal Minister was fully aware of the need to afford naval protection for French possessions overseas and for French trade routes.

Undoubtedly, the State, as in the case of the English and Dutch governments, conferred specific concessions, such as letters of marque, letters patent and grants of land also in areas which were exploited by private enterprise and private methods of finance for some considerable time; the charters issued to the great companies belonged to the same category as privileges and monopolies. But there was no infringement of the freedom of the individual entrepreneur.

In France, on the other hand, there was considerable state interference from the very outset, with a concomitant restrictive effect on private responsibility. Here as everywhere, Richelieu wanted to be the master planner and subject everything to central control. We have seen how he developed France's harbours, how he personally made all decisions concerned with the building and purchasing of new ships, and we have also seen that he frequently contested local or regional traditional rights and claims that impeded the progress of his work. He also concerned himself personally with the problem of emigration and the provision of ships' crews. In this sphere he used both inducements and coercion. The nobility were allowed to take part in seafaring and even in trade without loss of rank. Members of the bourgeoisie who volunteered for service at sea were allowed to adopt noble titles. Real seamen, however, a type whose best representatives tend to be of an extremely independent cast of mind, fought shy of Richelieu's methods. The Cardinal began to press men into service, and this soon led to the application of harsh measures. Because of the shortage of sailors there was a growing tendency to punish even the most trivial offences by sending the culprits to the galleys. The bureaucratic machine, which, as usual, was far removed from practical affairs and had little esperience of them, worked slowly and ponderously. The profitable practice of selling offices also crept into the sphere of seafaring. All these factors, combined with the military strain imposed by the Huguenot war, offer some explanation as to why Richelieu's colonial policy should have produced such modest results.

The French colonialization programme for Canada and the West Indies was entirely different from that pursued by the English. Because of its decidedly "directional" nature it remained relatively unsuccessful. In contrast to that of other colonial powers, French methods differed in that the Church played a leading part both by providing welfare for the emigrants and by pursuing missionary activities. In the early period of their colonial rule the Spanish and the Portuguese had exploited the natives. Subsequently, owing to the influence of men like Vitoria and Las Casas, this situation underwent a marked change. The Anglo-Saxon Puritans for their part kept the natives very much at a distance. They did not treat tham as fully equal human beings. By contrast, as early as the sixteenth century the French had already developed the notion of the "good savage", perhaps as a result of their encounter with the pacific tribes of the Canadian territories. The missions' objective was to educate baptized natives and turn them into Frenchmen with equal rights.

Ever since the sixteenth century the problems of the New World had exercised the imagination of the French. Numerous accounts of overseas travel and many economic treatises appeared. Rabelais' last book dealt with the quest for the North-West Passage. The character of Rabelais' "pilot" was an exact copy of Cartier.

The founding of the French trading companies under Richelieu began in 1626. Some never got past the planning stage; others, like the "Compagnie du Morbihan" and the "Compagnie de la Nacelle de St Pierre fleurdelisée", came into existence but remained inactive.

Richelieu's friend Razilly suggested that a "Compagnie des Indes Orientales" should be founded. But this proposal was not acted upon. A number of private individuals, however, made voyages as far as Madagascar and the island of Réunion. In the year of his death Richelieu founded a shipping company which was subject to strict state supervision and which was given the name first put forward by Razilly.

The "Compagnie pour la Rivière Sénégal", which was founded some years later, safeguarded the interests of the smaller companies operating in West Africa and also traded with that part of the continent. It was there that the evil traffic in slaves first began.

Eight years before this a small private planters' and trading settlement had been set up on the island of St Christopher in order to grow tobacco. As early as 1626 the "Compagnie des Seigneurs de St Christophe" was initiated in order to trade with this settlement. But disputes immediately broke out between the Company and the planters, who found it more profitable to deal with the Dutch. This situation remained unchanged even after the Company was reorganized in 1635 and extended its activities to the islands of Guadeloupe and Martinique. The planters needed workers, and the Company either delivered them too late or transported them in such poor conditions that many of them died during the crossing or were ill upon arrival. But despite these difficulties this foundation was the most successful of those operating during the Cardinal's lifetime; the changeover from tobacco to sugar cane greatly increased the value of the territories. After 1642

Richelieu renewed the Company's priviliges. At that time there were about nine thousand French settlers on these three islands as compared with eight thousand in Acadia and Canada.

Colonial problems, a subject that Richelieu had closely studied, were many and varied. As early as 1626 Razilly had submitted the Pontoise memorandum to him, in which the colonial situation was presented as unpromising. Richelieu had intended to turn Mogador into a French bastion. In 1631 a treaty opened up Morocco to French merchants. It gave France the right to set up consulates and offered the traders guarantees of religious tolerance.

Like Napoleon, Richelieu was particularly interested in Egypt, which, he said, was the springboard to the Middle and Far East.

France's relations with England and, in view of subsequent developments, Holland, should be considered against the background of the events sketched out above.

But in the year 1635, whether they liked it or not, the French and the Dutch had no choice but to collaborate for the sake of their common cause against Spain. The great unknown quantity at that time, which might jeopardize their chances of victory, was Britain.

CHAPTER VII

FRANCE GAINS BERNHARD OF SAXE-WEIMAR

On April 2, 1635, Feuquières had signed a draft agreement between the King of France and Bernhard of Saxe-Weimar. Duke Bernhard had insisted on being given guarantees for his Duchy of Franconia and for the family possessions of the house of Saxe-Weimar. But that was not all. He also refused to ratify the agreement since one of its clauses ran counter to his princely dignity. Feuquières' draft stated that, in the event of "Bernhard of Saxe-Weimar absenting himself," a French Lieutenant General should command his army.

In the end the Duke declared the agreement useless from his point of view, since the French did not have control of Alsace. What he needed was financial subsidies and soldiers for his exhausted army.

Why Alsace? In Feuquières's draft Bernhard had been promised eventual sovereignty of "the County of Alsace". These lands were always referred to as "the County of Alsace", although there was some uncertainty in Paris as to the constitutional position of the territories in question. But in the seventeenth century the designation "County of Alsace together with the fief of Hagenau" was quite customary. We find it in the Hapsburg family agreement, which, it will be recalled, was concluded between the Spanish and the Austrian lines in connection with the Imperial election. This provided for the cession to Spain of properties owned by the House of Austria in Alsace, a proposal which Richelieu rightly considered to constitute a great danger for his country: Franche-Comté, Alsace, firm overland lines of communication between Milan and the Netherlands, Spain in possession of the Palatinate and the Valtelline—the last link would be forged in the chain of Spanish possessions surrounding France. By this time the situation was no longer as dangerous as it had been in 1617; but although France was much stronger she still desperately needed Saxe-Weimar's army and his commanding personality to protect her eastern frontier against invasion. And so, apart from its capitular lands and the properties of individual estates, which Louis XIII was not in a position to dispose of, the Duke was offered the County of Alsace together with all revenues previously enjoyed by the House of Austria.

The negotiations were continued. On July 7, 1635, Richelieu informed the indispensable Bouthillier that Vignolles had already spoken to the Duke of Saxe-Weimar, who was expecting a powerful enemy offensive at any moment; the army then being formed by Cardinal de La Valette would have to be brought up to strength as quickly as possible. Immediately afterwards he had advised Servien that Saxe-Weimar's accountant, Ponika, had arrived in Paris. Over and above the 12,000 livres which had already been paid out to the Duke he was now to be given a further 60,000. In a letter to Bouthillier of June 30th Richelieu had painted a distinctly gloomy picture: "Meanwhile peace has been concluded in Saxony . . . Gallas and Piccolomini have crossed the Rhine, the King of Hungary is drawing nearer, Duke Bernhard is losing heart and will be lost [to us] if we do not provide the support which he is demanding; he has withdrawn to Saarbrücken. . . ."

Between October 17th and 19th, following Bernhard's arrival in Saint-Germain-en-Laye, the French negotiated with him in person. Once again the discussions were extremely difficult, but on this occasion agreement was finally reached. The Duke was guaranteed an annual subsidy of 4,000,000 livres for the upkeep of his army of 12,000 German infantry and 6,000 cavalrymen together with all necessary ordnance. It was proposed that he should command his army under the ultimate control of the French. In a secret clause he was promised that the Austrian territories in Alsace would be made over to him as his sovereign territory. Bernhard persisted in his refusal to ratify the agreement, and he would not hear of French influence on military decisions. In order to enforce acceptance of his own conditions he eventually threatened to acknowledge the Peace of Prague, and time and again he used the anti-French feelings of his officers and men as a bargaining counter.

Father Joseph declared: "If we fail to gain Bernhard we shall lose the whole of Germany."

On July 10th Richelieu had informed the Duke that, if they should be forced to give up their plans in respect of Alsace, he could offer him the prospect of considerable revenues in Lorraine and that, if the worst came to the worst and they also lost Lorraine, he would receive an equivalent income in France.

As for the principal French condition that all strongholds in Alsace were to remain in the King's hands, a compromise formula was agreed upon, which stipulated that at least those strongholds already taken from the enemy should receive French garrisons. As early as March 23rd Bernhard had written to his brother expressing his regret that the French should have gained possession of fortresses in Alsace. And in point of fact the clause providing for French occupation of the strongholds contradicted the other provisions of the agreement, whereby Saxe-Weimar had been promised all Hapsburg rights within the County of Alsace and the fief of Hagenau.

In the end the Duke added his signature. After long argument he received his 4,000,000 livres; it was this that had tipped the scales. There was one qualifying clause, which he was obliged to accept and which required him to pay out a proportion of this money to any German allies who put troops into the field. He was accorded the title of a Landgrave of Alsace and given guarantees that the Duchy of Franconia would be assigned to him upon the conclusion of peace; he was required to protect the Catholic religion in his future sovereign territories. The provision in the original draft agreement, whereby the King of France was to retain ultimate authority over the deployment of the army, was dropped from the final version, which was signed on October 27, 1635, in St-Germain.

The troops commanded by Cardinal de La Valette, 18,000 foot and 6,000 horse, were all that Bernhard, the Swedes and what remained of the German Protestant forces could count on in the way of French military support. La Valette and Bernhard maintained close liaison and in the year 1635 both commanders were highly successful. They took Zweibrücken and subsequently Bingen, but then they came up against Count Gallas, the victor of Nördlingen, and were forced to retreat. Their withdrawal was carried out in extremely difficult circumstances and with Gallas advancing in their rear at the head of 30,000 men.

Richelieu said at the time that all offensive actions undertaken by France were hampered by the fact that on the east bank of the Rhine the troops were unable to live off the land, since Gallas had laid waste the whole of the East Rhenish territories from Worms onwards, while the transportation of adequate supplies across the river posed insuperable problems. Gallas, for his part, stated that the miraculous withdrawal organized by Bernhard of Saxe-Weimar would have appeared quite incredible to him had he not witnessed it with his own eyes. At that time Bernhard actually succeeded in sapping the strength of an army greatly superior in numbers to his own and in the following year he was to destroy it.

But, as has already been mentioned, the most dangerous situation for France was to develop on the Flemish border in 1636.

The Flemish Front

Despite the persistent sabotage practised by most of those living at or visiting the Court, Richelieu's relationship with Louis XIII between 1635 and 1638 remained virtually unchanged. The King resisted all attempts to influence him against the Cardinal. In spite of temporary bouts of ill will he constantly defended his principal Minister, who was still indispensable to him. Henry IV's son and heir spent frequent and lengthy periods in the field, and Richelieu, plagued by illness, tried as best he could to keep close to him.

But the crucial relationship between the King and his Minister was subjected to one of its severest tests in the year 1636, which was to prove so calamitous for French arms. The armies were fighting on every front, in Germany, Alsace, Franche-Comté, Lorraine, Burgundy, on the Dutch border and, as we shall see, in Italy.

Condé was laying siege to Dôle when he received news that the forces led by the Count of Soissons were too weak to prevent the enemy, who was then advancing from Flanders, from crossing the Moselle.

At the end of July the Royal Council was in session in the beautiful house placed at the Cardinal's disposal by Bassompierre, who was then still being held in the Bastille. In the course of the meeting the Cardinal spoke in great anger of M. de St Léger, who had lost the town of Châtelet near Saint-Quentin, just forty miles from Paris, to Prince Thomas of Savoy and also of Du Bec, who had capitulated in the fortress of La Capelle.

The King was so indiscreet as to inform his favourite, Saint-Simon, in confidence that the two commanders must expect the most severe sentence. He had forgotten that St Léger was Saint-Simon's uncle; the latter immediately passed the information on to his brother, the *bailli* of Senlis, with the urgent request that he should warn their kinsman of his peril. This he promptly did and St Léger was able to take flight for Clermont. A reward of 60,000 livres was placed on his head, and both he and Du Bec were condemned in their absence to be dragged to death by four horses on the Place de Grève.

On August 23rd Richelieu wrote about this incident to Cardinal de La Valette, furious that the two men had eluded his sentence: "Their effigies were dragged by four horses and, if they are caught, they themselves will be subjected to the same treatment."

On August 2, 1636, Richelieu gave a grand reception in the Queen's honour. The very next day bad news began to pour in from all sides. Condé's Superintendent reported that an advance force of 6,000 enemy horse had already reached Clermont; Montdidier and Roye had been occupied and it was thought that the main body of the Spanish and Imperial armies was besieging Corbie, while Johann von Werth was burning and laying waste the whole countryside for miles around; the people were all fleeing to the woods. As if that were not enough, it was learned that Charles of Lorraine had forced Condé to abandon the siege of Dôle on August 14th, and shortly afterwards came the bitter news that Corbie had fallen on the 15th, which meant that the road to Paris lay open to the enemy. At this Richelieu informed the Count of Soissons that, if it should prove impossible to prevent the enemy from crossing the Oise, he must at all costs avoid being outflanked and should throw his weak forces into the breach to protect Paris from the enemy offensive. But von Werth's cavalry advanced boldly, reaching Pontoise, a small town only 34 km. from Versailles.

These were the Cardinal's darkest days. Everybody held him responsible. Mathieu de Morgues was triumphant and his words were on everybody's lips: "Why were the frontier defences removed, why are the state coffers empty, what possible justification was there for breaching the walls of Paris in order to build the 'Palais Cardinal'?"

While the Paris mob uttered threats against his life, the Cardinal, as always in such situations, went into a temporary stupor; sobbing convulsively, he issued contradictory orders, cancelled instructions the moment he had given them and promptly relapsed into fits of fury. But then, we are told, he pulled himself together following a long nocturnal discussion with Father Joseph. The Capuchin analysed the situation and dispelled the phantoms that plagued the Cardinal; he also spoke of the power of prayer, but above all he spoke of strange presentiments and predictions, with the result that he succeeded in guiding Richelieu's imagination, always highly receptive to such ideas, and restoring to the utterly shattered statesman the sense of mission and destiny which informed all his actions. The Cardinal was suddenly uplifted; he was everywhere at once, taking decisions in every conceivable sphere, and his powers of improvisation, his ability to conjure up soldiers and weapons as if from nowhere, the quality of his instructions, which often revealed a supreme command of detail, his capacity for extracting additional sums while at the same time restoring general confidence, appear almost uncanny. At a time when he was an object of fierce hatred, when panic was driving the people of Paris to flight, he drove unguarded in an open carriage and at a walking pace through the busiest streets of the city; and nothing happened to him. Once again his relationship to the King had stood the test, once again the monarch had protected his principal Minister. The people quickly forgot that Richelieu had been responsible for denuding the northern frontier of troops and ordering the main French force to Lorraine. Then, as in the previous year, everything that France had achieved in the unhappy Duchy of Lorraine was again placed in jeopardy; in Burgundy invasion threatened, for Gallas had crossed the Rhine with newly formed units and his vanguards were already ranging as far as Langres and Dijon. But Bernhard of Saxe-Weimar was at his post; he and Cardinal de La Valette maintained their positions around Montsaugeon and constantly harassed the Imperialists and their reserves with guerrilla attacks. Eventually Gallas dug in at Champlitte, whereupon his army again began to disintegrate; the tide was turning in France's favour. Meanwhile, however, the flood of refugees from Paris, citizens and magistrates alike, continued to make for Orléans, Lyons and Tours.

The *noblesse d'épée* were commanded to join the King's armies at once under pain of degradation and loss of all privileges. But these nobles, most of whom were out of sympathy with Richelieu's foreign policy, proved a disappointment. Many, whose estates lay in the territories occupied by the invading army, unhesitatingly espoused the Spanish cause in order to save both their lives and their lands. Everyone complained about the lack of courage displayed by the ancient warrior caste. In the preceding year, Louis XIII had written to Richelieu from Lorraine:

"I regret to have to tell you that our nobles are unreliable. As soon as they are asked to exert themselves, as soon as one tries to undertake some action with these gentlemen, [it soon becomes apparent that] all they are fit for is to help their King to lose his honour. If one sends them no more than three hours' distance from here in the direction of Metz or Nancy, they begin to grumble and claim that they are being sent to their perdition and threaten to decamp. What is to be done when one commands an army consisting, as mine does at present, principally of such people?"

At first the King simply condemned his nobles out of hand for their lack of concern. Later he admitted exceptions, as in the following instance: "The first to arrive, those from the Auvergne, Forez, Beaujolais and Burgundy are the best; the most useless are those from Poitou."

Then the parlement of Paris bestirred itself. A group of counsellors maintained that, in the tragic situation facing the country, they had a right to vet the King's sovereign decisions; twelve members of the parlement formed a committee, which then tried to set itself up as a board of control. But such things were not at all in keeping with the times. Louis XIII summoned the representatives to appear before him and hectored them: "It is none of your business to interfere in the affairs of my State; I am not referring to all of your members but to a particular group, which is full of envy and malice."

He then strictly forbade them to continue their discussions.

France was saved in 1636 by a *levée en masse*, in other words by the people, who were already groaning under the burden of taxation, by the guilds, the tradesmen and the farmers, who placed themselves unreservedly at the King's disposal and even contributed considerable sums of money for armaments.

Louis soon found himself at the head of a new army, in which a new spirit prevailed. Within a matter of days a force of 15,000 to 20,000 men had been formed as a result of Richelieu's levies and the influx of volunteers.

Johann von Werth, a man of great élan and the most audacious of the enemy commanders, was insisting that, having taken the enemy unawares, they must exploit the situation and advance on Paris with all speed. But both Thomas of Savoy and the Cardinal-Infante considered this far too hazardous, partly because of the problems posed by the movement of supplies and reserves but primarily on account of the purely military risk. The offensive lost its impetus, then came to a standstill, which was shortly followed by a general withdrawal; the great enterprise had come to nothing and France suddenly found herself saved from catastrophe. This turn of events was due above all to Bernhard of Saxe-Weimar, as we shall see.

The battle of Nördlingen had opened up favourable prospects for the Emperor, which he failed to exploit. But that great victory over the Swedes and their allies had not been gained by Count Gallas or by the Cardinal-Infante; the real victor of Nördlingen was a dead man, murdered at Eger, whom Ferdinand II had thought he could dispense with once Gustavus Adolphus was dead. Wallenstein was one of the supreme organizers of all time; it was not his skill as a strategist but his genius as an army organizer that time and again enabled him to redress the military balance; the army that he had created later conquered the Turks under Prince Eugene; this superb instrument of war only met its final destruction in the hopeless conditions imposed by a totally different world in the Great War of 1914–18.

From 1635 onwards the separate Imperial armies, led by rival commanders who maintained little or no liaison, were severely mauled by the French forces. Gallas met his master in Bernhard of Saxe-Weimar. Although Bernhard, after forcing the battle of Nördlingen, had lost it to Gallas, the mastery of the art of evasion, diversion and surprise attack that he displayed in his subsequent encounters with the Imperial General earned for the victor of Nördlingen his reputation as a "destroyer of armies". But though he had saved France's eastern frontier, Bernhard was to experience the Cardinal's ruthlessness, as so many others had done.

Richelieu, as we have seen, nearly always destroyed his political opponents or persons whom he had used and could afford to dispense with, provided he could do so with impunity. If his adversaries were persons whose rank precluded such action, he tried to win them over by appointing them to highly responsible positions. This he did in 1636, when he allowed the command of the army facing Prince Thomas and Johann von Werth to pass to his implacable enemies, Gaston d'Orléans and the Count of Soissons. In opposition circles it was assumed that he was simply giving them rope to hang themselves. Actually, however, they were asked to assume the command under conditions that were favourable; the Imperial attack on occupied Lorraine had been repulsed, attacks against the flank of the French army in Flanders, and those launched by the banished Duke Charles IV and his loyal Lothringians, had failed, owing in part to the heroic defence of St-Jean-de-Losne by a French garrison, whose spirit of sacrifice stood in marked contrast to the many capitulations characteristic of that era and often verging on treason. By persisting with the siege of this town, which subsequently received the name of St-Jean-de-Belle-Défense, the enemy merely brought on his own downfall.

By then both the King and Richelieu were in the field. The Cardinal took quarters in Amiens, while Louis stayed in a castle 24 kilometers outside the town.

On September 9th, when he was still in Senlis, the King had told his brother that he was appointing Marshal de La Force and his son, the Marquis, whom he regarded as two of the most experienced and capable men in the kingdom, to his staff. He went on to say: "They have always served me well and I wish you to accept their advice."

On November 5th Richelieu described the attempt to wrest Corbie from the Spanish:

"I do not know how the siege of Corbie is progressing; I favour neither a blockade nor an assult . . . it seems to me . . . that if, by blockading, we have to lay siege to the stronghold for six months—and this seems the best we can hope for—things would go badly for the King. If Gallas wins the battle which is about to be joined we would be badly placed if the King's forces were tied down at Corbie."

However, thanks to Châtillon's level-headed determination, the hotly disputed stronghold fell on November 14, 1636; the very next day the *Gazette* published an article, inspired and partially composed by Richelieu, to the effect that Marshal Châtillon's proposal to take the fortress by storm, a course considered by many too hazardous in view of the season, had "immediately received the energetic support of His Eminence." His Majesty, whose "sterling judgement is beyond question", had been in full agreement. Corbie was again in French hands, as was St-Jean-de-Losne following its relief by Condé, who had been entrusted with the "pacification" of Lorraine; fortune was changing.

None of the French leaders was willing to enter Corbie,

where the plague had broken out. Richelieu did so; he inspected the stronghold and then returned to his quarters in Amiens. But here, after such an unexpected and favourable development of the war, the Cardinal was soon to face again grave danger from a group of conspirators.

Attempts on Richelieu's Life

Gaston d'Orléans, refusing to be won over by the responsibility vested in him, was still eager to take his revenge on the Cardinal. The rancour accumulated in him over the years had found new fuel in the recent attempts to annul his marriage with Marguerite of Lorraine, in which the Cardinal was said to be the prime mover. Time and again the heir to the French throne had felt violently provoked by the Cardinal; on repeated occasions he had tried to turn feelings into action. But action was not what he was gifted for.

Once before, on January 30, 1631, shortly after the "day of the dupes", Richelieu had narrowly escaped death, and he had never forgotten it. He had just retired for the night in his well-guarded *palais* in Paris, when the heir-apparent forced his way into his room with a large retinue of young noblemen. Richelieu hurriedly rose and went to meet him. Orléans, with barely a word of greeting, burst out: "When I swore that I would be your friend I did so against my will; I now revoke that oath which I cannot and will not keep to a man of your kind; you insult the Queen-Mother!" At that moment Gaston's companions laid their hands on their swords. Richelieu was silent; with bowed head he faced the infuriated Prince, who continued to shout: "You also behave arrogantly to me, you nobody from nowhere, by rights I should have you struck down like a lackey." At this Gaston raised his hand, but then he said: "Your priest's robes prevent me from doing so!" His companions were all waiting for him to give the signal. But, curiously enough, when he did signal it was to stop them. Gaston spoke again: "I shall spare you, but

take heed! In future nothing will save you from the punishment which people like you, who transgress against persons
of my rank, deserve." Richelieu mumbled submissive protestations, and when the haughty throng made its noisy exit
from his *palais* he held the heir-apparent's stirrup for him.
But once alone he gave vent to his feelings: "I owe the Holy
Mother of God an *ex voto* for my deliverance, but I shall make
this company pay for it."

The exact circumstances of a far more serious threat to
Richelieu during his stay in Amiens in 1636 are set out in
the Memoirs of Claude de Bourdisle, Count of Montrésor;
all the accounts given by later reporters such as Retz,
Montglas, La Rochefoucauld and the younger Brienne are
derived from this source. Montrésor was Master of Hounds
to Orléans, who thought very highly of him, and his cousin
Saint-Ibar had attached himself, for better or for worse, to
the Count of Soissons. Goulas described Saint-Ibar as a "man
of high ideals and an enemy of tyrants". The two cousins
were bold, resolute men, willing to run every risk.

Montrésor reports that, following a session of the Royal
Council, which had been held in Amiens in the palace of
the Duke of Chaulnes, the Count of Soissons had addressed
Richelieu in the courtyard of the palace after the King had
already left. Contrary to his normal practice, the Cardinal
had appeared without his guard whereas Gaston d'Orléans,
Montrésor, Saint-Ibar, Campion and a number of other conspirators were all assembled. The moment was exceptionally
favourable. Orléans was to give the signal; a wink, a movement of his eyelids, and the hated Cardinal would have been
cut down, like Ancre before him. But, we are told, Orléans
again failed to give the prearranged signal; after standing like
a man transfixed he abruptly turned his back on his followers
and in extreme agitation hurried off to the palace, running up
the stairs to the first floor. Montrésor rushed after his master
and begged him to return at once. But by the time Orléans
had regained some measure of self-control and followed his

Master of Hounds, though with hesitation, indeed trepidation, the Cardinal had already disappeared; three days later the conspirators decided to try again, but they were not offered a second opportunity.

After this half-hearted attempt, Orléans and Soissons were understandably frightened. They made this quite evident by departing with all speed, the one to Blois, the other—and this was crucial—to Sedan; at that time Sedan was still uninvested.

CHAPTER VIII

THE ITALIAN FRONT

In December 1634 Henri de Rohan, as will be remembered, was in the camp at Rambervillers near Épinal in Lorraine, in command of a force of 12,000 foot and 1,200 horse. In March 1635 he was suddenly instructed to join up with part of his forces with the troops then stationed in the Grisons under the command of Colonel Du Landé; he was then to proceed at the head of the combined force to occupy the Valtelline. He was to march through the territory of the Confederation as quickly and unobtrusively as possible, avoiding all use of force; otherwise he was given an entirely free hand in the execution of this daring operation.

By that time the Protestant and Confederate Estates, especially Berne, had had enough of the internal strife in the Grisons between the Catholic and Protestant parties, one taking the Spanish Imperialist side, the other siding with the French. Initially the Swiss thought that Richelieu's strategic plans for the territory on the southern slopes of the Alps were designed to favour the Protestants. And so when Louis XIII appointed Rohan as a special envoy to the Swiss cantons and also as Lieutenant General commanding the French troops in the Grisons the appointment was greeted with satisfaction by the non-Catholic Swiss, precisely as Richelieu had predicted. The result was that Duke Henri was able to lead his little army from Alsace through Bernese Aargau via Basle, Zurich and St Gall to Chur without hindrance. He asked the towns whose territories he crossed for transit rights but did not wait for their reply. Only Basle gave immediate permission and also explained the reasons for its decision to the other Protestant towns in the Confederation. The march was executed with such speed that the Catholic towns knew nothing about it until it was all over. Berne had been informed at an early stage by Johann Ludwig von Erlach, Bernhard of Saxe-Weimar's friend, who was shortly to become his right-hand man. The transit was certainly daring, for an Imperial army was encamped in the "Forest Cantons" of the Upper Rhine and could have invaded Aargau. Rohan had told the Confederate Estates that his objective was to restore to the Confederation one of its member States, the Valtelline. This was why the Swiss Protestants had all placed their hopes in the great Huguenot leader; later, when he tried to ensure the preservation and defence of the Catholic faith in the Valtelline on behalf of the King of France, they were to be disillusioned. Berne informed the Catholic towns and the Imperial envoy that Rohan's march had taken them completely unawares. France had asked the Swiss cantons to provide a force of 5,000 men in support of the project; the five Catholic cities refused to allow any recruiting within their territories; the others quickly raised two Swiss regiments.

But in March 1635, before Rohan had arrived in Chur, Du Landé had taken his men across the Splügen Pass and reached Riva, while the Grisons Colonel, Andreas Brügger, had led a force of experienced mountain troops, through deep snow and in constant danger from avalanches, from Iglis to Zernez, through the Spöntal and on to Bormio. Both in Bormio and in Chiavenna the inhabitants failed to notice the approaching troops, who arrived by night, until it was too late. Rohan, who was still on his march through Switzerland, was advised of the outcome of these surprise attacks by his Secretary, Priolo, who was then returning from the Grisons.

Rohan

Rohan's campaigns in the Grisons and the Valtelline are among the most astonishing in the whole history of mountain warfare. Within the context of this book we can only touch upon their main features. In 1634 the great Huguenot leader had completely espoused the French cause. We have already seen how he brought his influence to bear on Bernhard of Saxe-Weimar to persuade him to join the French. In a memorandum bearing Rohan's signature and composed in the year 1632 we are told: "If the King is prepared to support the party which is opposed to the House of Austria, then, since the King of Sweden is dead, Louis XIII will be able to control events in Germany."

In 1635 the Spanish General Serbelloni was encamped on the Italian side of the Valtelline while the Imperial General Fernamont was stationed on the Tyrolean border. These two army commanders were intent on joining forces. The population of the Valtelline favoured the Spanish, while from the outset the inhabitants of the Grisons, who were split by internal strife, were unreliable allies for Rohan. But their support was absolutely essential to him. All in all Rohan had to defend fourteen Alpine passes and paths with his numerically inferior but highly disciplined troops. He knew that, if there was the slightest setback, his cause would be lost in France. By re-entering the King's service and fighting for his country he could hope that the restoration of his land would at least be made definite. It will be recalled that these lands had been awarded to the Prince of Condé following the collapse of the Huguenot revolt but that this measure had subsequently been rescinded "for the time being". Rohan, though he had fourteen Alpine passes and passages to defend, could not afford to divide his small force. Consequently, as soon as he had taken possession of the Valtelline, he set up a central base in Tirano. Operating from this centre, he conducted lightning campaigns and managed to beat his opponents one at a time.

On June 27, 1635, he defeated Fernamont at Livigno and on July 3rd a superior Imperial force at Mazzo on the Adda. It was then that Serbelloni tried to win over the Duke

through Clausel, who had originally been in the service of
Marie de' Medici and who is already well known to us. Acting
on behalf of the King of Spain, this agent offered the French
Commander rights of sovereignty over the fertile valley of the
Valtelline. Mistrusted by the French and surrounded by spies,
Rohan had the tempter, who had once been his confidant,
hanged on the spot.

The months of August and September passed peaceably.
By the end of October, Rohan had again moved into the
Frele Valley and was poised for an attack on Fernamont. If
Du Landé had arrived on time the Imperial army could have
been wiped out. But Du Landé did not come and the defeated
Imperialists were able to withdraw to the Tyrol. Up to the
end of Rohan's mission, Du Landé constantly worked against
him. Immediately following the defeat of Fernamont, which
the French had failed to exploit, Count Schick, another
experienced Imperial General, appeared at the head of fresh
troops. Rohan again found himself between two armies. And
the Spanish were also able to put crack troops into the field.
On November 10th Rohan attacked Serbelloni. The engagement lasted three hours and there was fierce street fighting in
Morbegno. Serbelloni was wounded and forced to leave the
field; Count San Secondo, his Cavalry Commander, fell in the
engagement. This was the fourth of the glorious battles that
Rohan fought within a brief period in the Valtelline. On
February 10, 1636, Louis had given Rohan firm instructions
to advance into Milanese territory. Rohan himself considered
this entirely feasible, but only if the Duke of Savoy mounted
a simultaneous offensive. This was not forthcoming. In fact,
none of the amazing victories that Rohan had won under conditions of extreme difficulty was exploited. Paris had other
things to think about and sent no troops and, even more
important, no money. Drunk with victory following the
Battle of Avesnes and later deep in despair over the setbacks
of 1636, the Royal Council left Rohan completely unaided.
And so did Savoy. Rohan wrote to Richelieu at the time that

he would rather die than relinquish his glorious achievements in the Valtelline. Within a year of his first victory he had advanced as far as Lecco but was forced to withdraw again to Sondrio in the face of superior enemy forces. He was exhausted, beset with cares and felt utterly abandoned. He fell seriously ill. His troops were hungry and the cases of plague were increasing.

The Grisons detachments harassed him for their back pay. Very soon their attitude grew threatening. They were demanding their rights, and consequently the pro-Spanish party was again able to strengthen its influence in their ranks. It was at this time that Johann von Werth was menacing Paris. The Spanish had failed to drive Rohan from the contested valley but they had succeeded in inciting the population of the Grisons against France. Spanish agents spread the rumour that, although Rohan had promised to return any territories he conquered to their original owners, he had no intention of doing so. The moment had come for Jürg Jenatsch, the Grisons pastor and popular leader, who had been embittered by the protection Rohan had extended to the Valtelline Catholics, to intervene. He gathered all the malcontents about him and told them that it was only by entering into an alliance with the Imperialists that they could take over the disputed territory in their own right. When Rohan was informed of this he was lying on his sickbed. He implored the Provisor of the Venetian Republic, the French envoy in Switzerland, Méliand, and the French Resident in the Grisons, Lasnier, to proceed to Chur with all speed and to pacify the malcontents. But Lasnier adopted the wrong approach to the mountain dwellers; he issued threats. Rohan, though barely able to stand, decided to intervene himself. He was carried to Chur in a sedan chair and arrived there on October 11, 1636. In Thusis he met the Commander of the Swiss auxiliaries from the Protestant cantons. He promised him that he would send couriers to France to get the pay claims settled. Time and again he gave assurances that the King of France was not pursuing secret aims for his own ends; the only reason why he had taken to arms was to protect his allies.

As early as April 1636 the text of a treaty had been drawn up in Chiavenna, which was intended to settle the relations between the inhabitants of the Grisons and their vassals in the Valtelline; the disputed territory was to be returned to its former suzerains, against assurances that they would respect the religious faith of the inhabitants. The Grisons signed, but in Paris the various provisions were subjected to constant critical scrutiny. Rohan did his best to get the treaty ratified, but Richelieu reacted to every reminder by demanding modifications. The tenor of his correspondence with a commander of such merit became increasingly harsh. Rohan's opponents had succeeded in stirring up latent mistrust. If Rohan asked for money to settle the pay claims of the Swiss or Grisons detachments he was accused of having wasted the money sent to him in the past. For more than a year Rohan and the three leagues were fobbed off by Richelieu with empty promises. While Rohan was in Chur without an escort, the "Kettenbund", i.e. the conspiracy led by Jürg Jenatsch, was maturing. Only a few days after his arrival in the Grisons capital an assembly was held at which the delegates referred angrily to the Treaty of Chiavenna. Rohan persisted in his view that immediate ratification was urgently called for. He reported to Louis XIII that the conclusion of the treaty would be entirely advantageous to French interests. But before he could enter into negotiations—and this is typical of the safeguards that hemmed him in—he had to obtain permission from the French Resident, Lasnier. And so the inevitable happened: at a provincial diet in Ilanz the Grisons decided to establish contact with the House of Austria in order to obtain full rights over the Valtelline and drive out the French troops. Three envoys were sent to Innsbruck to establish friendly relations with Claudia de' Medici, the widow of Archduke Leopold. The Archduchess accommodated the delegates from the Grisons in every possible way. In vain Rohan implored the Cardinal to agree to everything which both the Austrian Archduchess and the Spanish promised—rights of sovereignty in the Valtelline and money, above all money. Instead of the million livres, which were then owed to the Grisons officers, Richelieu sent two hundred thousand, part of which came from his own private resources. Eventually, on November 20th, Rohan received a communication from the King dated October 27th which at last authorized him to ratify the treaty. But it was too late. Once the Austrians and the Spanish had given their assurances nobody was interested in a treaty with the French. A few of the Grisons regiments had already stolen money from the intendancy. In the end Rohan distributed the rest of the money and even issued assignats. But ever since the Innsbruck delegation had received the necessary assurances the French troops in the Grisons were made to feel the mounting anger of the population. The pastors preached against them from every parish pulpit. The people armed themselves, military equipment was brought in from Lindau and eventually, on March 18, 1637, the revolt broke out. Although the conspirators gave Rohan a final period of grace up to May 1, 1637, they were in fact simply trying to mislead him, for from March 6th onward they had been making their preparations for the seizure of the Rhine fortress, which was then occupied by the French. In the general summons to the parishes of March 18th the French were accused of breaking their word. On the eve of the revolt Rohan was informed of the conspiracy. He left Chur and hurried to the fortress to secure it against a surprise attack. Jürg Jenatsch's plan was to cut off the French forces in the Valtelline from Rohan and the few French units in the Grisons. Spanish troops were waiting on the southern, Imperial troops on the northern border of the Valtelline, ready to move in. Under pressure from the insurgents, Rohan was forced to capitulate on March 26, 1637. It was agreed that between April 20th and May 5th the French troops were to withdraw from the Valtelline and surrender the citadel. On March 27th the Duke returned to Chur, and was required to

remain there until his departure from the Grisons as surety
for the agreement signed in the fortress on March 26th. The
Duke's personal papers were confiscated, his house was surrounded with spies and his every move was kept under
surveillance.

In a letter to Bullion Richelieu wrote:

"The misfortune which has occurred in the Valtelline . . .
is so great that I do not know whether it will be possible to
effect a remedy . . . God knows whether the Swiss will not
revolt over their back pay; God knows if Italy will stand
firm . . . this evil has come about through lack of money; for
every écu which we should have spent betimes we will now
need ten, and even then we will not make good our loss. For
some time I have been preaching to the gentlemen of the
Finance Department; I now implore them to believe me,
otherwise there is little hope that our affairs will prosper."

In a letter to the King dated March 29, 1637, Richelieu did
not blame Rohan for the catastrophe, although he was to do
so subsequently. As late as March 30th he wrote that he was
sending two hundred thousand livres to the Duke and an
equal amount for the Swiss.

On May 5, 1637, the Swiss cantons handed over the fortress
on the Rhine to the people of the Grisons; on the same day
Rohan was escorted to the frontier. Once there, threats and
raised voices were forgotten; things took on a festive air; a
speech was made, in which Rohan was assured that his
achievements on behalf of the Grisons had been so exceptional
that, even if they were to erect as many statues to him as there
were rocks in their mountains, they could not hope to give
adequate expression to the debt of gratitude which future
generations would bear him. The Duke had acted with such
despatch because he had considered it right to return the
territory which he had conquered to the Grisons and not to
Spain.

In his Memoirs Richelieu subsequently accused Rohan of

having fallen out with the people of the Grisons as a result of his ineptitude, his unjust measures and his illegal profiteering. He criticized the capitulation of March 26, 1637, which was put into effect on May 5th of the same year and in which Rohan, "contrary to Louis XIII's command", had handed over the Valtelline to the people of the Grisons.

Rohan went to Geneva a broken man. Once there, he was ordered to proceed immediately to Franche-Comté. Richelieu was suddenly convinced that the Duke had established new contacts with the Spanish and so tried to lure him into a trap. But Rohan, who was surrounded by agents and could never feel safe even in this Swiss town, finally took the step that he had long been contemplating: he joined Bernhard of Saxe-Weimar in his camp on the Upper Rhine.

CHAPTER IX

THE RHINE FRONT

In 1635 and 1636 contemporary observers were forced to the conclusion that the French declaration of war on Spain had been an irremediable error. For the Swedes the year 1636 was not so unfortunate as it was for the French. Banér's army, which was concentrated in Pomerania, had fought its way through Brandenburg and on October 4th had defeated a combined Saxon and Imperial army at Wittstock. But that was the end of Banér's offensive. In 1637, after failing to advance into Bohemia, the Scandinavian Commander was obliged to retreat as far as Torgau in the face of Imperialist pressure. At that time the Elector of Brandenburg would gladly have opted for neutrality. But when the Swedish general Wrangel seized Spandau and Küstrin as pledges and began to requisition supplies in Berlin he fled from his capital and declared "definitively" for the Emperor.

The most astonishing phenomenon in the early years of the war was Richelieu's achievement in the sphere of military organization. We have seen that he placed civilians and prelates in highly influential military positions, even at the front. But over and above this he allocated commissaries and intendants to the forces to supervise army pay and provisions, quartering and all legal questions; he also constantly raised the effective strength of the fighting units; and he did all this in the midst of serious reversals and bitter disappointments. One great setback for his German policy was the election on February 15, 1631, of King Ferdinand of Hungary as Holy Roman Emperor after Maximilian I, to whom Richelieu had repeatedly offered the Imperial Crown, had again refused it. At that time France was scarcely in a position to afford effective resistance to the Spanish, let alone support her Swedish allies in Germany.

But in the Imperial camp things were not quite as good as they seemed. The Princes who had gone over to the Emperor following the Peace of Prague were unreliable allies or wavering neutrals, likely to abandon him at a moment's notice and defect to the enemy. The revocation of the Edict of Restitution had been a heavy price to pay for such ephemeral relations. Germany was then in ruins and the devastation was growing constantly worse. No Emperor, no Duke, no Prince exercised effective control over the German territories; the real power lay in the hands of the sinister collective of armies that lived off the land.

As King of Hungary Ferdinand had roused great hopes in the Catholic world, especially after the Battle of Nördlingen. But these hopes were not realized because Ferdinand was no longer striving for victory but for an acceptable peace.

All over the continent of Europe men marched and countermarched, retreated, laid siege and fought off relieving armies.

At that time German troops under the command of a German Prince were defending France's eastern frontier against the Holy Roman Emperor. In the course of this protracted defence Bernhard of Saxe-Weimar led Gallas, the Count of Campo, and the Duke of Lorraine up hill and down dale, harassing them ceaselessly, until both of their armies were destroyed by hunger and epidemics.

Bernhard had rejected the French demands for an invasion of Imperial territory because he was bracing for a combined attack by the Duke of Lorraine and the Spanish army stationed in Franche-Comté. But Frederick Henry, William of Orange's youngest son and a maternal grandson of Admiral Coligny, who had conquered the fortress of Herzogenbusch in 1629 and taken Maastricht in 1632, now took the fortress of Breda, an act of bravery that was to prove of great consequence for the further course of the war. The loss of this crucial position in the Netherlands forced the Spanish to withdraw large numbers of troops from Franche-Comté. Bernhard of Saxe-Weimar suddenly found himself able to take the offensive, and he did so to the surprise of French and Imperialists alike. Paris had been urging him to invade the German territories in the Central Rhineland, and the Swedes had been constantly pressing for Bernhard to join forces with General Banér's army. Father Joseph had made particularly urgent representations: "this stronghold" must be taken, "this town that is marked on the Duke's map" must be occupied. And Bernhard had replied: "Your index finger, Father Joseph, is not a bridge."

There was no food for an army on the east bank of the Middle Rhine. And in point of fact it was the problem of feeding his army that prompted Saxe-Weimar, in 1637, to head for the relatively unravaged territories of the bishopric of Basle, whose former bishop, Prince Baldenstein, had renounced his neutrality and joined the Catholic League; his successor, Henry of Ostein, had then inherited this situation. The Emperor had imposed an annual contribution of thirty thousand florins and a levy of three thousand men on the bishopric. Both conditions weighed heavily on the impoverished population. The Rhinegrave, Otto Ludwig, had already passed through the territory on various campaigns; Hungarian, Lothringian, Scottish and Croat troops had plundered the bishopric. But the chances of feeding an army there were still better than in the mid-Rhenish territories. Moreover, this ecclesiastical principality, which Bernhard wished to punish for its allegiance to the Emperor, also offered strategic advantages, above all for a project which Bernhard then had in mind, namely the crossing of the Upper Rhine.

From the bishopric of Basle Bernhard launched a surprise attack on the forest cities of the Upper Rhine. He crossed the river at Säckingen; the following day he occupied Laufenburg and shortly afterwards laid siege to Rheinfelden. The Imperialist counter-attack was led by Johann von Werth and the Duke of Savelli. Saxe-Weimar's army suffered heavy losses and was forced to quit the field. But once again Duke Bernhard succeeded in quickly disengaging from the enemy and only three days later he took Johann von Werth completely unawares, attacking him near Rheinfelden, where he won a decisive victory and captured both von Werth and Savelli. Rheinfelden then fell into Saxe-Weimar's hands, to be followed soon after by the stronghold of Rötteln, then Neuenburg on the Rhine and finally Freiburg im Breisgau. Johann von Werth was conducted to Paris, where he was held in honourable captivity the Duke of Savelli managed to escape.

The Duke of Rohan, who had been abandoned by France following his campaign in the Valtelline, fought in Bernhard's ranks at Rheinfelden. Everyone had warned him of Richelieu's intentions, especially the Swedes. Consequently, after leaving Geneva, he had joined the army led by Bernhard of Saxe-Weimar, whom he greatly admired, to whom he was joined by bonds of genuine friendship and whom he had once hoped to have as a son-in-law. As always he stood his ground manfully and on March 28th he was wounded; he was then taken to the monastery of Königsfelden, a Hapsburg foundation on Bernese territory, to recover. Blandini, the Geneva doctor who was often in Bernhard of Saxe-Weimar's camp and who also maintained contacts with the French Court, was sent to attend him. At first the wounded man's condition gave no grounds for concern, but subsequently it quickly grew worse and on April 23, 1638, Duke Henri died in his fifty-ninth year. He had been the most able of the native French army commanders. His personal fate was one of the harshest of the entire era. Every one of his achievements was established in the face of tremendous resistance. Not only had he defied superior forces, he had also defied treachery and slander, which had been his constant companions and had finally reduced him to become a fugutive. He was buried in the Cathedral of St Pierre in Geneva.

In 1638 Saxe-Weimar's triumphs were celebrated in Paris and the Duke, the hero of the hour, the saviour of France, received endless protestations of gratitude; but behind all this glorification percipient observers like Grotius noted the cold political appraisal to which the victor was subjected.

The Conquest of the Fortress of Breisach

These victories of Saxe-Weimar's were followed almost immediately by the greatest event of the war in the period preceding Richelieu's death: the conquest of the fortress of Breisach, which was the key position in Spain's long line of communications on the Continent and was considered to be impregnable.

Because of its importance we shall have to consider this event in some detail and concern ourselves with a number of military engagements.

Breisach, situated on the east back of the Rhine, was a mighty bulwark surrounded by double walls and moats watered by the Rhine; chains fastened across the river made it impassable for enemy ships. In those days the numerous old tributaries of the Rhine flowed into the two main branches of the river at Breisach, which were linked by strongly fortified bridges. The town, built on a hill with a steep northern face, was crowned by a citadel; this was the castle of the Archdukes and the seat of the government of that part of Austria.

Saxe-Weimar laid what was called a Dutch siege. In other words, he began to build his own fortress around the fortress of Breisach. It was to consist of a semi-circular encampment equipped with all the resources of contemporary fortification technique and extending to the river bank at both ends, where the main defensive works would be; once it was finished, Breisach would be completely cut off. The Duke had known from the start that the only way in which he could take the town was by starvation, but he was in any case determined to win the "mistress of the Rhine" without destroying her.

For the erection of his camp he used his own force, two thousand local inhabitants and two hundred specialists trained in fortification techniques.

Vienna commanded that everything possible should be done to save Breisach. Three armies were allocated, the first led by Count Götz, the second by Savelli and the third by Charles IV of Lorraine. The Catholic inhabitants of the Black Forest were called upon to engage in guerrilla warfare; in the course of the siege their surprise attacks on Saxe-Weimar's raiding parties accounted for the loss of more than a thousand men. Duke Bernhard tried to cut off the Hapsburg armies intended for the relief of Breisach at the upper reaches of the Danube and force them to give battle. But the Imperial generals succeeded in avoiding him and eventually reached the Rhine valley while Bernhard pursued them through the Black Forest along devastated roads. Frequent attempts were made to get supplies into the beleaguered town; some succeeded, others failed. For both Götz and Savelli this remained their principal task and their principal problem; they were engaged in a race for time with the fortification workers who were slowly throttling the town. From Lake Constance to Freiburg every last scrap of food was used up. Privation was so great on both sides that special units were sent out to gather the windfalls from the fields. Time and again the armies tried to buy food in Basle or Strassburg but with little success. Saxe-Weimar had entrusted the defence of the encampment to his second in command, Johann Ludwig von Erlach, a native of Berne. Meanwhile he himself, the indefatigable warrior with his slim, youthful but powerful figure, had been taken suddenly ill in Colmar. Long before, he had been warned that attempts might be made to poison him. The warnings had come from France and the Spanish had been suspected. He had taken strict precautions for his personal safety.

His principal tasks at that time were to defend the Rhine crossings and above all to prevent the armies of Götz and

Savelli from joining forces with Charles of Lorraine. Two Colonels were in charge of the work in the Breisach encampment, which was pursued with great energy. But despite all his astonishing successes, the reinforcements that the ailing Duke had urgently asked for failed to arrive from France.

At this point the Imperialist attempts to relieve Breisach were brought to an end by a pitched battle followed by a short but decisive encounter.

The Spanish had always insisted that Savelli's army group should be used only in Burgundy for the defence of Franche-Comté. By now, however, it had become essential that it should join forces with the army led by Count Götz. But Savelli's abilities as a commander inspired little confidence. Johann von Werth had spoken of his "bad and ill-advised conduct" and had asserted that, although he might "have the wit to govern a piece of land, he was no good as a general". But assessments of this kind were not welcomed at the Imperial Court, and von Werth was advised to be careful when talking about the Duke in Vienna, for this Roman "Ghibelline" had a considerable backing both on historical grounds and in terms of actual political influence. In any case Götz was unable to operate in southern Germany without Savelli's army; divided, they were both too weak and risked destruction. But once they joined forces, the two commanders engaged in constant disputes over the artillery, over recruiting and requisitioning, over the purchasing of provisions. The Ministers in Vienna had thought of promoting Savelli to "Field Marshal" and attaching him to Gallas, for it was felt that he would get on better with him. But the relief of Breisach took precedence over everything and so in the end the two Generals simply had to make the best of it. The first attempt to reach the beleaguered town had failed. Götz had formed a detachment of nine mounted regiments, in which each man carried a sack of gunpowder and another of corn; Saxe-Weimar's troops had ambushed this detachment and wiped it out. Shortly afterwards three hundred Imperial Croats succeeded in carrying a few hundred sacks of flour into the town in the dead of night. But then one of Duke Bernhard's cavalry units seized and drove off three hundred cattle from the enemy near Offenburg while at virtually the same time Croat troops, who had approached along secret paths, had emerged from the Black Forest and made off with two hundred of Saxe-Weimar's draught horses. Considerable time was spent in such skirmishes. Meanwhile the steel clamp had yet to be closed around the town.

When the Imperialist troops eventually emerged into the Rhine valley, Götz, acting under constant pressure from Vienna, decided to join battle.

Saxe-Weimar continued to call for French reinforcements. The troops brought by Count Guébriant, a seasoned and courageous commander who had proved himself a true comrade to Bernhard in the field, were not enough for an all-out offensive. At last, on July 17th, a further French contingent arrived, although even this was smaller than the Duke had expected. It was commanded by the twenty-seven-year-old Turenne.

On July 27th Bernhard ordered his army to march. The advance guard under Taupadel pushed forward from Ettenheim to occupy the pass. The next day news was received that the enemy had been sighted between Ettenheim and Offenburg with a large column of supply wagons and appeared to be quite unaware of Saxe-Weimar's presence. Bernhard gave orders for his troops to march only after dark. At midnight his army arrived in Malberg, where they waited for dawn. At first light they advanced in battle order behind a powerful vanguard, which took possession of the unoccupied pass at Dillingen, near Lahr. The enemy had taken up positions in the village of Friesenheim. Bernhard sent the French infantry into attack. The Imperialists then set fire to Friesenheim and withdrew to the heights behind the village. From there they laid down a powerful artillery barrage which, however, was ineffectual because they were aiming too high.

Saxe-Weimar massed his own artillery in the vineyard opposite the enemy position and his cannon took immediate effect. He then ordered his infantry to attack, but the defence was so resolute that by midday his men were forced to fall back on Malberg. Götz and Savelli did not give pursuit. Instead, they waited for darkness to marshal their forces, whereupon the two Generals spent the whole of that night quarrelling. The next morning their troops were positioned between Friesen-heim and Schüttern. Savelli was insisting that he should command the vanguard; Götz disagreed, whereupon the Italian threatened to march off with his army. Eventually Savelli had his way and Götz even placed some of his own troops at his disposal. Savelli was to advance via Wittenweier and Kappel so as to reach the bank of the Rhine at Schlettstadt, where the provisions would be put on shipboard and taken to Breisach. The rearguard was to follow slowly. Götz had calculated that Saxe-Weimar would attack him and not the convoy. He was mistaken. On the morning of July 31st Savelli slowly advanced across the difficult country between the Kaiserwald and the Rhine towards his objective. Because of the boggy fields the artillery, the carriages and the enormous train, which included the officers' wives, the cannon, the baggage and the whole of the infantry, were soon left behind by the cavalrymen. Savelli nonetheless continued on his way, without sending out patrols, without even covering his flanks, and so marched blindly into the narrow pass of Wittenweier, where to his utter amazement he found himself face to face with Saxe-Weimar's army. His troops were soon routed and by the time Götz had hurried up in response to Savelli's appeals and intervened in the confusion it was too late. Although his men fought tenaciously, forcing their way in among Saxe-Weimar's batteries and even seizing seven cannon, although the tide of battle surged backwards and forwards for a long time, so that each side twice occupied the positions previously held by the other, in the end Götz, who, although wounded, had fought in the front rank all day long, was unable to prevent Savelli's cavalry from fleeing or to rally his own when it began to break. And so this battle, like that at Rheinfelden, ended in total victory for Duke Bernhard.

In the report in which he defended himself against the complaints that Savelli had submitted to Vienna Götz wrote: "If, apart from the cuirassiers, 300 to 400 horse had stayed with me on the battlefield or had returned when I sent for them I would have gained an ouright victory with my rearguard without any doubt whatever." No more than 2,000 to 3,000 men succeeded in fleeing from the field. Saxe-Weimar's losses were also considerable. The Imperialists fled as far as Offenburg with Saxe-Weimar's cavalry in hot pursuit. A few days later Götz reached Tübingen, where he set up his quarters. Bernhard's victory greatly impressed the signatories to the Peace of Prague, even the Duke of Saxony.

Following the battle Saxe-Weimar sent his chamberlain, von Truchsess, to bear the good news to Paris and to submit urgent requests for more money and more troops and to impress upon the French Ministers that, if only he was given adequate resources, the time was ripe for embarking on decisive operations in Germany.

Louis XIII received the delegate most graciously: "In this year nobody has done anything except the Duke of Saxe-Weimar," he said to him, and at the same time he wrote to Richelieu:

"With only a small force the Duke of Saxe-Weimar has achieved great things which other Generals with large forces are unable to achieve."

To this Richelieu sent the laconic reply: "We have no Duke of Saxe-Weimar in France."

And then, after the King had given verbal assurances of further support, Richelieu withheld it. The task that he had allotted to Saxe-Weimar was nearing completion; he did not want him to grow too powerful. A situation developed which was a repetition of what followed Gustavus Adolphus' occupation of Munich.

When Bernhard's chamberlain applied to Father Joseph and Chavigny he fared no better. By that time Richelieu himself was already beginning to treat von Truchsess with a hint of coldness. He once asked von Truchsess what Saxe-Weimar was doing with all his money, to which the chamberlain replied: "The Duke's services on behalf of France are so great that I did not expect to be asked such a question."

At that point Bernhard wrote a personal letter to Louis XIII, after first sending him the many enemy standards taken at Wittenweier. His words were bitter. He had the feeling, he said, that the French were bent on destroying him; this conviction had been strengthened by the news that Longueville had been instructed to place no fresh troops at his disposal. All the advantages which he had gained had already been lost and the road to France would soon stand open to the enemy once again. He stressed the fact that Guébrient and the young Turenne had brought him few troops.

But Paris was prepared to grant only one additional subsidy. It was not until mid-October that the first half of the troops that Bernhard had requested arrived, and they were badly armed.

Meanwhile Longueville was ordered to intercept the Duke of Lorraine and prevent him from making for the Rhine. But the Duke succeeded in leaving Franche-Comté with four thousand men, five cannon and adequate supplies of corn and marching to the help of Breisach.

It is clear that in the conditions then obtaining it was relatively easy for Saxe-Weimar to employ the old military strategem of picking off his enemies one at a time. Colonel Rosen, who was besieging the fortress of Landskron, was too weak to repel the Lothringian advance on his own and was obliged to ask for help. Bernhard immediately placed several regiments from the Breisach camp at his disposal. Only a few days before, the Duke had mounted his horse for the first time since his illness in Colmar and led his numerically weak force to Ensisheim. Although he arrived there completely exhausted, by midnight he was again in the saddle. The Duke of Lorraine, like Savelli before him, had no idea that Bernhard was so near. In fact he was waiting in the undergrowth at the edge of the forest in Wittelsheim for daybreak, and when dawn came on October 3, 1638, Charles suddenly found himself confronted with the enemy. Saxe-Weimar then addressed his men:

"It is written in the Bible that the spirit is willing but the flesh is weak; but you could say of those men over there that their spirit is weak and their flesh strong. Although my cousin the Duke of Lorraine may have a fine and powerful army, I hope that today, with my trust in God, I shall be able to prove to him that we too are soldiers."

This engagement also was murderous. Courageous as ever, the defeated Duke of Lorraine was one of the last to leave the field. He barely managed to escape to Thann on foot while Bernhard was being driven to Ensisheim in a carriage, where he arrived in such a condition that his companions feared for his life.

Meanwhile Savelli, who had again reached the west bank of the Rhine with newly formed units, hoping to join forces with the Duke of Lorraine, moved off down river as soon as he heard of his defeat. Götz too had rearmed and together with General Lamboy, who had come with troops from the Netherlands to reinforce him, was waiting at Sankt Peter for his artillery to arrive before risking a counter-attack on Saxe-Weimar's camp. But once again he was too late, for meanwhile Bernhard himself had arrived before the walls of the town. On October 9th the Duke mounted an attack from the west bank on the bridge leading to one of the islands in the Rhine and the great fort that defended it. By then Götz was at Freiburg; he gave orders for beacons to be lit on all the hills of the Black Forest to encourage the defenders, and on the very next day his troops succeeded in reaching Bernhard's earth-works. Throughout the whole of that night he kept up his bombardment of the camp. In the same night Saxe-Weimar's men took the great fort on the island from the Breisach garrison while Götz occupied the redoubt by the pontoon bridge. In their fifth assault his troops reached the third bridge. It was there that all of Duke Bernhard's supplies were stored. The battalions thrown in to save them were wiped out by the Imperialists. Bernhard at that time lay in his tent with a high fever. But he knew that everything was at stake and had himself lifted on to his horse. In his presence the Imperialists were driven from the bridge and pitched in their hundreds over the balustrade and into the raging waters. Guébriant, who had been unhorsed, fought as a foot-soldier with a lance. Several more attacks were beaten off until in the end Bernhard had won yet another victory over the Imperialists under Götz.

Meanwhile letters from Baron von Reisach, Commander of the Breisach garrison, had fallen into his hands. One of them, addressed to the Emperor and dated October 9th, stated:

"Since the arrival of the last letter holding out hope of relief several days have passed, during which hunger and privation have increased. There is bread for only a few days, the cattle have nearly all been eaten and unless there is some prospect that this distress will be alleviated despair will soon set in. The short rations have carried off many officers and soldiers and laid others low with sickness; many desert their posts so that it is difficult to maintain the garrison in its allegiance."

On October 19th, after having read this cry of distress, Duke Bernhard wrote to the Commander:

"Field Marshal Götz has been defeated with heavy losses and is trying to re-form behind the Black Forest. The Duke of Lorraine has suffered a similar fate, and now that the bridge has been cut off and the forts captured there is no prospect of supplies from the west bank. In view of all this the Master of the Ordnance [Reisach] should reflect that a sense of duty cannot achieve the impossible and that he is not dealing with an ordinary cavalier but with a Prince of noble German blood to whom God has at this present moment given greater power over Breisach than to the Prince whom the Baron obeys. Consequently both duty and justice require that he should pay greater heed to the Duke than to anybody else. But if he should be seduced by a false sense of honour and his own vanity into impeding the transfer [of the fortress] unnecessarily, the Duke would have to make an example of him as a warning to others."

Further severe attacks of fever prevented Saxe-Weimar from pursuing Count Götz, who had wrongly assumed that his opponent had already received the strong French reinforcements which he had been asking for. Acting on this false assumption, Götz marched with all speed up river. After fighting all the way and suffering heavy losses he arrived in the neighbourhood of Schaffhausen, where he built a fortified camp. The Protestant inhabitants of the canton were hostile, the weather was bitter and the privations suffered by his troops were in keeping with the fearful misery of the people in the territories through which his army had passed. Another report was sent to Vienna, informing the Court that the attack on Bernhard's camp had failed because Götz, again acting from envy, had failed to support General Lamboy.

Despite his wretched physical condition, Bernhard set out from Rheinfelden. Driven by hunger, the Imperial troops defected in hordes, and while Götz was still fighting desperately to maintain discipline and keep his army together Count Philip von Mansfeld appeared in his camp as Ferdinand II's representative and demanded his sword from him. Götz was conducted to Vienna under guard to answer a charge before a general court martial of having conspired with Saxe-Weimar.

The Emperor's endeavours to rescue Breisach at the expense of his armies in northern Germany were prodigious. Fresh troops had been sent time and again, although never in sufficient numbers. Now Götz was accused of having failed to launch an immediate attack on Bernhard's camp when the Duke had marched for Thann to engage Charles of Lorraine. Richelieu maliciously observed that the only way in which the Hapsburger was able to console himself for the misfortunes of war was by blaming his generals for everything and having Götz conducted from the field as a prisoner.

And in point of fact when Mansfeld succeeded Götz he too failed in his endeavours. As early as November 26th he began to withdraw from Schaffhausen through the Black Forest; a small number of his units reached Lake Constance. But because of the deep snow and the abatis set up in the Black Forest Bernhard's troops were unable to catch up with the remnants of the Imperial army.

Another of Ferdinand's commanders, General Horst, fared scarcely better. On November 12th he crossed the Rhine at Drusenheim with 3,500 men, having been ordered to prevent Longueville's army from joining up with Saxe-Weimar. In Remiremont Horst established contact with the Duke of Lorraine while Longueville remained in Upper Burgundy. This was why Charles IV of Lorraine was unable to intervene effectively in Alsace at that time. But under no circumstances was Horst prepared to serve under him, and when a false rumour was received to the effect that Breisach had fallen he again marched for the Rhine and recrossed on to the east bank. By the time his force had reached Colmar it was in almost total disarray; the men plundered their own baggage train and tore their standards to shreds. If it had been possible to spare any of Saxe-Weimar's troops from the camp in Breisach or if news of the failure of Horst's mission had reached the Duke in Rheinfelden in time, then this unit of the Imperial army, which had been ordered to advance without rhyme or reason, could scarcely have escaped destruction. Bernhard's Colonel

Reinhold von Rosen was sent in pursuit, but it was too late and he was unable to catch up with the fleeing Imperialists.

Meanwhile the distress within the beleaguered town had reached a peak; the people were eating dogs, cats, rats and mice; they hunted down children; they even consumed corpses, so that guards had to be posted in the graveyards. Reisach had bread made from bran, ashes and the bark of oak trees; the daily ration was one pound to three men. On November 15th Bernhard again wrote to the Commander of the fortress demanding his surrender. He informed Reisach that, since it was quite obvious that distress in the town had reached its peak, if he still refused to yield he could no longer expect to receive amicable terms; instead his obstinacy, which defied all logic, would be punished in such a way that it might serve as a warning to others.

Reisach replied that three days before and again on that very day he had been informed that relief was imminent. He was therefore obliged to respect the Emperor's orders and hold out to the last.

Upon receipt of this message Erlach hurried off to the Duke, who then had his quarters in Neuenburg. After their meeting Erlach himself wrote to the Commander of Breisach to say that he had not passed his letter on to His Grace the Prince since it would only have roused him to anger. He pointed out that there was no longer any hope of relief, that the Imperial army was itself suffering extreme hardships and because of constant desertions was quite unable to take the field; Saxe-Weimar on the other hand had just received powerful reinforcements from France. He then proposed to send a number of captured Imperial officers into the town to prove the truth of his statements. In his haste Erlach forgot to sign the document and Reisach sent it back to him with a note to the effect that he did not read anonymous letters, whereupon Erlach gave his signature. On November 22nd the letter was again in the hands of the Commander, who then explained that the Emperor had impressed upon him that it was his bounden duty to hold out until the town was relieved. However, since this relief had failed to arrive, he requested safe conduct for a few of his officers, whom he proposed to send to the Imperial army to ask for fresh instructions. This request was rejected on the grounds that it appeared to question the truthfulness of the Duke's statements.

Meanwhile the tower on the north side of the fortress, in which the powder was stored, caught fire and the ensuing explosion destroyed a number of houses and part of the city wall. At this Bernhard decided to make an end of the siege and take the town by storm. Erlach was not in favour; he argued that, since the breach was so near the river, access would be difficult; moreover, the ramparts were too high and the ditches too deep, while the palisades were still in good condition; and within the week starvation would have done its work anyway. Erlach was proved right, for on November 26th he succeeded in taking St Jakob, the last of the forts on the west bank of the Rhine; the exhausted garrison was no longer able to repel the assault and, after breaching the bridge, retired within the walls of the town.

At last the end was in sight. On the 28th Reisach agreed to send out two officers to discuss surrender terms provided they were granted safe conduct. The Duke accepted this proposal but added that the "traditional considerations of military courtesy" would not be extended to Reisach himself. The Commander then begged Saxe-Weimar not to be incensed with him for as late as October 27th he had received strict orders to hold out for as long as a dog or a cat was still to be found in Breisach.

At mid-day of December 3rd hostilities came to an end. Bernhard, who had meanwhile been in Rheinfelden, was then returning to Breisach. But upon arrival in Hüningen he came down with a severe attack of fever which lasted several days and Erlach was authorized to negotiate on his behalf. Bernhard advised him that the leading officials of the Outer Austrian government were to be detained in Breisach, that all documents dealing with military, building and supply matters were to be handed over and that the 50,000 gulden which Reisach had acquired from the moneys and valuables brought into the town before the siege had to be returned. Reisach was also to order the Commander of the Imperialist fortress of Landskron to capitulate immediately. With great fortitude Reisach rejected these conditions—but not for long. Soon the strength of the garrison was utterly spent. Saxe-Weimar then stipulated that Vollmar, the Chancellor of the Vorder-Austrian government, who was then in Breisach, should be excluded from the negotiations because he had made insulting remarks about the Duke of Saxe-Weimar. Reisach immediately interceded for the Chancellor and begged Bernhard to accept his apologies. No consideration was given to the petitions presented by the burghers, for Saxe-Weimar had reserved the right to decide the destiny of Breisach himself.

The capitulation which followed on December 7th was based on fourteen articles which were translated into French at Reisach's request so that the Commanders of the French auxiliaries might also give their signatures.

In the end it was agreed that Reisach and his garrison should withdraw in full military order with their standards flying; they would be allowed to take two cannon and would be escorted as far as Offenburg. In return Reisach was obliged to order the Commander of Landskron to surrender his fortress, whereupon he too would be granted an honourable withdrawal.

It was a full two months before the Outer Austrian government officials were given permission to leave Breisach with their personal possessions. All the archives had to be handed over and all the goods and chattels of the House of Hapsburg were confiscated by Saxe-Weimar, who regarded them as his rightful property.

But then the garrison's withdrawal was postponed until December 8th. A number of Saxe-Weimar's men, who had been captured during the siege, had been thrown into jail at the time and the Imperialists had refused to hand them over despite the ransom offered for them. Thirty had died, the rest had gone mad from hunger and had eaten their dead comrades.

When the Duke heard of this he was seized with such violent rage that he gave orders for the agreement to be broken and the garrison put to the sword when they withdrew from the town. His officers managed to pacify him but Reisach feared heavy retribution. When Saxe-Weimar's adjutant informed him that the garrison was to march through the town to the bank of the Rhine, as was customary in such cases, he replied that his troops would not get across the square alive let alone through the whole town and down to the river for embarcation. The Duke then gave him his word that no harm would come to his men.

Surrounded by his general staff, Bernhard waited on horse-back for the garrison to move out. The defeated Imperialists were led by the Master of the Ordnance, Baron von Reisach, the Vorder-Austrian Chancellor Vollmar, the former Commander of Freiburg, Colonel Escher, and all their officers. Reisach kissed the Duke's boots and wished him success in his campaign. For a long while the Duke was silent, then he hectored him over the prisoners who had died such an agonizing death in Breisach. Three times Chancellor Vollmar threw himself to the ground and craved the Duke's pardon. Saxe-Weimar then entered the town on foot preceded by three of his crack regiments. The mayor knelt as he handed him the keys. The four months' siege had cost the life of some 20,000 men and 1,800,000 reichstaler. The Duke reimbursed himself with the gold and silver and other valuables that he found in the Arch-ducal castle. On December 16th the victory was celebrated by a solemn high mass in the cathedral church of Breisach. The general military situation was completely transformed by this one success. The victor was praised and sought after on all sides.

The English envoy Olivier greeted him on behalf of Charles I and the Palsgrave Karl Ludwig; the Margraves

Friedrich and Sylvius of Baden-Durlach appeared in Breisach, and Duke Frederick of Württemberg also came to express his admiration.

After the Fall of Breisach

While the siege was still in progress not only Austria and Spain but France herself had been trying by diplomatic means to restrict the excessive power that Duke Bernhard had acquired.

The Hapsburger in Vienna could see his Austrian patrimonial dominions in Switzerland and Alsace being taken from him. Charles IV of Lorraine had been cut off from the Emperor; he had to fight on two fronts and had every reason to fear that he would now lose his State irretrievably. The advantages that Saxe-Weimar had gained for France were incalculable. Strassburg was on the point of losing her neutral status and the Spanish had little hope of retaining Franche-Comté. The Protestant territories of southern Germany were freed from the pressure to which they had been subjected following Nördlingen; one after the other they began to oppose the conditions of the Treaty of Prague. The Catholic cantons in the Confederation felt threatened.

Throughout the whole of Bernhard's campaign on the Rhine and even after the capture of Breisach the attempts to reach a peace settlement had continued. In the spring of 1638 John George of Saxony had asked Bernhard's brothers, Dukes William, Albrecht and Ernest, to mediate between the Emperor and Duke Bernhard. It was said that the Emperor desired reconciliation with all the German Princes, a declaration was issued offering to extend the amnesty granted under the Peace of Prague to all those previously excluded. Bernhard, it was reported, was held in the highest esteem in Vienna.

These attempts fell in with a visit Duke Ernest of Saxe-Weimar paid the Saxon Elector, John George, in order to draw his attention to the misery caused in his territory by both the the Swedish and the Imperial and Saxon troops. The Elector used the opportunity to enquire whether there was any likelihood of persuading Bernhard to conclude a peace. Duke Ernest replied that first they would have to know the precise conditions that Vienna was prepared to offer his brother. The Elector then gave assurances that Duke Ernest would receive a pass from the Emperor, guaranteeing him safe conduct to and from the negotiations. This discussion took place in February 1638 and a few weeks later the Emperor's letter of safe conduct actually arrived in Weimar. But this upset Duke Ernest's two brothers, for the pass was valid only for him or his personal representative. By mid-May the three Dukes finally agreed to entrust the mission to their illustrious brother to one Hofmann, a justiciary from Jena who had once been Bernhard's private secretary. They had to reckon with the possibility that their territory might be annexed by John George; they also feared that the Emperor might exploit their weakness and make them pay for the harm Bernhard had inflicted on him. And so, apart from asking Bernhard for subsidies in their support, they further pleaded with him to formulate any statements in a way that would avoid giving offense to either the Emperor or the the Elector of Saxony. If he was unable to effect a reconciliation with the Emperor and bring peace to the Empire, then he should at least temporarily renounce his own lands in Weimar for their benefit; his brothers had no intention of depriving him of what was lawfully his, but he should at least negotiate with Vienna for as long as it seemed likely that his part of the territory might be annexed. "The whole welfare of our princely house," Duke William wrote to Bernhard, "depends on Your Honour's decision. I therefore pray to God that He will guide Your Honour so that you may choose the right path."

Bernhard immediately informed Paris of the gist of Hofmann's mission, stating that the Emperor and the Elector were seeking some way of concluding a general peace but that he himself would never enter into any undertaking which ran counter to his obligations to France. At the same time he also informed Oxenstierna.

In his reply Louis XIII wrote that those who were trying to sound Bernhard through his brothers were well aware of the right way to reach a general peace settlement. If the "King of Hungary" genuinely desired peace he need only send his envoy to Hamburg to inform his allies of his conditions. But it was to be doubted whether he really had any such desire, for these were mere stratagems designed to split the allies.

When Elector John George learned of this correspondence he censured Duke Ernest in the strongest terms. He denied ever having advised Ernest to warn Duke Bernhard of the dangers that threatened him at the next investiture if he refused to subject himself to the Emperor. He could answer for nothing, he said, for he had left everything to the discretion of the Dukes of Weimar. At the same time he ordered his troops to stir up unrest in the Duchy of Weimar. Bernhard complained bitterly to Hofmann of the injustice being done to his completely innocent brothers on his account. He stated that France and Sweden had already sent plenipotentiaries to Cologne and Hamburg, where the question of a peace settlement was being discussed, in order to hear the Austrian proposals; if he was provided with the necessary passes, he too would send a representative.

The Emperor now instructed the Duke of Savelli to resume the endeavours, which he had first undertaken during his brief spell of captivity following the battle of Rheinfelden, to effect a reconciliation with the Duke. Savelli wrote one letter, then another, but Bernhard did not reply; he responded only upon the arrival in his headquarters of a third letter, in which he was taken severely to task. He wrote requesting Savelli to spare him further such unseemly imputations; though prepared to concede that His Excellency's ancient and noble house meant well by the Holy Roman Empire, he found it both strange and surprising that His Excellency should try to instruct a Duke of Saxony in love of country, a virtue that he had inherited with the noble blood of his great ancestors, and that the Field Marshal should deem it necessary to advise as to what was profitable to the fatherland or what detrimental or the means whereby it might attain peace, security and prosperity. In order to convince His Excellency of the seriousness with which he regarded the question of a general peace he was sending him a copy of the reply which he had recently given to his noble brothers, the Dukes of Saxony, in response to their enquiries, in the hope that this would satisfy His Excellency and persuade him to refrain from all future comment.

But still Vienna tried to come to terms. Time and again Bernhard was told how highly Ferdinand esteemed him and that he wished to appoint him Commander-in-Chief of the Imperial armies. Bernhard's brothers received their letters of investiture, although they were withheld from Bernhard himself on the grounds that he must first effect a reconciliation with Ferdinand; he was also refused letters of safe conduct for the journey to Cologne, for Vienna wanted the reconciliation to be effected without Bernhard's being able to seek support from Sweden and France. The Imperialists did not let up; the next move was made by the King of Denmark, Christian IV, who wrote to Bernhard: "Foreign enterprises are not enduring, for which reason I do not doubt that Your Grace will show himself in a light befitting a German Prince."

Erlach's Paris Mission

In May 1638—some months before the fall of Breisach—Bernhard had delegated Major General von Erlach to Paris. From his instructions we learn that the Duke wished the fortresses in Alsace to be handed over to him, especially Breisach; Erlach was also to sound the French as to their future intentions. But the Ministers in Paris refused to be sounded and roundly declared that, if Bernhard was to use his own troops to garrison towns and strongholds, he would be reducing his effective strength in the field and so breaking the terms of his agreement.

At that time Erlach urged his master's views with great force. His most productive talks were with Father Joseph, who still remained the leading expert on German affairs and always

insisted that without their German allies the French could
achieve nothing. When Erlach told Father Joseph that his
Prince was sacrificing his property and shedding his blood
and receiving nothing in return and that, since he himself felt
he was serving no useful purpose in Paris, he would like permission to leave and report back to the Duke, the Capuchin
declared that the King was thinking only of the Duke's fortune
and prestige and that, although a few misgivings still lingered,
these would be resolved in the fullness of time; when the final
peace was made the Duke would enter into full possession of
the territories he had conquered, for his interests did not clash
in any way with those of Louis XIII. Erlach for his part considered that France's lack of money and her opposition to
Protestantism were the real reasons underlying their remaining
differences.

It has been suggested that, despite the encouragement which
Father Joseph gave to Erlach, he was actually working against
the Duke. The Capuchin had merely been trying to nourish the
the illusion which the Duke as a result of French promises had
cherished for many a year and which, despite long-standing
doubts, he continued to cherish, because he believed in the
word that a King had given him. Total disenchantment was to
come later, after he had fulfilled his great task and Breisach had
fallen.

Father Joseph did not live to witness Saxe-Weimar's disenchantment and collapse. According to popular tradition, although there is no firm evidence to support it, Richelieu told
his friend and adviser as he lay on his death bed: "Courage,
courage, Breisach has fallen," at which a last smile of triumph
is said to have appeared on the face of the dying man.

Richelieu had chosen Secretary of State De Noyers to
conduct the crucial discussion with Erlach. De Noyers was
an outspoken opponent of the Duke of Saxe-Weimar, a fact
that Bernhard was well aware of. He nonetheless instructed
Erlach to continue presenting his original demands. Richelieu
then tried to win over the negotiator by authorizing Des

Noyers to offer him an annunity. This attempt failed, for the Major General declined.

As late as June 26th Erlach was still told not to leave Paris until he had received specific declarations. But on July 14th Saxe-Weimar informed him that he was to restrict his demands to money and reinforcements and, if these were refused, to leave Paris at once, and not listen further to any proposals with regard to Alsace. By that time dissatisfaction on both sides had reached a peak. It was also at that time that the first serious symptoms of Saxe-Weimar's illness manifested themselves.

After the victory of Wittenweier, when Bernhard's chamberlain, von Truchsess, was staying in Paris, the Duke had refrained from broaching the dangerous question of Alsace through him. Whether Richelieu's equerry, M. de Graves, who was sent to Bernhard at the end of November 1638 and was present at the fall of Breisach, had already forced the Duke to hand over the fortress and then brought Count Guébriant the decree appointing him governor, has not yet been established. But in Paris it was being said quite openly that Breisach belonged to the King, and it is clear that this was being done intentionally. And so, when Bernhard failed to mention France and Sweden or even the members of the Heilbronn League either in the provisions of the capitulation or in the course of the actual surrender, when he placed a garrison of three regiments of German troops in the fortress and then, on December 20th, issued a general order appointing Major General von Erlach governor of Breisach and all the other strongholds he had conquered, the King of France, his First Minister and the Royal Council began to contemplate harsh measures.

Although he continued to behave perfectly correctly towards the French Crown there is no doubt but that from 1638 onwards, while Vienna was making peace probes, Saxe-Weimar gradually began to withdraw from French tutelage and to pursue his own long-term policy.

Saxe-Weimar's Personal Conduct

Saxe-Weimar could count on the complete loyalty of the men under his command. German, Swedish, Italian and even French troops confirmed that he shared all their hardships and provided to the best of his ability for the sick and wounded. His officers were bound to him by comradeship and loyalty. He knew all their difficulties and he joined in their festivities. He tried to compensate those of his officers who had lost their lands as a result of their exclusion from the concessions granted under the Peace of Prague by allocating them estates in Alsace. Taupadel, the Saxon, and Rosen, the Livonian, were personal friends of his, as was Erlach, the Bernese, who enjoyed his absolute confidence.

From his letters we know how generous he was. He assisted George Frederick, Margrave of Baden-Durlach, when he was driven from his lands; Anna Sabina, the widowed Duchess of Württemberg, whose son served under him; Sibylle, Countess of Hanau, and also the widowed Countess of Rappoldstein. When the last-named sent him her jewels he returned them to her together with a present and wrote that, when times improved, he would do more for her.

His quarrelsomeness cannot be denied. This character trait appeared every time he was required to share his authority and, as we have mentioned, it tended to prejudice his relations with his own brothers. But when he was separated from them and they found themselves in difficulty the sense of family solidarity was very strong. He always cared for the House from which he was descended and from which he derived both his personal pride—which was intensified by the spirit of his age—and also to a considerable extent his sense of destiny. When his brothers adhered to the Peace of Prague, although this caused him great difficulties, he never reproached them for having done so. He once wrote to his brother William: "I can well imagine that in these difficult times Your Grace has had to endure many calamities. I fear they will not be the last; but the best way of countering them is by persevering in one's office and awaiting God's decision with patience."

The reason why he tried whenever possible to quarter his men in enemy territory was that his armies had to live off the land and this could not be done without coercion.

His administration was well planned and orderly. As soon as he gained possession of a new territory he tried—unfortunately often to no purpose—to help the population, to revive its trade and to maintain public order by dealing severely with all transgressions. He paid great attention to agriculture. In order to reduce the burden of contributions he set up a large number of storehouses. After his victories he was always tolerant towards Catholicism, although strangely enough he showed little mercy to the Commanders of fortresses who stubbornly defended untenable positions; instead of respecting these fellow-soldiers for their honourable conduct he had several of them executed. Within the territories which he controlled he constantly tried to win the gratitude and affection of the population by welfare measures against the time when he could be their sovereign Prince. In many cases these measures came too late—in the Forest Cities for example, where the war had surged backwards and forwards and so reduced the population that when Bernhard wanted to build fortifications along the Rhine he was able to find no more than three skilled masons.

For his armies, for the armies of his Protestant allies and also for their opponents naked necessity was frequently the driving force behind their heroic deeds.

Saxe-Weimar's Campaigns in 1639

The conquest of Breisach was followed by the winter campaign in Upper Burgundy, which was fought along the banks of the Doubs and the frontier of Neuchâtel as far as Pontarlier. Large supplies of stores were brought from the Jura to Breisach. Joux soon fell and the army headed for

Franche-Comté, where the Spanish, the Lothringians and the local farmers, who fought like grim death, were defeated. Within six weeks Bernhard had taken possession of the richest part of the territory.

What did he hope to gain by this offensive? Most probably he was simply trying to lay his hands on some valuable territory, which he could offer the French in exchange for Breisach and Alsace. But this only helped to increase the antagonism in Paris, which had already been exacerbated by his friendship with Henri de Rohan before the Battle of Rheinfelden.

It was a considerable time before Bernhard realized just how problematical his relations with France had always been. This was due partly to objective factors and partly to the mental reservations that Richelieu had entertained from the outset when he still desperately needed the Duke; but ultimately—and from 1637 this was apparent to keen observers—it was due to the fact that the Cardinal could not tolerate the emergence of a new sovereign territory under a German Prince between the Rhine and the Moselle, in other words the creation of a new Lorraine. And then Saxe-Weimar's personality, his consciousness of both his rank and his achievement, his high demands, from which he never deviated, his unbending, adamantine nature failed to please either Louis XIII or his entourage. The many protestations of gratitude, the festivities arranged in honour of the man who had defended and saved France's eastern frontier seemed to Bernhard a sheer waste of time, meaningless display; his conversations, in which he always came straight to the point, offered little scope for winning and gracious phrases. On his last visit to Paris he was nonetheless treated with every consideration. But when Bernhard asked for troops and money in terms that were close to rudeness, Richelieu, for all his cool courtesy, replied for the first time in a cutting tone and with an almost imperceptible expression of cold disdain.

On December 27, 1638, de l'Isle, a Court chamberlain, was

sent on an official mission to Bernhard of Saxe-Weimar to congratulate him on his victory. Louis's representative met the Duke in Upper Burgundy after first having contacted Guébriant, who was to advise him as to how to proceed. He handed over letters in which both the King and Richelieu, after expressing their gratitude and praise, assured the Duke that their desire to render further assistance in order to continue the war and maintain Breisach, which was of such great importance to the whole of Christendom, had never been greater. Guébriant tried to sound Saxe-Weimar as to his intentions, but Bernhard simply spoke in general terms of his obligations towards Louis XIII, after which he broke off the discussions. It was then rumoured that he intended to go to the French Court himself. At that time De Noyers was already speaking quite openly of the Duke's improprieties, although in doing so he was not referring to the possibility that France might lose Breisach but to the fact—one to which he took violent exception—that a Protestant service had been held in the Breisach minster to commemorate the victory. It was still assumed however that, once he was in Paris, Bernhard would listen to reason and give way.

And so de l'Isle was sent to the victor a second time. The letter that he handed to Bernhard on that occasion expressed the King's pleasure at the forthcoming visit. Richelieu wrote in a similar vein. But then Wicquefort called on Saxe-Weimar and, acting on instructions from Grotius, urgently warned him not to appear in person at the French Court; he was advised to conduct all negotiations from a distance and on no account to leave the territories he had conquered. The English Ambassador at the French Court, Leicester, also begged Wicquefort to do all in his power to prevent Bernhard from travelling to Paris; at the same time he let the Duke know that, if he should lose the support of the French, England would help him in every way. In the end Saxe-Weimar declined the French invitation on the grounds that it was then more important for him to remain in Alsace than to visit the

Court. Again he complained about the lack of support. A great reception had already been arranged and there was talk of the three to four million livres that Bernhard was to receive for handing over Breisach. In Richelieu's entourage it was said that, if the Duke was prepared to conclude an alliance with the Cardinal, France would procure the Imperial Crown for him. This was an expedient that had been used only too often. Rumours to the effect that the French were trying to persuade Bernhard to change his religion seem improbable, because his conversion would have resolved the difference between him and the Emperor. But the assumption that the French Ministers were thinking of arranging a marriage for him either with a royal Princess or with Marie de Vignerot et Combalet, the Duchess of Aiguillon and Richelieu's niece, who was still unmarried, and of guaranteeing him an annual income of eight hundred thousand livres is not so easily dismissed. The Duke is supposed to have said of Duchess Marie: "This lady is too beautiful for a mistress and too humble for a wife."

Richelieu complained both to his own agent, Hoeufft, and to Wicquefort about the Duke's attitude, which he found inexplicable.

Saxe-Weimar then decided to send Erlach to Paris again. But the Major-General's departure was delayed at the last moment. In Joux, where he had arrived in a fair state of health, the Duke suddenly became seriously ill; he was then taken to Pontarlier, whence he hoped to proceed to Alsace. In Pontarlier he was met by de l'Isle, who was then on his way to Alsace to negotiate with him. Bernhard rejected all the Cardinal's reproaches, explaining that the rudeness of which he stood accused had been prompted by his annoyance at France's failure to send the help he had constantly asked for and had always been promised. Other remarks that he was supposed to have made about his relations to the French Crown were again being disseminated in Paris. It was at that point that Erlach set out for the French capital. His official instructions were to congratulate the King on the birth of the Dauphin and to offer excuses for his master's absence, explaining that his sickness and general debility had prevented him from travelling. The General was also to ask for a further 2,400,000 livres as well as a special allocation for improving the artillery and purchasing more horses. Erlach first got in touch with De Noyers. But on this occasion the Secretary of State conducted him immediately to the Cardinal, who told him at his very first audience that Saxe-Weimar's absence was due entirely to the insinuations and influence of foreigners. Erlach was most cordially received by the King and Queen, who showed him the royal infant. He was even told that the heir-apparent would later be entrusted to the Duke of Saxe-Weimar so that he might learn the art of war. Meanwhile De Noyers had Bernhard's envoy closely watched. Chavigny and Bouillon also took part in the discussions. At that time Erlach still spoke with conviction on the Duke's behalf; among other things he argued that, if Breisach were to pass into French hands, it must inevitably appear as if the King intended to pursue a policy of conquest in Germany, and that could deprive him of his German allies. He said nothing of Bernhard's real intentions. As far as subsidies were concerned, he obtained assurances that Bernhard would receive 600,000 livres every quarter and also a special contribution of 200,000 livres to strengthen the cavalry and improve the artillery for the next campaign; a further 100,000 livres would be provided to bring the troops under Guébriant's command up to 8,000 men by enlisting German mercenaries. But in granting these new concessions the French also imposed new conditions. The Duke was to give a written undertaking to the effect that his garrisons in Breisach and the other strongholds he had conquered would come under the ultimate command of the King of France; he was also to undertake never to transfer these strongholds without explicit orders; he was to command the Governor of Breisach to give assurances that he would transfer the fortress to nobody except the King of France in the event of his own death. Duke Bernhard was further required to guarantee that France might freely dispose of all conquests he had made or would make in Germany and Upper Burgundy as a result of French subsidies. All new reinforcements provided by France were to remain under Guébriant's independent command. And then Erlach, the Governor of Breisach, agreed to accept an annual pension of twelve thousand livres from the French, which he had refused in the previous year. In those times such an arrangement was not unusual. The General also solemnly promised in the presence of the King, Richelieu and De Noyers that—should the Duke die—he would watch over Breisach and ensure that it remained at the disposal of Louis XIII.

While all this was going on Bernhard had made a tolerable recovery, although he was still weak, and he was about to set out with Frederick, Duke of Württemberg, and Charles Magnus, Margrave of Baden-Durlach, envoy from the Palatinate and Hesse, for Alsace. With a powerful escort he marched through the bishopric of Basle, then by way of Laufenburg and Hüningen to Neuenburg, where he boarded ship and sailed down the Rhine to Breisach, which he entered in state to the roar of the cannons and where, shortly after Easter, he celebrated the victory gained by Banér at Chemnitz on April 4th. Colonel Rosen again successfully repelled an invasion mounted by Lothringian troops. Bernhard himself came to his aid with the Flersheim regiment and six cannon. Thann was occupied; the town of St-Claude was conquered, pillaged and burned and its inhabitants were cut down, all because a trumpeter accompanying Saxe-Weimar's truce officers had been murdered by the townspeople. As a result of these conquests the Spanish were denied access to Franche-Comté. Spurred into action, the Catholic cantons appealed to France, who badly needed their permission to recruit new troops in the Confederation. And so the Duke was expressly requested by Paris not to make enemies of the Swiss. The first thing he did upon receipt of this admonition was to threaten the cantons and accuse them of having supported the enemy in every possible way while withholding all support from him. Moreover, although they had promised the Swedes and the German Protestants that they would remain neutral, they had persistently broken their word. They had also failed to prevent the Bishop of Basle from entering into an agreement with the enemy, even though he was a compatriot of theirs. The cantons responded in a similar vein: they made countless protests, they spoke of the atrocities committed within their territories and of the violation of their rights, they defended the Bishop of Basle, maintaining that he had been forced to negotiate an agreement with the Imperialists because his incomes and rents were subject to Austrian control.

In Upper Burgundy Bernhard had placed German garrisons in the most important strongholds and razed the indefensible fortifications.

He intended to keep control of Alsace and the Lower Rhenish territories himself, but, apart from Pontarlier, Joux, Sainte-Marie and a number of other towns, which he wished to retain as gifts for his allies and comrades, he was willing to transfer Franche-Comté to France in repayment for the subsidies and military aid he had received. He had never given up the idea of prevailing upon the German Protestant Estates to repudiate the Peace of Prague, of arming them and then leading them against the Emperor.

The Swedes meanwhile were also urging him not to surrender Breisach to the French; so too were the English, with whom Saxe-Weimar had entered into very close relations. We have already mentioned that Charles I had promised support, and it was only the Scottish rising that prevented him from keeping his promise. This too Richelieu was well aware of. Oxenstierna advised Bernhard to acquire the services of the Hessian troops under Melander. Negotiations were started with Amalia Elisabeth, the widow of William of Hesse-Cassel, who had died in September; they were conducted by Chancellor Müller, acting for Oxenstierna. But this immediately gave rise to tension between Calvinists and Lutherans. Amalia Elisabeth especially, whose marriage to Bernhard of Saxe-Weimar was being mooted, revealed a deep aversion to all things Lutheran.

Was Bernhard trying to create a third party or was he trying to mediate between the Protestant Estates of the Empire and the Emperor? There is much to be said for the first possibility. He wanted to align south Germany with Thuringia and promote a *rapprochement* between Hesse-Cassel and the House of Saxony. He sent delegates to negotiate with George, Duke of Lüneburg. By then the army of the disbanded Heilbronn League was a spent force. The States that had once belonged to the League had only a few weak forces in the field, and these were scattered between the Upper Danube, the Neckar and the Middle Rhine. The prospects for Saxe-Weimar's projected invasion of Imperial territory were favourable. It was because of this that Banér had censured the Duke so severely for his Burgundian ventures. He failed to appreciate the Duke's great need for bargaining counters with which to protect himself against France before undertaking any further projects. In 1639 both Vienna and Madrid rightly regarded the situation as serious. Bernhard also received far-reaching proposals from the Emperor: it was said that in return for the cession of Alsace he was to be offered Archduke Leopold's daughter in marriage and also considerable territorial compensation. There was even talk of restoring the Duchy of Franconia to him.

Imperial attempts to effect a *rapprochement* continued. A certain Häusner von Wandersleben, who had gone over to the Imperialist cause following the Peace of Prague, wrote to the Duke in February 1639 from Basle requesting an interview. He was asked through Rehlinger to name his principal. Häusner would only speak with the Duke himself. It was then learned that the Emperor was prepared to offer Bernhard of Saxe-Weimar the chairmanship for the peace negotiations if he would effect a reconciliation. The Spanish envoy to the

Catholic Estates in the Confederation, Don Diego de Saavedra Farjardon, wrote to Bernhard on behalf of Olivares: "I have been sent by one of Spain's greatest Ministers [Olivares], who greatly admires your heroic qualities, to say just two words to you on his behalf." Bernhard did not receive him, not even when the burgomaster of Freiberg interceded for him.

After Bernhard had returned to Pontarlier an important meeting took place on June 10, 1639, when Guébriant succeeded in obtaining a private interview with him. He showed the Duke a letter from the King, spoke of Erlach's negotiations with the Ministers and mentioned that Bernhard's Major General had asked that the King of France should leave Breisach to the Duke as a fortress and storage depot for future campaigns. If this request were granted, Guébriant said, Bernhard would have to give assurances that the King would have unrestricted use of the fortress. To this Bernhard replied: "I have a communication here which Erlach brought me from Paris. Read it. You may find that it contains the substance of your instructions." To his surprise, Guébriant saw that the memorandum did in fact correspond with his instructions. He then said: "It is only a little thing that the King is asking, you can easily grant it." But Bernhard replied: "Am I to be made into a slave, I who am fighting for freedom? The King gave me Alsace by agreement and in return I have given him loyal service; I have shed my blood for him and sacrificed my army. And now you are trying to take from me what I have won by force of arms!" Guébriant pointed to the paper which the Duke had handed him. "That is not stated in the articles," he said. "The King is simply asking you to occupy Breisach under the same conditions as those under which you exercise your office as commander, in other words under his ultimate command; he is giving you the substance and retaining only the shadow. If you consider the money he has paid you and the help he has sent you, do they not count for more than what you are now demanding?" "But these things cancel one another out," Bernhard replied. "In return for that money I have put brave men into the field and sacrificed large numbers of them on his account."

Then it was Guébriant's turn: "The troops are paid by the King," he argued, "and everything they have achieved was achieved with the help of French auxiliaries. You cannot claim all the credit. I beg you, Your Grace, consider well what you are about to do. Your most honourable course of action would be to satisfy the King, who, as you see, is again giving you money with which to strengthen your army."

"That is perfectly true," Bernhard replied, "but he expects me to play the commissar and place all the [newly recruited] troops under French command. I shall raise no new levies until such a time as my own army has been brought up to its full strength. The King also insists that I transfer all future conquests to him; but, if I agree, what am I do do if any of my relatives or those linked with my house by a joint inheritance wish to negotiate with me? Am I to reject them as honourable partners if they refuse to recognize French Governors?"

"If such a case should ever arise," the Count said, "then I am sure the King would give way. I am prepared to conduct further negotiations on this point." Bernhard rejected his offer.

Guébriant then made one last attempt to impress on the Duke the dissatisfaction that would be felt at Court if he should refuse to meet its requirements. But Bernhard's final word was: "That will be my misfortune, but I have to do what I think is right. Tomorrow I will give you my answer in writing. You will see that I am doing all I can. I shall never part company with France; and if I am driven out through one door I shall come back in by another. I shall never be ungrateful." And with that he brought the conversation to an end.

The next day he talked with Méliand; they discussed the Swiss demand that the bishopric of Basle should be evacuated, which Bernhard rejected. The written reply that he had promised to Count Guébriant was handed to the Frenchman on June 12th. Bernhard demanded the unencumbered possession of Alsace and the most important strongholds in Upper Burgundy together with their lands. He offered France his acquisitions in Franche-Comté in payment of the support costs but refused to give an undertaking that, in the event of his capture or death, his conquests should pass to the Bourbons. He also complained of past injustices and claimed that in 1636 Bullion had cheated him out of a full million livres. In his reply Guébriant pointed out that, while the Duke had enumerated all the unpleasant items, he had made no mention of the many benefits he had received and suggested that this would prejudice the fame he had acquired by his feat of arms.

Further discussions were held in the same vein until eventually the Duke stated quite unequivocally: "I have no wish to expose myself to censure for having dismembered the Empire." At this Guébriant interrupted him. "Who is asking you to do so?" he said. "The whole of Alsace, including Breisach, is a patrimonial dominion of the House of Austria; why should not a Prince of the House of Saxony or Bavaria be made Emperor?" Bernhard was silent. After a pause he asked the Count to use his influence at Court to expedite his projected campaign in Germany because Banér's victories might make the Emperor inclined to accept a peace.

He revealed nothing of his further plans save that he was negotiating with the Landgravine Amalia Elisabeth.

Guébriant submitted a detailed account of these discussions to De Noyers. He also wrote both to the King and to Richelieu informing them that he was unable to achieve any more than was set out in his memorandum. At the same time he asked for further resources with which to expedite the campaign.

Richelieu commented on these events as follows:

"If France is indulgent towards the Duke she will reveal her weakness, which he will exploit to his own advantage. He will cavil at every proposal that is made to him and . . . will make it quite impossible for France to force the Emperor to accept peace terms, for if he retains his [present] power he alone will be in a position to do so. Once he is made master of Alsace he would prefer to leave Lorraine in the hands of Charles IV, for he would rather promote his interests than those of France, who is intent on incorporating Lorraine into her own territory; to judge by his moodiness he would be likely to incite constant unrest with his neighbour, which could lead to open rupture at any time, and [for this reason] he would prefer to have a petty Duke rather than a mighty monarch as his neighbour. It is also to be feared that, if France adopts an indulgent attitude towards Bernhard, it will be thought that she is incapable of resisting either friend or foe."

Richelieu then proceeded to interpret the original contract by which he had bound Bernhard of Saxe-Weimar to France. He explained that "the land together with all rights previously vested in the House of Austria" was not to be understood in the sense propounded by the Duke, since these rights were restricted to the possession of the domains, the administration of justice and the receipt of incomes.

The French then decided that their best policy was to do their utmost to persuade Bernhard to open the German campaign as quickly as possible in accordance with Banér's wishes and to postpone the discussion of all questions relating to Alsace until after its completion.

Accordingly the French government complained to the Swedes that Saxe-Weimar was failing to exploit Banér's victories.

The instructions worked out in Chavigny's office about June 12th and intended for M. d'Avaux, the French representative in Germany, show how deeply disturbed Richelieu was over Saxe-Weimar's behaviour at that time:

"Having observed that the Duke is still perpetually complaining, that he dismisses out of hand the conditions which the King has made concerning the strongholds in Alsace, that he haughtily dismisses the massive subsidies which he has received, and the French auxiliaries, who made all his victories possible . . . , that he now dares to assert, although his troops are paid by the King and he himself owes his position of command to the authority vested in him by the King, that the strongholds which he has conquered are his rightful possessions. . . . His Majesty is of course extremely displeased with him. On the other hand His Majesty is prepared to believe that the Duke may yet prove amenable to reason and that upon more mature consideration he will comply with His Majesty's just demands. Up to now his recalcitrant behaviour has been ascribed to his obdurate nature, which is intent on personal gain. There are, however, two factors which make it appear highly improbable that he would ever change sides: the first is his personal reputation, by which he sets great store, and the second is the enormous amount of money which he has so far managed to extract from the King and which neither the Empire nor Spain would be able to provide."

Bernhard then decided to break camp and cross the Rhine. He informed Guébriant, who asked him to wait at least until the reinforcements had arrived. But an outbreak of plague in Pontarlier reinforced the Duke's determination. While Erlach was preparing for the Rhine crossing in Neuenburg Bernhard marshalled his four thousand to five thousand men, gave them their pay and ordered the Count of Nassau to remain behind with three regiments to wait for the French auxiliaries. On June 23rd he marched to Mont Benoît. Because of their hatred for the population of Pontarlier both German and French troops plundered and set fire to the town. Saxe-Weimar was so grieved by the news that he said: "I am loath to go on living, for I can no longer abide such Godlessness with a clear conscience."

In Mont Benoît he had talks with Erlach. Then he led his troops to Pfirt. There, when the people flocked to see him, he is supposed to have said: "I fear that I must share the fate suffered by the King of Sweden, for as soon as the people paid more attention to him than to God he had to die."

From Pfirt the army marched to Neuenburg; Bernhard rode on to Hüningen, where he met his advisers, Mockel and Rehlinger. But the next day he was again taken ill and returned to Neuenburg by ship, where his army crossed the Rhine. His condition deteriorated from day to day. He himself said that he had never felt so ill before. The doctors, including the celebrated Blandini of Geneva, who had attended Rohan when he died in Königsfelden, tried their numerous remedies, but to no avail. Bernhard summoned Erlach, Ehm and Rosen. He exhorted them to remain united in the event of his death, to guard against dissension and not to desert the cause. His Chancellor, the younger Rehlinger, was called to take down his last will at six in the morning, by which time the Duke was so weak that he could scarcely dictate it. Bernhard's principal concern was that the territories he had conquered should remain within the Empire; he therefore asked that his brothers should take them over and defend them with the help of the Swedes. If none of them was prepared to do so, then France should hold them with her own and the Duke's troops until the conclusion of a general peace, when they should be returned to the Holy Roman Empire. He gave control of the army to Erlach, the Count of Nassau, Ehm and Rosen but without stipulating which of them was to be senior commander.

He bequeathed large sums of money to his officers and servants; he left his horse to Count Guébriant and his treasure to his brothers.

When the Chancellor drew his attention to the vagueness of the most important provisions Bernhard replied in a weak voice that his will was being given, not as he would have wished but as pressure of time required. He insisted on absolute secrecy and made the Chancellor promise to do all he could to ensure that his wishes were carried out.

A few close friends and the doctors, Schmid and Blandini, then entered the room. The Duke pointed to the paper which Rehlinger held in his hand and said: "This contains my last will." He repeated these words in French to Blandini. Then he sent them all away: "I have talked enough, now I must speak with God." The Court Chaplain approached the sickbed and prayed with him. The Duke's breath grew shorter but his heart was still beating strongly. "I am surprised," Bernhard said, "that my heart is still so fresh and will not resign itself to death." Then he prayed again, called on Jesus by name and departed. It was 7 A.M. on July 8, 1639.

As soon as the Duke was dead there was talk of poison. Dr. Blandini, alleged to have fled to Geneva after Bernhard's death, was accused of the crime and it was rumoured that he had acted on Richelieu's behalf. The Spanish and the Austrians were also arraigned. One witness maintained that Bernhard himself had spoken of poison. The argument advanced by Gonzenbach, author of the copious monograph on Erlach, that Richelieu had not the slightest interest in Saxe-Weimar's decease is difficult to follow. Bernhard's death undoubtedly relieved Richelieu of an anxiety quite as great as that from which he had been released when the all-powerful Gustavus Adolphus had fallen at Lützen. But this does not prove that he was in any way responsible. What is quite certain, however, is that immediately Saxe-Weimar had been buried Guébriant hurried off to Breisach to win the services of his officers for the King of France.

Guébriant, Oisonville and Choisy, who arrived in Breisach one after the other, were all instructed to do nothing without first consulting Erlach. Erlach, meanwhile, sent Colonel Flersheim to Paris to continue negotiations.

On October 19, 1639, agreement was reached: all Bernhard's conquests, together with his army, were taken over by the French; in return Louis XIII guaranteed that Saxe-Weimar's officers and high officials would retain both their rank and their positions and that the estates which Bernhard had conferred on them would be regarded as theirs by right.

Bernhard's brothers had hoped to gain possession of their inheritance with Swedish help. But Duke William was on bad terms with Oxenstierna, while his brothers, who had adhered to the Peace of Prague, had to reckon with the possibility that, by accepting Bernhard's will, they might well gain nothing and could lose their hereditary lands in the bargain.

In August 1639 the Cardinal recalled the Duke of Longueville from the army in Italy; this was a wise move, for on October 9th Bellièvre, who was still in London, reported that he had learned from Queen Henrietta that Charles I would like to see the Count Palatine "at the head of the army previously led by the Duke of Saxe-Weimar". Shortly afterwards the King of England renewed this request in a conversation with Bellièvre. But Richelieu had no intention of giving up "the conquests which the Duke of Saxe-Weimar had made for France" to the son of the King of Bohemia. In his instructions Bellièvre was told: "The envoy may inform the King of England that if he now wishes to join the King [of France] and his allies in the offensive and defensive pact against Spain and is prepared to maintain a force of 6,000 foot for the Count Palatine in Germany, France will not forget the Count or the obligation to restore his lands to him at some future date." But the Count Palatine did not await the outcome of these negotiations. With the approval of his uncle, the Prince of Orange, and with 250,000 livres from his other uncle, Charles I, he secretly entered France in order to establish contact with the high-ranking officers of Saxe-Weimar's former army.

Bullion's spies were well informed; a number of them, who knew the Count personally, were set on his trail. On October 18th Secretary of State Bullion wrote to Chavigny: "I will do all I can to ensure that he is arrested with as little unpleasantness as possible." Charles Louis was captured in Moulins disguised as a lackey. He had been heading for Alsace. The

French envoy in England was instructed to advise Charles I that "the Count Palatine would be treated with every consideration owing to a person of his rank and would be detained until such a time as His Majesty had discovered why he had been travelling through his territory in disguise, a practice quite out of keeping with normal observances where powerful Princes were concerned." Charles Louis was conducted to the "bois de Vincennes" while Chavigny tried in vain to persuade Leicester, the English Ambassador in Paris, that Vincennes was a royal residence rather than a prison. The Count Palatine was kept there until 1640. He was then allowed to live in Paris after he had given the Cardinal his word of honour that he would not try to escape. This privilege took effect from March, and in September Danish, Swedish and English pressure finally procured his release.

The Duke of Longueville, who had taken over Saxe-Weimar's army, went into winter quarters in the Palatinate, where he had found food for his troops. By the end of the autumn he had occupied Oppenheim, Neustadt, Bingen, Kreuznach and Bacharach. By December 27, 1639, his second-in-command, the future Marshal Guébriant, had completed his preparations for their Rhine crossing. On February 9, 1640, Saxe-Weimar's old army mustered under Longueville near Limburg. For the time being this operation silenced the repeated complaints that Banér had made during Bernhard's campaigns in Burgundy and Franche-Comté. Longueville hoped to join forces with the Swede and then arrange a combined attack on Austria's patrimonial dominions.

When Banér had crossed the Elbe on February 1, 1639, he had commanded a force of 18,000 men; his army was equipped with eighty cannon but he was without food and virtually without money; 5,000 thaler was all he had. His soldiers were living on horsemeat and the bark of trees. They quickly advanced into the lush territories of the Dukes of Brunswick and Lüneburg, who were no longer members of the Swedish alliance. Halle, Zwickau and Chemnitz capitulated. Although

the Imperial General Marazzini forced the Swedes to give up
the siege of Freiberg, he failed to win back Chemnitz. On
April 14th the Imperialists attacked but the Swedes gained the
victory. The cities of Saxony then offered little resistance. On
May 21st Banér stood before the walls of Prague. His mercenaries demanded booty and Banér gave in to them. Refusing
to listen to Torstensson's advice, he began to bombard the
weakest points in the city walls. But before sending his troops
in Banér wanted to inspect the breaches and the dispositions
made by Counts Gallas and Schlick. He climbed on to the roof
of a mill and was astonished to see 15,000 men drawn up in
line of battle. He immediately retreated with all speed to
Thuringia. Discouraged by this setback, he then tried to
bring about a separate peace between the Emperor and the
Swedes, but Richelieu's agents exerted pressure in Stockholm
and Banér was refused the necessary authority. For the time
being nothing more was heard of the activities of Bernhard's
army under Longueville.

Peace Negotiations

From 1635 there was no let-up in the peace feelers put out
by all parties. Official, semi-official and secret contacts were
established time and again by various European powers, even
by Spain and France.

Richelieu's concern for the norms of international law—the
underlying reason for the flexibility of his claims, which he
adapted to meet the needs of the moment—becomes obvious
in this connection. As a result of his theological studies he
was undoubtedly greatly influenced by memories of the
medieval courts of arbitration. But as, with the onset of the
Renaissance and the Reformation, the traditional and long-
established safeguards of international law lost effectiveness,
new forms had to be found. The extent to which the relationships between the great nations were influenced by the
experiences of the Italian States is well known. Rucellai

exercised a crucial influence. The concept of the "balance of power" derived from his political thinking. But all endeavours to establish conditions of collective security remained questionable. Conquering coalitions have always created temporary new orders, but once they began to disintegrate those who had been obliged to join by force of arms entered into fresh alliances in order to achieve a new distribution of power, a process often involving catastrophe.

In Richelieu's conception of a secure European order France occupied a position of considerable power, if not indeed of pre-eminence. His policy of alliances, which he pursued with such energy and consistency, was directed towards this end. In his eyes all non-Hapsburg States were natural allies.

Ever since 1635, when France began to play an active part in the European war, Richelieu had not only maintained unofficial and secret contacts with his country's enemies, he had even refrained from offering open resistance to various official peace moves, contenting himself with tactical resistance.

As early as 1630, at the Regensburg Diet, serious consideration had been given to the possibility of convening a General Congress to stop the proliferating European conflict. In the instrument negotiated on behalf of the King of France by the official French representatives, Brûlart and Father Joseph, and subsequently so decisively rejected by Richelieu in Lyons, Louis XIII was referred to, not as an arbiter but as an important mediator. This agreement, signed by the French and the Imperial plenipotentiaries, was always regarded as binding by both Ferdinand II and Ferdinand III. In their view Richelieu's Lyons intervention was a flagrant breach of contract.

In assessing the peace moves of the 1630s we must give special consideration to the Pope's attitude. While expressly disclaiming all intention of trying to influence the parties concerned, Urban VIII had repeatedly offered to use his "good offices". From 1630 onwards a General Congress had been on everybody's lips. The chief obstacle in the way of such a project was Richelieu's insistence that all of France's allies should take part in any talks held by the opposing powers. Obviously, the Cardinal wished to prevent an exclusive agreement between the Catholic sovereigns. Quite apart from his own interests in the matter he owed it to his allies to adopt such an attitude. A contributing factor was his perennial hope that England might yet be persuaded to take his side.

But Urban VIII would not hear of the Protestant Princes' and the Republics' participating in general negotiations. In this respect he placed the spiritual welfare of the Church above political expediency. In seeking a solution Father Joseph suggested that two separate conferences should be held: the first would try to settle the points of issue between France and the Hapsburgs, while a later conference could discuss the question of a general agreement. The Curia's initial reaction to this proposal was to recommend that an assembly of Catholic plenipotentiaries should be held in Rome and a similar assembly for non-Catholics in Trent. Rome's reason in wishing to keep the two confessions separate was to ensure that the Protestants would not disrupt the talks between the Catholic powers. But this separation was the one thing that France could not accept.

France's allies also made proposals; the Protestant Estates from the Upper and Lower Saxon Circles even came up with a project for a three-stage congress, in which the Catholics would meet at Mühlhausen, their own representatives at Erfurt and the "mediators" at Langensalza. Although the French had always insisted that Louis XIII was not an "arbiter" but a "mediator", in actual fact Richelieu had always had an arbitration role in mind for his sovereign, which would have enabled him to take authoritarian measures if the opportunity arose. In order to frustrate any solution that ran counter to this general objective he made one absolute condition: his Protestant allies must be admitted to all negotiations with full powers; otherwise France would stand aside.

In his basic work on the Peace of Westphalia Fritz Dickmann has analysed the position of the papacy during the great confessional strife in the seventeenth century and drawn a clear distinction between the possibilities open to the Curia then and those enjoyed by the mediaeval Popes. The secularization of government and politics had also had its effect on curial policy. As territorial Princes the Popes of the sixteenth and seventeenth centuries entered into alliances and joined coalitions; at the same time they continued to claim precedence over all secular powers. But this claim had long been disregarded by the European States, which were then developing more and more into self-contained, collective entities concerned only for their own national interests.

At the beginning of 1635 the many peace initiatives seemed about to bear fruit. The fact that France was prepared to send plenipotentiaries to a Peace Congress casts a revealing light on the general situation; the Emperor was also prepared to participate, and eventually even Spain gave her approval. Although subject to fluctuation, the common need for peace and the determination to enter into negotiations continued to make themselves felt even after the French declaration of war on Spain. In 1635 Constance, Spires, Augsburg and Trent were proposed as possible sites for the diet, but when the plague began to spread through southern Germany Cologne was chosen instead. The beginning of negotiations was fixed for October, and on September 17th, the Pope announced that Cardinal Ginetti would be appointed as papal legate to the Cologne diet. Richelieu still insisted on his original conditions, while Olivares was demanding that the Pope should impose ecclesiastical penalties on France for having entered into alliances with the heretics. The Estates-General for their part maintained that they would negotiate only on their own soil. As usual, no country wished to give the impression that it needed peace.

The instructions to the papal legate were first leaked and then officially published in 1636. A number of the proposals reflected Urban VIII's personal views, while others followed purely ecclesiastical trends that were grounded in Catholic tradition. In adopting this traditionalist approach Urban was departing from the practice of many of his predecessors. The Pope still insisted that there could be no dealings whatever with the heretics. If the Catholics wanted to establish contacts with the Protestants they should not do so at the Congress. The instructions concerning the Valtelline were typical: for confessional reasons there could be no question of returning the valley to the Grisons. In Paris, of course, this attitude was regarded as unequivocally pro-Spanish. As far as the Palatinate was concerned the members of the Pope's entourage still hoped that the Count would convert, in which case the Curia would do its utmost to further the restitution of his territory.

Cardinal Ginetti arrived in Cologne in October 1636, but the French, the Swedes, the Dutch and the German Protestant Powers did not appear immediately. In the Swedish Council of State Oxenstierna spoke in favour of continuing the war, and the French diplomats in Stockholm worked to the same end. Before setting out on his journey home the Swedish Chancellor had talks with the French, in which it was agreed that their general objective should be a return to the conditions obtaining in 1618. This was in fact stipulated in the Franco–Swedish Treaty of Wesel in October 1636.

Both the French and the Swedes had assured the Landgrave of Hesse-Cassel that they would on no account enter into genuine negotiations unless their German Protestant allies were also invited to take part: "No peace without Hesse-Cassel," Richelieu declared. Meanwhile he continued to work for English participation. The French plenipotentiaries who were to appear at Cologne were not given their instructions until 1637. Richelieu failed in his attempts to persuade the Pope that on this occasion confessional questions were irrelevant, from which we may assume that, although France's entry into the war did not close the door on peace, it did make it more difficult. The concatenation of alliances, the countless separatist issues and ephemeral interests, made a clear-cut solution impossible. It was not only the adversaries who suspected one another but the allies as well. Fritz Dickmann has written: "The disputes over procedure, over the admission of delegates, over the composition, siting and date of the congress took up more time than the subsequent peace negotiations themselves. But these were not just questions of procedure, they were also decisions of great material importance. If the Imperial Estates were invited to the negotiations *in corpore* this would bring into question the authority vested in the Emperor to conduct negotiations on behalf of the Empire and to control Imperial foreign policy; if they were admitted individually and authorized to represent their own special interests this meant that they would be recognized under international law as independent members of the society of nations."

The Cologne Congress did not take place. But the will to negotiate remained and gave rise to diplomatic initiatives with which we shall deal later.

In the second half of the 1630s and the early 1640s internal opposition remained the greatest threat to France. Olivares constantly exploited it, and his chances of success were all the greater since the leaders of this opposition were to be found in the Royal House itself.

CHAPTER X

COURT INTRIGUES

We have had numerous occasions to observe the pro-Spanish sympathies of the Queen, Anne of Austria. This unfortunate lady became embroiled in serious political conflicts. Often she was close to despair and once even tried to flee the country. Madame de Motteville has provided a balanced and well-informed account of the Queen's life, from which it appears that it was thanks only to her innate cheerfulness that she managed to throw off her perpetual worries.

Richelieu's agents also spied on the exiled Queen-Mother, and to this end the Cardinal did his best to enlist the aid of Anne of Austria's ladies in waiting, among them Mademoiselle de Hautefort, Marie Louise de La Fayette and Mademoiselle de Chemerault. With the last of these he even achieved a certain degree of success. Apart from this, the strong affection that Anne of Austria inspired in her ladies always thwarted him.

Marie de Hautefort, the daughter of the Marquis, Charles de Hautefort, was orphaned at an early age; at Court she was assigned first to the Princess of Conti and then to the Queen-Mother, after which she came into close personal contact with Anne of Austria. All contemporary observers agree in praising her charm, her gentle nature, her tact and self-control. She is said to have exercised great influence over her mistress.

Louis told her all his troubles and had long talks with her about people, about religion, about love; the concepts of renunciation and sin furnished them with an inexhaustible topic of conversation and also with a kind of spiritual gratification grounded in "noble restraint". When Louis first saw this gently bred young girl he simply stood and stared until eventually he summoned the courage to address her; and when he did he spoke shyly of hunting, of dogs and of flower gardens. Marie de Hautefort was then fifteen years of age.

Very soon he was meeting his young *confidante* daily, and occasionally he would speak of the Cardinal and of the pressure that this powerful man brought to bear on him; he often criticized him. When he did so the young girl, who was growing up under the Queen's influence and was entirely devoted to her, concurred wholeheartedly and sought to strengthen Louis' rancour. Richelieu was of course informed at once, and de Hautefort's days at Court soon came to an end. As a replacement the Cardinal introduced the daughter of Jean de La Fayette, who was descended from a Marshal of France, into Anne's Court as a maid of honour. Unlike de Hautefort, who was blonde, Marie Louise de La Fayette was a dark beauty; as had been expected, the King soon turned his attention towards her.

This idyll followed much the same course as its predecessor. The King quickly found that Marie Louise was indispensable to him and sought her company daily. But she too remained loyal to the Queen and steadfastly opposed the Cardinal's influence. This relationship was also restricted to conversations and confessions.

And so once again Richelieu's attempt to use a woman's influence for his own ends failed. He had also brought pressure to bear on this young girl, and when it proved ineffectual he tried to get her out of the way by forcing her to take the veil. She anticipated him; in order to escape from an intolerable situation she withdrew into the convent of Sainte-Marie on May 19, 1637. For some months the King visited her regularly, and it would seem that she continued to assert a strong moral influence on him, similar to that exercised by the nun Maria de Agreda on Philip IV. De Hautefort is said to have been jealous of this young woman who had "fled from the world", and there was even a brief *rapprochement* between her and the

King, which caused Richelieu some anxiety, for he feared she might abandon her former reserve in an attempt to establish a stronger bond with the monarch. Women had proved a disappointment to him, and in his anger he generalized on the whole sex:

"This species is astounding. 'Occasionally one is inclined to believe that, just as they are incapable of doing anything really good, so too they are incapable of doing any great harm. But upon my life there is nothing more calculated to destroy a nation than women . . ."

These private affairs would seem of little consequence but for the fact that the opposition immediately exploited them.

It was not only the "women", however, who worked against Richelieu in the King's immediate circle. We have already mentioned Louis's confessor, the Jesuit Father Caussin; he also tried to influence the King against the Cardinal. For a long time Richelieu considered him to be "naïve and good-natured" and consequently harmless. But perhaps he was simply a man of strong character with the courage and determination to suffer any and every consequence. He consistently tried to bring about the downfall of the man whom he regarded as a tyrant. He held him responsible for the unspeakable misery endured by the nation and censured him, like the *dévotes* before him, for having concluded Protestant alliances. But he tolerated the King's friendships with women, especially his relationship to La Fayette, partly because they fitted in with his own plans but also because he was convinced that they were innocent; had not the King himself said: "There must never be adultery in my house"? He reproached Louis for other reasons; like Francis I, Louis was trying to unleash the Turk on Christendom. Louis' answer to this charge was that he would be happy to see the Turk in Madrid, although once he was there he would unite with the Spanish in driving him out.—But how could His Majesty take such decisions upon himself, the priest asked, to which Louis replied that he never took any decisions without first consulting learned theologians as to the justice of his cause. Paid agents, the confessor retorted, who had received 2,000 thalers from Richelieu! He urged Louis to authorize his wife to negotiate a peace with Spain and he spoke with warmth of the Queen Mother. Again and again he insisted that the sovereign should not allow himself to be governed by any one person but should listen to the opinions of all. The priest went very far when he expressed his surprise that the Cardinal should be treating the Queen so badly, for he had once loved her and still felt a deep affection for her. A friend of Richelieu's is said to have described this imputation as the blackest slander ever to have come from the mind of a cleric. One day the King himself admitted to Chavigny that the reverend father had got him into such a state in the confessional that he had been going in dread of eternal damnation. Caussin had blamed him for all the horrors and misery of the war, and time and again he had pressed for Richelieu's removal from office and even for his arrest. The Jesuit's political views were the same as Bérulle's and Marillac's. Matters then took their inevitable course.

Louis had been impressed by his confessor's exhortations, which had been reinforced by La Fayette, and the members of his entourage found him extremely pensive, almost dejected. Finally he decided to have a discussion with the Cardinal, at which Caussin would be called upon to put his case, which he would then support. He asked Caussin to travel to Rueil on December 9, 1637, explaining that he himself would arrive shortly afterwards and would immediately call him into his presence. Although loath to do so, Caussin complied with this request. Richelieu received him coldly and when the King's arrival was announced he showed the priest to the room where he was to wait. When the King asked, "Has Father Caussin arrived?" Richelieu replied: "Yes, but he has already left again." The King then reproduced the substance of his conversations with the priest, and Richelieu refuted all the charges made against him. Louis defended his confessor and claimed that he had acted in good faith. Richelieu then asked the King to choose between his confessor and his Minister. Louis did so unequivocally, and by the time the monarch left Rueil Caussin was already a lost man. Meanwhile the Jesuit, who had been outsmarted so quickly and so easily, remained quite unaware of the fact; he waited until late in the evening for the tripartite discussion to take place. Night had already fallen when he left the Cardinal's residence.

When the King received him only very briefly on December 10th, he still suspected nothing; twenty-four hours later his papers were confiscated and he himself was banished, first to Rennes and shortly afterwards to Quimper.

But prior to this incident other and far graver events had taken place.

Anne of Austria was being kept in isolation. She felt lonely and bored and, since she had no children, she feared Louis might repudiate her. This strengthened her attachment to Spain and her Hapsburg pride. In the course of that same year, 1637, she conducted a treasonable correspondence with Marie de Chevreuse, who had been banished to Tours and was doing her utmost to prevail upon the Queen to oppose Richelieu's policies and to establish contact with Spain. Anne of Austria then wrote to her younger brother, the Cardinal-Infante, and also—through the agency of Mirabel, the former Spanish ambassador to France—to Philip IV himself. Amongst other things, she advised the Spanish that the French government had sent a mendicant friar to Spain as a spy and urged them to keep a careful watch on his movements; she also told them of the negotiations then being conducted with Lorraine and even gave information about French troop movements. She had always written her letters in the convent of Val-de-Grâce, where she went to pray and where she had thought herself to be unobserved. Her faithful servant La Porte, whom we encountered during Richelieu's journey back to Paris from Montmorency's execution, had then put her letters in code;

those intended for Spain he gave to a Secretary at the English embassy by the name of Anger, who forwarded them to Brussels or Madrid, while those addressed to the tireless Marie de Chevreuse were delivered by a certain Chevalier de la Thibaudière, who paid regular visits to Tours, where the banished Duchess held her gay Court, which had become a centre for malcontents. Evidently Richelieu's police had won over this Thibaudière. One day, when La Porte tried to pass him a letter in the Louvre, he told him that he had to stay in Paris longer than he had intended and asked La Porte to keep the letter for him until the following day. La Porte, unsuspecting, paid a visit to a wounded officer with the Queen's letter in his pocket. He was seized on the street, bundled into a carriage and taken to the Bastille. Richelieu interrogated him there in person. He was given a choice: torture if he refused to talk, release if he agreed. He refused and withstood the torture; he did not betray his mistress by as much as a word.

Richelieu then sent Chancellor Séguier, accompanied by the Archbishop of Paris, Jean François de Gondi, to question the Reverend Mother of the Convent of Val-de-Grâce. She was ordered under pain of excommunication to state whether Her Majesty the Queen had written to the Marqués de Mirabel. She replied: "The Queen often wrote letters but nobody knew to whom." The Reverend Mother and three other sisters were immediately expelled from the convent and sent to the abbey of La Charité.

The Queen put up a spirited resistance. At first she had intended to flee to Brussels disguised as a pageboy but was obliged to give up this fantastic project; she then resolutely denied everything. On August 15, 1637, the Feast of the Assumption, she took communion and then sent for her secretary, Le Gras, and swore to him on the sacrament she had just received that she had never sent information abroad. After this she told Le Gras to inform the Cardinal of her oath. But when she discovered that far more was known about her than she had suspected, and after Richelieu had assured her that the

King was prepared to forgive and forget provided she made a full confession, she suddenly broke down and wept. She told him everything and repeated several times: "How good you must be, Monsieur le Cardinal."

She assured Richelieu that she would be grateful to him for the rest of her life, and then she did something that was most unusual in a Spanish *Infanta*: "Give me your hand," she said and held out her own right hand in order to set a solemn seal on their reconciliation. But the Cardinal retreated several paces and murmured that respect for Her Majesty forbade him to accept such a mark of distinction. He maintained his reserve, refrained from any expression of feeling and succeeded in prevailing upon the Queen to sign a document, in which all her misdemeanours were enumerated. Louis then gave a written declaration that he was prepared to forgive her and to continue living with her on friendly terms. But the Cardinal set down the Queen's perjury in detail and so informed posterity, not without malice, of her grave lapse.

Towards the end of that year an event occurred which totally transformed many aspects of the prevailing situation and banished hopes and fears that had been entertained for decades. At the beginning of December 1637, the King went to visit Mademoiselle de La Fayette in her convent—a practice that had become habitual with him—with the intention of proceeding subsequently to Saint-Maur, where he proposed to spend the night. While he was with the novice in the reception room a violent snowstorm began. It seemed inadvisable for the King to continue his journey and one of his retinue suggested that they proceed to the Louvre. But the King's apartments in the *Palais* were unheated and the beds unmade. Louis hesitated to spend the night with the Queen but eventually agreed to do so. Anne of Austria received him with great cordiality. The King stayed with her, and nine months later, on September 5, 1638, the new heir-apparent was born, the child who was later to become Louis XIV and who had been awaited for twenty-six years.

Gaston d'Orléans

It might be thought that the birth of a son and heir would have led to Orléans' eclipse, but that was not the case. He still drew all the malcontents, all the opponents of the régime, into his circle; France's external enemies went on trying to win this Prince for their plans and to use him in their undertakings. Until quite late in the period of the Fronde people continued to hope for effective action and leadership from this son of Henry IV, who never failed to disappoint but who never failed to enchant. As for the son of Louis XIII and Anne of Austria, he was already threatened in his cradle and was to remain so throughout the whole of his childhood, a fact that explains many of his later actions and despotic ways.

Orléans was always bringing his influence to bear both on Richelieu's work and on his private life. The Cardinal once said that the petty intrigues of the Court were more dangerous than the great designs of territorial Princes. And it is true that the friction in his life was provided by matters near to home, by day-to-day events, by the constant and incalculable influence brought to bear on the head of state, Louis XIII, by the need to combat the treachery and other base actions of the members of the King's entourage.

The relations between Louis XIII and his younger brother could well form the basis of a tragedy. In Richelieu's day the interest taken in the intimate affairs of powerful families was of a different order than that prevalent in later times. In the seventeenth century there was no analysis of the individual's psychological development; instead, everything was related to a highly specific typology. In fact, every case was assessed in terms of its social and above all its political consequences, as was done by both La Rochefoucauld and Vauvenargues.

Since the case we are considering involved a King and a Prince who had been heir-apparent from 1610 to 1638, the relations between these two Bourbons were not only highly charged but also had a very real significance. We possess an inordinate amount of contemporary comment on Orléans. On the basis of this abundant source material most later commentators have arrived at a distinctly negative assessment of the Prince. He has been described as dissolute, untruthful, treacherous and entirely self-seeking. But he has also found his partisans, who have stressed his kindness, his wit (which was so reminiscent of his father) and even his courage, which he occasionally displayed in the face of the enemy. Many have spoken of the wide scope of his foreign-policy conceptions, which, they claim, were intended to promote a balance of power in Europe. Reference has been made to special circumstances, which are said to have exercised a pernicious influence on his childhood and youth.

Like Frederick the Great on the death of his friend Katte, Orléans received an early and lasting wound when his close friend Chalais, whom he had loved and then abandoned, was executed in 1626 to be followed to the block a year later by another intimate friend, François de Bouteville Montmorency. Orléans never forgave Richelieu, whom he held responsible for these sentences, not even when, despite everything, the Cardinal took his part and protected him. Gaston participated in every attempt on the life of the hated First Minister. But because he was frivolous to the point of irresponsibility in matters of planning and lacked drive and stability in the sphere of action, in a word because he was weak-willed, he was never able to put his project into effect.

A strange triangular relationship existed within the royal household. When he was two years old Gaston lost his father and his mother's regency began. There is evidence that Henry IV preferred his youngest son. We have also seen that Marie de' Medici felt a positive dislike for the oldest boy and missed no opportunity of demonstrating her own preference for his young brother, whom she pampered. Louis, on the other hand, received an extremely harsh and strict upbringing. He once remarked: "I would prefer to receive less reverence and fewer whippings." At the time he was ten years old.

Gaston, so called after his ancestor Gaston de Foix, was first known as Gaston d'Anjou; Louis XIII used to refer to him as "my brother Anjou." In November 1611, when Henry and Marie's second son died at the age of four, Gaston inherited his title. From then on he was called "Orléans et Chartres" or, as was the custom, simply "Monsieur." When Henry IV chose the patronymic of Anjou for his third legitimate son he made the following characteristic remark:

"I would have liked to call him Navarre, but as Prince of Navarre he might have been tempted to harass and importune my first born." In point of fact the Orléans branch of the Bourbon dynasty was to pose a constant threat to the older line right down to the time of Philippe Egalité and Louis Philippe.

As a child Louis XIII was reserved and obstinate, and this always roused his mother's anger. By contrast, Orléans was enterprising and so communicative that he would often betray both himself and his friends simply for the sake of a *bon mot*. He was a womanizer and, unlike his inhibited brother, an un-restrained hedonist. We have seen that he was even able to charm his own mother. This tormented Louis and his torment grew into a gnawing jealousy which, despite the countless disputes and the countless solemn or sentimental reconcilia-tions that took place between the two brothers, never dimin-ished. But even in their most serious quarrels Louis and Gaston respected their "sanctified blood"; even when the King im-posed the harshest punishments on Gaston's confidants and helpers he always judged Gaston himself and his actions by a special standard.

After his older brother had died and when he himself was only three, Orléans was engaged to the seven-year-old Marie de Montpensier, the richest heiress in France. In fact Gaston inherited this engagement together with his title from his dead brother. On August 24, 1624, when the heir-apparent was sixteen years old, he danced with his fiancée in public at the ball held in the Palais du Luxembourg to mark the completion of the frescoes by Peter Paul Rubens. Many of those present were of the opinion that the time was not far distant when Gaston would eclipse the reigning King. This was why Louis constantly placed new obstacles in the way of his brother's marriage even though his mother approved of the match. Richelieu, as always, thought only of the dynastic succession and was therefore opposed to his sovereign on this issue.

On August 5, 1626, the Cardinal formally renewed the engagement between the heir-apparent and Marie de Montpensier in the King's antechamber in the royal castle of Nantes. The wedding was celebrated the very next day in the local Franciscan church. It was preceded by holy mass but accompanied by no festivities. One of the guests present at the ceremony wrote that there had never been such a dismal wedding; the bride wore a white satin dress and was adorned with her own and the Queen-Mother's pearls, but Monsieur had appeared in an old suit and all day long they had heard neither fiddles nor any other kind of music.

Marie de Montpensier brought to the House of Orléans the great wealth and the ducal title it was to retain until the French Revolution. One year after her marriage she died in childbirth. She had been quite convinced that her child would be a boy but in fact it was a girl, who subsequently came to be known as the "Grande Mademoiselle," the bold and manly Princess who played a leading part in the Fronde, opposing Mazarin and the young Louis XIV. In their reports the observers whom Richelieu had placed in Orléans' service expressed their surprise at the violence and duration of his grief. When Louis XIII heard that Orléans' wife had died in giving birth to a daughter his reaction was ambiguous. During Marie's pregnancy Richelieu had taken a keen interest in her welfare. It was then that he sold his castle of Limours to Monsieur for a very high price. In the course of that year, when Richelieu had sought closer contact with the young couple, Orléans once said to him: "If Madame should be delivered of a son I hope that one day he will become a Cardinal."

"Why a Cardinal?" Richelieu asked.

"Because in France the Cardinals control everything," the Duke replied.

The day following his wife's death Orléans said that God had taken her from him to punish him for his wanton ways but that it was not possible for him to live a chaste life, for he was the son of Henry IV, the great daredevil. Orléans never failed to criticize his own shortcomings, and his one great wish was to prove his worth. This wish was never fulfilled. There was only one brief time in his life when he was able to show his mettle, and that was at the siege of La Rochelle. Richelieu then wrote to him: "The fact that the Island of Ré is again receiving aid thanks to your presence, your authority and your prudence affords me great pleasure." And on another occasion he wrote: "You have made allowance for everything. ... Those who are further from the scene cannot judge the situation as accurately as you. You know precisely what needs to be done and what can be done. I place my trust in your leadership, your courage and your good fortune."

But on October 12th the King joined the army and Orléans' activities came to an end. He had been checked in his stride, thrust out of the limelight, and on November 16th the disenchanted Duke returned to Paris.

Although loath to do so, he then promised Marie de' Medici that he would contract a marriage with the House of Florence if she would obtain a military command for him. But immediately afterwards he began to pay court to the daughter of the Duke of Nevers, the Gonzaga who had passed such scornful remarks on the bourgeois origins of the Florentine suzerains; it seemed as if he was trying to touch the Queen-Mother on one of her sorest points. Marie gave the King no peace until he agreed to oppose his brother's Mantuan aspirations in every possible way. Orléans approached Bassompierre, who had been a close friend of his father's, and asked him what he thought the King would say if he were to marry Princess Marie Louisa, the Duke of Nevers' daughter.

Bassompierre replied morosely that that would be the least of Louis' worries.

It was thanks to Richelieu that, shortly after his return to the capital, Orléans was given the prospect of commanding the army intended for the protection of Mantua in the War of Succession, which was then threatening. Richelieu wrote: "In my opinion His Majesty should make this offer to Monsieur." But Louis could not bring himself to give his younger brother another opportunity of distinguishing himself and declared that he was not yet in a position to raise an army worthy of the heir-apparent.

Orléans' later development was greatly influenced by the King's early attitude towards him and also by the Queen-Mother's blind desire to see the downfall of the House of Nevers and the end of the Mantuan dynasty. These factors, coupled with Gaston's relations to the House of Lorraine and his marriage to Charles IV's sister, were the cause of all subsequent complications in the relations between the two brothers.

But whenever the nation was in danger or there was an opportunity of winning glory for France, Gaston immediately broke off the close ties that he formed with foreign powers as a means of bringing pressure to bear on the King and offered to take command of an army and fight in the field. The King was never able to bring himself to permit his brother to win real honour for himself. When he distinguished himself, as at the siege of La Rochelle, Louis withdrew his command. But when Gaston took the path of treason and placed his own honour in jeopardy reconciliation followed at once; the King took him to his heart, paid his debts and furnished him with money: Gaston was also the son of "Henry the Great", he was the brother of the "anointed King".

The heir-apparent, in whom so many had placed their hopes—for the King was a sick man and during the first twenty-six years of his reign had no direct heir—possessed a trait, which he revealed at an early age and which has since won him many advocates, especially among recent historians: Gaston d'Orléans had what we would call a social conscience. It has been assumed that this was inculcated in him as a child by Savary de Brèves, a former ambassador to the Sublime Porte; from 1614 to 1618 Brèves was his principal tutor but was sacrificed to Louis' mistrust at an all too early stage. Orléans said at the time: "If M. de Brèves is incompetent, why was he assigned to me as my tutor? If he is competent, why is he being taken from me?" This state of affairs was to continue. The position of private tutor to Orléans was a perilous one, as is clear from the case of Ornano (cf. Vol. I, Chap. XIII).

In 1615, during the civil war when the Court was away from Paris, the seven-year-old Gaston attended a meeting of the Council of War, which was being held at the Arsenal. The magistrates and military men were discussing the requisitioning of horses for the artillery. Suddenly the child interrupted them and said at the top of his voice:

"It is not necessary to take the poor people's horses away from them and disturb them in their work. It would be better to leave the horses [on the farms], where the artillery can always find them. To start with, draught horses should be hired in the city and the farmers should be left in peace."

Those present were greatly surprised and also amused. One of them said:

"Bring him something to drink, otherwise he will give us no peace."

But the lad replied:

"This is no laughing matter. You should save your laughter for other occasions."

On leaving the Council meeting he said:

"I spoke up on behalf of the people; some of the others were cruel. If M. de Bassompierre had not looked at me the way he did I would have said more."

On another occasion, when Orléans was travelling to Rouen, where he was to assist at the opening of the Assembly of Notables, his tutor said to him: "We have passed through many villages on our journey and everywhere we have seen people dressed in rags and looking like skeletons. And you, Monsieur, have not asked me the cause of their misery." Gaston then asked Brèves to enlighten him:

"Well, you see, Monsieur, if a body is covered with leeches it soon loses all its blood and is reduced to mere skin and bones. The comparison is apt, for that is the condition of our poor people; not only do they have to carry the whole burden of taxation, they are also being ruined by the eternal revolts of the great nobles. The miserable existence endured by these peasants, who wander through the land living off grass like animals, is due to the excesses of the rough soldiery, who are the King's subjects and are fed from the state coffers."

Fourteen years later, when Gaston faced the King at the head of a hostile army, he published a manifesto in which he addressed the monarch in the following words:

"I have not left the Court in order to sow discord in your State or disturb the peace of your subjects. But I have seen the misery with my own eyes and God knows that I would give my blood to bring relief."

He spoke of Richelieu as "an inhuman and perverted priest, if not indeed a Godless criminal, who is betraying his vows and has introduced a reign of perfidy, cruelty and coercion . . ." And he went on to warn Louis:

"Beware of the pitiable condition to which France has been reduced by the Cardinal's ambition. He is forcibly destroying all the natural orders of the realm . . . , throttling every independent corporation, silencing them and denying them access to His Majesty, thus preventing them from fulfilling their principal duty, which is to tell His Majesty the truth . . . I do not wish to enumerate in detail the various malpractices whereby he [the Cardinal] has brought France to such a pitch . . . I merely wish to say that I have seen it all. Today less than a third of the people living on the plains eat real bread. Some live on oats while others not only are reduced to begging but are in such misery that the greater part are dying from starvation. Those who survive do so on a diet of acorns, grass and the like, just like the beasts of the fields; or else they eat bran and drink the blood from the gullies of the slaughterhouses."

This actually was the state of affairs in large areas of the country.

But the King had had to choose between Marillac's policy of internal reform, Bérulle's plans for establishing a balance of power by peaceful means and Richelieu's anti-Hapsburg war policy. He had made his choice.

As leader of the opposition Orléans was not only the natural but also the inevitable choice. We shall come to see, however, that he was quite unsuited to the part.

When he was denied his command in the Mantuan War of Succession Orléans blamed the Cardinal. This was unjust. The truth of the matter was that the King wanted to lead the army himself. The offended heir-apparent had then proceeded to Grenoble, where he learned of the death of the Grand Prior of Vendôme. It was at this time that he was intent on marrying Maria Gonzaga against his mother's wishes. Acting on the false assumption that the Princess was still in the Louvre, Gaston returned to Orléans to await further developments. He did not know that Marie de' Medici, fearing the Princess might be abducted, had placed her in safekeeping in Vincennes. At first the heir-apparent wanted to effect a reconciliation with the King but only on the understanding that he would not have to return to Court. However, when he discovered that Louis was not interested in a reconciliation he followed the advice of his counsellors, Le Coigneux and Puylaurens, and crossed over into Lorraine. In Nancy he lived a life of splendour, incurred debts and, in order to pay them, demanded a larger appanage. To obtain it he gave in to his mother's wishes, whereupon, on January 2, 1630, he was immediately restored to favour and endowed with the Duchies of Orléans and Valois. He had a personal meeting with the King on February 17th, at which both brothers made great protestations of friendship and Gaston was appointed Lieutenant General of Paris and the adjacent provinces. As always when he thought he had been entrusted with a responsible office, Orléans took his duties seriously. In Champagne he set up frontier guards and required the governor of the province to keep him informed of all troop movements. Rightly anticipating revolts on account of the famine, he arranged for extra supplies of food to be brought into the northern cities. He remained in constant touch with Charles of Lorraine and subsequently often asserted that it was thanks only to his intervention that Imperial troops had not marched into Lorraine in 1630.

By then the strongest bond between Marie de' Medici and her youngest son was their shared hatred of Richelieu. Whenever Gaston appeared to be reacting positively to the many accommodating gestures extended to him by the Cardinal, his relationship to the Queen-Mother grew strained. However, there was no danger that he would ever forget what Richelieu had done to him. He never got over the Ornano, Chalais and de Bouteville affairs, and, like his father before him, he loved and favoured the great nobles; Richelieu's attitude to this class he found utterly repugnant.

But the moment Marie de' Medici was persecuted Gaston went over to her camp entirely. It was against this background that he undertook the strange attempt on Richelieu's life of January 30, 1631, which we have already discussed. We know that, following this escapade, he made for Orléans the same evening; once there, he raised money, recruited troops and entered into secret negotiations with the Spanish Ambassador. This persuaded Louis that it would be advisable to have his brother brought back to Paris, and to this end he ordered a powerful escort to set out for Orléans in early March. At this Gaston left the city accompanied by four hundred cavaliers.

On March 13, 1631, he stayed in Sully's castle on the Loire; it was as if he had stepped back into his father's world again. He then continued his journey to Burgundy, where he addressed the peasants, and returned to France via Franche-Comté. At this point his property was confiscated and certain members of his entourage were arrested.

Meanwhile Marie de' Medici had fled to Brussels and the conversations between mother and son then extended from Epinal to the capital city of the Spanish Netherlands. On January 3, 1632, Gaston and Marguerite of Lorraine contracted their sudden marriage, whose validity Richelieu proceeded to dispute with every conceivable legal argument and by constant diplomatic interventions. In the same year Gaston instigated the revolt which collapsed so lamentably at Castelnaudary. Following this defeat the heir-apparent accused his mother of having driven him into rebellion. In May 1633 secret meetings were held between Gaston's representatives, who included Guy d'Elbène, and Richelieu to negotiate the heir-apparent's return to France. But in June 1633 Monsieur was still with the Spanish forces in Maastricht. He then made outright proposals to the French Court. But, as we have already seen, his young wife then joined him in Brussels and he decided to make his marriage public. On March 30, 1634, he wrote a long letter to his brother entreating him to recognize his wife.

The Infanta Isabella, who had been well disposed towards Gaston, died on December 2, 1633. Her successor in the Spanish Netherlands, Francisco de Moncada, had always regarded Orléans as unreliable and dangerous and so made him give contractual guarantees that he would not effect a reconciliation with his brother for a number of years. An emissary, whom Orléans sent to the Pope to plead his marriage case, was intercepted by Richelieu's police. It was only after the Battle of Nördlingen that conditions were ripe for fruitful negotiations between the two brothers. By then Richelieu had become somewhat more flexible and Gaston was told that, although his marriage would be judged by the laws of the land, he would not be forced to remarry against his will. He was promised that his and his nobles' estates would be restored, that he would be given four hundred thousand livres with which to settle his debts and that Puylaurens, his principal adviser, would be made a duke. On October 21, 1634, Louis and Gaston met in Saint-Germain and, as so often before, all was forgiven. After his return from Flanders Gaston first lived in Blois and Paris. He wrote to his wife from La Capelle, assuring her that he would never desert her. Apart from a few diplomatic concessions, he kept his word; when asked if he was thinking of remarrying he replied that he was not for he already had a lawfully wedded wife. As for Puylaurens, he contracted a marriage on November 28th of the same year with a cousin of Cardinal Richelieu, Mademoiselle de Pontchâteau, and vowed that he would prevail upon Gaston to repudiate Marguerite of Lorraine. He was, he said, prepared to stake his life on it. But he vowed in vain and consequently he and his friends, du Fargis and du Coudray, were conducted from Montpensier to Vincennes and the Bastille. Gaston refused to sacrifice his wife for his friends. On July 1, 1635, Puylaurens died in Vincennes. Was he poisoned? Tallemant reports that saltpetre formed on the walls of the narrow cells and that prisoners, like Ornano for example, were wont to die of arsenical poisoning at the end of four months.

Puylaurens' disgrace was discussed in an article inspired by Richelieu which appeared in the *Gazette*:

"There are three points to be noted with regard to this affair: the King's affection for Monsieur, whom he loves not only as a brother but as his own son; the sensible attitude adopted by the Duke of Orléans, who showed . . . prudence and moderation and proved that the power of the blood royal and the voice of reason outweighed all other considerations, and finally the great zeal displayed by His Eminence in the King's service . . ."

Orléans, in his vacillating way, would also take a short-lived stand on non-political matters. The Cardinal therefore kept a strict watch on his relations to certain circles among the Paris intelligentsia. Although this group was still small, Richelieu recognized in it a potential threat to the myth of the monarchy; for the time being, however, he made use of it against the *dévotes* and ultramontanes.

Libertines and Atheists

In the age of great Catholic reform in which he lived Richelieu paid particular attention to the emergence of anti-religious currents in the intellectual circles of the capital, maintaining an ironical, indulgent and somewhat indeterminate relationship to the leaders of this movement, who were also closely linked with the heir-presumptive prior to 1638.

A certain Father Mersenne wrote a book entitled *The Unbelief of the Deists, Atheists and Libertines of our Time Refuted Point by Point on Philosophical and Theological Grounds, etc.* In this work, which he dedicated to Richelieu, Mersenne claimed that there were at least forty thousand atheists living in Paris. A contemporary teacher of rhetoric composed 106 atheist quatrains and disseminated them throughout Paris and large areas of the provinces.

The leading figure among these aggressive freethinkers was the poet Théophile de Viau, who wrote under the name of M. Théophile. Though frequently prosecuted and sentenced by the authorities, he was always released again thanks to the intervention of powerful patrons. Théophile exercised a strong influence on the wealthy young men in Court circles. He referred to himself as an Epicurean. Most of his *confrères* had passed through a phase of scepticism inspired by Montaigne. These Epicureans developed into a sect which spread from Paris to the countryside, propagating quite openly a hedonistic paganism that was both highly inventive and basically insipid; besides de Viau, Boisrobert, Saint-Amant and Faret were its exponents. Montmorency indulged Théophile de Viau for his wit, Harcourt kept Faret in food and drink, while Saint-Amant was appointed Chamberlain to Maria of Gonzaga. The Epicureans celebrated black masses, summoned up spirits and elicited the repeated approbation of Gaston d'Orléans, who, however, was just as apt to urge those of his friends who frequented such circles to return to the Church. That Richelieu—a statesman as well as a Cardinal—occasionally sought the favour and approval of these people was one of the facts that startled public opinion in the capital; his opponents, the *dévotes*, did not benefit from the activities of these libertines.

A letter written by Richelieu to Count Bautru de Serran, dated October 11, 1626, shows that he was in tenuous contact with the Parisian group. It reads:

"Monsieur, I am sending somebody for news from you but do not mention this to those of your comrades who attended Théophile's funeral, for I fear they might then think I was made of the same stuff as you are. Your young friend asserts that your soul stands in greater need of purging than your body, but my 'little doctor' assures me that the keening women of Paris would have good cause to weep if you were to disappear from the scene. From this I assume that he does not regard your illness as serious. Father Guron sees things in a different light and considers that decent people would have more reason to laugh than to cry if the world were rid of your person.... Cure your body, cleanse your soul and rest assured that I, who hope for your conversion, will remain your devoted servant, Cardinal Richelieu."

A light-hearted tone for such a serious man! But Bautru was one of his entourage, as was Father Guron (de Rechigne-voisin), the other wit in his circle, who spoke to the Cardinal as blithely as he was spoken to. After all, this was the century of Brantôme. Both Henry IV and Bassompierre, who had spent their lives on the battlefield, were close in spirit to these hedonists. As for the women—the Princess of Rohan, Marie de Chevreuse, the Duchess of Rohan and the Duchess of Longueville—they lived at Court in a Rabelaisian atmosphere. Often enough this free living led to a bad end, especially when its exponents approached the dark spheres of magic. There were affairs like those of the possessed women of Vervins and Chartres, there was the execution of the priest Gaufridy, who was accused of being in league with the devil. Vanino Vanini, a scholar and philosopher, was condemned as a blasphemer by the parlement of Toulouse: first his tongue was torn out, then he was burnt. In his "Instructions for a Christian Life" Richelieu the Cardinal harangued the superstitious, "people who are perturbed to find the moon on their left and not on their right when they first catch sight of it." The wits who succeeded in the *salons*, those great masters of the daring word, stood poised on trapdoors which might open at any time beneath their feet. But all these worldly activities were counterbalanced by an ecclesiastical and more especially a mystical revival. Since Henry IV's conversion the King of France was once again "His Most Christian Majesty". Nor should we forget that the Jesuits had returned to France in 1603.

But—quite apart from the great spiritual processes then being enacted—the strivings of the rational sceptics for liberation, the aberrant passions unleashed by frightful pagan visions from past ages, and brutal, undisguised greed which capitalized on every disturbance combined to create a seething current which from time to time engulfed individuals and groups. The State intervened as the swordbearer of justice and the representative of order that had to be continually reimposed since it was continually endangered by famine, epidemics of plague, revolts, abject poverty in contrast to the sumptuous display of riches.

The Loudun Affair

On May 13, 1622, Louis XIII, who was at the time in

Royan, conferred the domains, equipment, moats and ramparts of the fortified castle of Loudun, which had once served the Huguenots as a stronghold, on Monsieur d'Armagnac, a First Chamberlain, and Monsieur Lucas, the "secrétaire de main", by letters patent, the ostensible reason being that His Majesty might wish to have the castle razed; it was stipulated, however, that the tower, at the time occupied by the Governor, Jean d'Armagnac, should be left standing provisionally, to protect the town. When this bulwark was later demolished, the responsibility was wrongly attributed to Richelieu, who, it was alleged, regarded this powerful stronghold as a threat to his newly acquired Duchy. Actually, in 1622, Richelieu had no influence whatever in matters of this kind. Furthermore, it was only in 1631 that he was made a Duke and Peer of France. In 1622 the project was entirely a matter of the King's intentions and of his liberality towards two of his dependents.

Loudun itself, then the departmental capital of Vienna in western France, was a centre of considerable tensions between the religious parties. A treaty of 1606, which took its name from Loudun, had given the Protestants substantial benefits. In the early seventeenth century a Jesuit-trained canon, Urbain Grandier, exerted considerable influence there, as a well-informed, celebrated preacher. Talented and attractive—though more to women than to men—he was also censured by some of the townspeople for his vanity. Following the publication of a pamphlet in which he took issue with the vow of celibacy imposed on the priesthood, he became a subject of controversy throughout the realm. Grandier drew a clear distinction between monks and secular priests. The monk, he maintained, had chosen chastity because he found it attractive whereas the priest had been forced to accept it. Convinced by his own arguments, Grandier allowed "the law of nature" to run its course. But among the many relationships which he allegedly established with the weaker sex, one involving a young girl of good family was to prove a threat to him. The threat might well have blown over if Grandier,

263

who was on particularly good terms with the Governor, Jean d'Armagnac, had not become involved in the demolition of the castle, a measure which had aroused the indignation of the local inhabitants, especially the Huguenots. Grandier placed great hopes in his relationship to this nobleman, who frequented the Court, where he regarded himself as a kind of provincial emissary to the King, and who had gained some insight as an onlooker into Court intrigues, for example those conducted by the Duchess of Chevreuse and Châteauneuf.

With regard to the profits which were expected to accrue from the razing of the citadel, Armagnac and Lucas were of course natural rivals. Initially, however, it seemed as if both men were prepared to share the proceeds on an equal basis. But then, before Armagnac had realized what was going on, the King's secretary had begun to intrigue against him. As we have already seen, the original order was given in 1622. But in 1630 the citadel was still standing. Then, in 1631, the King at last commanded Marshal Schomberg to proceed with the demolition of the fortress with the exception of the tower. The man commissioned to carry out the work was Jean Martin, Baron of Laubardemont, a native of Bordeaux, an expert in demolition work and was also in summary trials.

A native of western France, Laubardemont was familiar with that part of the country and had already razed the castle of Mirebeau in 1629 and the citadel of Royan. In fact, he was a specialist in two spheres: demolition and forcible conversion. He had functioned with great success in witchcraft trials. Laubardemont was hourly awaited in Loudun but failed to appear. It was learned that he had been detained in Paris, and very soon it was known why: the little town of Loudun had been talked about in the capital and Richelieu had developed a keen interest, not only in the prompt and total destruction of the castle but also in rumours concerning certain happenings in this town that was situated so close to his new Duchy. Armagnac, who insisted on the original under-takings and wanted to keep the tower as his home, was becoming a nuisance. But he had his weak points. One of these was soon discovered by Laubardemont: the Governor was protecting Grandier, about whom so many scandalous tales were told, both true and untrue, and who had already preferred a charge of slander against the town apothecary and scandalmonger, a man by the name of Adam. Among Grandier's many enemies was a certain Manceau, an advocate and fluent orator who had wanted to marry the young lady seduced by the priest, Madeleine de Brou, the best match in the town. But jealousy operates in many spheres. A cleric with the endearing name of Mignon felt embittered by his colleague's success as a preacher. He gave passionate support to the campaign against Grandier, who promptly arraigned him before the courts on behalf of the canons of the Church of Sainte-Croix. Mignon was found guilty. At that point Jacques de Thibault, a member of the local gentry and a distant relative of the seduced girl, entered the scene; with complete disregard for Grandier's priestly robes he thrashed him on the main street of the town. At the same time the archpriest of Loudun appealed to the Bishop of Poitiers to deal with the anti-celibatarian.

This high prelate, La Rocheposay, was not only a bishop; he was also a militant and determined man. He had no love for the Jesuits and Grandier had come from their ranks; Rocheposay was a Jansenist and his Vicar General was the celebrated Duvergier de Hauranne, Bérulle's friend and later Abbot of Saint-Cyran.

While Grandier was charging Thibault with assault in Paris the bishop issued a warrant for his arrest, and when Thibault was summoned to appear in the capital the bishop's warrant arrived in Loudun commanding Grandier to proceed to Poitiers to give account of himself. Grandier had to obey. Once there, he was thrown into prison without ceremony. On January 3, 1630, sentence was passed: on every Friday for the next three months the insubordinate priest was to live on bread and water; he was also relieved of his ecclesiastical duties until further notice and forbidden to resume his pastoral office in Loudun. But Grandier remained in good spirits. He knew that in Armagnac he possessed an advocate at Court, and on the day of his release from prison he received a letter from his protector in which he was told: "I will not abandon you but will help you to the very end."

A complex case: already it was being fought by the secular authorities, who were soon to be joined by their ecclesiastical counterparts. A witness who had testified against Grandier, accusing him of sacrilege, withdrew his statement and Grandier won his case before the civil court in Poitiers after it had been transferred there by the parlement of Paris. Shortly afterwards he also appealed to Sourdis, the Archbishop of Bordeaux, who was senior to Rocheposay, and was acquitted of all the charges previously brought against him by the Bishop of Poitiers; this moral victory enabled him to return to Loudun.

Immediately after this incident an epidemic of plague broke out in the town. With complete disregard for his personal safety Grandier worked day and night to help the sick. This raised his prestige but it also revived his former boldness.

Meanwhile Armagnac had actually spoken to the King about his protégé and succeeded in convincing him of his innocence. He also fondly imagined that the arrangements regarding the demolition of the castle had been settled in his favour. But Schomberg had been instructed by the King to place Laubardemont in charge of the demolition work while Armagnac wrongly assumed that the Baron would be his ally. Behind the scenes the intrigues continued.

Laubardemont procured the services of correspondents who submitted biased reports to Richelieu on the Grandier case. The wildest rumours of all were spread by the Capuchin monk and a personal enemy of Grandier's, Mesmin de Silly, who enjoyed access to Rueil and enlarged on the sensational aspects of these reports, which were sent to the all-powerful Minister.

Laubardemont himself had a strong material interest in the revenues that would accrue from the castle and above all from its lands. Why should this simpleton, Armagnac, be allowed to profit from a mere whim which the King had entertained ten years before? Armagnac was easily dealt with; even the tower, his residence, would be demolished; the scandal of the "bad priest" offered a priceless opportunity for getting rid of the inconvenient Governor, for meanwhile the rumours had acquired a new dimension. Quite suddenly, and most opportunely, they had made their way into Laubardemont's special sphere; it was no longer a straightforward case of the dissemination of dangerous theories and of reprehensible conduct on the part of a priest; the devil himself was involved, the sinister omnipresent phantom of the age.

In 1626 an Ursuline convent had been founded in Loudun. The nuns came from the foremost families in the district. But the abbess, Madame de Belciel (Sister Joan of the Angels), and a number of her nuns were undoubtedly obsessed with the idea of the "God within"; Sister Claire of St John, née Claire de Razilly and a relative of Richelieu's, together with two other sisters, one from the great house of Nogaret and the other from the house of Sourdis, were among the most fervent. Laubardemont's own sisters-in-law allegedly were members of this convent. From 1632 onwards Richelieu took an enduring interest in this situation. The abbess later described herself as clever, perverse and arrogant. She received many visitors and delved into every rumour. She was vivacious, high-spirited and determined to be the centre of attraction at all times. These nuns, who had pledged themselves to God, went in for all manner of nonsense: at the stroke of midnight they would appear dressed as ghosts, they indulged in obscene behaviour and lost all sense of propriety. It was Grandier's misfortune that his rival, Canon Mignon, was father confesser to the convent. The abbess told Mignon gruesome tales about the sinister temptations with which she and her nuns were assailed. Satan had lately proved himself extremely active; he had been in Marseilles, in Chartres, in Marmontiers, he had been everywhere, *querens, quem devoret*, and at the moment he was in Loudun. Small wonder that in the course of the abbess's confessions the name of the handsome Father Grandier was constantly on her lips. Although it had been established that he had never actually entered the seclusion of the convent he was constantly present in the passionate fantasies of the nuns. Mignon conferred eagerly with Armagnac's and Grandier's opponents. The Bishop of Poitiers, who had lost face when the Archbishop of Bordeaux reversed his judgement, was informed. Exorcists, past masters of their art, were sought and found. The nuns were required to appear before these priests, and the demons residing within them were then interrogated and actually answered through the mouths of their victims; they stated their names, their qualities, their tasks; they used offensive and obscene language and forced their carriers to cut all manner of capers. Without exception these evil spirits named Urbain Grandier as their master, the man who had obliged them to take possession of the demoniacs.

It was then that Laubardemont made his extremely opportune arrival in Loudun. The tower was sacrificed, Armagnac ceded his interest in the enterprise, although Lucas retained his. The royal commissary immediately made contact with the Governor's and Grandier's opponents. An anonymous pamphlet from the year 1617, which contained an attack on Richelieu, was unearthed and its authorship ascribed to Grandier. Laubardemont was in his element; the whole of France was talking about the emanations in the Ursuline convent, and the Baron immediately requested instructions as to how he was to deal with the matter. After a meeting at which Louis XIII, Richelieu, Chancellor Séguier and Father Joseph were all present the following text was drafted and sent to him: "Monsieur de Laubardemont will proceed against Grandier as quickly as possible on all charges: moral depravity, seduction, scandalous behaviour and any other misdemeanours which he may discover relating to the demoniacal possession of the nuns and other persons who are said to have been plagued by evil spirits due to the magic practised by Grandier. . . ." The King's representative was granted full powers. He was instructed to participate in all the exorcisms and was authorized to pass sentence without right of appeal.

On December 7th Grandier was imprisoned. Then the witnesses were paraded. They stated: "This priest has led a dissolute life, his teachings were so harmful that the Bishop of Poitiers was forced to intervene; all his former friends have deserted him, for no decent man is able to defend him now, and he has been accused of advocating Théophile's doctrines."

It should be remembered that all this was taking place in Loudun, where it was witnessed by a large number of Protestants. Although they certainly laughed up their sleeves, they nonetheless sided with the Governor and the priest; in this way they hoped to preserve the independence of the town which had once afforded them refuge. Needless to say, their support was especially damaging.

The court hearings lasted throughout the winter, during which time disturbances broke out.

New exorcists appeared, including Father Tranquille, whose report of the proceedings Richelieu reproduced in his Memoirs.

But even if we disregard the theological implications and consider this matter strictly in terms of power politics, it is quite astonishing to see how many people refused to take the proceedings seriously. A well-known physician, François Pidoux, who was Dean of the Medical Faculty in Poitiers, disseminated pamphlets in which he attributed all of the fantastic emanations in the convent to perfectly natural medical causes. And the *Chevalier du guet* (the head of the Criminal Investigation Department in Paris) sent an alarming report to the First Minister on the scepticism and flippancy with which such a serious matter was being discussed at Court and in certain circles in the capital.

What was most impressive, however, was the quiet but resolute attitude adopted by Grandier himself throughout the whole trial. At the very outset Laubardemont sensed a shift in popular sympathy. He had to act quickly. He decided therefore to stage a great exorcist show in the Church of Sainte-Croix on June 23rd in the presence and under the chairmanship of a bishop and a royal commissary. He waived the power to pass sentence vested in him by the Royal Council and, skilfully calculating the effect, allowed Rocheposay to take the chair.

The next step was to confront Grandier with the "adversary"—Satan himself. It was a perfidious idea on Laubardemont's part to force the accused priest to appear in the role of exorcist to the demoniac nuns. Grandier submitted that in his view it would not be possible for a magician and sorcerer to transform a Christian into a demoniac without his or her assent. "That is heresy," the court replied, thus making it impossible for Grandier to opt out of the drama which the sensation-mongers in the church were eagerly awaiting. He did as he was told and asked the bishop: "Whom do you wish me to exorcise?" The bishop replied curtly: "These girls." Grandier then donned his surplice and began the ritual. The devil announced his presence immediately and forcibly. The abbess and Sister Claire distinguished themselves by the vehemence and the cynicism of their responses and even tried to use violence. They let out savage shrieks, "animal howls", they tore their clothes like mad women and stood there half naked and with no sense of shame. Eventually they threw themselves on the unflinching priest while he was still discharging the ecclesiastical office imposed on him by his superior. The onlookers felt cold shivers run down their spines. A number of women fainted. In the end the congregation had to rescue Grandier from the raving nuns.

On August 10, 1634, the bishop announced his verdict: "Grandier is to be subjected to the severest form of torture and then burnt alive." And so it was done. His legs were crushed between two boards until the blood spurted out mingled with the marrow from his bones while the attendant priest, who took an active part in the torture, constantly called out to him: "*Dicas, dicas.*" Laubardemont leaned over Grandier and shouted at him to extort a confession. But the tortured man remained silent right up to the moment of death.

Not long afterwards the abbess was miraculously cured. Quite suddenly, in the year 1638, she was liberated from the devil through the intercession of St Joseph. Bloodstains appeared on the shift which she wore during the final, near-lethal phase of the exorcism; they had been left there by Satan. From then on she herself was a miracle-worker. Richelieu gave her a large sum of money in recognition of her services; she visited him on repeated occasions. She also undertook a pilgrimage to the grave of St Francis of Sales and on her return journey she called at Saint-Germain where Anne of Austria was approaching her time. The Spanish Infanta insisted on wearing the miracle-worker's bloodstained shift during her labour; and so she gave birth to the child who was to become Louis XIV. "Joan of the Angels" did not die until 1665. Her grave became a shrine for pilgrims.

From a letter which Richelieu wrote on May 26, 1636, some two years after Grandier's death, to Gaston d'Orléans, who was suffering from some minor ailment, it is quite evident that the Cardinal did not take this affair very seriously: "Monseigneur, I have learned from one of the devils of Loudun, who has just returned here, that Your Highness has been taken ill and, although your malady is not as serious as that which continues to plague these poor girls and which they have so richly deserved, I thought it best to send this nobleman without delay so that he might extend my sympathy to Your Highness and offer Father Joseph's services as exorcist. . . ."

But what emerges most clearly from this episode is the power of the dark images which rose up from primeval depths and mingled bizarrely with the belief in established authority, the self-seeking materialism and even the critical scepticism of seventeenth-century France. One reason for relating this incident was to introduce the unjust judge, Laubardemont, who was among the most sinister of the horde of creatures whom Richelieu used to carry out menial and base tasks; we shall be meeting him again in the political sphere. But a much more important reason was to point out the extremely close bonds that still linked Richelieu's times with the Middle Ages.

And so once again we have encountered Orléans. Men like Goulas and La Rivière were always plying the Duke on Richelieu's behalf. They asked him to follow Chavigny's advice in all respects and even went so far as to suggest that he should marry Richelieu's niece, Combalet, after the dissolution of his marriage to Marguerite of Lorraine. Orléans laughed at this suggestion, paid court to the Cardinal and was more adroit and more elusive than ever. Richelieu remained extremely suspicious. Chavigny had reported that Gaston might conceivably have received an emissary from Duke Charles of Lorraine in Blois. In his reply Richelieu wrote:

"Once again we find that His Majesty's enemies are on friendly terms with Monsieur; this means that an attempt will be made, either on his authority or in his name, to have the Cardinal murdered or to force him to leave France. We must discover the names of all those in Monsieur's entourage involved in this cabal."

But to the Prince himself, who was causing him all this anxiety, he wrote: "Bouthillier will tell you how highly you are spoken of. Your servants will always offer a warranty of Your Royal Highness' good intentions." There then followed a veiled threat: "I am convinced that your conduct will always be of such a kind that certain persons will not have to pay for it."

Always the same narrow passages to negotiate, in which

the Cardinal was obliged to walk with bowed head, always
the same flattering words, which sometimes concealed genuine
fear.

And then came the sudden news that Orléans had left
Blois by ship on the Loire. Where was he going? Frightening
visions loomed up: was he making for England to join his
brother-in-law, Charles I? Chavigny ordered two fast vessels
to sail from Orléans in pursuit of the Duke. Accompanied
by Goulas and La Rivière, he himself tried to catch up with
him. He then wrote a reassuring letter to Richelieu: "The little
men who are with the Prince are not powerful enough to
persuade him to take such a decision; they aren't clever
enough for that." But in his mind's eye the Cardinal will
already have seen Gaston in the Loire delta setting sail for
Britain with a captured Chavigny on board, for he wrote to
his faithful associate:

"I am prompted by the love I bear you to send you this
word of counsel by express courier. If you should discover that
he [Orléans] has already passed Nantes and reached a position
which might give him the advantage and enable him to seize
and carry you off, you should on no account pursue him but
should simply send word to the effect that his journey is
giving rise to wild rumours and that it is his duty to dispel
them at once."

Richelieu ordered warships to sail from Brest, Le Havre
and Brouage to prevent the heir-apparent from fleeing the
country yet again. But it was all quite unnecessary. On
May 8th Chavigny stood at the window of a castle on the
Loire where a hospitable lady had offered him accommodation
and watched Gaston d'Orléans sailing up river towards
Saumur. It had never entered his head to take flight to England.
All he had wanted was to pay a visit to the sensational town
of Loudun, nine miles from Saumur. Once he knew his
destination, Richelieu wrote to the capricious and imaginative

Prince: "I am delighted to hear that the devils of Loudun have converted Your Highness."

But there were more serious grounds for concern than those furnished by the activities of a class which was slowly making its exit from the historical scene and which, in the midst of war, sought the backing of the King's brother and mother in order to establish contact with the enemies of the realm.

CHAPTER XI

POPULAR REVOLTS

France was threatened by dangers which had erupted from elemental depths.

The shooting war had consumed enormous amounts of money. The huge bribes and pensions paid out in the course of diplomatic warfare had imposed an ever-increasing burden from 1635 onwards, and the rapidly growing army of officials accounted for further vast sums. The basic trouble was the tax system, for which no equitable basis had ever been found. The improvised measures which were introduced to meet the needs of the moment further confused the situation and always oppressed the same social group, the Third Estate. This fact deserves serious consideration, for we have already noted that the Third Estate was prepared to make particularly heavy sacrifices in periods of wartime crisis. And yet both before and during the war it found itself obliged to take the law into its own hands and stage revolts which might well have led to national disaster. Throughout the years of his greatest achievement Richelieu was faced with this sinister and growing force; and he no longer had the time to calculate the limits of endurance of the oppressed masses, one of the great unknown quantities. When despair eventually erupted into fury his initial reaction, which was so typical of his method, was to recommend a policy of evasive tolerance; but subsequently, when the State found itself on the brink of national disaster, the Cardinal again appeared in the role of the strict disciplinarian who was prepared to take the most brutal action. But he was unable to effect any change in the system of taxation, which was the root of the trouble.

The peasant-farmers, who constituted 75 per cent of the population, led a miserable existence and continued to do so long after Richelieu's death. As late as 1653 an Englishman wrote that the fearsome misery in the country districts of France, especially in the frontier provinces, which were quite crushed by the burden of taxation, was not to be met with anywhere else on earth. It was extremely rare for a French farmer to acquire the kind of wealth possessed by certain of his English counterparts.

Many have borne witness to the wretched appearance of the agricultural class. A proverb of the time said: "When you came into the world you cried because you saw that your father's trousers were made of calico."

Time and again we have had to draw attention to what is virtually one of the *Leitmotifs* of this book: the fact that during his great war Richelieu's policies suffered in every sphere from lack of funds.

In France opposition to taxation has always been endemic.

In the spontaneous revolts of the early decades of the seventeenth century we have to distinguish between those which broke out in the towns and those which occurred in the country. It will be remembered that in a letter to Vienna, Lustrier, the Imperial Resident in France, advised the Austrian Emperor to exploit the ferment in the land by "fanning the flames of general revolt." Because of the immense burdens imposed on the Third Estate riots were constantly breaking out, first in one place, then in another. Popular resentment was sparked off by the most trivial events. The mere mention of the "tax collectors" or the "monopolists" was enough to rouse the masses. The authority of the State suffered most of all from the fiscal system; but the government could not possibly dispense with the revenue which it brought in, especially after 1635. In fact, the State was so dependent on the credit advanced by the great tax farmers that the Cardinal had no option but to express the nation's gratitude to them in a royal declaration; this was a great humiliation for Richelieu, for, as we know, he loathed such people and on other occasions spoke harshly of them.

The tax farmers often delegated their rights to subcontractors, a practice already in use in Roman times. A tax farmer in seventeenth-century France was authorized to raise indirect taxation for a period of six years. He acted on behalf of a finance company. The State received a yearly rental plus a percentage of the income from the taxes which it had farmed out. One of the evils of this system was the brutality and corruption of so many of the tax collectors.

In his *Political Testament* the Cardinal said of the tax officials: "They are the true cause of popular distress for there are so many of them."

In the political literature of the early seventeenth century the peasant-farmers and craftsmen, the *menu peuple* (little people), were denied all right to freedom. Although the opposition and Richelieu himself always talked about the need to bring "relief to the people," often this was simply a pretext for promoting the politico-economic interests and the legal claims of the ascendant *noblesse de robe*. The concept of "the people" had no precise meaning. It was only during the large-scale regrouping of the Estates in the seventeenth century that steps were taken to define the Third Estate. It is worth noting that the first public attempt to tackle this problem was made in the presence of the young monarch, Louis XIII, when he appeared before the nation's representatives at the States General of 1614. There, for the first time, it was decided that, strictly speaking, the peasant-farmers did not form part of the Third Estate. Robert Miron, once accredited as temporary envoy to the Confederation and subsequently Intendant of Finances in Languedoc, played a distinguished part throughout the 1614 Assembly as the President of the Third State. He was chairman of the merchants' deputation. In the course of the debate he said: "The peasant-farmers have to produce the food for Your Majesty, for the Ecclesiastical Estate, for the nobles and for the Third Estate." His bold, almost revolu-

277

tionary words deserve special mention; he apostrophized the nobles as follows:

"You spend your lives, noble gentlemen, in daring escapades, in gluttony, in extravagance, in acts of violence, both public and private. The ancient glory of your Estate is dimmed. The people go their way groaning beneath their burden and they do all the work. . . . If Your Majesty does not grant relief things could reach a point where these deprived people will open their eyes and suddenly realize that a soldier is simply a peasant with a weapon in his hand. It could even happen that a vineyard worker with an arquebus on his shoulder will suddenly find that the time has come for him to stop being the anvil and start being the hammer."

While Miron was delivering this prophetic tirade Jacques Bonhomme, a farmer from Beauvoisis, wrote with remarkable patience that the abuses were not so great that the calamity of a new civil war would not be greater; and he added: "We trust that in their goodness the King and the Queen, his mother, will gradually remove these abuses."

At this time a French nobleman also spoke of the Third Estate in an address to his fellow nobles. He said: "The Third Estate is composed of tradesmen, peasant-farmers and craftsmen and also of another type of person, who is neither an official nor a noble and is useless to both the King and the public."

It should be pointed out, however, that statements such as these were counterbalanced by others in which the impoverished provincial nobility expressed their solidarity with the peasant-farmers.

In the development from the medieval to the modern State the peasant-farmer was the last to be emancipated from feudal society, which existed in an integral form in France from the eighth to the eleventh centuries. Although seigniorial rights were still observed after the reign of Philip IV, by then the

feudal constitution as such had been largely absorbed into the
national State. The old feudal relations and bonds no longer
had any political significance. In socio-political terms, however, they still continued to play an effective role. Consequently it could not be a matter of indifference to the squires
if the solvency of the farmers, especially the tenant farmers,
was undermined by new and harsh fiscal measures. Time
and again in the letters written by Hugo Grotius to the Swedish
government we find evidence of a certain complicity between
the gentry and the rural population, especially in Normandy.
But we must distinguish between those relationships which,
although based primarily on self-interest, were also conditioned
by a sense of community, and the completely calculating
attempts of the insurgent nobles to manipulate and use the
rebellious peasant-farmers against the government.

As for the economic conditions in which the country people
lived and worked, these may be summed up as follows:

In large areas of seventeenth-century France agriculture was
based on a single-crop system. Consequently two bad harvests
in succession were enough to produce a severe famine. Often
fields were planted only three or four times over a ten-year
period because of the shortage of seed and fertilizers. Although
the owners of large estates were sometimes able to wait before
selling their products, the peasant-farmers had to take their
wares to market immediately following the harvest, when
prices were at their lowest. It has been established that the
mortality rate among the rural population was twice or three
times as high as among town dwellers and was highest of
all in the areas which concentrated exclusively on cereal
production; it was far higher there than in the provinces that
engaged in mixed farming and dairy farming. During
Richelieu's period of office there were two years in which the
mortality rate was particularly high—1629–30 and 1636–7.
The looting and vandalism of the mercenary armies, which
lived off the land in the frontier districts, the rise in the price
of food and the ravages of disease had left the peasant-farmers

in certain provinces so debilitated that the authorities considered it pointless to recruit them for any service.

But it would be wrong to assume that misery and privation were restricted to the countryside. The craftsmen, the tradespeople and the merchants could evade ruin by the pressure of taxation only by the greatest efforts, and they too were carried off by the epidemics which the troops were constantly introducing into the towns.

On August 29, 1631, Richelieu wrote to the Archbishop of Bordeaux: "I beg you to ensure that the burden of paying and feeding the 'La Meilleraye' regiment is not carried by the people. . . ."

In July 1636 the small town of Marle, near Laon, had to provide 20,000 livres for the upkeep of a cavalry unit which stayed there for ten days. On May 29, 1642, when 900 infantrymen spent the night in the same town, the cost of maintenance and damages was estimated at 10,000 livres.

Great bitterness was caused by a decree that required the poorest people, who often earned less than two or three sols a day, to pay a fee for the right to carry on their trade. This regulation applied to wood and coal porters, oyster and orange sellers, onion hawkers, commission agents and even rag and bone men, each of whom had to take out a licence from the State treasury.

The series of municipal riots was sparked off by the fiscal measures for the year 1623. The only details we possess of these events are those concerning the revolt in Rouen, which was the most dangerous for the government. But we do know where all these incidents occurred, thanks partly to the reports of the Venetian envoy but above all to the letters which Grotius sent to Oxenstierna.

A letter dated January 9, 1636, which the Secretary of State and Intendant De Noyers wrote to Chancellor Séguier from Amiens furnishes us with a description of the economic condition of a French provincial town shortly after the outbreak of open warfare.

"But for the fact that I know how precious your time is for our country I would have tried to tell you a great deal more about the effects of the 'sol pour livre'[1] which it is proposed to introduce in Amiens. . . . For the present I merely wish to say that, in the light of the knowledge which I have acquired of the popular distress and the disturbances which this threatens to unleash, I consider that, although the needs of the State oblige us to impose this new tax, it should at least be deferred until better times. By allowing a certain period to elapse after the evils which three years of plague and war have wrought in this city the poor people, who are at present virtually incapable of making further contributions, will find the burden imposed by the new taxes less onerous. The mere rumour that further tax measures were being envisaged was enough to paralyse half the city's trade and put more than three thousand people out of work, many of whom have since died or been reduced to begging. All this I have seen with my own eyes. After hearing the views of the municipal councillors I feel that we should wait before putting our plans into effect and should at least explain His Majesty's reasons and proposals beforehand in order to prepare public opinion for the allegiance which it is so difficult to exact from men whose bellies are empty . . . this would also be in accordance with the wishes of the more enlightened citizens and the whole of the municipal council."

De Noyers' letter was a perfect example of how to draft an Intendant's report prior to the outbreak of a revolt. He confirmed that even the wealthy citizens were inclined to give secret if not open support to the miserable and despairing masses. The Secretary of State considered that intervention by the volunteer militia would achieve nothing and that neither the governors nor the parlements were capable of restraining the people, who were set on revolt. A fact which strikes us time and again and which is borne out both by this and by

---

[1] This was a surtax over and above the normal taxation or added to the price of goods.

other letters written at the time was that none of these acts of desperation was planned in any way. Whether they were municipal or peasant revolts, whether they took place in the south-western provinces or in Normandy, they were always spontaneous eruptions, none of which was ever accompanied by any precise formulation of the insurgents' demands. In this respect they stood in marked contrast to the peasant revolts in Germany of the early sixteenth century, which revealed marked religious and political trends. The rebellious workers in Louis XIII's day were people who were no longer able to satisfy the most modest of all demands, the right to bread and salt. The vineyard workers of Dijon, the wine merchants of Paris, the innkeepers and coopers of Bordeaux, the silk and velvet ribbon weavers of Lyons, the tanners and shoe-makers of Rouen were all caught up in the rebellion. They were all deprived of the fruits of their labours by the treasury.

In the countryside the first spontaneous insurrection broke out in 1624 in Quercy. Resistance flared up again in several of the south-western provinces in 1636 and 1637 during the open war with Spain, when it posed a direct threat to the government. In those parts the peasant armies were called the *"croquants"*,[1] a name which went back to the closing years of the sixteenth century.

In Niort and Dax men took to arms in 1633 to resist the tax farmer's representatives and the *élus*, elected collectors. The same thing happened in Bordeaux in 1635 over the tax on innkeepers. Agen, La Réole, Condom and Périgueux then followed Bordeaux's example. But the biggest and most dangerous of these revolts was staged in Rouen in the summer of 1639. In Normandy the imposition of a duty on salt was the immediate cause of an armed insurrection on the part of the population. Until then the province had been spared this burden and the introduction of the new measure affected many people, chief among them of course the salt workers.

The significance of such internal upheavals in the midst of

[1] From the word *"croquer,"* bite.

a life-and-death struggle with external enemies should not be underestimated. Revolts in Provence and Languedoc: not only could they be exploited by the opposition groups at home, they also offered a possible basis for a successful Spanish invasion.

The disturbances in Aix, like the revolt of the so-called *lanturélus* in Dijon, were triggered by the government's decision to strengthen its hold on the provinces by establishing the *élus*. In his Memoirs Richelieu sought to justify this decision by pointing out that in the territories of Languedoc, the Dauphiné and Provence the annual tax assessment carried out by the provincial Estates had produced far too high a profit for the governors and their followers at the expense of the national treasury. He also voiced the suspicion that the Duke of Guise, who had caused him such great difficulty when he was carrying out his fundamental reorganization of naval affairs, was trying to use his position as governor to incite the people against the King. He said of him: "It was not that he was so devoted to the Queen-Mother and Monsieur but rather that he was obsessed with a passionate desire to undermine the King's authority and increase his own. For this reason he never failed to give secret support to any rising against the King in his province."

We have an account, which Richelieu set down in note form in 1631, of the situation in Aix-en-Provence. In it he gave brief profiles of all the rebel leaders and quoted statements made by them.

It was well known that at that time the Duke of Feria had been ordered to concentrate a force of 2,000 Italians and 500 Spaniards in Barcelona for use in Provence. These orders were subsequently rescinded when it was learnt in Madrid that the Duke of Guise had fled abroad. All these events took place in 1631 and should therefore be taken into consideration when we assess the foreign policy aims pursued by the Cardinal and Father Joseph at Regensburg.

But these actions were only a prelude to what was to come.

The popular revolts in France did not pose a really serious threat to national security until after the outbreak of open hostilities. But the great revolt in Bordeaux of May 1635 was followed in 1636 and 1637 by the so-called war of the *croquants*, the long-drawn-out disturbances in which the whole of southern and south-western France was embroiled.

Apart from individual and unpremeditated acts, the demonstrators in Bordeaux remained disciplined in the initial phases. There was no looting. But when their numbers swelled to 3,000 men they stormed the town hall and forced two treasury representatives whom they had taken captive to go on their knees and beg for mercy. Having achieved this, however, they immediately broke out into cries of "Long live the King." The next day, still with the same rallying cry, they marched through the town and declared that they were prepared to pay all duties save that on wine. While this was going on the governor, the Duke of Epernon—no friend of Richelieu's, of course—remained in his castle of Cadillac feigning illness and refusing to intervene on the grounds that the forces at his disposal were inadequate. It was only after he had received urgent and repeated petitions from the municipal council that he finally appeared in Bordeaux. But even this powerful man was unable to prevail upon a single one of the peasants in his extensive territories to help put down the demonstrations. Most of the men working for him, incidentally, were ex-soldiers. He appealed to Paris for military aid, but to no avail. Then, on June 15th, he was eventually obliged to enter Bordeaux at the head of a small formation and engage in street fighting with the powerful mob in the most important area of the town, where barricades had been set up on every street.

Disturbances soon broke out in the other towns in Guyenne. In a letter dated June 28th Richelieu informed his sovereign of the dangerous spread of the revolts throughout the whole of Gascony: "In Agen Your Majesty's officials have been murdered; between thirty and forty soldiers in the new regiments have also been killed. The fact that the native troops are loth to proceed against their fellow-countrymen gives cause for concern."

In his Memoirs the Cardinal points out that the revolt in Bordeaux took place virtually simultaneously with that in Toulouse. In August he informed M. de La Valette that the edict relating to the innkeepers in Bordeaux would be withdrawn together with a number of other fiscal measures which might cause discontent in the province. But no reduction in the *taille* could be considered, for the State was in urgent need of the revenue it brought in. In the same letter, incidentally, Richelieu assured La Valette that neither he nor his father had ever been suspected by the Court of having secretly promoted the disturbances in Bordeaux and the neighbouring towns. Later, in his Memoirs, he was to go back on this statement. La Valette, who held the command on the Spanish frontier in the bad year of 1636, was eventually ordered by the government to use the mailed fist against the *croquants*. This was in 1637, that is, one year after the majority of the French peasant-farmers and the municipal craftsmen had spontaneously offered their services in defence of their homeland. The revolt of the *croquants*, which did not collapse until 1637, was one of the greatest in the history of France in terms of the territories involved and the number of men participating. The links between these bloody riots and the municipal disturbances of earlier years are unmistakable. Later Richelieu wrote:

"The insurgents were not induced to take action by the war itself, which they knew was raging on every frontier of the realm, but by the false rumours which were being put out on all sides to the effect that the military situation was serious and the enemy was going from victory to victory."

The peasant-farmers of Périgord announced in a proclamation that they regarded themselves as true servants and loyal subjects of the King and that under the command of Antoine du Pay de la Mothe, M. de la Forêt, they were prepared to sacrifice their lives and their possessions in defence of the

Crown and the country; they had only taken to arms to defend their freedom and to throw off the bonds which enslaved them and of which they were quite certain that their King neither knew nor approved. The same attitude is revealed by the *arrêts* which the peasant-farmers of Saintonge composed for submission to the government. They made no demands on the authorities, they "humbly petitioned" them, begging to be released from their "compulsory solidarity", that is, the provision whereby the solvent members of a parish were liable for the debts of the insolvent. They requested a reduction in the duties on wine, salt, fish, iron and livestock and also the abolition of manorial rights and tithes. Another of their requests—one which was to have grave consequences—was directed against the tax exemption granted to the nobility, the clergy and other privileged groups. In conclusion they stated that the peasant-farmers were being exploited to such a degree that the only course left open to them was a "revolt of despair"; they hastened to add, however, that they acknowledged their "grave guilt" and appealed to "His Majesty's clemency and goodness."

The tax exemption enjoyed by the nobility was based on the age-old precept, then still generally accepted, that the nobleman should pay either with his goods or his blood. The special position of the clergy, on the other hand, derived from the disputes between the Kings of France and the Curia. Philip IV had already quarrelled with Boniface VIII over the question of taxing the Church. The Pope had given way only to the extent of agreeing that national or provincial synods should be authorized to raise voluntary contributions.

If we are to concern ourselves with the position of the Third Estate we shall have to take account of such historical precedents. The nobility had served the State to its utmost for centuries on end; many noble houses had been wiped out in the process, others had been ruined. This service had become greatly attenuated, primarily because of the links which this class had established with the life of the Court, a fact which was to constitute one of the principal causes of the French Revolution. But as far as the revolutionary movements of Richelieu's own day were concerned, we must not forget that in the midst of war the internal security of the State was constantly threatened by a powerful force of armed peasants, whom the government could not hope to appease by trifling concessions. On June 21, 1636, the Cardinal wrote to the King:

"The revolt in Angoumois, which appeared to have died down, has recently revived. 7,000 to 8,000 men, 3,000 to 4,000 of them armed, have banded together. Their fury is so great that they tore a poor surgeon to pieces, having mistaken him for a *gabeleur* [tax official]. I am told that the only way of dealing with them now is by force. If possible we should send in the regiments of La Meilleraye, Calonge and Montmège. Four companies of light cavalry will also be needed."

But first the government tried to negotiate with the rebels, for at that time the French armies were fighting in Burgundy, in Lorraine and on the Flemish and Spanish borders. In the autumn royal decrees were published announcing the removal of the most unpopular taxes. Well-informed spokesmen were sent out into the provinces to explain the provisions of the various decrees and to pacify the population. But throughout the whole of the winter, even after the reconquest of Corbie, the situation remained extremely tense, and in the spring the riots broke out again with renewed force.

Meanwhile the Treasury had tried to obtain new revenues by raising a compulsory loan in Guyenne. Verthamont, the intendant attached to the army on the Spanish frontier, urged that, in view of the misery and bitterness of the population, this measure should be dropped. According to his estimate, Bordelais could not even meet the demands already being made on it.

Although the export of 50,000 barrels of wine per year at 20 écus per barrel brought in 3 million livres, some customers, notably the English, paid in kind and not in cash. And so

Verthamont declined to exact a compulsory loan and in June 1637 he advised the government that the troops stationed at the foot of the Pyrenees should no longer be allowed to live off the land and that other sources of supply should be found for them.

Apart from the peasants led by La Mothe de la Forêt in Périgord, who were well disciplined, all the other insurgent groups, whose leaders were constantly changing, were quite disorganized. The net result was murder, plunder and pillage. Although large numbers of finance officials were killed, by and large the peasants did not vent their wrath on either the nobility or the citizens. Châteaux and suburban villas were seldom looted. At that time no ill will was felt towards the property-owning classes. In a memorandum drawn up for the Super-intendent of Finance, which dealt with the disturbances between 1629 and 1643, we read: "The *croquants* held meetings at which the priests and the nobles demonstrated their approval . . ."

The leaders of the various movements always tried to win the support of whole parishes and then to establish contact with the towns. But the peasant-farmers were extremely loth to leave either their lands or their native district. Come what may, they wanted to remain within the immediate vicinity of their homesteads; at the same time they sought the protection of city walls, with the result that many of the insurgents banded together in small fortified market towns. In the course of the punitive expeditions mounted by the army this sealed the fate of many such groups. In his Memoirs Richelieu calmly observed:

"Because of a revolt by a number of peasant-farmers in Périgord, which then spread to the other parts of Guyenne, La Valette was obliged to abandon his project [on the Spanish frontier] in order to deal with the insurgents; this he accomplished quite easily, dispersing the rebels by conquering Sauvetat and subsequently Bergerac; in this second operation he was aided by La Mothe de la Forêt, the Peasant General, who claimed that he had only undertaken the task because he, his wife and his children had been threatened with death."

There then followed a passage which was crossed out in the manuscript of the Memoirs:

"A few other parishes, which had been incited by the insurgents, rose in Poitou but were brought to their senses by Lieutenant General de Rochers Baritaud. . . . His Majesty had granted an amnesty [through Baritaud] to all those who had taken part in the insurrection but had subsequently submitted."

In his Correspondence the Cardinal was far more direct but also far more severe. On June 13th he wrote to the King:

"The defeat of the *croquants* is certain. M. de La Valette has sent a courier confirming this. Fourteen hundred rebels died in the actual fighting and many more, who had gone back to their homes, have also been killed. M. de La Valette says that he is now proceeding against Bergerac, where the rest of this rabble—some 5,000 to 6,000 men with cannon—have entrenched themselves."

And five days later:

"Espenan suggests that, now that twelve of the guilty parties have been hanged, the *croquants* should be granted an amnesty on condition that they place an armed force of 4,000 men at the disposal of the Crown for a period of two months; in his opinion these reinforcements would enable the King's troops to drive the Spanish out of Saint-Jean-de-Luz and Soquoy. If this suggestion should prove practicable it seems excellent."

On June 7th a force of 3,000 foot and 400 horse under the

Duke of La Valette had forced the suburb of Madeleine in Bergerac into submission with little loss of life. At that time Louis XIII said to one of his governors that he was so vexed by the popular revolts that nobody could render him a greater service than by helping to stamp out these dying embers.

In extending his gratitude and congratulations to the Duke of La Valette Richelieu wrote:

"The subjugation of the *croquants* is so important for the welfare of the monarchy and of the State and brings so much honour to your own person that, although I have already expressed the pleasure I feel at such a happy outcome ... , I find myself compelled to reaffirm it. Above all I wish to inform you of His Majesty's satisfaction with your conduct throughout this whole undertaking and to express his gratitude to you for the way in which you have acted ... "

It is quite evident that no matter where this great but extremely localized revolution flared up it nearly always lacked real leaders and inspiring ideas.

The important seventeenth-century chroniclers concerned themselves primarily with the peasant revolts in Normandy. There is good reason why they should have done so, for after the suppression of this particular revolt Richelieu set exceptionally severe examples, partly in order to blunt the ardour of any other provinces which might have been contemplating similar ventures but more especially because, throughout the entire Norman revolt, he had feared armed English intervention at every moment. The threat of English support for the revolt in Normandy was due primarily to the marked increase in tension which had followed recent French moves with regard to Flanders and the Channel ports. But traditional motives, which had their origin in the medieval history of the two peoples, also played their part. England still regarded Normandy as a Crown dominion. And of course Richelieu also knew that Charles I had repeatedly toyed with the idea of military action on the Continent to divert attention from political difficulties at home.

The man who suppressed the Norman revolt with such severity was Chancellor Séguier. Verthamont, who accompanied him as *maître des requêtes*, kept a diary in which he recorded countless details of the action carried out by the Chancellor and his General Staff. This document tells of the complaints and demands made by the peasants, of the penalties imposed upon them and also of the administrative measures instituted following this punitive expedition. The diary covers the period from December 15, 1639, to March 27, 1640. Séguier was sent to Normandy in 1639 and returned to Paris upon completion of his task in 1640. Verthamont's observations are drafted in the form of an official record. Besides this diary there are numerous other sources, of which the most informative are the reports submitted to Chancellor Oxenstierna by Hugo Grotius, the most independent of all observers.

Normandy was more heavily taxed than any other French province: the Normans paid one sixth of the entire *taille*. Between 1628 and 1634 the cloth merchants, the tanners and the paper and cardboard manufacturers of Rouen had opposed —sometimes successfully, sometimes in vain—the special duties on leather, cloth and paper. The history of those years reveals an unrelieved sequence of penalties, executions and reprieves.

It was probably following the executions carried out by the government in the southern and south-western provinces in the second half of the 1630s that the major burden of taxation was shifted to Normandy.

In the year 1632–3 the government had promised the Estates that direct taxation would be decreased by a quarter. But, according to the Estates' *cahiers* (that is, their records) for the year 1634, this undertaking was not honoured: "Far from being able to report a reduction in taxation, we poor people are subjected to constant increases."

These complaints were repeated in the *cahiers* for 1638:

"Four years ago Your Majesty promised to reduce the *taille* by half. We are still waiting for this promise to be put into effect; the tax imposed by the commission for this present year . . . doubles our liability . . . and in view of this increase we are prompted to suggest that, if we are to be asked to pay a double tax, then we should be given two autumns and two . . . harvests."

Later we are told:

"This poor province has been afflicted by all manner of calamities; in a number of towns and parishes, which had already suffered at the hands of the soldiers, the plague has carried off the entire population; because of last year's bad harvest, which was caused by the protracted drought, the poorest of our people have been forced to feed themselves like animals. Our cup is full . . . "

Since the beginning of Louis XIII's reign Normandy had been a centre of opposition. As early as the second half of the 1580s there had been peasant revolts in Normandy. These had been sparked off when the local inhabitants had taken up arms against marauding mercenaries. Then, too, the insurrection had been put down by troops. The Normans were imbued with a powerful sense of freedom and also with a marked propensity for subterfuge, which they practised right up to the moment when the underlying elemental forces suddenly broke their bonds. The first signs of opposition, which were apparent only to the skilled observer, usually appeared during Carnival week. On such occasions the revels generated spontaneous and bitter lampoons before finally erupting into sudden acts of violence. In 1634 a revolt was triggered by new duties on leather and playing cards. Street fighting broke out at once and after the initial insurrection had been suppressed there were serious differences of opinion between the local parlement and the government, which was accused of having greatly exacerbated the situation by its precipitate intervention. But Paris disregarded the complaints and sent an intendant to punish the guilty parties. Many were sent to the galleys while others were fined. The parlement's worst fears were then realized: the spirit of revolt spread from the town to the countryside.

The outbreak of disturbances on a large scale was ultimately due to the imposition of a salt duty in parts of Normandy which had previously been allowed to exploit this commodity free of charge. Richelieu adopted a very independent attitude to this question; he even went so far as to advocate that salt should be exempt from duty.

The bitterness caused by the salt duty, which had existed for centuries, broke out again during the war with Spain, in the 1630s and 1640s, when it assumed an extremely violent form. A certain M. de Beaupré, an estate owner whom the peasant-farmers wrongly thought to be in favour of the duty, presented himself at the audit office in Caen and advised the authorities of the growing danger. When they disregarded his warnings he approached the King himself. At the time Louis XIII was in the camp at Mouzon on the border of the Spanish Netherlands. Beaupré informed him of the state of affairs and showed him some of the rebel tracts which were in circulation. The King then ordered the immediate abolition of the salt duty. But it was to be a long time before this provision was put into effect.

We have already noted that the bureaucratic machine worked very ponderously. On this occasion no attempt was made to expedite the implementation of the royal decree or to make its contents known in the province. By the time action was taken it was too late.

In July 1639 in Avranches, where a fierce resistance movement had already been active under Henry III, innocent people were murdered because they were taken for tax collectors. This movement spread to the whole of Lower Normandy.

The Governor of Avranches had no troops at his disposal. He remained within the walls of his castle, which was besieged by the rebels day and night. Eventually he managed to send a messenger to the Governor of the province, but all that he was able to raise was a force of four hundred men.

It was then that the name Jean Nu-Pieds was first heard. Countless pamphlets purporting to have been written by this Jean Nu-Pieds passed from hand to hand and made a powerful impression.

In the early days of the revolt many innocent people were maltreated and the *bureau des cinq grosses fermes* (Office of the Five Large Estates) was plundered. In Vire, a small town in Lower Normandy, the mob broke into the building in which the *élus* held their tribunals. The aged president of this body was murdered and his house was burned down; similar incidents occurred in Mortain and Caen.

The organization of the revolt was evolved in the course of the summer. Nobody had ever seen Jean Nu-Pieds; he is thought to have been an imaginary figure named after a poor salt worker, who always walked barefoot on the beaches.

The brigades of the peasant army were led by men who evidently maintained no liaison with one another; most of these leaders were desperados from the upper classes. But there were also ecclesiastics in the ranks; a vicar from one of the suburbs of Avranches distributed pamphlets to his parish priests which he asked them to read from the pulpit and in which the people were urged to take up arms.

The parlement of Rouen prohibited the formation of armed bands and the posting of seditious bills.

In Chancellor Séguier's memorandum on the events in Lower Normandy we read: "At first it was just a small group of unimportant people who were easily dispersed, but once certain of the great nobles had lent their support and low-ranking representatives of the discontented provincial nobility had banded together a well-armed corps of 5,000 to 6,000 men was formed which was divided up into eight to ten regiments, each under the command of its most experienced leader. These forces then spread out over the whole province. Pontorson was the first town to welcome them, Coutances furnished them with troops and money, Vire gave reinforcements, Bayeux supported them and Caen tolerated them. The major part of the population was involved."

The priests in Normandy were forced by the insurgents to read the following manifesto in their churches:

"We, General of the 'Nu-Pieds,' command the inhabitants of this parish, irrespective of rank, to provide themselves with weapons and ammunition in order to serve their King and defend his realm; this they are to do within a fortnight, after which, upon receipt of further orders from the above General, they are to proceed in good order and fully equipped to the place which will then be designated."

On September 3, 1639, Grotius reported to his Chancellor that the revolutionary army in Normandy numbered twenty thousand men. This figure is too high. There were six thousand men near Avranches and further divisions were spread out over the whole of Lower Normandy. These army units were made up of suburban dwellers and peasants and also of impoverished nobles, most of whom occupied positions of command; but there were very few citizens in their ranks. The insurgents had adopted John the Baptist as their patron saint. In his name they murdered Capuchin priests who had allegedly or actually tried to conceal tax officials. There is no evidence that the Huguenots took any part in the revolt. When two Capuchins died in Rouen in August the parlement directed that they should be buried in a secluded spot to prevent the populace from giving vent to their fury on their corpses.

The Nu-Pieds showed no mercy to deserters and traitors. Recalcitrant villages were visited by punitive expeditions. But the insurgents lacked funds. Although the populace secretly provided them with food, force was needed to make "the enemies of the people" contribute to the cost of arms. Far more plundering went on in the revolt in Normandy than elsewhere. The rebels marched from town to town, from hamlet to hamlet. The poor were forced to join their ranks, the rich to pay forfeits; some had to give money for muskets, others for pikes. To make the peasants join the movement the armies drove off their cattle. It should be pointed out, however, that most of the accounts of rebel atrocities were put out by their adversaries and that nearly all of these reports were written after the revolt had been suppressed.

It is worth noting that in many of the seditious pamphlets, although the King himself was never attacked, Cardinal Richelieu was always a butt for criticism. During the revolt in Rouen Richelieu's coat of arms was torn down from the Jacobin monastery which he owned. Grotius said that the monks went in peril of their lives because of his coat of arms. This incident was symptomatic of the hatred felt by all classes for the King's First Minister.

By and large the only members of the landed gentry to be attacked were those who had been in some way involved in the administration of the tax system or were related to the financial officials by family ties. The provincial nobles were sufficiently versed in the art of war to repel sporadic attacks on their castles, which were still fortified in the traditional way.

The differences which arose between the parlement of Rouen and the government were due to the fact that the members of the parlement thought that the strict punishment demanded by Paris would merely serve to increase popular resentment. But in its letters to the King and the Governor of Normandy, the Duke of Longueville, the parlement did not reveal its true motives but spoke instead of clemency and forgiveness. Its members were afraid to show too much understanding for the insurgents lest they be censured. But when a government official arrived from Paris to impose penalties it soon became apparent how much sympathy was felt for the rebels and how great the tension actually was. Between 1635 and 1639 this tension constantly increased. During that time the large municipal corporations also came into action.

The chronicler Bigot de Monville wrote: "The news of the incidents in Lower Normandy doubled the courage of the 'little people' of Rouen. . . . Having nothing to lose, they decided to risk everything."

By this time the revolt was not simply an eruption of popular resentment but a series of well-organized military actions. Jean Nu-Pieds, who had meanwhile become a mighty symbol in the mind of the populace, was said to have given the order to strike. The arsenal was captured and adequate supplies of weapons were obtained. Then the houses occupied by the treasury officials were stormed. An eye-witness gave an account of these assaults: "We saw them running across the roofs of four-storey houses like cats and rats without a sign of fear; one after the other, with wooden clogs on their feet, they clambered over the cornices and tore down the lead flashings to make bullets."

The siege of the town house belonging to Le Tellier de Tourneville, the tax farmer authorized to collect the *gabelle* for the whole of Normandy and a man renowned for his severity, aroused widespread enthusiasm. Le Tellier had long since been advised to move into the parlement buildings or the town hall to ensure his personal safety and place himself and his possessions under the protection of the parlement, but he had refused to do so. He had no confidence in the officers of the law and intended to arrange for his own protection. He barricaded his house and hired sixty powerful men, whom he armed from head to foot. But the rumour soon got about that he was laying up supplies of food and ammunition in his house and turning it into a fortress. The siege was laid at once and lasted two days, the house becoming the focal point of the revolt.

At the eleventh hour, when the garrison was about to crack, two courageous councillors from the parlement appeared on the scene accompanied by two magistrates and a number of armed citizens. They succeeded in cordoning off both sides of the road and placing guards in front of the house; they also managed to talk to the people, giving assurances and also issuing threats. They were trying to gain time so that Le Tellier could escape and remove his money. But the attackers soon realized what was going on and rushed the cordons, with the result that the councillors themselves escaped only by the skin of their teeth and returned to the parlement with bloodstained faces and torn clothes. Meanwhile Le Tellier had left the house disguised as a trumpeter and mingled with the crowd. A smith then broke down the front door of the house; gold and silver dishes were thrown into the well and the pitfall. Le Tellier sought refuge in a church, where he exchanged his trumpeter's uniform for a priest's robes. But his pursuers had found his trail and forced their way into the church after him. He was discovered in the belfry. But once again a councillor of the parlement, who arrived with a few armed men, succeeded in saving him from the mob; he took him back to the parlement, locked him up in the cells for his own safety and announced that he would be tried together with his accomplices. "We'll try him ourselves . . .", the mob cried. Eventually Le Tellier was able to escape to Paris.

As soon as the peasants gained the provincial nobles as their leaders the citizens grew frightened. This strengthened the hand of the parlement. Its First President announced that the people, greedy for loot, would soon be storming the houses of all wealthy citizens. It was only then that the Civic Guard placed itself at the disposal of the parlement. The President ordered that the rebels must be forced to withdraw, after which the Guard was to take the offensive and, if necessary, open up on the insurgents with musket fire. On August 22nd the councillors of the parlement walked through the streets dressed in their robes of office and escorted by the Civic Guard. Their primary object was to pacify the people, and at first they succeeded in this. But suddenly the mob fell on the solemn procession, striking out at the councillors with swords, long daggers, halberds and iron bars. At this the President at last gave the order to open fire. Eighty dead were left lying on the street. Covered by the musketeers, the parlement which, according to its secret records, was "too weak to annihilate the seditious mob" withdrew into its offices. Meanwhile the provincial nobles, who had first supported the revolt but were eager to disassociate themselves from it once they saw that it was getting out of hand, had appeared on the scene. The first victory over the insurgents was not won by the councillors of the parlement, who had given proof of such understanding and moderation before they were finally obliged to intervene, but by these mounted gentry from the local estates. The councillors had been caught in a crossfire with the government on one side, which accused them of cowardice and complicity, and the insurgents on the other. However, it is evident that, well meaning though they were, the councillors were crippled by their own indecisiveness. Their first intention was to proceed against the captured ringleaders and make an example of them; five days later, on August 30th, the President insisted that the most reliable members of the Civic Guard should be present at the executions. But on August 31st the attorney-general declared that the flames of revolt were still too strong and that they could not risk executions. A fortnight later this high magistrate (Salet) died, according to one of his contemporaries, from his dual fear of the populace and the government but in point of fact in a condition of extreme moral anguish. The government then decided to refuse the parlement's request for special powers and to order the army to intervene. The delegates urged them to reconsider this decision.

Meanwhile the Nu-Pieds had achieved their most important objective: for three months no taxes had been paid. During this time most of the Norman nobles had been with the armies in Germany fighting alongside the German Protestants for the Swedes against the Imperialists. Those nobles who had intervened against the insurgents had been older men.

The revolt in Normandy became well known at the time not so much because of the actual events as because of its fearful conclusion. The official government mouthpiece, the *Gazette*, made only brief reference to it lest it should excite the interest of enemies abroad. But others provided detailed information, the most accurate, impressive and sustained despatches coming from Hugo Grotius.

As late as August 27, 1639, Richelieu had written to the Finance Department: "We must try to deal with the Normandy affair as best we may by means of prudent and skilful diplomacy, for there can be no question of sending in troops at this present time." It would seem that he was then thinking along the same tactical lines as the councillors of the Norman parlement. On August 28, 1639, he had written to Bouthillier, the Superintendent of Finance: "I cannot understand why you do not give more thought to the consequences of the measures which you take in your finance council. It is an easy enough matter to take precautionary measures even against incurable evils; but once they have set in there can be no remedy."

The fear that the revolt might become nation-wide while France was still hard-pressed on her fighting fronts was undoubtedly an enduring nightmare for Richelieu. The fact that these sporadic uprisings revealed the influence not only of the opposition but also of a certain anti-absolutist trend did not escape Louis XIII's First Minister. He also knew that Olivares' agents had a hand in the disturbances and that Spanish money was being circulated. But in Normandy there was a further factor to be reckoned with: England's attitude.

The sudden decision to withdraw a powerful contingent of troops from the front line was taken in the light of English preparations on the Channel coast and Lord Leicester's activities in Paris. Effective and speedy action had to be taken; the command of the punitive expedition was given to Jean Gassion, who had already acquired a considerable reputation fighting under Gustavus Adolphus and who was promoted Maréchal de Camp in 1638. He had six thousand infantrymen and four cavalry regiments under him; all the men in his force were foreign mercenaries, who were accustomed to the methods of the German war and could be expected to show no mercy whatsoever to the population of Normandy.

To appreciate the significance attached to this armed intervention it must be remembered that Chancellor Séguier was also sent to Normandy at the same time as Gassion's armed force and that he was furnished with truly regal powers.

If we are to believe Tallemant des Réaux then it would seem that the majority of the Norman nobles joined the punitive expedition.

Gassion's force set out in November 1639. He marched at the head of his main force in the direction of Caen, laying waste wherever he passed in accordance with his instructions. From Caen he advanced in line of battle with troops posted to cover his van, rear and flanks against Avranches, where the main body of the Nu-Pieds was concentrated. Although they had occupied the suburbs, most of the insurgents were quartered in the surrounding villages, largely on account of the food shortage in the town. The dispersal of the peasant troops was to prove their undoing. When the decisive battle was joined many of them arrived too late. On November 20th the King's force was sighted. The Nu-Pieds split up into two groups, one of which constructed a fortified camp on the bank of a small river at the point where they assumed that Gassion would try to force a crossing. Meanwhile, however, there were many who were intent on informing the Maréchal de Camp of the insurgents' movements, with the result that he was soon acquainted with their precise dispositions. While the major part of the Nu-Pieds watched the river crossing some 4,000 of their comrades, who were drawn up in front of Avranches, were subjected to a surprise attack. The royal troops were halted by the musketeers of the peasant army, which fought with the courage born of despair. But then, angered by their losses, the troops attacked in force and after a battle which, according to the *Mercure François*, lasted no more than two hours, put the enemy to headlong flight. Countless numbers of the peasants were drowned in the river. Those who were captured were cut down on the spot. Detachments arriving too late from the villages met with a similar fate. After wreaking fearful vengeance in the suburbs Gassion's army forced its way into the town. Montglas wrote: "All those behind the barricades were taken prisoner and all the prisoners were hanged."

Gassion himself maintained that in dispensing summary justice he had ordered the execution of only twelve men; the rest had been sent to the galleys. In the light of Richelieu's naval policy this claim appears credible.

Richelieu congratulated Gassion on his victory in extravagant terms and held out the prospect of high rewards. And then the Cardinal, who had repeatedly urged caution in the past, wrote to Chancellor Séguier: "I beg you to remember at all times that the example which you are to set cannot be too severe. . . . Quite apart from the punishment of individuals it is a matter of urgency that the city walls should be razed."

From Avranches Gassion marched to Rouen, where he was required to place himself at Chancellor Séguier's disposal. During the whole of their march the troops were allowed to plunder at will, and they made good use of the opportunity. They arrived in Rouen on December 31st. According to an eye-witness report the inhabitants of the Norman capital had lost everything; they were harassed, destitute and in despair; many had fled to the woods. No food at all was being brought into the town from the countryside and no peasants were seen in the city. The only people exempted from quartering in Rouen were the tax officials and the clergy. Even the wealthy citizens were harshly treated, just as if they had taken an active part in the revolt. The Chancellor even went so far as to suggest that the splendid town hall should be razed to the ground. Here, however, Richelieu advised restraint.

The insurgents who had been captured in August were still being held in prison: Séguier made short shrift of them. They were tortured, then broken on the wheel. These proceedings created such an enduring sense of horror that even during the Fronde a pamphleteer said of Séguier that it was impossible to forget the barbarous way in which he had acted in 1640. But Le Noble, a councillor of the parlement of Rouen, and various other contemporary observers refuted these allegations.

In the end those who profited most from the revolt were the finance officials. They were more than handsomely compensated, and it was the people of Normandy who bore the cost.

The day following his arrival in Rouen, Chancellor Séguier summoned the magistrates to appear before him. They arrived dressed in their robes of office, wearing their skullcaps and adorned with their golden chains. A royal declaration was then read out to them, in which they were severely censured for their indulgence in allowing the insurrection to go unchecked. The councillors of the parlement of Rouen were forbidden by the King's emissaries to continue performing their official duties in any fashion or form. The parlement was then dissolved and its jurisdiction passed partly to the parlement of Paris, partly to royal officials, councillors, presidents, attorneys and advocates. All the officials of the old parlement were required to leave Rouen within four days, to contact the King's retinue and await further orders. The administrative officials were dealt with in the same way; the mayor and the magistrates were removed from office and their functions suspended. All the property and revenues of the municipality were confiscated and transferred to the Crown. The cannons, which were the symbol of the town's independence, were carted away. The court of the *aides* was closed and the *aides* were replaced by officials known as *officiers d'en haut*.

There is no need to go into further detail about the fearful methods employed in suppressing the revolt in Lower Normandy. The revolutionaries had acted out of desperation, and as soon as the State was assured of victory it hit back with relentless force. In 1639 Hugo Grotius reported that the despair which had seized the province was so great that new revolts would always be flaring up.

In fact, they set in with great violence; complete regiments of the King's troops were stripped of their arms and equipment. Martignon, the Governor General of Lower Normandy, openly expressed his fears of the consequences of renewed military intervention on the part of the State. All these forces of resistance, which rose up from the depths of popular feeling, continued to assert themselves throughout the extremely difficult final period of Richelieu's life and even after his death. It is not surprising that Normandy should have become the chief centre of the Fronde during the regency.

CHAPTER XII

THE GENERAL SITUATION

Lorraine

While these events were taking place in France sporadic and indeterminate battles were being fought in the colonial territories, on the high seas and in all parts of the Continent of Europe.

In Lorraine, the tribulations suffered by the people continued for a full ten years after the Peace of Westphalia. The atrocities committed in the Duchy, where the people had remained loyal to Charles IV of Lorraine, have been recorded in all their horror by the great Callot in a series of pictures that anticipate Goya. The towns and strongholds of the territory had frequently changed hands, passing back and forth between Charles IV and the French. The latter had pursued a scorched-earth policy so extreme that eventually even Condé found it intolerable. After the fall of Breisach Charles and his followers succumbed to a sense of hopelessness. When the tension between Richelieu and Bernhard of Saxe-Weimar became threatening, the Cardinal had again approached the Duke of Lorraine. Although it had nothing whatsoever to do with the substance of their discussions, a love affair played a part in the negotiations: despite the fact that his wife Nicole was still living, Charles IV had contracted a second marriage in Besançon with a lady of Cantecroix. Richelieu offered to have the first marriage dissolved and the second recognized in France and also to intercede with the Holy See. This persuaded the Duke to travel to Paris in March 1641, "where he laid his fortunes and his territories at the King's feet". . . . But, as on all previous occasions, he immediately drafted a secret protest, in which he declared that the oath which had been forced from him was null and void; he then instantly proceeded to fortify the strongholds still left to him and re-entered his territories to the tumultuous acclaim of his martyred people, who paid homage in a manner reminiscent of the adoration of the saints in medieval times. A further rising ensued, in which Charles participated. The horrors of war were unleashed yet again in Lorraine. Within two months the French had occupied every stronghold and Charles was forced to flee to Swabia as an exile, where he cursed the halfhearted leadership of the Imperialists and their complete lack of purpose.

Without going into the subsequent fate of Lorraine and its incorporation into the structure of the French State, it should be remembered that, despite all this distress, the people of Lorraine were to find their beloved homeland in France and that ever since—and especially following the French Revolution of 1789—their descendants have willingly risked their lives and their lands in its defence. This must give pause for thought: what in fact are the values for which a human generation pays by its sufferings? The heroic defenders of the fortress of La Mothe, who held out with such remarkable fortitude as late as 1644–5 against a French siege, were the forefathers of the Lorrainers who have since referred to themselves with pride and devotion as the defenders of "France's eastern bastion".

Events in Germany

On October 6, 1635, the Elector of Saxony had declared war on Sweden. At the beginning of 1636 the Swedish Marshal Banér occupied the town and citadel of Halle. In the face of the Imperialist army under the command of the Duke of Saxony, he then withdrew to Magdeburg before taking up positions at Havelberg and in the fortress of Werben. Swedish contingents were then stationed in Magdeburg. The Saxons laid siege to the town at the beginning of May 1636. Banér, who was awaiting the arrival of Marshal Leslie, made no attempt to relieve it, and to Richelieu's surprise the town capitulated on August 13th. The Cardinal wrote in his Memoirs with great indignation: "This was all because of Banér's new marriage. He had been celebrating so much that it seems he was no longer able to think clearly." Shortly afterwards, however, the Swede acted with great determination. He conquered Uelzen, which brought him in 3,000 Reichstaler, and there he was at last joined by Leslie. On September 27th Richelieu wrote to Chavigny:

"Banér and Leslie have joined forces. They have conquered the whole of Luxembourg. Now they will attack Saxony, and the 4,000 cavalry led by Colonel Götz have already been forced to retreat instead of reinforcing Gallas, who had been expecting them. The Landgrave of Hesse is no longer threatened on his flanks and things are going well on this front."

On April 20, 1636, Saint-Chamond, the King's representative at the Imperial Court, had succeeded in concluding a treaty in Wismar with the plenipotentiaries of Queen Christina of Sweden. Under the terms of the treaty Louis XIII agreed to pay the 500,000 livres which France then owed Sweden. He also agreed to pay another million livres in subsidies throughout the further course of the war. In return Sweden promised to carry the war into Silesia and Bohemia in order to immobilize Ferdinand's armies far from the French frontiers. This treaty was to run for three years. As always during Richelieu's conduct of affairs, both parties undertook to make no separate peace with the Emperor or his allies. Meanwhile the possibility of concluding a general peace was to be further pursued in Cologne.

Now that he was able to count on the co-operation of a powerful collaborator in the Elbe district, Saint-Chamond

sought a further ally to support the French armies on the
Rhine. The man he had in mind was the Landgrave of Hesse-
Cassel, whom Richelieu had described as the "most courageous
and high-minded Prince in Germany." The Landgrave had
already broken the armistice he had concluded with the
Emperor, and he hurried to the aid of Hanau, which was on
the point of surrender. However, he was not yet prepared to
sign the treaty proposed by the French. He was waiting for
Banér to come; but the Swede sent his apologies, explaining
that he had been obliged to lead his exhausted troops into
Saxony to take rest and booty.

Meanwhile Saint-Chamond had learned that the Landgrave
had set out for The Hague to obtain provisions and ammunition from the Dutch. He suggested that on his way back the
German Prince should break his journey in the Duchy of
Cleves so that they could meet for discussions. The meeting
took place and the Landgrave was in the best of dispositions.
In the Netherlands, Charnacé had handed him 20,000 écus as
a gift from the King of France with which to buy corn, salted
meat, butter, linen and medicines. Despite all these attentions,
the Landgrave still refused to sign the treaty; he argued that,
compared with the risks he was being asked to take, the
pension of 15,000 Reichstaler which the King was offering him
was far too small. In fact, the "most courageous and high-
minded Prince in Germany" could be won over only if France
was prepared not only to honour her original undertaking in
full but also to pay him an additional 100,000 talers at once.
He was intent on obtaining immediate help from the Swedes,
in order to recapture Hermenstein. Saint-Chamond had
written to Charnacé, asking him to persuade the Dutch to
send 4,000 auxiliaries and the Waldenburg and Mulard regiments, which were maintained by the King of France. But
these two regiments were in a wretched state, their Colonels
were unreliable and the Prince of Orange would not hear of
troops being sent abroad. Charnacé still went in constant fear
lest the States General should conclude a bilateral treaty with

Spain, and this fear was shared by Richelieu. The representative appointed by the Dutch to negotiate with Louis XIII,
an official by the name of Musch, was the man of whom
Charnacé had said in a report written in 1634 that he would
render valuable services provided the King showed him a few
favours. Richelieu had not forgotten this and had already set
aside the sum of 92,000 livres. Charnacé then received the
following instructions: "The plenipotentiaries present when the
treaty is concluded must also receive some personal gratification. You tell me that you propose to present them with
golden chains, but it is the King's wish that the whole of the
92,000 livres should be distributed to the best possible effect.
The King is relying on you."

On December 27th Richelieu again wrote to Chavigny: "A
courier has arrived from M. de Saint-Chamond with excellent
news. Thanks to Saint-Chamond's initiatives the King of
Denmark will remain . . . neutral; this has greatly pleased the
Swedes."

When Richelieu learned that the Polish ambassador, who
was then recovering from a serious illness, would be returning
home, he wrote to thank him in advance for the kind services
which he would render Louis XIII on his journey across
Germany.

Shortly afterwards Father Joseph spoke of the sympathy
which the Polish representative felt for France and mentioned
the pleasure the Cardinal's letter had given him.

The news from Rome was far less favourable. The Pope
and the nepotists, with the exception of Cardinal Antonio
Barberini, were quite out of sympathy with France. The
Pope was then trying to negotiate a peace settlement that
would be favourable to Spain. The two French representatives,
Marshal d'Estrées and the Count of Noailles, made little
headway with the Holy Father. In order to give the appearance
of acting on the Pope's proposals and trying to accommodate
him, the French agreed to the convention of the preliminary
peace conference in Cologne. The Imperial Diet which was

due to be held in Regensburg was a source of concern to Richelieu. In his memorandum of October 7th he told Mazarin that there were two reasons why the House of Austria was convening the Diet: firstly, to have the King of Hungary elected as the titular King of the Romans and, secondly, to form a pan-German League to oppose France and its allies. Ferdinand of Hungary, who was later to succeed his father as Emperor Ferdinand III, was duly elected King of the Romans on December 22, 1636. After studying the golden bull, Richelieu's jurists and theologians discovered four grounds on which the resolution passed by the Diet might be declared invalid. Firstly, the Electors had been convened to discuss the question of peace and not that of the Imperial succession; secondly, they had met in Regensburg whereas, according to the terms of the bull, they should have met in Frankfurt; thirdly, since Maximilian I of Bavaria had usurped his electorate his vote was invalid; fourthly, the Elector of Treves, one of the three ecclesiastical Electors, had been held prisoner by the Spanish because they considered him to be francophile. Richelieu added by way of conclusion that the Electors had undoubtedly been won over by promises.

In 1637, when Ferdinand II died and his son succeeded him on the Imperial throne as Ferdinand III, Louis XIII refused to recognize him as Emperor; the only title he was prepared to accord him was that of King of Hungary. But Paris went into mourning for Ferdinand II's death and also for the subsequent death of the Cardinal-Infante.

As to the Spanish, in his Memoirs Richelieu said of them: "They sought new excuses and pretexts every day. They hovered between war and peace, trying to steal advantages and to guide the negotiations along paths that were most profitable to themselves." Any other form of behaviour would surely have been too altruistic.

In 1638 Maximilian of Bavaria joined with the Elector of Saxony in pressing for an Electoral Diet. He asked if the Estates of the Empire should be expected to go on fighting a war that was essentially a duel between the Bourbons and the Hapsburgs.

By then things had greatly changed from conditions prevailing three years before, when the Peace of Prague had been widely accepted. On this occasion the Catholic Princes also pressed for a far-reaching amnesty, and confessional questions receded even further into the background; the only point on which there was almost total agreement was that a settlement with Sweden could only be reached by granting some territorial concession. The territory in question was Pomerania, and the Prince who would have to pay the price was the Elector of Brandenburg; he of course was opposed to this project.

At this juncture the Emperor appeared in person at Regensburg, where only a few of the German Princes were present, most of them having sent representatives. Thanks to his personal stature and dignity, the Emperor was able to eliminate his fiercest opponents.

But all contacts between Ferdinand III and the Swedes were broken off following the renewal of the Franco–Swedish alliance, which had expired in March 1641. Richelieu was determined to extend the alliance to the end of the war. The Swedes had asked for two separate congresses, one in Cologne, the other in Hamburg, while Richelieu had been working for a single comprehensive conference. Both Münster and Osnabrück were mentioned as possible sites. Then, on June 30, 1641, the Swedish Envoy, Johan Adler Salvius, signed the Franco–Swedish treaty in Hamburg. From then on the Emperor was unable to conclude a separate peace.

Franco–Spanish Battles

Louis XIII was constantly visiting the army camps. Despite the great hardships which this imposed, Richelieu always tried to follow him. At one time he travelled extensively in Picardy and sent a humorous report to Chavigny of the reception accorded him by the Governor, the Duke of Angoulême. Richelieu had asked Angoulême to dispense with the long speeches and addresses customary on such occasions. In his letter to the Secretary of State the Cardinal wrote: "M. d'Angoulême has never been in better form; as a rule he only gives two or three speeches but on this occasion they were so numerous that they proved too much for the day of my arrival and several had to be held over until the following day. . . ."

It was always at times of extreme tension that Richelieu was most prone to pen humorous passages for his associates. He himself was not at all interested in receptions. But he was interested in the border territory of Picardy, where the Flemish front lay; he regarded this as the most important of all the fighting fronts, for he had still not given up his original plan of joining with the States General in attacking Spain at what he considered to be her weakest point. In this way he could cut off Philip IV's territory in the Netherlands from the Empire and gain control of all the strongholds from the Bay of Biscay to the North Sea, including those on the Channel coast.

But the Franco–Spanish war, which was commonly referred to as "his war", made little progress. Reversals alternated with minor territorial gains. Essentially it was a matter of siege warfare, in which victories and defeats tended to cancel one another out.

In May 1638 the French laid siege to Saint-Omer and in September they conquered Câtelet, near Saint-Quentin. On August 22nd Sourdis, the Archbishop of Bordeaux, won a naval victory over the Spanish in the Atlantic. This was one of the first major achievements by Richelieu's new navy. But on September 7th the French were defeated at Fuenterrabia, the fortress situated on a promontory four miles to the north of San Sebastián and controlling the river Bidassoa, which formed the frontier between France and Spain.

Following the naval victory gained by the Archbishop of

Bordeaux Richelieu wrote to Chavigny: "I have so much to tell you that I scarcely know where to begin. Let me start with the victorious naval battle, as a result of which M. de Bordeaux [Sourdis] is now asking for money with which to make an attempt on San Sebastián in order to take this important town from the Spanish and fortify it. I consider that we should send him at least 60,000 livres at once." The day after this letter was sent the breach in the defence works of the Spanish fortress was so large that an assault was feasible. But for some time the Duke of La Valette, one of Condé's officers, had been refusing to take part in military conferences. This sort of dissension, which was constantly occurring among the High Command, had an extremely disruptive effect. On September 7th a general assault was launched by the Spanish relieving army. The Marquis de La Force repelled the enemy's initial attack on his left wing with ease, but this only made the *tercios* redouble their efforts. La Force himself hurried to the scene; but he was too late, for his men were already breaking. Condé was no more successful than La Force. By evening the French army had been defeated. Condé managed to escape to Bayonne in a barque. Richelieu, who always treated him with forbearance, wrote to him: "His Majesty does not judge a man's intentions by results."

The Duke of La Valette, however, who had stayed in his tent nursing his anger, was severely censured by Richelieu: "If his failure was motivated by a desire to harm the public cause, then he deserves to make public atonement for his guilt." But La Valette did not allow himself to be caught. He told his brother that he intended to undertake a journey, went on board a Scottish ship at Castillon and sailed to England.

This happened in 1638, the year in which the fall of Breisach changed the course of the war, in which the future Louis XIV was born and Father Joseph died.

The pattern of alternating military success and failure continued throughout 1639. On June 7th the French suffered a reversal in Lorraine at Thionville but on June 29th they took the fortress of Salces in Roussillon. Condé was the victor on that occasion, but by December he was forced to give up the fruits of his victory. In the same year, the year in which Bernhard of Saxe-Weimar died, Banér advanced as far as Bohemia and Gassion suppressed the desperate revolts in Normandy.

On October 21, 1639, the Dutch fleet under Van Tromp defeated the Spanish off Dunkirk.

The Italian Front

On April 26, 1631, the Peace of Cherasco had been concluded by the following parties: France, the Emperor, acting on both his own and Spain's behalf, Venice, Savoy and the Curia. This treaty provided for the withdrawal of the Austrians from the Grisons and the Valtelline and of the French from Piedmont. The Duke of Nevers was given Mantua and Montferrat with the exception of Trino and Alba, which passed to Savoy. At the instigation of Louis XIII's sister, Duchess Christine of Savoy ("Madame Royale"), and her adviser, Father Monod, Duke Charles Emmanuel of Savoy, who urgently needed peace after the battles he had just fought, placed himself under French protection. The texts of three secret agreements had already been brought to Turin from Paris in the course of the winter. The bearer was an extremely dubious personality, a certain Perdicelli d'Emery. The bait offered was contained in an article whereby France undertook to procure a royal crown for the Duke of Savoy, a desire which Christine had long cherished. The House of Savoy was also promised future rights of sovereignty over Genoa and Geneva, although the latter was still to remain a French fief. Victor Amadeus of Savoy did not give his signature to this article. But he did give it to another relating to the fortress of Pinerolo, which—according to the official treaty—was to pass to Louis XIII only on a temporary basis but according to the secret treaty was to form an appendage to the Dauphiné "together with the tributaries flowing into the Po."

In publishing the Treaty of Cherasco in the *Mercure François* Richelieu added a typically emphatic peroration: "And so this great confusion, which was created by Spanish ambition, has disappeared. The horrors of war, which were the product of injustice, and the privations, which plague and hunger raised to such grievous heights, have disappeared; the mighty storm which darkened the whole earth has been dispersed, the storm which threatened to deprive France of her lilies, Mantua of its fortresses, Italy of its independence, the French nobles of their glory and the whole of Europe of its freedom. The Germans and the Spanish had forced their way into Italy and have been driven out again in disgrace. All that remains of this great persecution of a Catholic Prince is an eternal reminder for posterity, which testifies to the most heinous crime that has ever been perpetrated between Christian Princes during the past eight hundred years." Very strong words for a military episode of this kind! Four years later, on June 11, 1635, the original articles were further extended under the Treaty of Rivoli. On this occasion the principal questions were those relating to the Valtelline and to the agreements with the Swiss Protestant Estates, with Venice, Parma, Modena, Mantua and above all Savoy. This document also contained a supplementary clause, in which the French again undertook to cede Genoa to Savoy and to confer on Duke Charles Emmanuel the title of "King of Upper Liguria" (instead of the purely decorative title "King of Cyprus"). The French representative in Rivoli was M. de Bellièvre, who did all he possibly could in the tough negotiations which he conducted with Father Monod, the representative of Savoy, to persuade Charles Emmanuel to renounce his neutrality and accept the supreme command of an Italian League to oppose Spanish Milan.

This Jesuit, Monod, was an interesting man. In dealing

with him in his Memoirs Richelieu—rather ironically—asked the question first put by Virgil: "To what lengths will ambition go when it overpowers a religious mind?" He described Father Monod, who was undoubtedly the originator of Savoy's pro-French policies even if his ultimate concern was for the Duchy and its greatness, as an intruder who meddled in affairs of State and was one of those fanatically industrious people, whose activities merely served to produce confusion.

Charles Emmanuel of Savoy always thought highly of Monod. His successor, Victor Amadeus, Christine's husband, was less enthusiastic, while Duchess Christine herself, to whom Monod acted as confessor, tried repeatedly to have him replaced. In a letter to her brother, Louis XIII, she asked him to help her remove the troublesome priest, but he would have to act cautiously, she said, for nobody must know who had instigated the move.

Although Richelieu had been prepared to make fantastic promises in order to win Savoy over, he nonetheless found the idea of an enlarged Savoy that might well turn anti-French an oppressive one, especially if it were headed by a man like Monod, who considered himself as the Cardinal's double.

In May 1637, when Rohan was being driven from the Valtelline, Richelieu had wide-ranging talks on the Treaties of Cherasco and Rivoli with Monod. The Jesuit painted a dismal picture of the political situation: the Valtelline was as good as lost and the Duke of Parma had seceded; the Duke of Mantua was seeking refuge in neutrality and the Count of Montferrat was embittered with France; the whole of Italy lay open to the Spanish, who were ready to fall on the Duchy of Savoy in great strength.

Richelieu did not take kindly to this sort of talk; any allusion to one of his failures always provoked a violent reaction. And when, after giving this depressing view of his affairs, the priest went on to offer him advice and to impress upon him the need to come to terms with the "King of Hungary", because all the Princes of the Holy Roman Empire regarded him as their Emperor, Richelieu, enraged, told the Jesuit that every one of his words would seem to indicate that Savoy wished to relinquish the French alliance. Richelieu had prepared himself thoroughly for this discussion. In a letter to Chavigny, which the Cardinal sent on April 24, 1637, we read:

"Tomorrow morning, before the Savoyard envoy and Father Monod arrive here, M. de Chavigny is to send an extract from the treaty concluded between His Majesty and the Duke of Savoy so that I can see which articles Savoy has broken and also any remarks which the King made to the Duke over and above the points established in the articles themselves; this I need to know in order to answer Father Monod."

Louis XIII also wished to be informed, for on April 29th he wrote to Richelieu:

"Father Monod is calling on me tomorrow at ten in the morning to take his leave. If you should consider that he will want to discuss State business with me, would you please tell me how I am to answer."

Richelieu fulfilled this request immediately. His anger is revealed by the title of his memorandum: "Arguments with which to refute Father Monod's impertinences."

After Monod's arrival in France the Duke of Savoy had asked Richelieu whether it would be preferable to wage an offensive war in Italy or to remain on the defensive and thus enable all the Italian Princes to participate. He estimated that the offensive would cost two million livres more per year than a holding action. Despite the Jesuit's urgent representations and the advantages an offensive would have brought, Richelieu decided, in view of the financial situation, to conduct a defensive campaign and to reinforce the garrisons of Pinerolo, Casale and Bremo; there was, after all, nothing to prevent him from sending additional troops at any time and going over to the offensive. We now see why it was that Rohan received no help from Savoy in the Valtelline.

At that time it was hoped that the European powers would also discuss all Italian questions in Cologne. This hope was frustrated by the death of Emperor Ferdinand II.

Richelieu's aversion for his self-styled double, Monod, grew from day to day. On December 1, 1638, Duchess Christine wrote to the Cardinal: ". . . no matter how depressed I may have been, I have always been aware of the great debt which I owe you for your services and also of my own desire to afford you every assistance. I know that people who are not well disposed towards me, especially M. d'Emery, have tried to impugn my good intentions. . . . But you will, I am sure, have the goodness to recognize what I have done, not only during my father-in-law's lifetime but also during my regency."

Richelieu knew that, upon the death of Duke Victor Amadeus in 1637, the Emperor, acting in his capacity as liege lord to the Dukes of Savoy, had declared the late Duke's will null and void and subsequently withdrawn the regency and the guardianship of the young Princes from his widow, Duchess Christine.

On May 17th Louis' First Minister wrote to Cardinal de La Valette:

"I do not doubt but that Prince Thomas[1] will do all he can to ensure that his journey to Piedmont brings the greatest possible benefit to Spain and will try to intimidate 'Madame' into helping him. . . . But I consider this Princess too intelligent to be caught off her guard . . . and you yourself, M. le Cardinal, too shrewd not to see through these evil designs and frustrate them by prudent action." But Richelieu's final comment was: "If Madame should make any mistakes we would have no other choice than to act on your proposal, by arresting Prince Thomas and occupying Turin."

The same day a letter bearing the King's signature was sent to La Valette, commanding him to seize Prince Thomas and

[1] Thomas of Savoy, brother of Duke Victor Amadeus of Savoy.

detain him in Pinerolo. Louis also wrote a letter to his sister Christine which was dictated by Richelieu and in which he said: "I am bound to inform you that I would be forced to withdraw the confidence which I have always placed in you if Prince Thomas, who is so closely allied to the Spanish, were to stay in your territories with your approval; if such were the case you could no longer count on receiving those marks of affection which I have always paid you in the past." From the King's point of view this was not unjustified. Thomas and his brother, the Cardinal of Savoy, had concluded a treaty with Spain, under whose terms the territories governed by the Duchess were to be divided among them, and Spain would be given possession of all the strongholds which they conquered.

Meanwhile Thomas had arrived in Piedmont at the head of his troops, while the Spanish General, the Marqués de Leganés, who was Governor of Milan, was marching against Montferrat. La Valette was trying to force the Spanish to give up their siege of the castle of Cencio, near Asti, when a courier sent by Duchess Christine informed him that her brother-in-law, Thomas, after having taken Chivasso, was only six hours' march from Turin. Christine had already sent her elder son to Savoy to defend the Duchy against attack. In Piedmont one fortress after another opened its gates to the Spanish. Richelieu wrote at the time to La Valette from Rueil to say that the lack of care exercised by the Duchess in choosing the garrisons for her strongholds was both "deplorable and intolerable".

The King of Spain had not only permitted Prince Thomas to leave Flanders but had actually commanded him to join with Leganés in staging an armed intervention in Piedmont. By then the above-mentioned treaty had already been drawn up between Philip IV of Spain, Thomas of Savoy and his brother, Cardinal Maurice, which specified how the territories then governed by Duchess Christine as Regent of Savoy were to be divided. The people of Turin had been completely won over by Prince Thomas.

Meanwhile Christine had agreed to place Carmagniola,

Savigliano and Cherasco under French protection. But by the beginning of June the Spanish had gained possession of Moncalvo, Pontestura and Trino. There then followed a hard-fought battle for Chivasso, at which Thomas and Leganés were defeated by Longueville.

Louis XIII attached such great importance to the threat to Turin that he himself advanced as far as Pinerola with a combined force of Swiss and French troops. But in Italy units of Prince Thomas' army succeeded in infiltrating into Turin in small groups—according to the French, they were aided and abetted by the guards—and shortly afterwards the population opened the gates to the Prince's army with great enthusiasm. The important thing then was to gain time, and so the French negotiated. La Valette and Prince Thomas concluded an armistice which was to run from August 14th to October 24th. The Spanish began to hope for a *détente*. In the course of conversation Leganés informed La Valette that in the whole of Europe no man had rendered greater service than Richelieu and that he would like to effect a reconciliation between him and Olivares.

Thomas was hoping to negotiate a special agreement. On one occasion he informed La Valette that he would be happy for his daughter to marry Duchess Christine's son with the open approval of the King of France. He would like his own son to marry Mademoiselle de Longueville. If this could be arranged, he said, then he would even be prepared to change sides. Richelieu considered the pros and cons, and he certainly did not reject the possibility of transferring the regency to Prince Thomas summarily. At that time there were very few of Duchess Christine's domains left anyway. In real terms her powers extended only to Savoy, Susa and Villefranche. Richelieu called this the "flotsam from the shipwreck." Cardinal Maurice of Savoy had already taken Nizza and shortly afterwards Villefranche also fell. Richelieu, who was then in Lyons, was preparing to follow the King to the front when he heard that Cardinal de La Valette was seriously ill; he died on September 28, 1697, from a pulmonary abscess. On September 27th the

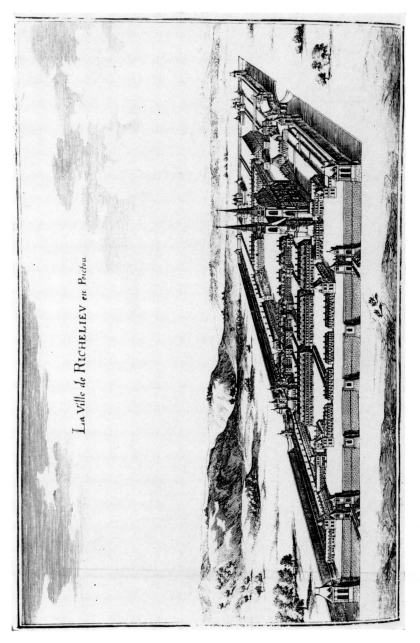

La Ville de RICHELIEU en Poiƈou

6. The town of Richelieu (Poitou) from Merian's *Topographia*

7. Cinq-Mars, by Mathieu Le Nain

command of the army in Italy was given to Count Harcourt. On September 23rd Richelieu had arrived in Grenoble, where he met Duchess Christine. He is said to have harangued and censured her most severely for having lost the respect of the population. She remained unbowed and adamantly defended the interests of her territories in the face of Richelieu's demands. Her uncompromising attitude led the Cardinal to think seriously of binding himself to Prince Thomas and the Cardinal of Savoy. But things took a new turn when Harcourt defeated Thomas and Leganés at Quiers.

In 1642, which opened with Guébriant's victory at Kempen and the occupation of Jülich but which then saw the French reversal at Honnecourt, Savoy's problems were at least temporarily resolved. In 1640 Harcourt, who had already relieved Casale, besieged Turin for four months before entering the city, where he received the regent, Duchess Christine, on November 19th. At that time Richelieu treated Savoy as if it were a French province. The pro-Spanish Princes were just as dissatisfied with Spain and Spanish ingratitude as Christine was with her motherland, France. Eventually the followers of both great powers in Savoy realized that their dissension must inevitably lead to the loss of their country's independence as a sovereign Duchy. The Pope, Urban VIII, then sought to reconcile the opposing parties. It was a matter of great importance to Rome that this Catholic State should continue to exist on both sides of the Alps. Once again Mazarin negotiated in this sphere. On this occasion, acting as France's representative, he persuaded all the parties concerned to agree to the division of Piedmont among the young Duke's uncles. Nobody regarded this as a definitive solution. Duchess Christine wrote at the time: "Moved by the love We bear Our people, We have deigned to accept this solution but have no intention of sharing Our authority as regent with the Princes." The confusions in Piedmont, the guerrilla warfare in that territory, continued until after Louis XIII's death.

The really astonishing thing about Richelieu was his omniscience. He was a master of both Italian and German politics, he had a complete grasp of internal conditions in the Scandinavian countries, he was conversant with the workings of the Stockholm parliament and was as well informed about events in Poland and Russia as he was about those in Constantinople. His knowledge of English internal affairs enabled him to take daring initiatives in that sphere, and he reacted to any shift in the balance of power in the Netherlands like a seismograph. Every insight he gained was immediately transformed into action with the object of bringing influence to bear on individual persons or groups of persons. From the mid-1630s onwards the secret negotiations which he conducted with his ill-starred adversary Olivares were never broken off. In the Spanish provinces, especially in Catalonia and Portugal and even in Andalusia, the Cardinal kept himself informed and involved. Although he lived intensely in the present, he learned his lessons and drew his consequences from the past and his tireless endeavours were always dedicated to building for the future, on which nobody in his century exercised a greater influence than he; thus the Peace of Westphalia, although concluded after his death, was essentially his achievement.

Richelieu did not suffer from the ceaseless pressure of external events, he suffered and exhausted his reserves of strength in the narrow circle of his everyday life, in other words at the Court, to which we must now return.

CHAPTER XIII

OPPOSITION AT COURT

In 1640 Anne of Austria was again expecting a child. Eleven days before her confinement, before the birth of the Duke of Anjou, who subsequently founded the fourth house of Orléans as Duke Philip I, the Queen's intolerable situation, the confused and morbid attitude of her husband and the father of her children and her absolute dependence on the Cardinal's good or ill will towards her were demonstrated with particular clarity.

On September 10, 1640, Louis XIII wrote to his First Minister from Saint-Germain:

"I deeply regret to have to inform you of the great aversion which my son[1] feels for me. Things are so bad that he cries, as if he were being flayed alive, when he catches sight of me from his window as I cross the courtyard; the mere mention of my name is enough to make him turn purple. Since I last wrote to you I have visited him twice in his room but without coming into close contact with him; the moment he sees me he begins to roar. What annoys me most of all is that everybody knows about it and that the First President, who came here this morning from Paris to see me, broached the subject with me. The thought of staying here any longer to await the Queen's confinement is so abhorrent that I feel it would kill me. I could not bear to sit and watch this degenerate child positively devouring her with his caresses, to hear him always mentioning her name and despising mine. I could not endure it

[1] The Dauphin, Louis XIV.

323

and so I ask you, the best friend I have in this world, to advise me what I should do in this situation. I intend to take the boy away from here at once either to Chantilly or some other place, so that he will not see the Queen any more or any of these women who spend all their time idolizing and flattering him. The Queen shows a positive aversion for everything which she thinks might be connected with me. I find that more than strange. There are certain women whom I intend to remove from my son's presence, though I will not take away his nurse or the two sick-nurses whom Madame de Lansac assigned to him; the others (whom I shall dismiss) are intended for the new child. Because my son has seen M. le Grand [Cinq-Mars] in my company he feels the same aversion for him as he feels for me. I beg you again to advise me what I should do in this affair. Please express yourself quite freely. As soon as I have dealt with the many new recruits [soldiers], I shall go away at once and I do not intend to leave this child here any longer. Do you take a different view? Tell me it. Please believe me when I say that I shall act according to your opinion. Louis."

It is somewhat frightening to see that Richelieu's influence reached into such intimate family matters.

The King had left the army in the early days of September 1640. On September 7th, i.e. three days before the above letter was written, he sent a personal message to the Cardinal from Saint-Germain: "I arrived here today to find the Queen and my son in good health. My son is very handsome but very obstinate; I do not intend to tolerate his bad moods."

Richelieu had instructed Madame de Brassac to keep him informed; he was always in close contact with "eavesdroppers". On September 10th, the day on which the King had implored the Cardinal for help, M. de Brassac also wrote to him:

"One of the services which I can and must render is to furnish Your Eminence with reliable information on the events that take place here. Alexander [Louis XIII] arrived yesterday from Notre-Dame in quite a good humour until last evening.

But then, when he came into Carnation's [the Dauphin's] room in order to see him, the boy, who was not accustomed to meeting so many people, began to cry when Scipio [Cinq-Mars] tried to fondle him. Alexander instantly fell into a rage. As he was returning to his chambers he met Diana [the Queen] and stopped to talk to her, his face distorted with rage: 'Carnation cannot bear the sight of me', he said. 'He is being fed on a strange diet, but I shall remedy this.' He then walked off, leaving her in utter perplexity. After she had retired to her room she began to cry and said to Aminte [Madame de Brassac] that she was innocent and greatly distressed, for she knew only too well what was afoot: they intended to take Carnation away from her and in point of fact Alexander's subsequent comments tended to bear this out. Scipio and Jasmin [Cinq-Mars and M. de Brassac] tried as best they could to ease the tension but Alexander remained in a black mood. . . . Last evening, when Diana retired to bed, she told Aminte that Alexander had written to Mark Antony [Cardinal Richelieu], adding that her only hope was that he in his kindness would prevent them from subjecting her to the pain of being separated from Carnation; she also expressed her conviction that, if he were to put himself in her place, he would feel sympathy for her. He will surely understand my distress, she said, and, like everybody else, will see why I feel offended. Her confidante assured her that she did well to place her hope in Mark Antony, who daily showed her so many tokens of his good will. These are the events with which Jasmin felt he should acquaint his master; otherwise nothing noteworthy has occurred."

The Queen then decided to make a direct appeal to the Cardinal. On September 13th her secretary, Le Gras, sent a letter of hers to Chavigny. He also enclosed a covering letter of his own, in which he wrote:

"This morning she is still disconsolate, despite the caresses which the Dauphin has lavished on the King; he kissed him

325

twenty times, called him Papa, ran after him to kiss his legs till in the end sorrow gave way to joy."

There is no evidence that the Cardinal replied to the King's letters of September 7th and 10th. It would seem that he made use of the services of intermediaries to relieve the situation. The child was urged to show special affection for his father.

We shall come to see that from this point onwards the Queen lived in constant fear of being separated from her children, which explains her subsequent behaviour.

Cinq-Mars

Meanwhile, before the dynastic succession had been ensured, Richelieu had hit upon an unusual idea.

Since the young ladies in waiting had not fitted in with his plans—even Mademoiselle de Chemerault had eventually given her undivided allegiance to the Queen—he decided to introduce an attractive young man into Louis' intimate circle. On this occasion Richelieu felt quite sure of himself, for the person in question was the son of a man on whom he had bestowed every possible favour, who had distinguished himself before La Rochelle and in Piedmont, who had proved his abilities as an ambassador in Flanders, England and Germany, attained the high office of Governor of Auvergne, shown himself to be a compliant, extremely moderate and loyal Super-intendent of Finance (cf. Vol. III, p. 138) and, as Commander of the French army in Germany, had ultimately achieved the exalted rank of a Marshal of France. This man was Antoine d'Effiat, the Marquis of Cinq-Mars. In 1632 he succumbed to an illness in Alsace, and Richelieu—as always where his faithful servants were concerned—helped his family as friend and adviser and provided for their every need; he often visited d'Effiat's widow in her castle and he saw her children grow up.

The Marshal's younger son, Henri d'Effiat, who was born in 1620, was given the command of the newly formed company of the Royal Guards when he was only sixteen. In order to procure a position for him at Court which would enable him to come into closer contact with his sovereign, Richelieu successfully opposed the claims of Henry III's former favourite, M. de Bellegarde, and the young Cinq-Mars was appointed *Grand-Maître de la Garde-Robe* in August of the same year. It was at this point that Mademoiselle de Hautefort was made to feel the full force of Richelieu's aversion.

A letter from Secretary of State Chavigny to Cardinal de La Valette of December 6, 1638, indicated that this lady was destined to fall from favour. But things did not immediately go according to plan. At first the young Cinq-Mars failed to make any impression on the King, and after a while Louis actually disliked him. It was only during the campaign in Artois between June and August 1639 and Louis' journey to the Dauphiné that these prejudices were dispelled.

Nicolas Goulas, the best contemporary chronicler of the life of Gaston d'Orléans and of the Fronde, reported a change in the King upon his return from this journey: he had taken a lasting dislike to Mademoiselle de Hautefort, while Cinq-Mars, aided and abetted by the Cardinal, had completely captivated him; Louis' original aversion had been supplanted by a violent passion. In fact, when Louis returned to Fontainebleau, if he ever spoke to Hautefort and Chemerault it was only to reprimand them; he even threatened to banish them from Court, if it should ever come to his ears that they had cast the slightest aspersion on Cinq-Mars. Shortly afterwards Marie de Hautefort was in fact commanded to retire into a monastery at least forty miles from Paris.

Marie-Louise de La Fayette had taken her vows in 1638; she died as the Reverend Mother of the Convent of the Visitation in 1665.

Cinq-Mars, who was already *Premier Ecuyer de France*, received the County of Dammartin as a royal gift. But he wanted more, he wanted to become *Grand Ecuyer* (Chief Equerry), and on this occasion Richelieu tried to frustrate his plan because he had reserved this Court office—one of the highest—for his gifted nephew Brézé. Cinq-Mars achieved his goal, however, without the slightest effort and from that time onwards was always referred to as "Monsieur le Grand."

Tallemant once said that the King loved what Cinq-Mars hated while Cinq-Mars despised what the King esteemed. This was an accurate assessment: the King was Spartan while Cinq-Mars loved comfort; the King preferred a simple life and dressed like a gamekeeper while his favourite strove after elegance. Henri was a gourmet while the King, although he liked to cook, was quite happy to eat the same food as his troops or his beaters. Louis derived satisfaction from frugality and small economies and yet at first he fulfilled the hopelessly spoiled young courtier's every wish. The slim, elegant youth with his rather doll-like good looks and girlish gaze could not live without high society, which he sought out whenever he could in the fashionable Parisian suburb of Le Marais. He had dabbled in literature and poetry and read Ariosto and Tasso with delight; he had an innate sense of taste for fine furniture, choice jewels and rare trinkets. He was the best-dressed man at Court and was a keen judge of ladies' gowns. Erlanger has furnished an inventory of the articles in his luxurious household. His coaches and teams were soon famous while the stock of horses in his model stables and his well-kept harness rooms were considered remarkable. His principal residences were the Hôtel de Clèves near the Louvre, the Palais d'Effiat in Saint-Germain-en-Laye and the family castle of Chilly, which he furnished and fitted out; these residences were far better equipped than the Cardinal's State rooms. Henri d'Effiat collected tapestries from Bergamo, Flanders, Auvergne and Rouen, Persian, Turkish, Chinese and Savonnerie carpets; his furniture, which bore the signatures of the foremost cabinet-makers, was renowned, and his great wealth of porcelain and silver was both praised and envied. His fifty quilted jackets shot with gold and silver, his coats embroidered with sarsenet and with golden and silver ribbons, his fifteen sabre belts of velvet and rare leather, his countless suits of black, pink and green velvet or shot silk and his dark red, nut-brown or brimstone-coloured suits of Dutch cloth were legendary. In his dressing rooms, next to the ornamental copper baths and the silver wash-basins, there were bottles of perfume by the score. This sort of thing would have annoyed the King at any time. It annoyed him all the more at that particular time, when the country was embroiled in a bitter war and the people were suffering fearful privations; it annoyed him because he himself resolutely resisted all excesses of fashion; on one occasion, when a lady appeared at Court with an extremely low-cut dress, it so irritated him that he spat a mouthful of red wine straight into the opening of her gown. But Louis nonetheless continued to place at his favourite's disposal the means with which to pay for such luxuries, while the favourite responded by placing himself less and less at the disposal of his ecstatic monarch. Cinq-Mars had absolutely no inhibitions where women were concerned. At the very beginning of his rise at Court he had become the favoured lover of the great courtesan, Marion Delorme. He called on her four times a day, wearing a different suit for each visit. He also succeeded in seducing the "spy" whom Richelieu had placed in the Queen's household, Mademoiselle de Chemerault. He possessed all the qualities lacking in the shy and awkward monarch, whom he had bewitched: a sparkling personality, self-assurance, unconcern and a rather impudent, childlike, uninhibited wit. At the beginning of the Cinq-Mars period there was dancing, there was drinking and the night was turned into day. But Louis XIII soon tired of these revelries, which he found distasteful and which were also bad for his health. Completely blinded as he was at that early stage of infatuation, he claimed that his favourite also had little liking for such carousals. And in point of fact Cinq-Mars often absented himself from these gatherings, but only because he was leading a double life. Every evening after the monarch's *coucher* he would ride from Saint-Germain or

Versailles to Paris to pass a few hours with his lover before riding back again. In the morning, Louis, who was an early riser, would ask in vain for Cinq-Mars, who seldom rose before midday. Eventually the monarch's eyes were opened. He was then assured that Cinq-Mars was married to Mademoiselle Delorme and that the reason why he rode into Paris was to visit his wife, who was referred to as "La Grande Madame".

The King had always been greatly upset whenever one of his favourites married. When he was told about Cinq-Mars he locked himself up in his room for several days, refused to receive the young profligate and had him informed that he was suffering from severe attacks of fever. But Cinq-Mars kept his grip on the tormented monarch by the strongest of all bonds, jealousy.

The King then began to complain to Richelieu about this youth, whose mind was "gilded copper". He spoke of his unbelievable idleness and his impertinent remarks, and then he said something which told Richelieu a great deal about his protégé: that he took a passionate delight in being the bearer of bad tidings. If, on the other hand, good news arrived, he would try to undermine it with a display of scepticism; he criticized every order that was given and treated his King "like a doorkeeper".

The tone which the favourite adopted towards his monarch was in fact disrespectful if not outright offensive. On one occasion, when Cinq-Mars was rebuked by the King, he replied: "It would make more sense if you thought about your armies than devising ways of tormenting me from morning to night." And another time he said: "You have no loyalty, you do not keep your word, it is impossible to have any dealings with you." This was a reference to the fact that Louis had once promised to give him one hundred thousand talers, which he had asked him for, and had subsequently denied all knowledge of the promise despite the fact that the Cardinal, the Chancellor and various intendants had been present at the time; people would be well advised to bring a notary with them, Cinq-Mars suggested, when they spoke with the King.

For a while Richelieu found it expedient to mediate between the two men, and it was as a result of his mediation that a series of astonishing documents were drawn up and signed by the King and his favourite, among them the following:

"We, the undersigned, declare to all whom it may concern that we are well pleased with one another and have never been in such a state of harmony as we are today, for which reason we have signed this statement. Saint-Germain, November 26, 1639, Louis and, at my command, Effiat de Cinq-Mars."

And again:

"Today, May 9, 1640, His Majesty, being at present in Soissons, has seen fit to promise 'Monsieur le Grand' that throughout the whole course of the campaign He will refrain from any outburst of anger towards him and that if 'Monsieur le Grand' should afford Him some slight provocation He will appeal to the Cardinal without rancour in order that His Eminence may intercede and prevail upon the said 'Monsieur le Grand' to mend his ways and desist from any action which might displease His Majesty. . . ."

This undertaking was given by the King and "Monsieur le Grand" in the presence of His Eminence. Louis and Effiat de Cinq-Mars signed the document.

On August 2, 1640, a Spanish relieving army attacked the French forces besieging Arras and soon gained the upper hand. At first Marshal Châtillon was loth to throw in the volunteers under Cinq-Mars; he was afraid of what might happen to him should the "youth" suffer some mishap and his beauty be marred by a wound. The Duke of Enghien, who was later to be known as the Great Condé, and the Dukes of Mercoeur and Beaufort were all present at this engagement, and they began to mock the "Grand Ecuyer" on account of his pallor.

One of them said: "He looks healthier at a ball than under fire!" Henri took part in an attack, lost his horse and remounted at once. But at that point Châtillon intervened; he had been wounded himself and was not prepared to run any further risks with Cinq-Mars. He wrote in his despatch:

" 'Monsieur le Grand' arrived with a large number of volunteer nobles. If M. le Maréchal de Châtillon had not restrained him . . . he would have forced his way into the fort, which the enemy had again stormed. His arrival greatly pleased the officers and men, who had been resisting the enemy for two hours."

According to the *Gazette de France*, "Our volunteers were led by the 'Grand Ecuyer de France', who so distinguished himself in the attack on the enemy cavalry that it was immediately apparent to all present that he had inherited the merits and virtues of that courageous Marshal who, as Commander in Chief of his Majesty's armies in Germany, had inspired fear even when he was a dying man." It was at the siege of Arras, incidentally, that the valiant Charnacé fell.

Théophraste Renaudot (cf. Vol. III, pp. 386 ff.), the author of this short panegyric, received a severe reprimand from the Cardinal; he had to print a second, official version of the engagement in his columns and announce that the first account was false. His second version was edited by Richelieu. Neither Cinq-Mars nor François de Thou, his closest friend, was mentioned. The Duke of Enghien, Richelieu's nephew, figured as the leader of the volunteers. The Cardinal even spoke to the King of Cinq-Mars' cowardice and made fun of him. This no man in his twenties, who has overcome his fear and done his duty, will ever forgive.

Richelieu always denied that he installed favourites. But in the case of Cinq-Mars the facts are indisputable. The Cardinal was soon forced to the conclusion, however, that the young man was not complying with his wishes and the question arises as to why he should have constantly offered his services

as mediator between Louis and his favourite: in the beginning
it was probably because he wanted to prevent the King from
succumbing to more powerful political influences. Louis complained to Cinq-Mars about Richelieu and to Richelieu about
Cinq-Mars. And every single aspersion, which the King cast, or
was alleged to have cast, on the Cardinal, was passed on by
Cinq-Mars with obvious relish to the guardian of his childhood
and the founder of his "fortune". Eventually, when things
had reached a point where Louis was obliged to inform his
favourite that he could not allow him to remain in his immediate
presence if he continued to oppose the Cardinal, this hopelessly pampered young man realized that he could not take
up the struggle against his former benefactor alone but must
join forces with other malcontents. And so he became a conspirator. It was a long time before Louis realized this, but it
was not long before he noticed that the favourite was tending
more and more to give free rein to a kind of nervous antipathy
which he had meanwhile developed for him. And so Louis
himself began to bring pressure to bear on the youth.

After having first anticipated his every wish he now began
to refuse his repeated requests.

One day, when Cinq-Mars asked for the Governorship of
Verdun, Louis told him that it had been reserved for the children of M. de Feuquières. When he asked for the command of
the troops besieging Arras, it was given to du Hallier; he
himself received only the command of the Horse Guards.
Once the handsome young man tried to force his way into
the Royal Council and was quite literally thrown out.

Eventually this once so successful enchanter overreached
himself. Since all things seemed possible to him he decided
that he would marry Princess Maria of Gonzaga, who had
once been courted by Gaston d'Orléans. Richelieu wrote at
the time and also told all who were prepared to listen that this
was "too big a match for such a little man."

Cinq-Mars knew that he was being watched. He unmasked
three spies one after the other. Meanwhile the King vacillated

between suffering and anxiety and confessed to the Cardinal every one of the ups and downs in this violent and ill-fated relationship. But there were also instances when his bitterness against the Cardinal showed. He is supposed to have told him one day, when passing from his chamber to one of the public rooms: "After you, Your Eminence, since it is said that you are the real King."

The monarch's sense of thrift, which was always gaining the upper hand with him, worked in Richelieu's favour; after the initial period of blind passion it had again asserted itself. Richelieu wrote: "He wishes 'M. le Grand' to content himself with his caresses; he does not wish him to make further demands on his purse." And on another occasion he wrote: "Cinq-Mars' role must be reduced to that of a well-paid jester."

But Louis could not bring himself to break with this handsome, boyish, somewhat lascivious and languorous ephebe, who was amenable only to the charms of women and once declared in disgust that he could not abide Louis' bad breath.

Cinq-Mars, who grew up under the strict régime of his widowed mother and the admonitions of the Cardinal, who was not even allowed to talk at table until he was sixteen, now lived surrounded by drawing-room heroes and self-styled warriors, by womanizers, gamblers and brilliant conversationalists. The "libertines" who, as we have already seen, formed an important element in Orléans' entourage, also belonged to this group. Their most prominent member was Louis d'Astarac, the Marquis of Fontrailles, a vindictive little hunchback, who was a native of Languedoc. For a while he was Richelieu's most dangerous adversary. It goes without saying that he sought out Cinq-Mars, who was impressed by him. Always better informed than anybody else, he attended occult séances and had black masses celebrated. We shall see more of him later. This extremely intelligent cripple with his aura of brimstone stood in marked contrast to the pure and naïve mentor, the representative as it were of the powers of good, who became a true friend to the much wooed "Grand Ecuyer".

This friend was François Auguste de Thou, who was born in 1607 in Paris as the son of Christophe de Thou, a magistrate and member of the *noblesse de robe*. The father had been a leading public figure under Henry III; he had conducted negotiations with the King of Navarre, acted as the King's commissary in Normandy and Picardy and played a crucial part in the reconciliation between Henry III and the future Henry IV; he was one of the chief authors of the Edict of Nantes and one of the three men chosen by Marie de' Medici to take over the wide-ranging duties previously performed by Sully. Throughout his life he had worked on his *Historia sui Temporis* only to find that this book was to cast a gloom over his declining years when it raised violent controversy and was ultimately placed on the Index. It was from this serious environment, from contact with such a free and objective mind, that François Auguste originated.

He was appointed councillor in the parlement at the age of nineteen and shortly afterwards a councillor of State. He himself nearly jeopardized his career by allegedly acting as go-between for the Queen and Marie de Chevreuse following the latter's hasty flight to Madrid. Among other things he redeemed the Duchess' jewels and tried to buy the silence of people who could have borne witness against the Queen. On these occasions de Thou had already entered into personal contact with the Spanish. But, although this may have checked the considerable momentum of his career, these transgressions had been forgiven. Louis d'Astarac, the Marquis of Fontrailles, was no doubt the very opposite of this honest and even pedantic magistrate, but on one point the two men were in total agreement: the Cardinal had to be overthrown. In his memoirs Vassor wrote that de Thou had quite made up his mind that the Cardinal must be destroyed and was convinced that he would be regarded as a hero in the eyes of the world if he were to remove the tyrant. But this assertion is belied by the facts: the truth of the matter was that this virtuous man shrank from political assassination.

However, things had not yet reached such a pitch; the Cinq-Mars conspiracy was still in its opening stages.

But this matter has to be considered within the context of other internal affairs. Many different forms of opposition arose and had to be overcome. Chief among them—despite all that Richelieu had achieved in this sphere—were the revolts of the great nobles.

The Soissons Conspiracy

If we consider the conspiracies staged by the great nobles during Louis XIII's reign we find that the principal actors were always the same. They were led on every occasion by members of the royal House, very often by Gaston d'Orléans, but also by a descendant of the House of Condé, Louis de Bourbon, the Count of Soissons, who was commonly known as "Monsieur le Comte". We have often encountered him, the last occasion being at the fall of Corbie in 1636. He was the only one of the Princes of the blood who had managed to escape entirely from Richelieu's authority. There came a time when the Cardinal tried to arrange a marriage between him and his niece, Marie-Madeleine de Vignerot, the daughter of his sister Françoise and M. de Pont-Courlay, who had been widowed in 1622 and had lived in close contact with her uncle ever since as his principal confidante (cf. Vol. II, pp. 140–1). Soissons had simply laughed at such marriage proposals. He had quite different plans (cf. Vol. I, p. 193). Because of his involvement, indirect though it was, in the Chalais affair he had long been under suspicion, and although he had been able to rehabilitate himself at the siege of La Rochelle he was now about to disillusion the Cardinal by taking direct action against his own person.

Following the incarceration of the Vendômes (cf. Vol. I, p. 201) in 1626, Orléans, who again feared for his safety, had turned to Soissons. The Count, who was then Governor of Paris, had offered him generous help: 500,000 talers, 8,000 infantrymen and 5,000 cavalry men, on condition that the Duke plucked up the courage to come to Paris and make common cause with him (Soissons) against the Cardinal. That would have meant civil war; as always in such situations, the King's brother remained undecided, refused to commit himself either way and let the opportunity pass by. Richelieu soon knew about these negotiations and it was not long before Soissons was aware of the fact. Since the Cardinal had shown how far he could go when he had had Chalais executed and Henry IV's sons imprisoned, Soissons thought it advisable to pay a visit to his relative, the Duke of Savoy, and then make for Rome with all speed. Richelieu instructed the French Ambassador to the Curia to request that Soissons be denied the reception due to a member of the House of France. But the Ambassador in question, M. de Béthune, replied that if this Prince was guilty of some transgression he should be brought before a court and condemned; until then he preferred not to fail in the respect which he owed to the royal House. Richelieu did not insist.

Soissons did not return to France until La Rochelle was invested. Two years later he accompanied the King on the Italian campaign. He then kept his peace for a time. As Governor of Champagne he proved an excellent administrator. When war was declared in 1635 he was given the command of the army of Picardy. We have already seen that, owing to inadequate support, he was unable to prevent the Cardinal-Infante from crossing the Somme. And then followed the disaster of Corbie. As always when panic takes over and even more so when it begins to ebb, somebody had to take the blame and—not without the Cardinal's support—Soissons was used as a scapegoat. As a result he became fiercely opposed to Richelieu and his policies; it goes without saying that the countless numbers of malcontents immediately and enthusiastically greeted him as their long-awaited leader and began to ply him from all sides.

At this point we encounter François de Baradat, the Marquis

of Damery, in the role of *provocateur*. The expression, "the fortune of Baradat", is used in French to denote a period of short-lived luck or prosperity. It goes back to François de Baradat, who, after first serving at Court as a page and subsequently as equerry of the "small stables", became the object of one of Louis's sudden sympathies. As was his wont, Louis gave him rapid promotion, but then, after just one year, allowed him to fall from favour. It was this Baradat who subsequently convinced Soissons of the need to remove Richelieu, for he considered the Cardinal to have been responsible for his earlier misfortune.

The threat of assassination was always present.

It will be remembered that, following their unsuccessful attempt in Amiens, (cf. Vol. III, p. 182), Orléans and Soissons were understandably afraid. They showed their fear quite openly by withdrawing with all speed, the one to Blois, the other—and this was a decisive step—to Sedan, the Duke of Bouillon's territory. Orléans again confessed to his brother, the King, and effected a reconciliation. But Soissons had burned his bridges; he remained "abroad", for at that time Sedan was still independent.

How was it possible that the opposition continued to trust Gaston d'Orléans and to rely on him? Many of those who were fighting for their ancient liberties and privileges thought they detected traces of Henry IV in Gaston's easygoing ways and witty manner; his unscrupulousness, his lack of courage and his constant willingness to surrender were for a long time regarded as flexibility.

Bouillon was still an independent Prince, no less than Charles of Lorraine had been. But Duke Charles' position had been immeasurably stronger than Bouillon's, whose sovereignty over Sedan literally hung by a thread. His only hope was that he might receive help from the Emperor and the King of Spain, but both of these rulers had already strained their resources to the utmost and Ferdinand III's freedom of movement depended entirely on the outcome of events in the

German theatres of war and on the Pyrenees border. In such circumstances Bouillon had to be prepared for any compromise.

But once Soissons had been won over by Baradat the new conspiracy began to gather momentum. Sedan, Brussels and Madrid all took an active part. This latest attempt to overthrow the Cardinal, which had powerful financial backing, was placed on a firm footing by the participation of Prince Frederick Maurice of Sedan, the son of Henri de Bouillon and the elder brother of the great Turenne. Frederick Maurice had distinguished himself in the Netherlands under his uncle, the Prince of Orange, at an early age; for a while he was Governor of Maastricht; then, in 1635, at the age of thirty, he entered the service of the King of France. It was not until 1641 that he decided to step outside the law in order to overthrow Richelieu. He then joined Soissons and was prepared to risk everything, including his life, in order not to share the fate of the Duke of Lorraine. But like many other prestigious persons within the opposition movement, he was denied the opportunity to prove himself in action. He also believed that Orléans was indispensable to the pursuit of his plans, especially since his personal relationship to Soissons was strained. We have already mentioned that Montrésor, as determined as he was embittered, and Orléans' cousin, Saint-Ibar, were members of his retinue, which also included Fiesco, Aubijoux, Brion, La Rochepot, d'Espinay and Fontrailles. Fontrailles, Aubijoux's cousin, was entrusted with the most difficult task; it was he who was asked to win over Cinq-Mars.

The conspirators referred to themselves either as "the Princes of Peace" or as "the Representatives of a Reunited Christendom". They addressed themselves to the suffering masses and promised to end the war and relieve the intolerable misery. In their search for influential helpers, understandably, they first set their sights on Cinq-Mars. That he was on bad terms with the Cardinal, his former protector, seemed to them a singular piece of good luck, though they must have been aware of the risk that, like Richelieu, they might one day lose control of the wayward "Monsieur le Grand", in which case he would be dangerously well informed about them.

The affair started with a blunder: Soissons sent Count Fiesco, a Genoese nobleman and a member of Cinq-Mars' personal circle, to sound out the favourite. But Fiesco approached his task with a curious lack of psychological insight. He tried to win the young man over by openly promising him rewards. The Court gossip had ensured that d'Effiat's ambitious marriage plans and the fact that it was Cardinal Richelieu who had thwarted them had become common knowledge. And so Fiesco, assuming that Cinq-Mars would be feeling aggrieved on this account, bluntly offered him the prospect of an alternative marriage into a princely house: if he was prepared to collaborate he could marry Maria of Gonzaga's cousin, the sister of the "Great Condé".

But Cinq-Mars saw his prospects in quite a different light; he showed Fiesco that he was offended by such tactlessness and—not without a hint of menace—dismissed him.

The Princess of Gonzaga

We first caught sight of Maria of Gonzaga when Gaston d'Orléans, then a young widower, tried to win her hand, thus provoking the anger and intervention of Marie de' Medici (cf. Vol. I, p. 337). Cinq-Mars was convinced that in her he had found his great love (in Corneille's sense of the word), although this did not prevent him from continuing his more earthly relationship with Marion Delorme, Mademoiselle de Chemerault and various other ladies. He saw Maria as the crowning glory of his dizzy rise to eminence. She was beautiful, the consciousness of her high birth filled her with pride and dignity, but the days of her youth were passing. And now she was being approached by this irresistible youth who, like Luynes before him, might easily have woken up one morning to find himself a Duke and Peer of France. But most important of all from Maria's point of view, her new admirer was

Richelieu's enemy, for although Maria's father owed his throne in Mantua to the Cardinal, she nonetheless hated him fiercely; she held him responsible, firstly, for frustrating her marriage to Soissons and then for breaking off her engagement to the heir-apparent; she also asserted that he himself had approached her with intentions which were not compatible with his priestly office. But these were only emotional reasons. Politically highly conscious, she also opposed the Cardinal on objective grounds. She belonged to those among the aristocracy who criticized his policies, his Protestant alliances and his break with tradition on a basis of reasoned argument. The nation meant nothing to her; her world was the whole of Christendom, encompassed within the network of interrelated dynasties and to be saved by the Counter-Reformation. Like her sister Anna, the wife of the Palsgrave Edward of Bavaria, she was a woman of a political cast of mind. Of Anna the Cardinal de Retz had once said that not even Queen Elizabeth of England was better equipped to govern a state than she. Maria Louisa, who subsequently married King Vladislav of Poland, an unglamorous widower, was to lead a melancholy life in later years, when cruel ballads were sung about her in the streets of Paris. But for the present she still lived in the capital, where she took part in all Court activities; having been initiated into Soissons' conspiracy at an early stage, she too considerd Henri d'Effiat to be of incalculable value for this great venture; if he was properly handled crucial influence could be exerted on the King.

Cinq-Mars was nine years younger than Maria. Before she could bend him to her political will she had to bind him to her person, and this she did by keeping him suspended between hope and fear; indeed she gave him hope until she herself came within an ace of acting upon it.

Effiat's former mentor, Richelieu, was determinedly opposed to this relationship and constantly berated him: "What do you think you're up to?" he would ask. "What has got into you?" Cinq-Mars, who had fallen out with his strict mother over his relationship with Marion Delorme, now made his peace with her and asked for her help in his marriage plans; not unsurprisingly, she backed him strongly, something he immediately reported to Richelieu, who reacted with irritation: "If your mother really is supporting you, she must be mad!" This in turn infuriated Cinq-Mars. The Cardinal had insulted his mother, the widow of the great Marshal!

Cinq-Mars now had only one aim in mind, and he swore eternal allegiance to Maria. In return she gave him embroidered ribbons in her own colours and an occasional gracious smile.

"Monsieur le Grand" was able to call on the Princess almost daily from Saint-Germain. Richelieu was informed about every one of these visits; he was well aware of the antipathy which Maria of Gonzaga felt for him.

But the Court was not always in Saint-Germain, and whenever it took up residence elsewhere or whenever the favourite was required to accompany his King to the front he would work off his rancour on him; and the worse he was treated the more useless it was for Louis to try to free himself from his bondage. Cinq-Mars' cruel game was not consciously thought out; he acted instinctively. There were times when he succeeded in causing a serious rift between the Cardinal and the King; but in the end he always went too far and then Louis would turn to Richelieu again and write him pitiable letters. The following excerpt is typical:

"I have remained patient until now for, before writing to you, I wanted to wait and see whether 'Monsieur le Grand's' bad mood would pass; but in fact it has persisted ever since my arrival in Rueil, although I went twice to his room to ask him to forget anything I may have said or done which might have annoyed him. . . ."

The favourite was being backed up by every one of the Cardinal's adversaries, most of all no doubt by the Princess. More than ten years had passed since her detention in Vincennes when she had believed herself to be engaged to the heir-apparent. The slender young girl had grown into a woman of stately beauty, who had learned from her disenchantment and was extremely well versed in all the manoeuvres of Court life. She constantly urged Cinq-Mars to demand more from the King, but when he did Louis told him that he could not make gifts which transgressed against "justice or the social code".

Within "society", this typically French phenomenon, which in the early seventeenth century was entirely self-sufficient and regarded itself as "the world", Richelieu was judged and found undesirable by the great majority. How could Cinq-Mars have withstood such a powerful current of opinions equally strong at Court, in the elegant quarters of Le Marais, and in the provinces? Everybody fed the bitter anger which this undiscerning youth had conceived for the Cardinal, and so, despite Fiesco's unsuccessful venture, Soissons was soon able to send a second and more skilful negotiator to work on Cinq-Mars. On this occasion Soissons chose Fontrailles, an intelligent man, who proceeded with exquisite prudence. He also told the favourite of the Princes' plans, but he warned him not to enter into contact with these great nobles who were about to take up arms against the sovereign, whose closest confidant Cinq-Mars could claim to be.

This was undoubtedly the best way of winning him over.

The Further Course of the Conspiracy

In 1640 and 1641, while Charles IV and the French representatives were doing their best to mislead one another in a series of talks that led to the utterly unreliable agreements between France and Lorraine, Richelieu's agents discovered that a certain de la Vigerie, a nobleman attached to M. de Soubise, the former Huguenot leader who was then living in England, had entered France as an emissary. De Noyers was able to intercept de la Vigerie, detain him and search his effects; he made a rich haul, for he found letters from Soubise and also from the Duke de La Valette, Epernon's son, whom Richelieu had condemned to death on May 24, 1639, for dereliction of duty at Fuenterrabía but who had just managed to escape across the channel to safety (cf. Vol. III, p. 313). All these letters were addressed to the eighty-six-year-old Duke of Epernon. Although the Huguenots had been quiescent ever since the Peace of Alais and had kept out of the revolt of 1632, it was claimed in these dangerous documents that one reason why it would be advantageous to strike against the Cardinal's hated régime at that particular time was that they could rest assured of a Huguenot rising in Guyenne, i.e. in Epernon's province. As soon as the battle was joined, it was argued, a large number of brave patriots as well as the leading nobles of France would certainly join their ranks.

Despite all the blows that Richelieu had dealt them, the military resources of the Provincial Governors even in the early 1640s still compared very favourably with the forces available to the Crown. The seemingly immortal Duke of Epernon had troops at his disposal in Guyenne which enabled him not only to hasten to the aid of the Queen-Mother but also to defy Louis XIII. Although, thanks to Henri de Rohan, Montmorency had been unable to incite the Huguenots, he had been joined by the nobles of Languedoc. Richelieu understood the workings of this kind of network only too well. When he was returning from La Rochelle and broke his journey in Poitou, the Governor, La Rochefoucauld, committed the same error as Fouquet when he received Louis XIV with excessive pomp and was subsequently destroyed for his pains; although his brother d'Estissac advised against it, in the fourteen days that the Cardinal spent with him La Rochefoucauld invited more than fifteen hundred nobles from his province, all of them friends or relations. This was enough for Richelieu to have him replaced immediately as Governor by M. de Parabère, a man without influence. At that time insurgents could still count on the support of whole provinces and conspirators availed themselves of all possible resources, whether they came from Sedan, Brussels, England or Spain. La Vigerie was interrogated under torture in the Bastille and disclosed all he knew; it was a great deal.

Richelieu then proceeded with extreme caution. He was convinced that, as always, the Queen-Mother was involved and he also immediately thought of Soissons. Why was the Count still in Sedan? What were the reasons underlying his new friendship with Bouillon? As for Epernon, the Cardinal entertained no illusions where he was concerned. He considered the possible repercussions of a revolt; it might well trigger off a chain reaction. Frederick Henry of Orange, who had always been on close terms with the suspect Duke of Sedan, had recently entered into extremely cordial relations with Marie de' Medici, who had utilized her time in England to promote a marriage between her granddaughter, the daughter of Charles I of England and Henrietta of France, and William of Nassau, the son of the Prince of Orange. The French Court had been consulted in this affair, and in a letter to Richelieu Louis XIII wrote: "As for the marriage of Orange's son, I find it has been undertaken precipitously; the Prince might have sent me word before the ceremony."

Meanwhile Soissons was behind the walls of Sedan and so, for the time being at least, safe from any attack on his person; Henri II de Guise, the frivolous, foolhardy and capricious adventurer who was born in Blois in 1614, had joined him in the principality as a fellow conspirator.

As soon as de la Vigerie's statement had been taken down the King declared "Monsieur le Comte" to be the instigator of the plot, and this declaration was of course promptly reported to Sedan. The suspect Count tried to clear himself; he wrote to Louis XIII to say that he would send a mediator to him and he asked the King to accept his representative's assurances that the charges against his own person were pure calumny. He wanted the matter to be thoroughly investigated so that the truth could be brought to light.

The man chosen by Soissons for this mission was Campion,

who had taken such an active part in the abortive attempt on Richelieu's life at Amiens. In mid-December 1640, after a brief audience with the King, he appeared in Rueil. Richelieu had put on "kid gloves" for the occasion: he received his visitor with great consideration and appeared to be playing down the whole affair.

Campion reported to Soissons on this audience:

"After I had assured the Cardinal that you had entered into no contacts either with England or with Flanders His Eminence remarked that the Abbot of Mercy, who had come from Brussels, was still in Sedan. He then sent for M. De Noyers. Before he appeared the Cardinal said that this Abbot had gone to Sedan to hold talks with M. de Guise and M. de Bouillon and that Don Miguel de Salamanca had appeared in Mont-médier in order to confer with these gentlemen. . . . I immediately replied that both Guise and Bouillon were also completely innocent but that since no charges had been made against them I had not been authorized to speak on their behalf. At this point De Noyers appeared and confirmed the statements made by de la Vigerie under interrogation."

When Campion observed that there was nothing easier than to make a prisoner talk the Cardinal replied with a smile: "You are becoming a little excited, Monsieur. I will inform His Majesty of what you have told me, and of course I believe you"—a subtle pretence—"I believe you implicitly when you tell me that 'Monsieur le Comte' is innocent."

Immediately after this interview Richelieu went to see the King in Saint-Germain, and on the same evening Campion was given letters from the monarch and his First Minister for Soissons.

Louis' letter reads:

"My Cousin, I have gladly listened to Campion's statements which differ greatly from those which I have heard from other quarters. Until now I had confidently assumed that your thoughts would remain within the limits proscribed by the love I bear you. I now pray to God with all my heart that you may afford me an opportunity of demonstrating my affection for you. May God keep you." (Dated Versailles, December 13, 1640; the text is in Charpentier's hand.)

And now Richelieu's letter:

"M. de Campion has discharged your commission. I am obliged to say that the King has received information which is completely at variance with that which you have sent him. I would be only too pleased if time should prove your intentions to be honourable and so afford me the opportunity of assuring you that I am your . . ." (from Rueil, December 15, 1640).

Understandably enough, Soissons was far from satisfied with these replies and Campion soon returned with two more letters for the King and the Cardinal. This time Soissons asked that his case should be investigated by the parlement, which in view of his rank was the only authority he could recognize. Campion subsequently said that he had been received far less cordially on his second visit. Although Louis had read Soissons' letter carefully, as soon as he had finished His Eminence's first "Valet de Chambre", M. de Chamarande, had appeared and handed the monarch a note from Richelieu. After reading it the King immediately brought the audience to an end and told Campion that he would receive a reply the following day.

This account differs from that given by the King in his letter to Richelieu of December 28; according to Louis, Campion had assured him that, contrary to what had been said, his master was not asking to be judged by the parlement but only by the King. He (Louis) had then promised to give his reply by the following day.

The King's second letter to Soissons was also edited by Richelieu, who had meanwhile proved to his monarch that the conspirators were trying to persuade the Dutch to conclude an armistice with Spain—in other words, to secede from their alliance with France. Upon receipt of this letter Soissons was again able to inform the Cardinal:

"In the last letter which the King graciously wrote to me, he expressed his belief in my innocence. I am surely right in assuming that it is thanks to your good offices that His Majesty has been made aware of this truth. I wish to thank you for this."

And so Richelieu tried to convince the conspirators that he was completely oblivious of their activities. This was doubtless the reason why Campion himself, whose protracted stay in Paris was causing concern to Soissons, was not thrown into the Bastille. Campion commented on this point in a report to Soissons. From this and other reports it is clear that he kept trying to impress on the Count that the King himself was basically well disposed and that it was his pernicious adviser who was spoiling everything. He wrote:

"In pursuing your interests here I am at liberty to do as I please, for the Cardinal will not have me arrested while he still hopes to lay hands on you. Consequently I am so unconcerned that I even rode with the Princess [Charlotte Condé] in her carriage to see the comedy *Mirame*; at the theatre we met Mademoiselle de Bourbon [who later became the Duchess of Longueville] and also Her Grace's niece [Marie d'Orléans-Longueville]. . . . My seat was very close to the Cardinal's, who was so intent on following this production of 'his comedy' that it seemed his only object was to admire himself in his own work."

And so we see that Campion was not even able to form an accurate assessment of his own situation. Although Richelieu probably was hoping to entice Soissons to Paris or at least on to French soil, the principal reason why he was holding his fire was that he first wished to establish the precise nature and extent of the conspiracy.

Of the many measures which Richelieu took to this end,

that involving the Count of Gassion, who was then serving as a Colonel in the army camp at Arras on the Belgian border, is particularly intriguing. Richelieu wrote to Gassion, whom we have already encountered in connection with the revolt in Normandy (cf. Vol. III, p. 300), and commanded him to appear at Rueil. It may well be that the Cardinal feared lest the illustrious conspirators should win over this young but exceptionally gifted officer, for this would explain the rather unusual request.

When Gassion received the Minister's summons he was afraid that he was about to be arrested, for at the siege of Arras he had quarrelled with his superior officer La Meilleraye. But Secretary of State De Noyers, whom Gassion's brother contacted on his behalf, wrote him a reassuring letter, telling him not to worry about his visit to Rueil, which could only be to his advantage. He advised him to agree to all the Cardinal's proposals, and after his arrival De Noyers repeated this advice: "Say yes to everything, without questioning it." Gassion then appeared before the awe-inspiring Cardinal, who, after first exacting an oath of absolute secrecy, told him:

"I have enemies, M. de Gassion, who are known to you and who also know you. They will undoubtedly try to turn you against me and involve you in actions which they have planned against me and the State. I would be extremely sad to see you become ensnared in such an unpleasant enterprise and want to advise you to be on your guard."

To this Gassion replied that nothing could sway him from the path of duty when the Cardinal's interests were involved. (On hearing this Richelieu is said to have taken a magnificent diamond ring from his finger and to have handed it to Gassion, adding that this was merely a token payment to show him how greatly he loved his friends when they proved their worth.)

On another occasion the Cardinal said to Gassion: "I was afraid that, knowing your courage and ability, the rebels might have tried to persuade you to join them so as to deprive

the King of the great services which you could render him
when the time came to dispose of these 'dissidents'." Gassion
replied: "With enough troops and artillery they could easily be
routed."

The Cardinal then took him to the King. Louis told the
Colonel that he was extremely pleased with him, whereupon
Gassion declared that he would undertake the duties proposed
to him by the Cardinal. But as soon as they were alone again
in Rueil Richelieu looked him in the eyes and spoke quietly
but forcibly: "The King intends to employ you in the affair of
'M. le Comte' and I have vouched for your secrecy, your zeal
and your allegiance."

It was only then that Gassion realized that the rebellious
princes did indeed mean to try to win him for their undertaking;
infuriated, he declared: "I shall kill the first man who dares to
speak to me about such matters."

Richelieu countered: "No, that you must not do. On the
contrary, you must listen calmly to their proposals, you must
make conditions, must give these rebellious nobles the impression that you are prepared to place your troops at their
disposal so as to prevent them from recruiting others. And then
when the day comes to do battle you must inform them of your
absolute loyalty to the King."

But these proposals did not elicit the desired response;
Gassion was repelled by them and answered brusquely:
"Your Eminence, I will devote my life to your service, I will
sacrifice my life in your service, but you must allow me to do
so without intrigue and without betrayal."

To this the Cardinal responded with an air of resignation:
"Monsieur, the King is asking you to perform a very special
kind of service"; and then he added with conviction: "He is in
a position to reward his loyal servants."

Strange as it may seem, the following day the Minister again
tried to persuade this bluff and honest soldier to change his
mind: "My poor Colonel, my friend," he said, "I am causing
you great trouble, but I am most grateful to you. Who knows,

perhaps you are more on my side than you know and perhaps you are even more displeased with the answer you gave me yesterday than I myself."

But Gassion replied firmly: "I can only give you my life and my allegiance; I would gladly lay down my life for Your Eminence but I will not place my honour in jeopardy."

To this Richelieu replied: "Very well, your career may suffer as a result of your attitude but not the respect which I feel for you."

One thing, however, Richelieu had achieved: he knew for certain that he could rely on the Colonel's allegiance to the King.

The Collapse of the Conspiracy

Soissons and his followers now had their backs to the wall. They had only two alternatives: they must either submit unconditionally or do battle. They were pushed into action by the whole of the opposition movement and also by Olivares and the Cardinal-Infante, who applied every possible pressure. Shortly before his sudden death, brought on by pneumonia on November 9, 1641, in Brussels, the Cardinal-Infante stated that he could see only one way out for Spain: she would have to rely on partisan action in France to make the government in Paris see reason. But in the event it was his French adversary who was to enforce this "reason" with such relentless zeal. Richelieu's astounding diplomatic achievements in the beginning of 1641 appeared quite miraculous to all competent observers, and the Cardinal himself felt that there were some facts that even his most impenitent detractors both at home and in émigré circles abroad could not deny—for example, the deposition of Philip IV by the Catalan Cortes, Louis XIII's appointment as Count and Protector of the rich border province of Barcelona, the secession of Portugal and Torstensson's victory over Archduke Leopold and Piccolomini at Wolfenbüttel. Yet in spite of all this the conspirators still

dared to take the field against the Cardinal. As Commander of
the royal troops sent to oppose the insurgent army, which
consisted of the garrison from the fortress of Sedan stiffened
with Spanish contingents, Richelieu chose Marshal Châtillon.

Why Châtillon, who had failed in the initial phase of the
Flemish war? He was a Protestant and had always annoyed
Richelieu by insisting on addressing him as "Monsieur" and
not "Monseigneur". But the Cardinal valued him for his
courage, his self-assurance, his equanimity. He was relying
on the man who, when his horse was destroyed beneath him
by a cannon ball, had blandly remarked: "Tiresome people,
that was a good horse." But this present occasion called for
more than equanimity.

The two armies met on July 6, 1641, at the forest of "La
Marfée" on the western bank of the Maas not far from Sedan.

Châtillon's troops suffered a crushing defeat which ended
in a general rout; he himself owed his escape to the courage
of his son Andelot, who hacked a way out of the turmoil and
saved his father from captivity.

News of the catastrophe soon reached Richelieu, and for
five long hours the Cardinal was completely beside himself
and close to despair. The frontier was breached and Champagne,
which had sided with Soissons, would be lost if the enemy
exploited their victory. The Cardinal envisaged a simultaneous
offensive on two fronts by Soissons and the Spanish, which
could carry them to the gates of Paris. He issued hurried
orders to Marshal Guiche and La Meilleraye, which he immediately countermanded; but then a second messenger arrived
and reported that Soissons was dead.

What had happened? The Duke of Bouillon reported in his
Memoirs that when "Monsieur le Comte" was riding across the
battlefield following the victory he had used the barrel of his
pistol to raise the visor of his helmet and accidentally shot
himself. This account was adopted as the official version. But
the majority of French historians are of the opinion that
Soissons, the only great leader whom the feudal nobles had

8. The Prince of Condé

9. The Church of the Sorbonne

produced up to that time, was murdered in his hour of careless triumph by an agent of the Crown who had been planted in his entourage.

The effect of Soissons' death was remarkable: despite their victory, the conspirators were so shattered that they disbanded and Bouillon indicated that he was prepared to negotiate. But he still made conditions. He insisted that there must be no encroachment on his sovereign territory and that Soissons' body should be brought back to France for honourable burial. He also requested a position of command in the French army for himself and benefices for his children. All this was granted, which shows the great importance attached to Sedan as a buffer state. The Spanish for their part could do nothing to restrain Bouillon; their units were no longer strong enough to launch an offensive on the Flemish border.

It was with the greatest difficulty that Louis XIII could be prevailed upon not to take revenge on the dead Soissons. In his initial access of rage he had ordered that the Count's body should be "dragged over the ladder", a practice customary in the case of common criminals. Richelieu warned the King not to subject a Bourbon to such infamy; Puységurs asked his monarch why he wished to wreak vengeance on a corpse when vengeance was in the hands of God. Between them they dissuaded Louis, who then ordered Puységurs to proceed to Sedan and inform M. de Bouillon that the King would allow the body to be removed from the town. The coffin, draped in black, was to be placed on a carriage, also draped in black, and accompanied to Pont-Audemer by an escort of five mounted noblemen; there it was to be taken on board ship and carried to Gaillon for burial in the family vault of the Bourbons-Soissons.

As soon as Puységurs arrived in Sedan with this authorization Bouillon was prepared to negotiate. He entered his coach and drove to the French Court, where he bent his knee to the King and dined with the Cardinal the same evening. His reception was as cordial as if nothing had happened. The

King felt relieved, for once again the threat to his eastern frontier would be contained by a Prince of the Empire, and he said: "Now I have won another brave man [for my cause]."

The best source for the events and intrigues which then followed is Fontrailles' Memoirs, which provide a dispassionate and objective account, whose principal points have never been refuted. When he heard of the outcome of the battle of La Marée and of Soissons' death Fontrailles was at Court. He immediately called on Cinq-Mars, whom he found in a state of panic. The favourite positively clung to this intelligent little man from Languedoc, and in his agitation he spoke with complete abandon. He admitted having been in league with the conspirators, for which he blamed Fontrailles, and feared that his involvement in the plot might come to light at any moment and bring about his downfall. At first the wily Fontrailles made no attempt to interrupt him; but subsequently he did all he could to strengthen his fears and then to work upon them in order to inculcate in this heedless young man an even greater hatred of the tyrant who had held Fontrailles up to public ridicule for being a hunchback. As was only to be expected, Cinq-Mars' marriage plans and Richelieu's opposition to them also came up for discussion until in the end tears of fury were running down the young man's cheeks. But then Fontrailles told him that he might set his mind at rest, for Gaston d'Orléans was prepared to support him—indeed a most reliable assurance.

This conversation took place at the beginning of August. Before the month was out "Monsieur" went to join his brother in the army headquarters for the defence of Picardy, which had been set up in Amiens, the town in which Richelieu had once escaped assassination by a hair's-breadth. There Cinq-Mars had many opportunities of establishing contact with Orléans. "If the Cardinal were to die," Gaston once casually remarked, "it would be a blessing for us," to which Cinq-Mars replied, as he always did on such occasions, "All that is needed is for Your Excellency to give the command." Fontrailles, who was

Gaston's shadow, repeated the favourite's words; but Gaston remained silent. He dismissed the two gentlemen and the next morning returned to join the Queen in Saint-Germain-en-Laye.

According to Fontrailles' account, Bouillon called on Cinq-Mars during the first few days of his negotiations with the French Court and was told by him that the King was growing more and more embittered with the Cardinal and that this was why the recent reconciliation had pleased him so much; the fortress of Sedan was of the greatest importance to His Majesty for, if things should reach breaking point between himself and the tyrant, there was no other fortified town in which he could seek a safe refuge; he was placing his hopes in Bouillon and the town of Sedan. To this Bouillon is said to have replied: "I am astonished and find it difficult to believe what you have told me. I know that the Cardinal is one of the most accomplished, indeed one of the greatest statesmen of our day and also one of his master's most loyal servants. If the King of Spain had a minister who was his equal things would go better for him." And when Cinq-Mars persisted in his allegations the Duke added: "If the King really should be thinking of breaking with the Cardinal then, if you have the power, you yourself should prevent him from doing so, for he will never find a more capable minister to run the affairs of State."

But this was not to be Bouillon's final word on the subject.

Meanwhile Fontrailles continued to play a leading part. Although he did in fact agree to approach Cinq-Mars on Soissons' behalf, fundamentally he was always an Orléanist. As far as Soissons was concerned he had never for one moment doubted that this rebellious Prince would come to a bad end, for he considered his methods to be far too direct.

Louis XIII spent most of the winter of 1640–41 in Saint-Germain. Consequently Cinq-Mars was able to pay regular visits to Princess Maria of Gonzaga, who used her influence in order to coach him. No more moodiness, she told him, no more quarrels with the King! Part of the time Cinq-Mars

355

followed her advice; he did his best; once again there were moments when Louis would pour out his heart and complain about the demands which his First Minister was making on him. Princess Maria constantly urged "Monsieur le Grand" to be alert and to prepare everything so that he might at last take action against the Cardinal; she was extremely well-informed, especially about the Queen's attitude. But time and again there were difficulties in the relationship between the favourite and his master, and in moments of exasperation Louis was unable to conceal the fact that—if he were forced to choose— he would have to sacrifice Cinq-Mars to his First Minister. This heightened the young man's insecurity and fear. When he had occasion to talk with Orléans, he exaggerated every-thing: he alleged that the King insisted that he break with the Cardinal and assured the Duke that his own occasional differences with the King were only a feint with which to deceive Richelieu. In fact, he said, the King had promised to protect him against everybody, including the Cardinal, and had even gone so far as to ask him to find reliable followers; once such men were available in sufficient numbers and were in a position to arrange a peace with Spain—which the King himself ardently desired—he would not hesitate to join them. After listening to such pseudo-logical outpourings Gaston put the question: "Have you suggested to the King that the Car-dinal should be murdered?" To this Cinq-Mars replied: "No, I did not want to act without being quite certain of Your Royal Highness' protection."

Gaston had already heard similar, albeit far less vehement, complaints about the Cardinal from his brother's own lips, and so he believed the young man and assured him of his assistance.

In December Fontrailles had convinced the favourite of the need to send his friend de Thou to Bouillon in Sedan in order to advise him both verbally and in writing of Orléans' "defini-tive attitude" and to acquaint him with the Queen's views. Henri d'Effiat had simply intended to give de Thou a sealed letter without explaining the full implications of his perilous journey. It says much for Fontrailles that he resisted this proposal; he told Cinq-Mars: "De Thou is risking his life and his liberty. You should not leave him in ignorance of the great responsibility which he is assuming." Cinq-Mars' answer was on the cynical side: "If we don't leave him in a state of ignorance he won't make the journey or will do so with such aversion that it will serve no purpose. He will certainly refuse to have any part in the Cardinal's murder, but even treason would place too great a strain on his loyalty, for he is far too much a man of honour."

Murder was being contemplated and de Thou had declared that he was against bloodshed of any kind. But it would seem that in the end the Queen, who was kept fully informed by Maria of Gonzaga, persuaded François-Auguste to overcome his scruples and take part in the conspiracy. He undertook this mission and proceeded, not to Sedan but to Bouillon's castle of Limeuil in Périgord. Bouillon kept him waiting; de Thou was informed that the Duke was unable to leave his wife, who was then approaching her confinement.

Shortly before, Bouillon had received a letter in which Richelieu tried to bind him to the King's cause by offering him the post of Commander-in-Chief of the army in Italy. But in the end his concern for the sovereignty of his petty State and the greater security, which he considered this new venture had acquired from the active participation of the Queen and—incredible as it may seem at this late stage—the Duke of Orléans, won the upper hand. After long deliberation he left Limeuil and was received in the "Marais", the *palais* of a M. de Mesmes. At the same time Orléans took up residence in the palace of his equerry, the Count de Brion, who was the Venetian envoy and an arch-enemy of the Cardinal.

Orléans, Bouillon and Cinq-Mars then drew up a draft treaty in January 1642 for submission to the King of Spain. Under its terms Spain was to provide twelve hundred foot soldiers, six thousand cavalry men, the support costs for an army, four hundred thousand talers for levies, a garrison for Sedan, the support costs for this garrison, pensions of one hundred and fifty thousand talers for Orléans, forty thousand for the Duke and forty thousand for Cinq-Mars; Spain was also required to grant Orléans absolute control of the army and of any territory that was conquered by the army in France. In return Orléans offered a lasting peace between Spain and France, the return of all Spanish fortresses and territories then occupied by France and the relinquishing of all Protestant alliances.

If we consider the position of strength that Richelieu had created by his persistent efforts, then the proposed surrender of all the advantages that France had gained, the proposed betrayal of the Protestant Princes of Germany, Sweden and Holland appear monstrous. But the sheer extravagance of this offer also shows the extent of the aversion felt by the French opposition for the "heretical policies" that Richelieu had been pursuing for decades. The Counter-Reformational forces were still as strong as they had been at the time of the wars of religion and all the states, especially the despairing peasantry, longed for peace.

The basic motif of the treaty was provided by the slogan: No harm to the King of France, all power to him and consequently none to his usurping First Minister. In the following passage this motif is particularly evident: "We unanimously declare that we intend to take no measures which might prove prejudicial to His Most Christian Majesty or to His territories or to the rights and authority of Her Most Christian Majesty, the Queen."

This allusion to the Queen is most surprising, for it would suggest that her regency was already being envisaged. Apparently the Spanish Infanta, the highly intuitive woman who then stood at the side of the quickly ageing Louis, was already setting her sights on the regency and, if necessary, was quite prepared to oust her brother-in-law Orléans, on whom she had always exercised such a powerful influence.

Fontrailles has stated that Anne of Austria was given a copy of the treasonable draft treaty by Orléans, from which we may assume that it was she who initiated de Thou into the conspiracy. As for Cinq-Mars, the dominant influence in that late phase of his short life was his passion for Maria of Gonzaga. Everything he ever thought, said or did was determined by this one basic feeling. But at that point he was once more obliged to leave Saint-Germain, for—despite Richelieu's warnings and anxious advice that he should not jeopardize his extremely fragile health—the King had again taken to the field.

At the beginning of 1642 French troops occupied Artois; they already held Alsace, and Lorraine was beginning to collapse; under constant pressure from Richelieu's agents the Spanish Imperium was creaking at every joint. It was being said that Naples and Sicily would follow the example set by Catalonia and Portugal and secede from the Spanish Crown; as for Franche-Comté, it seemed as if this outpost would also soon be lost to His Catholic Majesty.

Despite the famine and empty coffers the French armies continued to swell their numbers on the Rhine and along the Netherlands border; in fact, the widespread distress within the country ensured a constant supply of soldiers for the army. Louis XIII, frustrated in his quest for personal happiness, sought compensation by throwing himself into a "glorious" Pyrenees campaign with the object of consolidating all of France's previous gains and forcing the enemy to his knees. But his martial ardour was never enduring. Although he loved battles and victories, he soon tired of the vicissitudes of war because of the ceaseless tension which they imposed and also because of his dependence on the instructions, not to say the orders, of his great companion. More and more frequently he lent his ear to the growing numbers of the war-weary, to the opponents of the Protestant alliances and the pro-Spanish Counter-Reformationalists, only to scurry back to the policies of the conqueror who considered it a sacred duty to extend the frontiers of the Realm. A process was then initiated which, although its implications were not yet entirely clear, was historically inevitable. The old order began to recede; crucial changes took place; personages who had long played leading parts were deprived of their powers or went the way of all flesh. On March 7th Louis learned in his army camp that his sister, Queen Henrietta of England, had fled from London with her daughter and was expected to land in Vlissingen on March 8th. England was in the throes of revolution and thus eliminated from Continental politics for the foreseeable future.

The Cardinal's Internal Policies

Although all important decisions were taken through the King and within his immediate circle, the parlements still existed, and Richelieu's attitude to them will now have to be considered. The decline of this institution was speeded up under Richelieu. We have already seen how the members of the Paris parlement were put in their place in the year 1635, and we have noted the harsh treatment meted out to the Norman parlement in Rouen; in both cases the traditional rights vested in these institutions were completely disregarded.

Originally the parlement had been a council of peers, i.e. of the King's paladins. In practical terms, however, the parlement was an assembly of the leading nobles of the realm, convened in order to decide the affairs of State and administer justice under the chairmanship of the monarch.

In the days when the nobility was all-powerful no bourgeois assembly was allowed to deal with government business. But a gradual and almost imperceptible change then took place in the composition of the various parlements. The King began to delegate his authority to a representative, who passed judgement on his behalf, whereupon the peers and bishops followed the King's example and also absented themselves from the assemblies. At the same time, however, the list of cases was constantly growing and so jurists were called in to take their places and the assemblies were held every quarter instead of every six months. The parlement, which was accustomed to following the King wherever he went, began to complain about his constant changes of residence, and in 1308 Philip IV established a permanent chamber in Paris.

The Kings, of course, always pointed out that the parlement had been their creation, while the *noblesse de robe* always reminded the Kings that the parlement had passed from the magnates to them without being renamed. The transition from a feudal to a bourgeois parlement was a very gradual process; even before it had acquired its permanent seat in Paris some of its members had been bourgeois. Although the French parlement and the English parliament were identical in origin, their development was entirely different. We may say, approximately, that in France the King joined with the Third Estate in opposing the great nobles, while in England the Third Estate joined the Barons in opposing the King. In England there was a continuous development, in which preservation and innovation were nicely balanced. In France, conversely, everything was destroyed: first the nobility, then the Third Estate and eventually the absolute monarch.

When Cardinal Richelieu was still one of the malcontents, on the road to power, he wrote: "Honest people receive new hope when they see how discontented the parlement of Paris is and how courageously it speaks up."

But in 1638, when he was in power, he said to Chavigny: "We must deal firmly with the parlement, not negotiate with it." And as soon as the parlement showed the least sign of resistance Richelieu called its members a pack of rebels. But when he needed its backing, especially in his dealings with foreign countries, he spoke of the great senate whose authority must not be undermined. In his *République* Bodin expressed the view, which was shared by many older writers, that no royal decree involving the cession of French territory was valid unless it was ratified by the "sovereign parlement".

In the seventeenth century the Spanish monarchy, so often

described as the most tyrannical in the world, declared that the transfer of Flanders to the Infanta Isabella was invalid because it had not been approved by the Flemings. Here, as on other occasions, the Spanish Crown invoked the right of the people to decide the cession of their natural territory, a right which was not even recognized as late as 1815 and which is still constantly transgressed in our own day. Richelieu, on the other hand, was to declare that the parlement's only function was to ratify the decrees placed before it by the Crown. But the parlement and above all the *noblesse de robe* were resilient. Even at the height of the absolute monarchy, despite the many humiliations and constant persecution to which it was subjected, the parlement continued to wield influence. Among other things it played its part in deciding the question of the succession upon the death of a reigning monarch. Even after Richelieu, even after Louis XIV, the parlement still appointed the new King and, if there were valid grounds, was able to set aside a royal will. If, as we have said, this institution received its powers from the King, then it would be logical for it to have been dissolved upon the death of the King and thus debarred from deliberating on the appointment of a regent. But that was not the contemporary view either in Richelieu's day or during the three reigns immediately preceding the Revolution. Even if it was allowed to play only a minimal role, it remained a permanent institution. It was only after a new King had presided over a major session of the parlement that he could really claim to have taken possession of his throne. In 1643 Anne of Austria was told that, unless her regency was ratified by the parlement, she would lose prestige and authority. And yet, although there were still occasions when the councillors refused to ratify an edict and although they maintained their dignity and independence even when faced with exile or imprisonment, once Richelieu appeared on the scene the original function fulfilled by this institution ceased to exist, save when it was able to join forces with members of the royal House or with the Court opposition. But its former independence was lost. Louis XIII stated that he was always prepared to give friendly consideration to any recommendation that the members of the parlement chose to submit to him but that he would not permit them to use any other means of influencing the course of events. The last vestiges of independence were finally eradicated by Louis XIV in his declaration of October 21, 1653.

Owing primarily to the education but also to the economic power which it had acquired, the *noblesse de robe* was to become more and more important as a social class in the course of the seventeenth and eighteenth centuries, while the impoverished hereditary nobles were to enter into a period of steady decline. Its really great hour was to come in the years immediately preceding the Revolution, in which the great nobles were decimated. Although the *gens de robe* were also engulfed in this great event, their descendants were to reassert themselves in the nineteenth century. However, we are still concerned with the first half of the seventeenth century, when the ultimate victory over the great nobles had yet to be won, as was to be made only too apparent by the Fronde during Louis XIV's minority.

So far we have been discussing the developments within French constitutional law and the influence which Richelieu brought to bear on them. But his activities outside the strictly institutionalized sphere, his constant and intensive contacts with the instruments of "public opinion", to which he paid more attention than one would have expected of a seventeenth-century statesman, were far more important. In his day there was already a multiplicity of parties, powerful groups with powerful ideas and programmes, which are such a common feature of big-city life. And then there were the representatives of the various provinces, including a number of radical Gallicans who sought to defend their ancient priviliges, while in Paris and certain university towns Sorbonne-trained scholars disseminated their libertarian principles. Having spoken so often of Richelieu's adversaries in the course of this book, we should not forget his followers, who also formed a powerful contingent. But no matter how different their background or outlook, all of these French contemporaries of his, even the *dévotes*, protested to a man the moment the Curia tried to assert its supremacy.

In 1625, when the Jesuit priest Antonio Santarelli published a book in Rome under the title *De heresia schismate, apostasia et de potestate Romani Pontificis in his delictis puniendis,* it was not only the French "politicians" and the so-called *bons français* who were indignant. Everybody was up in arms, for the members of all groups subscribed wholeheartedly to the principal aims of the militant Gallican party.

Santarelli launched a full-scale attack. He condemned even the slightest deviation from "orthodoxy" and censured not only the heretics but all Catholic governments which permitted religious deviations within their territories. He declared war on indifference, expediency and every form of tolerance. In his view the Pope was the spiritual and temporal sovereign of the whole Christian world. *"In Summo Pontifice jure divino est utraque potestas spiritualis et temporalis,"* he declared.

Richelieu stated quite openly that in view of France's system of alliances and the rights of absolute sovereignty vested in the French monarchy, this publication was not only uncalled for but positively provocative.

Santarelli's book contained a brief synopsis entitled "Admonitio ad Regem". This was evidently directed against Richelieu, and his followers maintained that it had been inspired by the Spanish. The defenders of the French monarchy took immediate action and the Sorbonne also condemned Santarelli's thesis. Then the parlement of Paris entered the scene. The Court of Justice, the Great Chamber, the *Tournelle* and the Edict Chamber jointly decreed that the Provincial of the Society of Jesus must require the priests in the College of Clermont and in the three Jesuit houses to give their signature to the statement issued by the Sorbonne, which condemned the book for its "scandalous contents" and "seditious tendencies". If they failed to do so they would be seized and punished for lèse-majesté and sedition.

Thanks to this unanimity between even the most opposed parties in all matters concerning France's relations to Rome, Richelieu was able to regard theses such as that advanced by Santarelli with comparative calm. This could not be said of his attitude to Jansenism, in which he saw a direct threat to his own objective, which was to promote collaboration between the Crown, the Church, the intelligentsia and society within the framework of the absolute monarchy—witness the good-natured tolerance with which he treated the libertines and agnostics. In his day such people appeared of little account; he sensed danger only in great theological innovations.

We have frequently mentioned his relations to Bérulle, an adversary whom he respected. But although the Cardinal never failed to acknowledge his rare qualities, Bérulle remained one of the champions of a united Christendom until the day of his death (1629). Tension also arose between Richelieu and Father Joseph, his closest associate in foreign affairs, when the Capuchin, who normally executed the Cardinal's plans with a great deal of latitude, occasionally raised moral and theological objections to the boundlessness of his master's projects. But the Cardinal was always able to dispel his adviser's inhibitions and Father Joseph continued to place his amazing tactical skill at his disposal.

Richelieu's relationship to Duvergier de Hauranne, Abbé de Saint-Cyran, developed along quite different lines. Saint-Cyran, who was born in 1581 in Bayonne, pursued his studies, first in France and subsequently at the great anti-Lutheran university of Louvain. At the seminary in Bayonne Saint-Cyran then studied patristics, specializing in the works of St Augustine, after which he returned to Louvain for a brief period; subsequently he was given a post as canon and, in 1620, the abbacy of Saint-Cyran by the Bishop of Poitiers. It was at that time that he made the acquaintance of Richelieu, then still Bishop of Luçon. From Poitiers Saint-Cyran went to Paris, where he worked as a secular priest. His influence on society was considerable. Zamet, the Bishop of Langres, wanted to make him his coadjutor, but Richelieu was intent on procuring his appointment as Bishop of Bayonne. Saint-Cyran had attacked Father Garasse, the famous Jesuit orator. The authorship of *Petrus Aurelius*, a polemical work in which the Society of Jesus was severely criticized, was also attributed to him. The Jesuits retaliated with equal force and complaints about the Abbé soon reached Richelieu. At first he reacted with cautious benevolence and protected Saint-Cyran, but subsequently he was unpleasantly surprised when the latter refused the Bishopric of Bayonne. The first indication of the theological differences between the two men arose in connection with the article on "Contrition" in the catechism of Luçon. Things finally reached breaking point when Saint-Cyran argued that Gaston d'Orléans' marriage to Marguerite of Lorraine was a valid contract. On March 14, 1638, he was duly arrested and imprisoned in the tower of Vincennes. His papers were confiscated and, although they failed to furnish evidence for the prosecution, Laubardemont, who is already well known to us and who was placed in charge of this enquiry by Richelieu, was able to produce friends of Saint-Cyran who provided him with incriminating statements allegedly made by the Abbé. This persecuted prelate was not released until after Richelieu's death. His book on St Augustine appeared in 1640 while he was still in prison; Urban VIII's Bull denouncing this work, which is dated March 6, 1642, was not promulgated until 1643. Saint-Cyran knew nothing of this denunciation, for he died shortly after his release from prison.

It should be remembered that the Bishop of Poitiers was well disposed toward both Jansen and Saint-Cyran and that Chasteigner de La Rocheposay, who was a very close associate of his, tried to help Marie de' Medici. At that time Poitiers was an important academic centre, which produced many great scholars; Descartes studied jurisprudence there.

The spirit of Poitiers found its manifestation when Saint-

Cyran roundly condemned the Cardinal's policies during the grave Lyons crisis of 1632. This condemnation was in line with *Mars Gallicus*, the sensational work which had appeared in Flanders at the request of various dignitaries including the Archbishop of Malines and which brought the most serious charges, not only against Cardinal Richelieu, but against the policies pursued by all the French Kings from the Merovingians, the Carolingians and the Capetians onwards. All were condemned as usurpers, as heretics and as allies of the Mohammedans and the Protestants. They were proclaimed enemies of Christendom. Richelieu was made responsible for the war in Germany and censured for his alliance with the Dutch insurgents. The author of this work was Saint-Cyran's friend and teacher Jansen. Saint-Cyran was also in touch with Mathieu de Morgues, whom Richelieu had once tried to win as a collaborator but who eventually became his most intractable polemical opponent. The powerful Arnauld family, who always supported the Queen-Mother's policies, were also associates of Saint-Cyran. This whole group, which was tied up with the Marillacs and the rebellious French Princes, maintained constant contact with Spain. These men even considered the possibility of embarking on a new campaign against the Huguenots and reviving the French Holy League. A great deal of information on this project may be found in the correspondence of Peter Paul Rubens. It was Rubens who had brought the letters of credit from Madrid with instructions to hand them over to Soubise, but only on condition that England agreed to allow recruiting in her territory and to furnish warships.

Richelieu foresaw that these endeavours were calculated to bring about the two things which he dearly wished to avoid: the revocation of the Edict of Nantes and the bitter struggle with the Jansenists, both of which took place under Louis XIV. The simplicity and the rigour of his preventive measures were characteristic of his methods. He once said to Hardouin de Péréfixe: "If Luther and Calvin had been arrested at once mankind would have been spared many afflictions." He also tended to assess all the great phenomena in the history of ideas in terms of their political implications, and consequently he paid close attention to all contemporary innovations within this sphere. It is for this reason that he first consulted Vincent de Paul and other ecclesiastical dignitaries before taking definitive action, i.e. before employing Laubardemont in the case of Saint-Cyran.

Even outside the theological sphere the Cardinal tried to establish contact with all persons of particular merit both in order to orient himself and also to enlist the services of the French intellectuals for his political purposes. This is equally true of his approach to the art, the architecture and the literature of his day.

CHAPTER XIV

CULTURAL ASPECTS

In the age of Richelieu French classicism reached its peak. Its principal ideas were derived from the writings of the great contemporary philosopher Descartes and they orbited, in accordance with strict rules of symmetry, around his central concept of "reason". It was Descartes who called for a rational architecture.

Reduced to its simplest terms, the essence of classicism may be stated in the requirements *génie, art, science*, qualities which the Cardinal possessed to such a high degree and constantly demonstrated in his building enterprises. Tradition has attributed to him the maxim: "I am my own architect." Richelieu's ever growing need for representation was one of his defence mechanisms. At the same time, of course, these great edifices were also meant to provide a lasting memorial to himself. But there is something disconsolate about these endeavours. The "Cartesian" town which he had built next to his greatly enlarged ancestral castle and to which he devoted so much energy was occupied only briefly by a conscripted population; apart from a few sparse remains the town has retained nothing of its original character. Richelieu's favourite residence in Rueil has been destroyed, the castle of Richelieu razed to the ground in the French Revolution and the Palais Cardinal in Paris (subsequently the Palais Royal) has been rebuilt beyond recognition. Only the Church of the Sorbonne has remained relatively unspoiled. It is hardly surprising that the erection of the Palais Cardinal met with fierce resistance, for in order to extend the gardens a large section of the city wall had to be torn down. This, the Cardinal's town residence, was completed in 1639. It contained the gallery of twenty-six "famous men", including Champaigne's masterpiece, a life-size portrait of the Cardinal. In his will Richelieu left his *palais* to the King. Subsequently it was to pass into the hands of the junior line of the Bourbons, who were to cause so much trouble for the senior branch of the family.

Richelieu bequeathed his castle to his own family, and although visitors spoke of it in glowing terms, the Cardinal never saw it himself, owing partly to infirmity and partly to the pressure of work.

We have already encountered Richelieu as a collector when we were discussing Lopez, who was the most active of the many agents whom he commissioned to purchase precious objects. Although the Cardinal did not pursue this passion quite as insatiably as Mazarin and did not have his successor's expert knowledge of contemporary sculpture, he nonetheless succeeded in acquiring an abundance of treasures, which it eventually proved impossible to accommodate in Rueil and the Palais Cardinal, with the result that the castle also had to be used for this purpose. He is said to have possessed an excellent collection of antique sculptures and products of the goldsmith's art as well as tapestries, paintings and valuable furniture. But it is characteristic of Richelieu that his outstanding acquisition should have been his library, which was unequalled.

The Medici Gallery in the Louvre was created during the period when French hostility to Spain was still masked. There could be no more striking way of allaying Spanish fears than this glorification of Marie de Medici's policies created by Peter Paul Rubens. Richelieu had a large say in the choice of the subject matter. His object was to ensure that the credit which he had gained during the civil war was underlined by the artist. The reconciliation between the Queen-Mother and Louis XIII, which had brought him his Cardinal's hat, had to be brought out as clearly as possible. It was necessary to show that Marie was merely continuing Henry IV's policies. She had to be presented as the innocent victim of Richelieu's enemies, for the times in which Rubens was painting were extremely uncertain for the Cardinal. Later, when he was at the height of his power as the King's First Adviser, a passage appeared in his Memoirs, which was superbly formulated by Harlay de Sancy, Richelieu's secretary, and corrected by the Cardinal himself, in which Marie was described as a courageous and innocent person who had been driven to flight by fear. This was the impression which the great painter had created in his portraiture. In 1623, while he was working on the pictures for the Medici Gallery, Rubens was also active as a diplomatist and negotiated an extension of the truce between the Spanish Netherlands and the States General. He always used his visits to Paris to conduct political talks. If he had achieved his objectives in full a great deal of misery would have been avoided, especially in central Europe. Richelieu had, of course, kept a very close watch on the painter's diplomatic activities in Brussels. As soon as he came to power he entered into negotiations with the States General; three months later he concluded the Franco–Dutch military alliance against Spain, which was a diplomatic defeat for Rubens. But despite their political differences the Cardinal allowed the great commission for the glorification of the Queen-Mother to be conferred on his opponent; this series of pictures, twenty-one in all, became known as the "Medici Cycle".

But the full range of the upsurge in painting, which accompanied the revival in architecture, was not exhausted by Court commissions. We need only think of the brothers Le Nain, who movingly portrayed the life of the peasants and artisans, or of Georges de la Tour, who has come into his own only recently and whose compositions, in which line and form are of uncompromising purity, are in complete harmony with the spirit of French classicism.

The force of such paintings is greatly enhanced by their austerity, which is in marked contrast to the extravagant Baroque gestures and the pathos of contemporaneous Italian work. But this should not blind us to the continuing presence in French art of parody, irony and wit, which are also essential attributes of the French national consciousness. Living proof of their survival is furnished by the fifty engravings of the Lothringian Jacques Callot, which bear the title "Capricci; Balli die Sfessania" and portray a series of grotesque figures from the Commedia dell'Arte; by his drawings, which reveal his genius for improvisation, and by his "Misères de la Guerre," the series of war sketches which were engraved on copper by his friend Israel Silvestre and reached a wide public. Following the death in 1621 of Cosimo II de Medici Callot was appointed Court painter to Duke Charles IV of Lorraine. Strangely enough, Louis XIII was greatly attracted by his work and also, as it happened, by the works of the Cardinal's favourite painter Champaigne. He commissioned Callot to make a series of engravings celebrating his military achievements, in particular the siege of La Rochelle. But those which have survived can hardly be said to glorify his battles, while the above-mentioned "Misères de la Guerre" mercilessly record the atrocities committed by the licentious soldiery and the misery endured by the populace as a result of the war.

Philippe de Champaingne has been mentioned as Richelieu's favourite painter before. This Flemish artist even painted the Cardinal on his death bed, wrapped in his funeral shroud. Richelieu also gave Poussin commissions and was one of the few people in Court circles to promote him.

But the Cardinal's connections with literature were far more important and far more revealing than his relationship to art and architecture.

We would be missing the point, however, if we were to accept the interest which he took in contemporary authors at its face value. His principal object was to bend the writers to his political will. The seventeenth century in France, especially the first half, has frequently been described as a time of settled and harmonious proportions. In actual fact, however, it was rife with revolution. The establishment of harmony, order and a central authority was Richelieu's objective. At a very early stage he engaged a number of competent *littérateurs*, who built up and maintained relations for him with the contemporary literary scene; the three most important were Bautru, Boisrobert and Desmarets. Jean Chapelain, who was to play a leading part in the 1630s, was a member of the Cardinal's more intimate circle. He is said to have won Richelieu's support for the new dramatic rules.

The French theatre had long been viewed with a certain suspicion not only by the Court but by the upper classes in general. It was not until the end of the sixteenth century that it began to establish itself as a genuinely effective force. In 1599 the "Passion Brothers" hired out their theatre in the Hôtel de Bourgogne to Vallerant le Comte's troupe of strolling players. In the early seventeenth century this was the only theatre in Paris. Vallerant's ensemble was authorized by Louis XIII to call itself "The Royal Theatre Company". But it was not until 1628 that it was permanently established in the Hôtel de Bourgogne; its official manager was Alexander Hardy (1570–1631). Not much later a new theatrical group was formed under the actor-manager Mondoru, which performed in the Jeu de Paume in the fashionable suburb of Le Marais; Corneille's first successful play, *Mélite*, was staged there in 1629. From the early 1630s onwards there was a marked reaction in the French theatre away from Hardy's Spanish-style drama, which had reigned supreme for two decades. Between 1630 and 1637 some crucial events took place. Corneille made the acquaintance of Rotrou, Scudéry and Mairet. Prompted by the Italians and the Dutch, these new French dramatists reexamined the rules of the "ancients" and urged their observance. At Richelieu's instigation Chapelain defended the three unities in his "Letter on the twenty-four hours." Chapelain exercised a powerful influence in the development towards a classical dramatic style. In 1634 Mairet wrote the first play strictly based on the new rules of dramatic composition. The theatre then began to arouse widespread interest. The younger authors turned to play-writing. This was clearly the way to make an impression at the Court, to enjoy the favour of the First Minister, to obtain support from the general public, in short: to gain entry into the extremely sociable community of the French *littérateurs*.

We know that Richelieu extended his protection to Mondoru's company in the Marais at a very early stage. From 1631 onwards he mentioned on numerous occasions that he intended to control the further development of French drama himself. He commissioned Chapelain to work up Richelieu's ideas into dramatic form. He also took into his service Jean Desmarets de Saint-Sorlin who agreed, after much persuasion, to stop work on his epic poem *Clovis* and write for the stage. As to the frequently discussed question of Richelieu's share in Desmarets' work, it is impossible to establish with certainty whether or to what extent he actually participated in it. Fontenelle refers to Desmarets as the "Head Clerk in the Cardinal's Department for Poetical Affairs."

Theatrical performances were one of the few Court amusements which Richelieu appreciated. In his own household, ballets, pastorales and tragi-comedies with extremely elaborate technical effects were staged for his own entertainment and that of his guests. For one of these private performances he commissioned five different authors to work simultaneously on a five-act play in order to have it ready for staging within the month. Among the five dramatists was Corneille. Corneille worked for Richelieu from 1635 onwards and received a yearly stipend of fifteen hundred livres. Up to 1637 the Cardinal had made do with an improvised theatre in a hall which seated some six hundred people. But in 1637 he commissioned the architect Mercier to build a proper theatre in his *palais* in Paris. This building, which had many novel features and accommodated an audience of three thousand, opened in the winter of 1640–41 with the first performance of *Mirame*, a play for which Richelieu showed a marked preference. Johann von

Werth, who had been held captive since the second battle of Rheinfelden, and Eggenfort were taken from prison to attend the performance. The evening began with a ballet entitled *De la Prospérité des Armes de France,* which was followed by *Mirame.* Asked whether he had enjoyed the performance, von Werth is said to have replied that it had all been very agreeable but that he had been surprised to see bishops in the audience and saints in the dungeons. Sainte-Beuve, who relates this anecdote, said that the Cardinal had pretended not to hear von Werth's remark. As with all other institutions on which Richelieu exerted his influence, it may be said that the Cardinal regarded the theatre primarily as a means of pursuing his political ends.

The French Academy

The idea of founding a French Academy did indeed originate with Richelieu. At first this initiative met with opposition. Not all of those who were invited to join the projected institute approved of the plan for its organization. Two of the projected members maintained connections that opposed Richelieu's policies: M. de Sérizay was an intendant in the house of La Rochefoucauld and Malville was secretary to Marshal Bassom-pierre. Chapelain pointed out to these recalcitrants that they were dealing with a man who never indulged in half measures. And the energy with which Richelieu pursued this project was anything but half-hearted. He approached a group of authors who held regular meetings in the house of Conrart. As early as 1634 he had used the poet Boisrobert as a go-between. The minutes of the initial negotiations relating to the founding of the Academy are dated March 13, 1634. Work then began on the formulation of the statutes: those engaged on this task sought to define the aims of the organization and to draft the text for the *lettres patentes,* without which it could not be registered as a legal body. All drafts were submitted to Richelieu. The *lettres patentes* were signed by the King at the end of January 1635. But for more than two years the parlement deferred ratification of the documents. Eventually Richelieu intervened personally and asked the parlement to implement the decree since the project in question was beneficial and even necessary to the public at large. But when this appeal produced no result—it was feared that the Cardinal would simply use the Academy as a new instrument of power —Richelieu threatened to deprive the members of the parlement of their authority. On July 10, 1637, they finally yielded and gave their ratification but with the rider that "the aforementioned institution is only to seek to adorn, embellish and enrich the French language." From the outset the French Academy was regarded as the Cardinal's personal creation. It was not for nothing that it came to be known by such names as the "Eminent Academy". "There were many", Pellisson wrote, "who at least suspected that this foundation was a new pillar in the reign of the dreaded [minister] and that he was paying [many of] its members to serve his ends and to uncover the inclinations and activities of other men."

In January 1635 the Academicians were in fact instructed to elect no new members unless they had been recommended or approved by the Cardinal. We know that the Cardinal was constantly exhorting the members to exert themselves, but it was some time before this produced any tangible results. From a letter dated January 6, 1639, which Chapelain wrote to Bouchard, who was then in Rome, we learn that "the members of the Academy usually spent their time checking their own works with very great care, from which both the language and its [grammatical] rules were expected to benefit." It was only after Richelieu had complained that nothing of value was being done for the general public that a serious attempt was made to plan a French dictionary. Once again Chapelain was one of those who genuinely aimed at a positive contribution. In 1639 Richelieu approved the plans worked out by the young grammarian Claude Vaugelas and arranged for him to receive a stipend of two thousand livres. But it was not until 1694 that the Academy published its dictionary. Thanks to Vaugelas' "observations on the French language" and also to the influence of Rambouillet, an austere but elegant style was evolved between 1636, when the *Cid* made its début, and 1656, when Pascal's *Lettres Provinciales* appeared.

The Cardinal bestowed annuities on a large number of writers, the amounts involved ranging from four hundred to twelve hundred livres.

Today the names of most of these men are of interest only to the historian. But it is worth noting that, at Richelieu's instigation, Chapelain founded a new art of poetics and that the generation born about 1600, which came to the fore in the 1630s and disappeared from the scene by the 1660s, was the generation of Descartes and Corneille, of Chapelain and La Mesnardières, of de Scudéry, d'Aubignac and Guez de Balzac. These men were called upon to place authority above personal freedom and discipline above insubordination. They built their lives according to a set of rules, of a method, which corresponded to the view of the common weal conceived by the all-powerful minister.

Although there was some individual resistance to the process, during the great European war and for a short period of the ensuing peace the subjugation of literature to the requirements of politics established a common viewpoint between the intelligentsia, society, the Church and the Crown. The French poets celebrated heroism.

By 1650 French literature, which in the first three decades of the century had been permeated by the exuberance of its Spanish and Italian models, had undergone a remarkable process of compression and austerity. And yet, despite its obvious aspiration toward clarity and purity of style, and toward the presentation of utilitarian theses, this literature developed within the initial phase of the universal movement of the Baroque within which it took its distinctive place.

Richelieu's attitude to the intellectual currents of his time was always a political one. He was a comprehensive and a rapid thinker and he wrote like a man who had too many ideas: sometimes he tried to say everything at once and lost himself in endless elaborations; but there were other times when his razor-sharp mind enabled him to achieve the precision of the ancient *apte dictum*. His style contains pronounced elements which derive from the sixteenth century, from his theological studies. These always remained the primary influence in his life. As a theologian he became acquainted at an early age with the tensions which marked his period and was confronted with its principal problems.

The enormous mass of material assembled under his personal supervision, which he had intended to use as the basis of a factual and critical book on contemporary history and his own part in it but which has come down to us in the form of his Memoirs, shows his personal view of contemporary events.

In assessing Richelieu as a writer Sainte-Beuve said:

"We should not expect of the great Cardinal the same simple and precise good taste which is so characteristic of Henri de Rohan. Richelieu has a powerful imagination and he shows it; he is a skillful *littérateur* and he shows that too. There are times when his writing flashes, gleams and glitters, like the crest on a helmet. This suits him, just as it suits the nation which he leads and embodies. His bad taste is that of a Chateaubriand; it is a bad taste which deludes and prevails and there are times when it achieves far more than fastidious reason. It becomes the oriflamme of St Denis, the banner of Charlemagne."

In his noteworthy study, *Richelieu's Staatsidee* (Richelieu's conception of the state), Stephan Skalweit has pointed out that in Richelieu's writings and especially in his Political Testament "the dominant impression is one of unsystematic and fortuitous organization"; we have the feeling that we are not confronted with a didactic tract or with a government programme but with a "potpourri of historical narrative, objective proposals for reform of a strictly limited nature and general precepts of political behaviour."

What the Cardinal envisaged was a system in which all the contemporary disciplines, from theology and philosophy to the natural sciences and literature, would be combined in a joint operation.

The so-called classical age of French culture, in which artistic creations were based on ideal models, formed part of the Counter-Reformation period, the time of the *ecclesia triumphans*. It warded off the influence of the Baroque, which had made itself felt as far afield as China and the new territories of America. But without the European Baroque and this determination to resist its impact the specific culture of seventeenth-century France would have been inconceivable.

By consciously setting up strict artistic rules France created the necessary premise for her "modern" innovations. And yet contemporary French epic works were still rich in traditional motifs. Allusions to epic themes from the most distant past were to be found in the novels written in Richelieu's day. Slowly but surely, however, they were discarded. The French epic then began to deal with the tremendous experience of the overseas discoveries and with the adventures, the fortunes and the crimes which these produced, although it must be conceded that within the epic sphere France created nothing comparable to the works of a Milton. The spontaneous upsurge in missionary activity was accompanied by a powerful development of the sermon as an art form, which reached its peak in Bossuet's works. Incidentally, it was the Jesuits who were the first to grasp the full implications of the discoveries. In a letter to Francis Xavier, Ignatius Loyola said of the new peoples: "These nations are a gift from God." And the reaction to this gift was the injunction: Go out and teach!

Prodigious feats of will were the hallmark of this tortured and fermenting century. The process of ordering the language had begun with Malherbe. The absolute insistence on methodology, which was exemplified by Descartes, created an intellectual *élite* among the members of the upper class who were highly skilled in the art of self-denial.

In this process, which was accelerated by Richelieu's initiatives, the Spanish century was succeeded by a French century and eventually, as the concept of absolute monarchy imperceptibly hardened into a fixed and abstract principle of government, the monarchy itself became expendable. This last development becomes readily apparent if we recall that in 1789, when the "États généraux" were at last reconvened, they were unable to establish any link with the earlier assemblies which had withered under Richelieu.

CHAPTER XV

FINAL STRESSES

In moments of solitude Richelieu, like so many of the statesmen who have influenced the course of history, formed an
extremely clear and far-reaching view of future developments.
His ceaseless endeavours, which in the final analysis aimed
at the establishment of a general peace, were influenced by
such considerations. But he did not put his prophetic insights
into words; if he had they would not have been understood.
He was always hemmed in by immediate events. Of the daily
problems which accompanied him throughout his life the
presence in the heart of enemy territory of Marie de' Medici
and his own indisputable connection with this royal personage
was one of the most onerous. The ill-used Queen-Mother,
wife of Henry IV, who had fled the country in the face of
Richelieu's threats—what perfect grounds for impugning the
Cardinal's integrity. But death arranges such matters.

The Queen-Mother, who had been received in the Spanish
Netherlands in 1631 with royal honours and was then treated
with great consideration, which had not noticeably diminished
even after the outbreak of hostilities between France and
Spain, felt that it was improper for her to be staying in a
country which was at war with France. As early as 1636 she
had wanted to join her daughter and son-in-law in England
but Richelieu had successfully intervened against the project
in London. In 1639 Marie de' Medici then went to Holland,
where she was given an enthusiastic reception by the war-
weary populace. But under pressure from Paris the Dutch
government was obliged to inform her that their alliance with

381

Louis XIII made it impossible for them to permit a Princess, who had become the focal point of all opposition to French foreign policy, to establish residence in their country. Richelieu was fully informed about the popular desire for peace in Holland and he went in constant fear of an armistice between the States General and Spain—the very thing for which Marie de' Medici had always been working. This time the Queen-Mother succeeded in reaching England. The French ambassador in London was advised to ignore her presence. The draft copy of the instructions for this diplomat, M. de Bellièvre, dated January 20, 1639—i.e. two years before the battle of Marfée—discloses that Louis XIII had learned with considerable displeasure that his mother intended to ask for her daughter Henrietta's intercession so that she might return to France. This, the instructions said, would be entirely contrary to the interests of the State; both her character and her designs were well-known and had not changed. Even when she had held a position of great power in France she had always been discontented; if she were to return, she would prove even more recalcitrant, since it would be quite impossible to grant her a degree of authority in any way comparable with that which she had previously enjoyed. Once living in France, she would give new hope to the malcontents, her former followers. Furthermore, if she were able to reacquire political influence in France, the Spanish, who had shown little interest in her when she had lived among them as an exile in Brussels, would do their utmost to help her. They had always wanted her to return, in order to exploit the ensuing situation. Finally, there was the fact that only recently the Queen-Mother had fomented the formation of a dissident group in Sedan led by the Count of Soissons and the Duke of Bouillon for the purpose of invading France in concert with Count Piccolomini. From earlier occasions when she had made promises that were never kept it was obvious that the Queen-Mother would never change —and if the English were to argue that she should be allowed to return, it simply meant that they wished to be rid of her.

The King, therefore, wished to renew his proposal that his mother should go to Florence, where he was prepared to grant her an appanage befitting her rank and dignity. This proposal, he thought, would allow him to face God and the world with a clear conscience.

A document dated March 23, 1641, which gave the exact itinerary, proves the serious intention of this proposal. The Queen-Mother was to have travelled from London to Cologne via Rotterdam in a stately ship belonging to the Prince of Orange; from Cologne she would have continued her journey up river via Breisach to Basle, disembarking there and proceeding by sedan chair to Constance, crossing Lake Constance by boat, then going to Venice via the Arlberg and the Brenner Pass, from Venice by water to Bologna and so to Florence. Louis XIII was prepared to advance his mother one hundred thousand livres for her journey to Italy. As for her jewelry, which she had pawned, he declared himself unable to authorize the payment of the fifty-eight thousand and four hundred *écus* needed to redeem it, but proposed to pay the interest for one year to prevent its being disposed of.

The sixty-eight-year-old Queen-Mother actually did get as far as Cologne, arriving there at the end of October. But there was no question of her continuing her journey; her health was rapidly deteriorating. Acting in Louis' name, Richelieu sent Riolan, her former physician in ordinary, to attend her. Although this was meant to convey the impression of filial solicitude, here too the Cardinal was pursuing a dual purpose, for this doctor was instructed not only to submit a detailed account of the course of the illness but also to report every meeting the Queen-Mother had, every word she uttered.

Riolan's letters, which were unsigned, were directed not to the Cardinal but to the Abbot of the Preaching Order which Richelieu had founded, Father Carré, one of the Cardinal's most active informants. All doors were open to him; he had access to the ladies-in-waiting and even to the Queen herself. He copied Riolan's reports or made extracts, adding further information which he had acquired from other sources. This correspondence began on January 21st and continued until after the Queen Mother's death. It is perfectly clear that a conscious attempt was being made to inject as much venom as possible into the accounts of the Queen-Mother's statements and the trivial events in which she was involved.

Henry IV's widow was understandably afraid of the doctor sent to her by Richelieu. "She has told me nothing of her affairs and I do not dare to broach the subject", Riolan wrote at the end of January. On February 11th he reported that the Queen-Mother's body was heavily swollen and that she was also suffering from an eye complaint. He then added an observation which must have been particularly distressing for Richelieu:

"She is spreading the rumour that His Eminence will die of the illness which he has contracted and has had this published here in the *Gazette*; she claims that Cinq-Mars has the King in his power and controls all his affairs and claims that the Cardinal is suffering from 'Antiochus' disease' and is covered with hideous boils. A number of priests who had wished to write to the Cardinal had asked the Queen-Mother which form of address they should use in their letter, to which she had replied: Address him as 'the most ungrateful and evil man in the world.' "

Marie de' Medici's illness rapidly grew worse; she complained of her wretched financial situation, saying that she was being left to starve to death. Riolan reported that she had cursed the Cardinal and was simply waiting for the King to die, but in point of fact, if her laboured breathing and her coughing continued unabated, she might die at any moment. (There is an alternative version by a different observer, according to which the Queen-Mother is supposed to have forgiven everyone before her death.)

Eventually, on July 3, 1642, the unfortunate Princess

breathed her last; on July 15th Richelieu was notified by Father Carré:

"I wish to inform Your Eminence of the death of the Queen-Mother, which occurred last Thursday between twelve noon and one o'clock. She was so beguiled by her belief in the astrologers that on Wednesday, the day before her death, she assured her doctor that she would not succumb to this illness. Riolan had the audacity to advise her not to cling to her belief, for she would be dead within twenty-four hours."

Marie de' Medici remembered this man in her will, who was then base enough to remark: "Her will has been badly drawn up and could be declared invalid; I pray that this will not be the case for, like M. d'Aquin, I have been left twenty thousand livres."

On July 26, 1642, Richelieu wrote to Chavigny: "I enclose a short memorandum from M. de Riolan in which he comments on the annulment of the Queen-Mother's will."

And on August 12, 1642, he wrote to him again from Tarascon: "I have read a letter from M. de Riolan in which he says that if the Elector of Cologne [the executor] intends to implement this latest will those members of the Queen-Mother's retinue who are on the right side should contest it. If it should prove possible to inform people that the King approves of their project then, provided their case is well formulated, I believe it might be to our advantage. In my opinion they should also be told that the King will compensate those who are well disposed towards him. But they should be informed verbally by M. Chanteloup and not in writing. . . ."

This is a dismal story. It would seem that a dying man was persecuting a dead woman, who had once been his benefactress and the instrument of his rise, but who subsequently opposed his policies with intense hatred and with every means at her disposal. Now she too had left the scene; Richelieu was to follow her just five months later; her son, the King, despite his apparent severity towards his mother, morally suffered to his dying breath from his quarrel with her. He was destined to outlive these two personages who had held him in an insoluble quandary, by less than a year in the case of his mother, and by only five months in the case of his sinister mentor.

No Let-Up

The closing years of Richelieu's life were unremittingly bleak; languishing away but still unbroken despite his great burden of work, his reward was stark ingratitude. But though the ultimate success of his design still seemed highly uncertain, time and again some happy chance favoured his work, presenting it in the light in which he himself saw it. A happy chance is not the same thing as happiness, however. Richelieu was incredibly lonely; with every shortening breath he inhaled the hatred of those around him and in their faces he read their satisfaction at the sight of his racked and failing body.

At the outset of his career Richelieu had had a number of hostile pamphlets burned on the Place de Grève, and throughout his life both French and foreign publicists had kept him under fire—a fire always returned either by his associates or by himself.

One of the most vicious attacks, which probed into painful and intimate family affairs, consisted in an alleged exchange of letters between Richelieu and his brother, Cardinal Alphonse of Lyons, who ended his days in madness. These letters, appearing as pamphlets, were entirely fictitious; their author was Mathieu de Morgues.

But attacks of this kind were so immoderate in content and so shrill in tone as to be self-defeating. Others were more controlled and consequently more dangerous. And Louis XIII's First Minister gave intensive thought to the organization of an effective defence against them.

Father Joseph had introduced him to Théophraste Renaudot, a native of Loudun, the town so richly endowed with strange phenomena. Renaudot had been used by Father Joseph as a publicist. A Protestant by birth, he converted to Catholicism in 1612 and was made Physician in Ordinary in the same year. In 1618 the King's Council appointed him General Commissioner for the Nation's Poor, and in 1625, somewhat against his will, he settled in the capital. In 1630 he opened his "Bureau for Addresses and Contacts". On May 31, 1631, this Information Centre published the first issue of the so-called *Gazette Renaudot*, which appeared under a royal patent that was also dated May 31, 1631. On November 28th the *Gazette* doubled in size and from then onwards Renaudot's Bureau published a *Cahier* containing four pages of news.

There was no proper press in France at the beginning of the seventeenth century. Apart from the *Mercure François*, the official organ for government announcements which Richelieu used extensively, the only sources of news were the *"Feuilles Volantes"* or *"Feuilles Occasionelles."*

Renaudot was subjected to violent attacks by the book-sellers, who accused him of plagiarism. They also claimed that he merely translated the news bulletins which arrived in Paris each week together with a number of bankers' reports from Amsterdam, Antwerp, Brussels, Frankfurt, Hamburg, Zurich, Venice, Rome and various other towns. But by 1632 Renaudot had already amassed an amazing amount of information.

Because he was attacked on all sides but supported by Richelieu and the King, Renaudot was always prepared to serve the French Crown and its First Minister. Throughout the entire world the Cardinal had official and semi-official agents working for him, while in Paris he made liberal use of the *Mercure François*, which, however, had only a small circulation, and also of the *Gazette Renaudot*, which reached a far wider public and until recently was generally regarded as the precursor of the French press. The *Gazette*, which reported both domestic and foreign news, astonished its readers by its coverage; this exceeded their requirements at first but soon roused in them a desire for further information. The following memorandum is one of a number which Louis XIII sent to his First Minister: "I think it would be to our advantage if we were to publish this news in the *Gazette* so that everybody could see that we were the ones who were attacked." People were beginning to attach importance to the phenomenon which has since come to be known as "public opinion." Although no other period has ever shown such a ready appreciation for the vanity of human endeavour, seventeenth-century society nonetheless attached great importance to the individual's standing within the social hierarchy and to his personal fame. Richelieu also constantly sought to raise his social position to a point where it would be invulnerable to the attacks of his enemies. Nobody was allowed to encroach on his rights or to show even a semblance of disrespect.

This explains his determination to perpetuate his memory by erecting the town of Richelieu and the various buildings which bore his name. The most important of these have since been destroyed, but the ornate memorial which covers his remains is still to be found in the Church of the Sorbonne.

The grave of his great opponent Olivares, who died in disgrace and madness two-and-a-half years after the Cardinal, has no name, no title, no ornamental coat of arms. It bears the plain inscription: "*Pulvis, cinis et nihil.*" (Dust, ashes, and nothingness.)

With the passage of time most of those who had known Richelieu in the early part of his life had vanished from the scene and the great critics of French foreign policy, witnesses of the distant era of Henry IV and antagonistic to the present, had dropped out of the fearful race which the Cardinal in his declining years was still set on winning, thus fulfilling the grim maxim Talleyrand was later to coin: "One must outlive one's personal enemies." The great Sully had died on December 22, 1641, in Villebois at the age of eighty-two, and on January 13, 1642, the eighty-seven-year-old Duke of Epernon at last followed him to the grave. Meanwhile, on November 9, 1641, the most able and chivalrous of the enemy leaders, the Cardinal-Infante, had died of pneumonia and Louis XIII had ordered his Court to go into mourning.

But if the old monitors were silent, many members of the younger generation were passionately vocal in their attacks against the menacing minister, whose work and achievements they did not understand and whom they regarded as as unbearable oppressor. Calling for conciliation, for freedom and for the right to live their own lives without hindrance, they were all followers of Cinq-Mars.

But the conspirators had failed to realize that their own era, in which treason appeared to offer a viable solution, had long since been overtaken by Richelieu's new era; they remained unaware that the whole situation had been completely transformed, not because frontiers had been crossed or city walls had been breached or battles had been fought, but because certain events had taken place in Spain whose roots lay in the distant past but whose repercussions were to change the whole course of the war: long years after the secession of the Netherlands, Catalonia and Portugal also defected and other Crown lands threatened to follow their example.

The principal cause of these events is not to be found in Richelieu's skilful diplomacy but in those deeply entrenched medieval liberties and privileges which the French Cardinal had so consistently opposed in his own country and which now came to his help in Catalonia.

CHAPTER XVI

CATALONIA

When Mediterranean trade began to decline, the previously prosperous State of Catalonia declined with it. Ferdinand the Catholic made no attempt to exploit either her weakness or the marked racial differences which existed among her population in order to assert the supremacy of the Spanish Crown. On the contrary, he was intent on ratifying the Catalans' liberties, their chartered rights and privileges, so as to preserve the medieval structure of the territory while at the same time promoting its interests and enabling it to hold its own *vis-à-vis* Castile. He wanted to be King, not only of the whole of Spain but also of every one of her constituent territories. But the fact that he rarely appeared in person in the provinces worked very much against him, for the constitutional forms of their ancient independence were still a marked feature of provincial life. This was especially true of Catalonia.

In Madrid there was a separate "Council" to deal with the internal affairs of each province, while any matters which exceeded the competence of a particular provincial council were dealt with by the *Consejo de Estado*, the Council of State, which was subsequently replaced under the Duke of Olivares by a smaller and less unwieldy body, the so-called *Junta de Ejecución*. And then of course there were the Viceroys, who resided in their respective territories. But every administrative act, every military arrangement, every legal decision was undoubtedly hampered by the existence of chartered rights. These privileges had been granted by the monarch in the course of the wars of liberation fought against the Moors to cities, towns and powerful landowners, especially in Castile, by royal deeds known as *Fueros*. Their influence was felt in every sphere of government, from constitutional law to Customs administration. As far as Catalonia was concerned, the work of the Council in Madrid was hampered, among other things, by the fact that, on the death of the King, no new Viceroy could be appointed and no incumbent Viceroy appointed until the King's successor had sworn to uphold the *Fueros* on Catalan soil.

In 1588 the Catalan rights and liberties were codified in the form of "constitutions" in three printed volumes, the most important section of which, entitled "*De Observança*", was the list of legal recourses against any transgression of the law on the part of the King or his officials. From this codex it appears that it was possible to modify the constitutions; they were a flexible arrangement depending to a large extent on precedent, which could be quoted or ignored to suit any particular case. Actual laws could be passed only in the Cortes and then only in the presence of the King. On the other hand the monarch's decrees could receive the force of law only if they did not violate the constitutions.

One particularly complex problem was posed by the administration of royal justice when it clashed with the special jurisdiction vested in both the municipalities and the feudal lords. Just as in France, robber bands went their lawless ways in every corner of the land; in times of peace they often received support from the inactive nobles and not infrequently they enjoyed the protection of the great landowners. Because of the traditional internecine feuds, the landowners often found themselves obliged to treat the robbers as allies. Consequently the bandit chiefs were able to seek refuge in territories which, according to the constitutions, were not subject to royal justice.

One circumstance fraught with the most serious consequences for Spain in the event of open warfare was that military service—especially in Catalonia—was subject to discussion and negotiation. In principle it was possible to conscript armed contingents in the towns by proclamation while by special proclamation it was even possible to call the whole country to arms. But these powers were based on ancient customs which weakened with the passage of time and by the seventeenth century were no longer regarded as absolutely binding.

The Cortes were convened by the King. They comprised three Estates: the nobles, the clergy and the municipalities. Each of the three delegated one deputy and one auditor and these six men then formed a permanent commission, which was called the *disputació*. In the intervals between the sessions of the Cortes, which were often very long, this commission was supposed to safeguard the country's interests, defend all rights and liberties and supervise the collection of taxes, the administration of current expenditure and the payment of the subsidies granted to the King. The political significance of the *disputació* fluctuated. Whenever the power of the *disputació* declined, Barcelona was the only centre capable of conducting a dialogue with the Crown. In such circumstances this town spoke for the whole of Catalonia, by means of an executive body consisting of five councils, each chaired by a President who was chosen by lot. This corporation was advised and to some extent controlled by the Council of One Hundred, a parliamentary institution. In principle Catalonia, like Bohemia, was allowed to elect her own Princes.

The supreme court was the *audiencia* and was composed of jurists. The Viceroy, who was not allowed to violate the constitution, depended on them for legal advice and consequently the court often exceeded its legal function and assumed a political role.

When the news of Philip III's death, which took place on March 31, 1621, reached Barcelona on April 9th there were rumours of imminent reforms. At that time the Duke of Alcalá was Viceroy of Catalonia. His predecessor, the Duke of Albuquerque, who had relinquished his office in 1619, had already been accused of violating chartered rights, even though he had acted from necessity in an attempt to end the lawless rule of the bandits. As for Alcalá, he was said to have transgressed against local privileges out of sheer dislike of the Catalan people, a fact which earned him the hatred of the population. Because the King had not visited the province the Catalans refused to recognize Alcalá as their Viceroy. They found it intolerable that the monarch should have authorized the Duke to continue in office without regard for their chartered rights. There were two reasons for their indignation: firstly there had been a violation of the constitution and secondly they would have been only too pleased to be rid of Alcalá. On the other hand the Catalans did not want to fall out with the new sovereign, in whom they had placed such high hopes. Consequently, when the three Estates convened, the majority was prepared to accept the unconstitutional ratification of Alcalá's appointment but only on the strict understanding that this was to be regarded as an emergency measure. Alcalá was then duly sworn in on April 15, 1621. But the tension between him and his subjects continued to grow. In the following spring, when the Catalans discovered that Alcalá was to continue as Viceroy until September, they sent a delegation to Madrid to entreat the King not to defer his visit any longer. In the end Philip IV promised to come in the spring of 1623. The reason given for this further delay was the pressure of State business. In actual fact there was no money with which to finance a visit commensurate with the monarch's personal dignity and his need to represent the majesty of the State.

Meanwhile, Alcalá, subjected to hostility on all sides, tired of his office and asked for permission to resign. This was granted and the King appointed the Bishop of Barcelona, Juan Sentis, a man without any influence whatsoever, as his successor; he then asked the deputies to attend the attestation ceremony for the new Viceroy on August 6, 1622.

And so the constitution was violated for the second time. The monarch had again failed to fulfil the condition which required him to be present in Catalonia when a new Viceroy was appointed; and now he proposed to affirm the inviolability of the privileges, against which he had himself transgressed, by proxy. In an attempt to save the situation and accord his representative's installation the greatest possible measure of legality Philip turned to the Catalan nobles. He made an urgent personal appeal to them, asking them to attend the Viceroy's attestation in their capacity as representatives of the nobles, no matter when the ceremony was held. In view of their ancient customs and their military code of "service and reward" the nobility could scarcely refuse this request; some even abandoned their hostile attitude altogether. The members of the Council of One Hundred, on the other hand, abided by their sense of civic duty and adamantly refused to take part in the ceremony.

The Council of State in Madrid had always left the Council of Aragon to deal with Catalan affairs. Consequently it was this authority which decided, in December 1622, that the Bishop's attestation must take place at all costs. But there were those who had their reservations: it was suggested, for example, that, if force were used, there was a risk that the Barcelona mob might try to prevent the Bishop from entering the cathedral; it was also feared that an attestation, from which the public was excluded, would not be valid; yet others argued that the Crown should play for time. It was at this point that the Council of State began to concern itself with the problem.

Since the Duke of Olivares had not yet established himself as the undisputed leader of the Council of State the other members were able to express their conflicting opinions quite freely. Some wanted to use force against the Catalans, others preferred patient diplomacy. The principal argument against coercion was the proximity of the French, although its repercussions in other provinces also gave grounds for concern. The Council of State was aware that if the King were defeated this could trigger off tremendous upheavals, especially in Valencia and Aragon.

By and large Olivares favoured a conciliatory solution;

"a modicum of force", he considered, should be sufficient, and he recommended that the Count of Osona be sent to Catalonia, where he was extremely popular. Osona, who was also a member of the Council of State, was instructed to threaten the Catalans but to add that Olivares would do his utmost to prevent any reprisals, that he would even beg the King on bended knees to exercise restraint, if only the Catalan dignitaries would take part in the Bishop's attestation. When Osona arrived in Barcelona on January 10, 1623, the Council of One Hundred, the great majority of whose members were still quite unyielding, happened to be in session. Osona's difficult negotiations ended in failure, for the nobles insisted on receiving compensation before they would agree to his proposals, while the citizens demanded that the King should forgo the *Quint*, a tax whereby one fifth of all municipal income in Catalonia was diverted to the Crown.

In February 1623 Osona received new instructions authorizing him to adopt a more accommodating attitude. He was then able to give assurances that the King would appear in Catalonia in person and that the *Quint* would not be raised before the dissolution of the first Cortes.

Meanwhile brigandage had been on the increase throughout the territory and without the authority of a Viceroy it was impossible to check this evil. Consequently the province at large became hostile toward Barcelona, which was the centre of Catalan opposition. The general situation, coupled with large-scale bribery and the above-mentioned concessions finally persuaded the Council of One Hundred to allow their dignitaries to participate in the attestation ceremony. This vote was taken on March 3, 1623. Contrary to all expectations, the attestation, which took place in Barcelona on April 12th, aroused general enthusiasm. Nonetheless, the Catalans were still able to use the deferment of the King's visit as a pretext for refusing to pay financial levies, for example the contribution traditionally made to the Crown by every province upon the accession of a new monarch.

In discussing Duke Olivares we have already mentioned his centralizing trends. In his memorandum to Philip IV of December 25, 1624, he had stressed that the King should not content himself with his position as King of Portugal, Aragon and Valencia and Count of Barcelona but should secretly strive to introduce Castilian ways and Castilian law into every one of these provinces with the ultimate aim of removing all existing differences between the various Spanish territories.

Olivares saw three ways in which this union centred on Castile might be brought about. He first spoke in terms of a natural synthesis, by which he meant that offices previously distributed among the various provinces should gradually be concentrated in Madrid. He then proposed that the King should negotiate with the provincial authorities provided he could do so from a position of strength, i.e. provided the army and navy were not engaged in a foreign war. The Duke's third proposal met with the most violent opposition from the Catalans, an opposition which has since received the approval of historians. Its substance is as follows: A third way, perhaps not entirely legal but still a particularly effective way would be—provided the necessary forces were available—for His Majesty to pay a personal visit to those territories where intervention was necessary; large-scale popular unrest would then have to be sparked off to justify the use of royal troops. Under the pretext of restoring law and order and ensuring against any resurgence of such disturbances it would be possible to alter the constitution, treating the province as a newly conquered territory and so bringing the local constitution into line with that of Castile.

One of the principal reasons for these projects was Olivares' desire to tighten up army organization; this was essential both in view of the ever growing threat of war and on account of the widely scattered key positions which the King had to defend around the world. This was also why the Duke had evolved his plan for a "brotherhood of arms", i.e. a combined army, consisting of units from the Spanish kingdoms and provinces. If, as in Richelieu's case, Olivares' projects had led to ultimate victory and not to defeat, they would have been highly commended. His object was to divide the support costs for the army and navy among all the peoples living under the Spanish Crown, for this burden had long since proved too onerous for the heroic Castilians. By introducing his system of common service he also hoped to create a Spanish national consciousness. According to his calculations, the basis of this mutual aid program would be a permanent reserve of one hundred and forty thousand men, composed of contingents from each of the Spanish territories.

Given such an organization, it would have been possible to come to the aid of any province which was attacked with roughly one seventh of this reserve force, i.e. twenty thousand foot and four thousand horse.

Until then the provinces had been virtually exempted from military obligations. Thus Olivares' project constituted a serious encroachment on their rights. In Aragon and Valencia, for example, the King's vassals were not bound in any way to render military service beyond their own frontiers. In the event of a French offensive against Catalonia, a situation which would call for general mobilization, a Catalan force could be conscripted only by the proclamation of the afore-mentioned *Princeps Namque,* which would be legally binding only in the highly improbable event of the King's being present in the province at the time. From this it is clear that the chances of recruiting Catalans for military service beyond their borders were remote, even when the King bore the cost. Only the monarch's vassals were normally liable for military service. In the circumstances it appeared virtually impossible to raise a Catalan force paid from Catalan funds.

In the autumn of 1625 Olivares began to pursue this under-taking seriously. He chose three representatives from the Council of Aragon in Madrid and sent them to Aragon, Valencia and Catalonia respectively to gain the support of these territories for his project.

Barcelona had been passing through a protracted economic depression, which had grown worse from year to year. In 1623 there had been the demonstrations against the Genoese colonies. The free trade sanctioned by the Cortes in 1599 had been operating against the interests of the indigenous merchants for some considerable time. On top of all this there came a foreign-policy crisis. The Duke of Guise, who was then Governor of Provence, had captured three Genoese galleys, which were carrying one hundred and sixty thousand ducats. Olivares retaliated in early April by seizing French properties in Spain of equal value. At this Richelieu forbade all further trade with Spain, whereupon Madrid confiscated further French properties. For the time being, however, trade was still carried on between the two countries through improvised channels. At this point, in view of the growing threat of war and because the Viceroy, Bishop Sentis, was ill-equipped to deal with military affairs, Don Jerónimo Pimentel was appointed military commandant for Catalonia, which the Catalans probably regarded as a stepping up of Castilian pressure and certainly as a sign of mistrust.

A member of the Council of Aragon by the name of Fontanet, a Catalan who came to Barcelona towards the end of the year, found the political climate there decidedly tense. He was told that in the final analysis all of Olivares' plans were based on the formula: "*Un Rey, Una Ley, Una Moneda*" (the Catalans still had a harder currency than the Castilians). Consequently Fontanet reported to Madrid that nothing could be achieved in Barcelona until the King had made his long expected visit.

At about this time, the Cortes received royal summonses to convene in January 1626; the Aragonese Cortes were to proceed to Barbastro, the Valencian to Monzón and the Catalan to Lérida. Their date of departure was fixed for January 7, 1626. Despite threats and bribes, the discussions conducted by the Aragonese in Barbastro dragged on. Not only was there disagreement among the delegates about their own internal affairs, they also questioned the subsidies for the King. Barcelona for its part sent two of its five syndics to the King to protest against the choice of Lérida as a meeting place for the Catalan Cortes. This town had been proposed by the Viceroy with the object of safeguarding the assembly from the disruptive influence of the capital. The syndics pointed out that any decisions reached by the Cortes would not be legally valid, since the King had not yet come to Barcelona to ratify the constitution. As a result of their intervention the Duke of Cortona informed the Council of One Hundred on March 25th that the Cortes were to convene in Barcelona and not in Lérida.

On March 22, 1626, the King at last set foot on Catalan soil. He entered Barcelona in state on March 26th and on March 27th gave his solemn oath that he would not violate the rights and privileges of Catalonia. The Cortes were opened on March 28th.

From the outset the Catalans did their best to drag out the negotiations. They succeeded in doing so thanks to a procedural device whereby they were able to insist on a full discussion of all preliminary questions, which had to be settled before any major problems could be considered. Olivares did all he could to oppose these delaying tactics and even resorted to bribery. But, although many of the proposed amendments were withdrawn, there were quite enough left to contend with.

On April 21, 1626, the Duke of Cardona advised the nobles that the principal French negotiator had informed His Catholic Majesty at the conclusion of the Peace of Monzón that he deeply regretted the refractory attitude adopted by the Catalans and had offered him French military aid. We recognize Richelieu's influence here. (The news was widely circulated!) The initial reaction was just what the French had intended. Philip received numerous declarations of loyalty but the negotiations between Catalonia and Madrid still dragged on. The representatives of various cities received specific instructions that they were on no account to agree to any proposal for military aid.

There were three points that appeared quite insoluble: the *Quint*, the levy of one fifth of all municipal incomes, which the Catalans now wanted to see abolished entirely; the list of privileges, which had meanwhile been extended by new claims and which the King was being asked to ratify; and finally the jurisdiction of the Inquisition, which the Catalans wished to have defined.

If Philip IV had renounced his right to the *Quint* he might conceivably have won over the whole of the nobles and established an alliance between the Crown and the municipal oligarchies, for there was no single question of such direct concern to the merchant class as this one. Questions regarding legal jurisdiction and—most important of all for Olivares—military service were of greater interest to the nobility. But given the state of the nation's finances it seemed quite inconceivable that the Crown could forgo the income derived from the *Quint*. And so Olivares decided to make a partial concession: on May 3rd he authorized the Protonotario Villanueva to announce to the nobles that once again the King would not impose the *Quint* until after the next meeting of the Cortes.

This announcement, which was immediately recognized as a half measure, was badly received and the delegates prevented it from being discussed. Violent quarrels then arose between the Speaker and the Duke of Cardona. In the end the Duke drew his sword and forced his way out of the chamber, calling on all those loyal to the King to follow him. But of the four hundred present only one hundred and forty-two did so.

Without waiting for the formal dissolution of the Cortes and without having ratified anything, the King left the capital in the early hours of May 4, 1626. In the general consternation the President of the City Council was sent after him with a gift of fifty thousand lliures (roughly equivalent to the ducat) and with instructions to ask him to return to Barcelona to preside over the official dissolution of the Cortes.

Meanwhile both chambers resumed their debates; votes were taken amidst great confusion, with complete disregard for procedural requirements and to the accompaniment of constant protests. At last it seemed that the Cortes was prepared to agree to grant a subsidy of two million lliures.

By then the President of the City Council had caught up with Philip IV. The King listened to his requests, accepted the gift of money and thanked him but did not turn back, and so the Cortes in Barcelona were eventually prorogued in an atmosphere of indignation and dejection.

The King had had to borrow money for his journey from Bartolomé Spinola and had undertaken to repay this sum in August 1626 in Italy. Faced with this situation Philip was obliged to have further recourse to the "Donativo", a theoretically voluntary donation first raised in his territory in 1625, which was now to be extracted once again from these same Castilians, who should in fact have been relieved of part of their burden by the subsidies the King had hoped to bring back with him.

None of the territories had agreed to provide troops, and Catalonia, despite her apparent willingness at one point, had even refused to provide money. Olivares behaved as if nothing had happened. On June 25, 1626, he promulgated a decree setting up his "brotherhood of arms".

But from 1626 onwards Catalonia moved away from the territories loyal to the Crown: of that there can be no doubt.

Between 1626 and 1630 most of the disputes in Catalonia arose over the distribution of ecclesiastical offices. The bishops were seldom Catalans, owing largely to the low level of education among the Catalan ecclesiastics. Naturally, the opposition between Bishop and Cathedral Chapter was exacerbated when the Bishop was a Castilian.

Throughout the 1620s the conditions in the areas north of the Pyrenees had deteriorated. There had not been a single good harvest since the turn of the century; in Perpignan the number of habitable dwellings had been reduced from six thousand to two thousand and even the fortresses were falling into decay. The prosperous south gave no help and in 1627 the city of Perpignan again took steps in Madrid to have Roussillon and Cerdagne separated from Catalonia.

When in 1630 Cardona, the only native Catalan Duke, succeeded the Duke of Feria as Viceroy, Olivares hoped that the new Viceroy would be able to promote a greater sense of generosity among his fellow Catalans, for the war in Mantua and the reversals in Germany had made the need for subsidies more urgent than ever.

Actually the Council of One Hundred in Barcelona approved a subsidy of twelve thousand lliures on February 14, 1631, while other towns also decided to grant financial support. But only a year later, in view of the desperate situation in Italy and Flanders, Olivares was again obliged to ask the Castilians for further donations. On top of all this the Silver Fleet was lost in February 1632 on its way home from America. It was this more than anything else that prompted Olivares to recommend a second royal visit to Barcelona. Accompanied by his two brothers and the Conde-Duque, Philip IV arrived on May 3, 1632, in the Catalan capital. It proved possible to reach an agreement whereby the city loaned the monarch one hundred and ten thousand lliures to cover the cost of his journey. The whole of the King's possessions in Catalonia were offered as security.

On May 18, 1632, despite violent opposition, Philip's highly gifted brother, the Cardinal-Infante Don Fernando, was appointed, not only as the King's representative in Catalonia but also as Viceroy and President of the Cortes. But the conflicts continued nonetheless. Indeed, there were times when it seemed as if the delegates were consciously promoting them.

By late summer it had become extremely dubious whether the Cortes could be brought to an end without open conflict. On September 21, 1632, Don Fernando had handed the city authorities a letter from Olivares which contained precise demands but only vague undertakings. In the Council of One

Hundred the name of every delegate who showed even the slightest inclination to discuss these demands was immediately noted.

Meanwhile Madrid had decided to support the Duke of Orléans in order to deter the French from embarking on foreign ventures by creating difficulties for them at home, for by that time Catalonia was already a very tempting prospect for France. On September 25, 1632, the Cardinal-Infante drew the attention of the Council of One Hundred to the troop concentrations which Louis XIII was organizing at Narbonne. This news was received with great equanimity. Philip IV then commanded his brother to prorogue the Cortes on October 24, 1632, to inspect the frontier defences and to avoid any measures that might lead to the secession of Catalonia.

In the following April conditions in Italy required the presence there of the Cardinal-Infante and so once again Cardona had to take on the office of Viceroy.

At this point the people of Catalonia slowly began to realize the inevitability of the process in which they were caught up. New disturbances broke out. A fresh attempt was made to raise taxes from the ecclesiastical estate. The clerics fought back. The Viceroy then sent two doctors of the Audiencia to the town of Vic, which was the centre of the opposition movement; but the canons, who had organized their defence, branded them as traitors and sent them back again.

When a royal force, consisting of foreign mercenaries, passed through the territory en route for Roussillon there were serious clashes with the population. The Catalans had reached a point where they had to choose between total subjugation and rebellion; there was no other way. And then the question of the *Quint* was raised again, although the King had promised not to do so until the next Cortes had assembled; at that time the first Cortes had not even been properly dissolved.

On February 25, 1634, Jeroni de Navel, a member of the

Council of One Hundred, travelled to Madrid to negotiate on the *Quint*. He was received by the King, who censured him because, while the other cities had paid their contributions, Barcelona had not.

Acting on instructions from the King, Cardona then announced in Barcelona that the city's accounts must be submitted for examination and that if the authorities refused to comply voluntarily he would have to confiscate their books. But when the King's officials approached the Council building they found themselves confronted by armed men; at this Cardona had four of the Council delegates arrested. But Madrid shrank from a forcible solution for two reasons: in the first place it lacked the means with which to mount a punitive expedition and secondly the proximity of France meant that Catalan loyalty, however uncertain it might be, was absolutely indispensable. On August 16, 1634, Cardona was sent to Perpignan. When he pronounced the "Princeps Namque" there because of the French threat there was no response.

Navel, having returned to Barcelona to find the four Councillors behind bars, and already embittered by his experiences in Madrid, made sure that all requests for troops were ignored; he is said to have been responsible for thwarting every attempt to negotiate a compromise. It so happens that at this very time, the autumn of 1634, Navel drew the lot which made him President of the City Council. But the fact that he had broken the law on previous occasions enabled Olivares to have him barred from office. The situation grew more and more tense and Cardona was instructed to move his Residence to Gerona and to arrange for the Audiencia to follow him.

Early in 1635 the Marqués de Villafranca, a member of the House of Toledo, arrived in Barcelona to organize troop movements to Italy and also to negotiate once again with the city authorities on the subject of the *Quint*. It was in 1635 that open hostilities began. The councillors in Barcelona and even Navel suddenly realized how dangerous the situation had grown; the Council of One Hundred voted a subsidy of forty thousand lliures, which Madrid gladly accepted but without granting any concessions or privileges in return. Nor did it enter Philip's mind for one moment to abolish the *Quint*, which was to have brought in five hundred thousand ducats, in return for these forty thousand lliures.

And then from May 19, 1635, onwards Spain was at war with her great neighbour. As a result relations between Madrid and Catalonia entered into a new phase. Pressure on all the Spanish provinces was increased; there was no shortage of money, there was a growing and urgent need for troops and there were relatively few companies of young men capable of bearing arms.

Olivares had decided to make Catalonia the base for his operations against France. There Philip IV would take command of an army of forty thousand men, ten thousand of whom were to be supplied by the kingdom of Aragon. According to Olivares' plan, this army would either be used in Italy while the French were tied up in Flanders and on the Rhine or, if Louis XIII were to try to intervene in Italy, it would be sent to Flanders to launch an offensive against Paris; and if all went well in Italy, then the Spanish army would march into southern France. Objections were raised to this plan in Madrid. There were those who argued that a province as unreliable as Catalonia was totally unsuited as a general base. But in the end it was decided that the King would set out for this frontier province on January 21, 1636, at the head of his contingent.

Once again difficult constitutional questions were raised: the final dissolution of the Cortes now became a matter of the greatest importance. According to the Catalan constitution, the Cortes could not remain in session while an army was stationed in the province. But without the army the King lacked the authority which he needed for his negotiations with the Catalans. Olivares was determined to defend Catalonia and to use this great frontier territory as his base. But at this point his opponents got the better of him: the Catalan Cortes refused to sanction the necessary subsidies for troop concentrations within their territory. The whole project was called off and the situation in Catalonia remained completely unpredictable. This in turn jeopardized the authority of Viceroy Cardona in Gerona. The Catalans refused to supply either troops or money. When Olivares ordered the Viceroy to embark with a Catalan contingent and sail for Genoa at once the Viceroy was obliged to inform him that the Catalans were not even prepared to defend their own frontier; a few days before an infantry unit, which had been recruited with great difficulty, had deserted into France, taking their weapons with them, simply because it had been rumoured that they might be shipped off to Italy.

The King again offered to defer the legal battle over the *Quint* until the next Cortes had assembled if Barcelona would agree to raise three thousand to four thousand men for a period of six months. The city declined.

One result of the Catalan attitude was that the neighbouring provinces were required to provide more soldiers than they would normally have done. At last Olivares stated quite openly in the Council of State that the time had come to procure respect for the Crown in this rebellious province. Then, as on many previous occasions, the Catalans again baulked at the idea of actually breaking with the monarchy and at the eleventh hour they tried to mend their ways. Meanwhile the absence of the Viceroy and the removal of the Audiencia to the town of Gerona had had particularly unpleasant repercussions in Barcelona. Consequently, when Cardona was sworn in for a further three-year period in Perpignan the inhabitants of Barcelona, who were the real obstructionists and the source of all difficulties, insisted that he must give his oath in their city as well, especially as they wished to put aside their disputes with the Crown. The Viceroy then returned on January 17, 1637, and resumed his negotiations, in which, as always, the *Quint* was the principal

item on the agenda. As a token of the city's submission the
President of the City Council authorized the gift to the King
of forty thousand five hundred escudos. All in all since the
outbreak of war Barcelona had paid out eighty thousand and
five hundred lliures in subsidies—the equivalent of one year's
municipal income and consequently no mean sum. But the
gesture came too late. Relations between Madrid and Catalonia
were past repair. True, the Audiencia was recalled to Barcelona
but the ministers in Madrid were less impressed by the Catalans' generosity than the citizens felt they should have been.
From then onwards Madrid regarded every Catalan move as
an artifice while the Catalans saw in everything emanating
from Madrid signs of suppression and "Castilization". This
mutual sensitivity, which France naturally did her utmost to
foster, was constantly exacerbated by new conflicts. One of
the most harmful of these was the language dispute. Castilian
had gradually been adopted as the usual language of the upper
classes in Catalonia and a large number of Castilian terms had
also been taken over by the broad mass of the Catalan people.
Now, quite suddenly, it was branded as the "instrument of
foreign rule" and the Council of the ecclesiastical province of
Tarragona ordained that in Catalonia all sermons were to be
preached in Catalan.

As far as the "brotherhood of arms" was concerned,
Catalonia remained intractable. Since Philip IV's accession
its total contribution to the combined force had consisted of a
few reprieved criminals, whereas Valencia, for example, had
raised five thousand men for the Italian campaign. Consequently
the "Junta de Ejecución" informed the Viceroy that he must
prevail upon the Catalans to raise a contingent of six thousand
men; Cardona was required to explain that the garrison
stationed in Catalonia was needed in Italy and that the Province
must see to its own defence. In actual fact Olivares' plans went
far beyond the defence of Catalonia; by then it was his firm
intention to launch an offensive: an army of fifteen thousand
men (including six thousand Catalans) was to attack France

from the Pyrenees. This was why he ordered the Viceroy to proclaim the "Princeps Namque", the general mobilization of Catalonia, in Perpignan on June 13, 1637. As so often before, the Catalans maintained that this proclamation transgressed against the constitution, since general conscription could only be ordered in the presence of the King. True, this objection was overruled by the Council of Aragon; but when the Spanish army crossed the northern frontier on August 29th there was not a single Catalan soldier in its ranks. In response to Cardona's repeated representations Barcelona eventually sent three hundred of the five hundred men they had promised, who then behaved like the lowest of the foreign mercenaries and merely helped to strengthen the general aversion felt for the "King's war".

And then of course the Spanish attack on Languedoc was a failure; their army was defeated by the French militia and the provincial nobles at Leucate.

As was only natural, the sudden collapse of the offensive led to deep gloom in Madrid. Olivares blamed Giovanni Serbelloni, the Commander of the Spanish army, for the defeat but in the eyes of the public it was the Catalans' fault: the finger of scorn was pointed at them. Cardona, who did not consider himself in any way responsible for the defeat at Leucate, asked to be relieved of his post as Viceroy.

Despite everything, the Catalans felt extremely concerned at this military setback and thirsted for revenge no less than the rest of Spain. But their concern did nothing to encourage recruiting. In spite of their onrush of patriotic feeling, they were openly annoyed at the inconvenience caused by the quartering of troops or at the fact that the Spanish army had to winter in Catalonia.

In February 1638 a new Viceroy appeared on the scene, also a Catalan nobleman but less exalted than his predecessor; he was Don Dalmau de Queralt, the Count of Santa Coloma, an ambitious, excitable, insecure and pretentious man who aspired to the rank of a Marqués, but who exercised a certain influence over his fellow Catalans, even those who disliked him. His first task was the disagreeable one of establishing a tolerable *modus vivendi* between the local population and the marauding troops in winter quarters. He also had to repair the frontier defences; this too was a matter of urgency. But none of the Catalan towns was prepared to contribute to the expense without receiving concessions in exchange. And so Santa Coloma had to ask Madrid and above all Barcelona to grant further privileges, the so-called *"mercedes"*, in order to create a more favourable atmosphere for his negotiations.

Contrary to expectations, the French spring offensive was not directed against Catalonia but against the Basques, in the extreme west. Fuenterrabía was besieged. Meanwhile Santa Coloma had worked out a compromise solution with Barcelona only to have it rejected out of hand by Madrid. And yet Barcelona had been prepared to write off all previous credits advanced to the King, which meant that its contributions up to that time would have been the equivalent of four years' municipal income. Over and above this the citizens had agreed to present Philip with ten thousand lliures—over one tenth of the city's annual income. But the ministers declared that they were not interested in this account of services rendered and that what the Catalans ought to be doing was bringing relief to the beleaguered fortress of Fuenterrabía by attacking Languedoc. Once again Madrid blandly disregarded the clause in the Catalan constitution which made it illegal for native troops to be sent on an offensive beyond their own borders. The Viceroy was unable to levy troops because Catalonia did not consider that it had been attacked. In this instance Catalonia displayed a distinct lack of solidarity, which was in marked contrast to the reaction of the rest of Spain. From every other province volunteers were heading for Fuenterrabía, which had become a sort of national symbol. There for the first time ever a Spanish "brotherhood of arms" based on genuine devotion to a common cause and free from all coercion spontaneously manifested itself. Consequently the initial French victory at Fuenterrabía, like their victory at Leucate, brought disgrace on Catalonia, the province that had stood aside yet again out of "ruthlessness, avarice and cupidity".

Each year thousands of mountain dwellers gathered in Barcelona to hire themselves out to the estate owners as *segadores* (harvest workers). They were unruly and violent men, many of whom were armed. In 1640 they arrived in the towns, as always, for the Feast of Corpus Christi on June 7th. On this occasion they openly complained about the tyranny of the Viceroy and the excesses of the soldiery and adopted a threatening attitude towards all Castilians. The smouldering riot was finally sparked off by a single musket shot fired into the air from a window of the Viceroy's palace. The *segadores* then fell upon the Castilians; they even pursued them into the churches and killed large numbers of them. The militia sided with the insurgents, and a few Genoese galleys that had been chartered by Spain and were lying at anchor in the harbour were fired upon. Coloma, who tried to escape in disguise, was recognized and cut down. The scenes enacted in Barcelona were repeated throughout the whole province. The troops, hard pressed on all sides by the peasantry, withdrew either into Aragon or to the Catalan district of Roussillon, where they fared no better. In Perpignan the Spanish commander in the citadel had to bombard the town before the inhabitants would open the gates to the King's force. Perpignan, Collioure and Salces were the only strongholds in Roussillon to remain in Spanish hands. The Catalan authorities implored Philip IV to leave them to defend their territory on their own, to grant a general amnesty and to withdraw his armed forces. These requests went unheeded. Instead, all available units were massed for the forcible suppression of the insurrection. As a result the Catalan Cortes came out in open support of the general revolt against the Crown. They also appealed for help to Aragon and above all France. Richelieu sent Du Plessis-Besançon, an army engineer and diplomat, to Catalonia.

He soon came to terms with the rebels and signed a treaty of alliance with them on December 16, 1640.

The full extent of the rift between the Catalans and Philip IV became apparent as soon as the French launched their offensive in Roussillon. Richelieu had foreseen it all, for he had been kept fully informed for some considerable time of events in Catalonia, especially of those in Barcelona.

Faced with the reversals that France had suffered in Flanders and Italy and also the protracted and inconclusive nature of the war in Germany, the Cardinal had realized that offensive action against Spain's land and sea frontiers offered an effective means of aggravating the difficulties which confronted Philip IV at home. The first French offensive had been directed against the province of Guipúzcoa in 1638 and was accompanied by naval attacks on the most important Spanish and Portuguese harbours. But the initial outcome of all these endeavours was the severe defeat the French eventually sustained at Fuenterrabía. The action initiated in Roussillon in 1639 was also unsuccessful. It thus became clear that military offensives against the mainland of Spain would not in themselves procure a favourable peace for France. Once again it was Richelieu's diplomacy that was to produce the desired result. Using methods similar to those he had employed in Germany, Italy and the insurgent Netherlands, he proceeded to exploit the situation in Catalonia for his own ends. As early as August 22, 1635, he had asked the Duke of Halluin to send him ground plans of Barcelona, Perpignan and Salces. In the same year a memorandum was received in his chancelry which dealt with the various ways in which France might provoke a Catalan secession; the document laid particular emphasis on Catalan resistance to mobilization. From 1636 onwards Richelieu also received numerous letters from the government of Languedoc and the County of Foix together with reports from private individuals who furnished detailed accounts of the difficulties between Catalonia and Madrid.

The Governor of the fortress of Leucate, M. de Saint-

Aunais, was not trusted at the French Court, because of his extremely independent behaviour and disregard of orders. It was even believed that he was informing the Spanish about French troop movements—something he had already done during the Italian campaign. Early in October 1639 Richelieu instructed Condé to have M. de Saint-Aunais placed under instant arrest. But the Governor had already left Leucate. Following his repeated refusals to appear in Narbonne or Paris, orders were given for his dismissal. Shortly afterwards he joined Spinola in Salces, acting as his adviser throughout the long months of the siege of Barcelona, and in mid-February 1640 he rode into the city at Spinola's side as victor.

Du Plessis-Besançon, the agent whom Richelieu had sent to Barcelona in the summer of 1640, later reported that a written order had been issued by the Spanish requiring those regiments which had taken part in the campaign in Roussillon in 1639 to remain in Catalonia. It was assumed that this measure had been recommended to Olivares and the Spanish generals by Saint-Aunais with the object of provoking an anti-Spanish reaction among the population and arousing their indignation at the oppressive presence of what was virtually an army of occupation. It is interesting to note that, when Saint-Aunais later returned to his mother country, there was no mention of treason and he was immediately reinstated as Governor of Leucate. His journey to Barcelona might well have been a carefully planned and highly original piece of intelligence work.

La Mothe, who was in command of military operations in Catalonia during the early years of the French occupation and was Viceroy of the province from mid-1642 to the end of 1644, later wrote in his Memoirs: "Once revolution had been incited in Catalonia and Portugal by the late Cardinal's [Richelieu's] prudent measures France found ways and means of furthering her plans beyond the Pyrenees."

Since the end of August 1640 Richelieu and his army commanders had been backing every move to establish French military occupation and political control of Catalonia. In one of De Noyers' letters we are told: "Turin has been taken, the harbour of Rosas is being blockaded by the Catalans and new and important successes have been reported from Germany, all of which would suggest a revival of French fortunes." He might have added that Arras, the key fortress in the Flemish campaign, had also fallen into French hands, thanks principally to Richelieu's nephew, La Meilleraye. At that time Banér's setbacks in Bohemia were yet to come.

The correspondence dealing with Catalonia, then the burning question of the hour, was voluminous. On September 26, 1640, Chavigny wrote: "the King's affairs oblige me to remain in Paris or its environs. . . . So many commands are being issued in respect of Turin, Casale and Catalonia . . . that it is impossible for me to leave."

Even before it was known whether treaties had been signed with Catalonia orders were issued as a matter of urgency. On September 26th Richelieu was forwarded the following royal command to the Archbishop of Bordeaux, then Admiral of the French fleet: "The Catalans have appealed to me for help. . . . They have offered to cede the harbour of Rosas which they are at present blockading. I command that part of my fleet be sent without delay to the islands off Marseilles to take possession of the harbour of Rosas and its fortress . . . to force them into my service and to hasten to the aid of the Catalans."

These orders were accompanied by a letter |from De Noyers who informed the Archbishop that he must act on them immediately since they came from the King and the Cardinal. De Noyers also informed Du Plessis-Besançon of all these measures in a letter of the same date. In it he spoke of the great and glorious day which was about to dawn for Catalonia, the new province of which so much was to be expected. He then mentioned the orders for the attack on Rosas, whose harbour, it was hoped, was already in the hands of the Catalans, adding that Condé was on his way to Languedoc to prepare the army for a great military action.

In September 1640, the Duke of Halluin, since 1637 Marshal

Schomberg, who was General Espenan's and General Du Plessis-Besançon's superior, began to take an active interest in the course of events. During September and October he constantly informed Richelieu about all matters connected with the Catalan rising, about the support given by the French to the inhabitants of Illa in their battles against the undisciplined troops led by General Garay, about the French preparations for the invasion of Catalonia. Richelieu responded by coolly asking Schomberg not to interfere in matters which had been entrusted to the Prince of Condé; the Prince bore the sole responsibility for the defence of southern France and was also authorized to take any diplomatic measures necessary for the seizure of Catalonia. And in point of fact Espenan, Du Plessis-Besançon and Francisco Villaplana, a close follower and partisan of the President of the "Generalidad" and of the canon, Pablo Claris, always approached Condé direct in all matters calling for an immediate decision. On October 31st Richelieu gave orders that all troops in Languedoc be kept at the alert, so that they could march to the aid of the Catalans at a moment's notice. He wrote to Condé: "In view of the importance of this affair I do not doubt that you will give it your special attention, especially since there is some danger that the King of Spain might take action against Catalonia in the winter."

And on November 1st he wrote in still more urgent terms:

"I am writing to you again to beg you to march into Catalonia as soon as the Catalans provide Marshal Espenan with the opportunity and to employ on this operation double the force of three thousand foot and one thousand horse requested by the Catalans; this would deal a heavy blow to Spain, for if the Catalans are able to resist the assaults of the Spanish forces throughout the coming winter the campaign will drag on long enough for us to establish favourable conditions for an advantageous peace. If money is required, spend as much as you need."

In mid-November he plied Condé with the same request. By

this time he was almost pleading with him: "I am taking up my pen yet again to beg you to do all that is humanly possible to increase the size of the force that is to march into Catalonia. The matter is of the greatest importance and calls for speedy action and consequently I have no doubt that you will outdo yourself in this affair."

On September 25th, when the Spanish attacked Illa, French officers appeared on the scene, followed shortly afterwards by French troops, to conduct the defence of this Catalan town. This may be regarded as the first armed French intervention on behalf of the rebellious province.

In the battles fought in mid-November near Tortosa between Spanish soldiers and Catalan volunteers many Frenchmen, who had joined the rebel ranks, were taken prisoner. Marshal Schomberg, who despite Richelieu's warning not to take the initiative, had exercised absolutely no restraint, not only informed Du Plessis-Besançon that he was holding fresh infantry and cavalry forces in readiness at the border near Narbonne but also urged Marshal Espenan to apply to him immediately if there was anything he needed.

Eventually Claris and Du Plessis-Besançon completed the treaty drafts. These contained a provision to the effect that they must be returned within one month bearing the signature of Louis XIII together with all requisite endorsements. Shortly afterwards this provision was dropped and Claris agreed to accept Du Plessis-Besançon's signature instead, which the French delegate had been authorized to give from the outset. On the day on which the treaties were signed an important event took place in Barcelona: the deputies appointed Marshal Espenan "maestro de campo general" of Catalonia and the auxiliary army and Du Plessis-Besançon "Sargento Mayor" with absolute powers over the commanders of all military forces then available. Du Plessis-Besançon wrote to Richelieu immediately:

"We have lost no time in carrying out our allotted tasks . . .

The treaty of alliance between France and Catalonia was signed today in accordance with Your Excellency's instructions and is being forwarded to M. de Noyers. We wish to take this opportunity of affirming [our belief] that important though the contents of this treaty may be, they are as nothing compared with the consequences to which they will give rise."

At almost the same time Chavigny also received a letter containing a similar prognosis. Among other things he was told: "The conditions are very favourable for France. But they are as nothing compared with what we may expect. We shall soon see."

We must now deal briefly with certain military actions which were initiated by Richelieu himself for strategic reasons.

In a letter to the Archbishop of Bordeaux, the Admiral commanding the French fleet, Richelieu wrote that France did not possess a single stronghold in the interior of Catalonia and could not count on the loyalty of the population.

"If we are to conduct our future operations systematically and prudently we must occupy the coastal strongholds, which can be secured against surprise attack and military stratagems on the part of the enemy and to which it will be easier to bring succour at all times of the year than to inland towns. We shall have to form a complete infantry and cavalry corps, which will be accompanied by artillery and be fully provisioned and will arrive from Collioure under the command of Marshal Schomberg a few days after the fleet has assembled in the Bay of Cadaqués. The attack will be mounted from both sea and land."

A certain René de Voyers d'Argenson, who had worked for Richelieu against the Spanish in every part of Europe, was now sent to Catalonia. D'Argenson was commissioned to put the agreements concluded by Plessis-Besançon in Barcelona between January 18 and 23, 1641, into effect.

Throughout this undertaking Richelieu knew that he was running a very considerable risk. This explains why he was so determined to consolidate his gains by conquering the coastal towns. From the very beginning of the talks on French military aid for Catalonia it was considered that for French troops to penetrate into the interior of the province was an enterprise which might quite conceivably come to a very bad end: the French forces might be encircled by the Spanish units stationed in Roussillon or, if there were a rising by pro-Spanish elements in Catalonia, they might be forced to shed Catalan blood. Hence Richelieu's decision to use the fleet in an attempt to establish French garrisons in the coastal towns, thus avoiding the hazards of the interior. But from the very outset the project met with resistance from the Grand Admiral. He regarded it as impracticable, arguing that the harbours were unsuited for mooring ships and adding that what he had seen of the Catalans' attitude toward France did not inspire him with confidence. This was the beginning of Richelieu's conflict with Sourbis, the seafaring Archbishop of Bordeaux, whose political career was rapidly drawing to a close. He was plied with arguments in support of Richelieu's view, but to no avail: on February 1, 1641, the War Minister, De Noyers, wrote informing him that Catalonia had decided to submit to the King and his armies and that their willingness to do so called for some response; France must give the Catalans some proof of her good will. The Cardinal made Sourbis swear under oath that he would do his utmost to contribute to the success of this undertaking. He explained that the Catalans were prepared to help take the harbour and fortress of Cadaqués and to hand them over to the French once they were conquered; the time had come for action. The King was forming a new army, which was intended for Catalonia, and it was hoped that Portugal would also intervene. It was imperative that they should gain possession of the harbours of Rosas and Collioure and for this they needed Cadaqués as a base. Sourdis was to contact the Duke of Halluin (Schomberg) at once and work out a plan of campaign. But the Admiral continued to resist and on February 11th he received fresh orders, which were signed by both the King and Richelieu and which spelt out the instructions

o   417

previously sent to him in unmistakable terms. The Admiral was informed that as a result of developments in Catalonia, Louis XIII had had to instruct the Duke of Halluin to march into the territory at the head of powerful forces with all speed. Sourdis was to render assistance by mounting an immediate attack on Collioure and Rosas. Richelieu did not mince his words. He told him that there could be no possible excuse for him if the enterprise miscarried through his fault. Sourdis then obeyed. On March 5th three of his ships forced their way into the Bay of Cadaqués and landed four hundred infantrymen, who took possession of the town and three small forts. On March 19th three larger ships arrived on the scene, followed on March 26th by the main body of the fleet under the Admiral's command. On March 27th a fierce naval battle was fought in the Bay of Rosas, in which five Spanish ships were captured, and on May 28th two Spanish galleys were taken off Port-Vendres. The official communiqué on these actions stressed "the joy felt throughout Catalonia as a result of this heaven-sent blessing, which had been accorded to the territory when His Majesty had placed it under His protection".

It was Du Plessis-Besançon's reports on the politico-strategic situation in Catalonia that prompted Richelieu to change his plans. Du Plessis-Besançon succeeded in convincing the French ministers that their immediate objective must be to prevent the Spanish from landing new troops in Rosas and Collioure since this might enable them to cut France off from Catalonia. The troops stationed in Tarragona must not be allowed to advance via Conca de Barbera to Urgel, for this could lead to the loss of Lérida. Moreover, the rumours of imminent operations against Roussillon, which were then circulating in Barcelona, had aroused the suspicion that the French were more interested in occupying this district than in driving the Spanish forces out of Catalonia.

Richelieu then concentrated on the conquest of Tarragona which he undertook with the object of diverting as many Spanish troops as possible from Catalonia. The French navy succeeded in landing a powerful siege army beneath this Mediterranean fortress. On June 12th Fernandina approached with the evident intention of attempting to relieve the Spanish garrison, but when he saw that neither the Duke of Marqueda's galleys nor those from Naples had arrived he confined himself to cruising off the coast. On July 3rd Fernandina reappeared with his fleet, which had been reinforced by Neapolitan and Genoese vessels. Fierce battles were waged both at sea and on land. A local Spanish chronicler reported that after the fighting some three hundred bodies were washed up by the tide.

In spite of the confident communiqués sent to Paris by La Mothe, in which he claimed that Tarragona would soon fall, Richelieu was not optimistic. He brought every conceivable pressure to bear on the officers involved in the action. He wrote endless letters to Condé, La Mothe, d'Argenson, Admiral Sourdis, the Financial Intendant and his brother-in-law. He either made them promises and spoke of their prospects of fame and promotion or he threatened them with disgrace at Court. He instructed Brézé, who was about to sail for Portugal, to pursue the Admiral of the Spanish Atlantic fleet as far as the coast of Catalonia if he should discover that he was making for Mediterranean waters. Meanwhile La Mothe declared that the fall of Tarragona could well procure an immediate and highly favourable peace for France. A few days later Richelieu urged Sourdis on with the words: "If I were able to change myself into a ship I would gladly do so in order to help you in your struggle against the King's enemies."

On June 8th he informed Condé that he had given instructions for further galleys to be sent and expressed his opinion that the critical factor both in the campaign in Roussillon and in the two Catalan campaigns was supremacy at sea. On June 14th he again wrote to Condé, La Mothe, d'Argenson and various others and he kept up this barrage of letters for months. During that time he seldom referred to other events in Catalonia. He concentrated grimly on the operation against Tarragona.

But despite all the pressure he brought to bear, the Cardinal was unable to prevent this extremely costly operation from foundering. Tarragona was Richelieu's Gallipoli. The high hopes entertained in Paris were dashed, while a deep depression descended on Barcelona. From the official records of the *generalidad* of Barcelona we learn that forty-five Spanish ships laden with stores fought their way into the harbour of the fortress. The recorder then added: "This news cast the province into despair, for while the surrender of Tarragona was hourly awaited the fortress was suddenly relieved and the French army raised its siege."

Two months after these events Richelieu wrote to Sourdis informing him that his disloyalty had brought him into disgrace at Court.

In his reply and also in various other writings Sourdis claimed that he had fought against a fleet twice as powerful as his own and that he had been short of artillery, water and ammunition. Moreover, he said, he had warned De Noyers, Condé and various others beforehand that it would be pointless to try to attack Salou.

Richelieu hesitated for three months before having the treaties negotiated by Du Plessis-Besançon and d'Argenson ratified. The mood of the Catalan population was ambivalent. Much of the information reaching the French Court was decidedly pessimistic. But when the point had been reached where all these contractual agreements threatened to break down entirely he submitted the documents to the King for his signature and instructed Maillé-Brézé to proceed at once to Barcelona, where he was to take over the government of the new province as Viceroy and swear on behalf of Louis XIII to uphold both the provisions of the treaty and the constitution of the land. This was yet another attempt on Richelieu's part to promote his brother-in-law. Meanwhile d'Argenson had arrived in Barcelona armed with the ratified treaty documents and also with letters from Louis XIII and Richelieu. The following day the Council of One Hundred ratified the treaty.

They also agreed that the Viceroy should be allowed to attest the articles of the treaty and the constitution on the King's behalf. After informing Richelieu that the amendments had been accepted d'Argenson expressed his opinion that confusion and dissension would soon return unless the Viceroy arrived immediately.

Richelieu knew that the present solution was only a temporary one, but what mattered to him was the fact that it would deal the Spanish monarchy a blow that was likely to prove far more critical than any military victories or defeats. As for Maillé-Brézé, his appointment as Viceroy was to prove as unfortunate for Richelieu as the battles which had preceded it. By contrast Richelieu's nephew Jean Armand, the son of Maillé and the unhappy Nicole, whom the Cardinal had educated himself and who greatly distinguished himself as a naval officer, was a source of great joy to him. This young man fell at the naval battle of Orbitello shortly after the Cardinal's death.

At the beginning of 1642 Richelieu changed his policy; the main stress was shifted from Catalonia proper to Roussillon. It became imperative that the conquest of this county should be completed. But despite his mortal illness, despite the web of intrigue which was then closing in on him, the Cardinal did not lose sight of the over-all problem of Catalonia. On May 13, 1642, he instructed De Noyers to write to Marshal La Mothe and inquire whether, since French squadrons were shortly expected in Cadaqués this naval unit might perhaps be used to give support for a military operation in Valencia by seizing either the harbour of Vinaroz or that of Tortosa. But he was also obliged to advise him, even at this early stage, of the necessity for removing Marshal Brézé from his office, for which he was quite unfit; he stressed the desirability of appointing Marshal La Mothe in his place in order, as he put it, to avoid the dangers which might ensue from the presence in Barcelona of two persons of equal rank. At about this time Richelieu drew up an undated memorandum for the King, in which he insisted that everything possible must be done to ensure the security of Catalonia and Roussillon and preserve the inhabitants from the devastation which the King of Spain was determined to inflict should he succeed in inciting them to rebellion (against France). Once again he stressed the fact that neither Catalonia nor Roussillon could rest secure until Tortosa, Tarragona and Rosas had been conquered. He then added that, since it was not possible to achieve these three objectives simultaneously, they would have to decide which of these towns was to be taken first. Many believed that Rosas should be their objective, but, since the Catalans felt oppressed by Madrid and could not exist without a large army within their borders (which of course they would also find oppressive), he considered that they should first attack Tortosa and then Rosas.

During the closing months of his life Richelieu was constantly preoccupied with the political problems of Catalonia, and there are those who maintain that his desire to conquer Perpignan, capital city of Roussillon, was virtually obsessive.

Olivares was then staking everything on a single card, the conspiracy against the Cardinal's life. But here too he miscalculated. Richelieu was not eliminated and he continued to take every important decision himself right up to the moment of his death. Fourteen days before the Spanish tried to besiege Lérida he wrote to Chavigny and De Noyers:

"I would request the King to send one of his most capable and intelligent engineers to Lérida as quickly as possible in order to fortify the town. This is a matter of the utmost importance for, if the King of Spain gains possession of this stronghold, he will be in a position to defeat the Catalans."

In the same letter he pointed out that d'Argenson urgently needed a warrant enabling him to force the Catalan bishops to swear an oath to the "new régime" under pain of instant banishment.

Before focusing again on the French Court, where the events on which Olivares was pinning all his hopes were then taking place, we must first deal briefly with Portugal.

Portugal

Developments in Portugal were similar to those in Catalonia. Olivares had constantly tried to make changes in the act of union, which Philip II had respected on all occasions and Philip III on nearly all. He had forced the Viceroy, Marguerite of Savoy, a daughter of Charles Emmanuel, to accept one of his own pages, an extremely violent Portuguese by the name of Vasconcellos whom she detested, as the Spanish representative. In 1635 Olivares' favourite had imposed a 5 per cent tax on every Portuguese estate and he also tried to recruit troops in Portugal for use in the Netherlands and Catalonia. The Portuguese opposition was looking for a leader and it found one in John of Braganza, a descendant of Dom Manuel, who was urged on in this affair by his wife, the sister of Duke Medina Sidonia, a woman with a great lust for power. The Portuguese nobles had long since established contact with Richelieu and had asked him for naval support. On December 1, 1640, the Viceroy's Castilian and German guards were overpowered by conspirators and Vasconcellos' corpse was promptly dragged through the streets of Lisbon. Marguerite was courteously conducted to the frontier and John of Braganza was swept on to the throne by a great wave of patriotic fervour. Philip II's work was utterly destroyed. After the failure of the punitive expedition led by Monterrey, Portuguese troops advanced into Galicia. The colonies joined the revolt and Medina Sidonia tried to incite the Andalusians and set himself up as King of their territory.

France, England, Denmark and Sweden immediately recognized John IV and used their influence to promote a peace between Portugal and the States General. But Holland was not then prepared to return the territories seized from the Portuguese in the East Indies and Brazil. A ten-year armistice was concluded and Portugal gave an undertaking that she would not negotiate with Spain without first consulting France. Richelieu had repaid Olivares with interest for having interfered in every single French conspiracy.

We have seen from the Perez affair that even during Philip II's reign, which immediately followed the period in which Hapsburg power in Spain was at its peak, the King's freedom of action was greatly restricted by the many special privileges enjoyed by the provinces. Events in Catalonia provide an extremely telling illustration of the centrifugal tendencies which operated in Spain, while the fact that a Medina Sidonia could even think of setting himself up as the sovereign of an independent kingdom of Andalusia shows how weak the Hapsburg realm in the Pyrenean peninsula really was as compared with the fertile and densely populated country of France, whose unity Richelieu had ceaselessly promoted with every means at his disposal. Encumbered as she was by the medieval liberties enjoyed by her provinces, whose constitutional significance cannot be overestimated, Spain was ultimately bound to succumb in the life and death struggle which she conducted with her neighbour France, whose power was so much more concentrated. Once her eastern frontier was safe, the whole of France was safe. This frontier was secured in the period 1635 to 1638–9 and the episodic and often extremely heroic siege warfare which then ensued, the small-scale naval battles and the skirmishes on the various frontiers were not of crucial importance. The activities of the Swedes in Germany and the pressure brought to bear by Turkey prevented the Emperor from opposing the Bourbons on a large enough scale to decide the issue. The war against Spain, which continued long after the Peace of Westphalia, right up to 1659, was decided by the Catalan revolt and the secession of Portugal, both of which were largely brought about by diplomatic means. Although the victory of Rocroi, which was won by Richelieu's nephew-in-law the Duke of Enghien in 1643, failed to break the incomparable will of the Spanish, especially of the Castilians, even their heroic sacrifices were rendered useless by the absence of a sense of solidarity in a single Spanish province and a territory bound to the Spanish Crown by an act of union. The Spanish decline proceeded inexorably.

But at that point an event occurred which might well have called this whole development into question. Pablo Claris, the chief architect of the Catalan *Anschluss* with France, suddenly died. During his lifetime he had been highly praised as his country's protector. He had also been severely criticized.

The death of a man like Claris, who had been able to act on his own initiative in the negotiations with Richelieu's emissaries and in the drawing up of the Franco–Catalan treaties, was bound to have powerful political repercussions. It seemed quite impossible to find a replacement for him who would be acceptable to both the Catalans themselves and the French. Eventually the choice fell on José Soler, a canon, whose only recommendation lay in the fact that he was related to Claris and was a member of the same Cathedral Chapter of Urgel. During his five months of office he was little more than a puppet of the French representatives.

But it was not only Claris who made his exit at that time. In 1641 Du Plessis-Besançon also left the political scene an embittered man, who felt that he had not received the recognition and reward he deserved.

The question of foreign influence, especially French influence, on the Catalan revolt has not yet been fully clarified and presents a wide field for research. In his fundamental work on this subject Sanabre has said that the analysis of the documents relating to this problem which have yet to be dealt with and which are to be found primarily in the records of the French War Ministry and in Spanish archives, would be a lifetime's work.

While he was planning the risings on the Iberian peninsula and especially after war had been declared, Richelieu obviously did his utmost to turn the countries of the world against Spain and to draw her allies over into his own camp. His endeavours were not restricted to Europe but reached as far afield as the colonial territories of America and Asia. No discord between Spain and the States within her sphere of influence or those linked with her by constitutional bonds and no dissension between Spain and her allies escaped his attention; wherever he saw differences, whether newly emerging or of long standing, he offered his help. Like his adversary Olivares, who brought his influence to bear in Naples, Sicily and Portugal, Richelieu always took direct action; he applied the same methods, but with greater intensity, in the border districts of Roussillon and Catalonia. French agents undoubtedly infiltrated into the political and military hierarchy of these territories. But the only concrete knowledge which has been published so far about the province of Catalonia concerns the events in Roussillon in the last four months of the year 1639 when Du Plessis-Besançon, Richelieu's representative, began operations there. The memorandum which he composed on his diplomatic activity shows how he prepared the whole territory for attack and enabled the French to enter Catalonia as liberators with flags flying.

In a book which he wrote in 1649, i.e. five years after his brief reign as Viceroy, and in which he sought to justify his political and military actions, the French Marshal La Mothe stated:

"After Louis XIII had restored peace within his realm he had the gratification of being able to take his revenge for the many affronts he had received. . . . He began with a few enterprises in Biscay, in Salces and Laredo but when, thanks to the late Cardinal Richelieu's prudent diplomacy, risings had been set afoot in Catalonia and Portugal, France found ways and means of furthering her projects beyond the Pyrenees."

The Cinq-Mars Conspiracy

While all this was taking place the King of France was riding along roads covered with snow and slush to meet the enemy. The moment Louis was on horseback he was a different man, and anybody who tried to prevent him from going to the front was soon made to feel his displeasure. He had left Saint Germain-en-Laye on January 27, 1642, and by the evening of the same day had arrived at the castle of Chilly, which the courtiers interpreted as a sure sign that Cinq-Mars was back in favour: he and his mother were the King's host and hostess. But Louis felt indisposed and retired early. Scarcely had the doors of the royal chambers closed when Cinq-Mars called for his friend Gaspard de Chavagnac, who subsequently recorded the events of that night in his memoirs. Cinq-Mars told his friend to follow him, and the two men then made their way by a devious route through the rambling building until eventually they reached a door on which "Monsieur le Grand" knocked. He asked Chavagnac to wait outside and prevent anyone from entering. He himself then went into the room, where he remained all night. Inside he found the Marquis of Fontrailles, Aubijoux and someone else. De Thou was not present. Someone else? The "someone" was none other than Orléans; and on this occasion he gave his full approval to all proposals. Once this had been clearly established Cinq-Mars instructed Fontrailles to proceed at once to Madrid to deliver the treaty draft. The little hunchback was justifiably surprised to find that he was suddenly being asked to undertake such a mission without forewarning. But after the favourite had brought his powers of persuasion to bear and "Monsieur" had backed him up with the full weight of his authority Fontrailles asked for time to consider their request and withdrew with Aubijoux into a corner of the room. They talked for a long time, for they were well aware of the risk Fontrailles would be taking, since his physical deformity alone would draw attention to him. But they also realized that it was no longer possible to withdraw from the project; it was quite conceivable that by then Richelieu's police were on their trail and if they were seized they would both have to pay for Orléans and the "Premier Ecuyer" in any case. They had reached the point of no return; like Soissons before them, they had only one option, to act at once.

When "Monsieur le Grand" had all but given up hope Fontrailles accepted. He made only one condition: that during the King's forthcoming stay in Lyons not only the Duke of

Bouillon but also Orléans should be present in the city, for then he would at last be obliged to keep his word and see things through to the very end. But, whereas on previous occasions it had been the ambivalent Prince who had always recoiled at the last moment, this time it was Cinq-Mars who began to take fright at the thought of the actual assassination. Although Princess Maria had spoken to him in the most energetic terms he was seized by a strange dread of this deed; in his mind's eye he saw in frightful detail the corpse of his former benefactor lying before him. And yet the Cardinal had to be removed during his visit to Lyons. When the King's train met the Cardinal's at Briare, on the Loire, the young guards officers wanted to strike him down there and then, thus repeating the procedure adopted at the assassination of the Marshal of Ancre, which had also been sanctioned by the King's presence. But in Briare Cinq-Mars declared that they must not act until they reached Lyons, because then not only Orléans but also the Duke of Bouillon would be present, who was the only person able to offer refuge should the attempt fail.

And so they reached Lyons. Everything was prepared. But when Richelieu called on the King he was accompanied by the captain of his guards, De Bar. This was not his customary practice, and Cinq-Mars, who was thrown into confusion by this unexpected turn of events, found that, like Orléans before him, he was unable to give the prearranged signal.

Richelieu had set out from Briare two days after his sovereign. He was carried on a canopied litter suffering from open and festering sores. On February 19th he arrived in Lyons. On the 21st the King held a parade and on the 22nd he joined Richelieu to attend a Te Deum offered in the Church of St Jean for the victory of the Franco–Hessian troops under Guébriant over the Imperialist forces led by Lamboy at Kempen. The same day he received the Venetian envoy and delegations from Catalonia and Geneva. But the following day Louis was on his way again. On February 25th he met Valemani, the Papal Chamberlain, who handed him the Cardinal's hat for Mazarin, which the King himself placed on the Neapolitan's head. Only those with political insight realized that the isolated and indefatigable Richelieu had succeeded in the most difficult task of all: he had found a successor and had promoted and protected him in time.

On February 27th Louis set out for Montélimar, arriving in Bagnols on the 28th, Nîmes on March 2nd, Montpellier on the 7th and Narbonne on the 8th.

Richelieu's brother-in-law, Marshal Brézé, had entered Barcelona in state on February 23rd to an enthusiastic reception from the populace. His attestation as Viceroy was then duly carried out in the cathedral.

Meanwhile Marshal La Meilleraye had advanced through snow storms at the head of a powerful force, fighting all the way and conquering various enemy strongholds, until he stood before Collioure in Roussillon, which he besieged for twenty-four hours before this Spanish bulwark also capitulated on April 2nd. Even then the Spanish still held the citadel, but on April 10th the Swiss took the well which had supplied the defenders with water. The Spanish commandant, Mortare, was then forced to sign the document ceding the whole stronghold to the French. At virtually the same time La Mothe-Houdancourt defeated the combined Castilian and Aragonese armies in Catalonia. Like Guébriant, the victor of Kempen, he too received his Marshal's baton. Both of these commanders were loyal followers of the Cardinal's.

As a result of this last feat of arms the road to the key position of Perpignan lay open.

Cinq-Mars, Enghien and the young Turenne had taken part in the siege of Collioure. Whenever there was a lull in the fighting the favourite would appear in the King's intimate circle, where he did his best to follow the advice given to him by the lady of his heart. But despite "Monsieur le Grand's" determination to exercise self-control his relationship to the monarch was unstable. A monotonous sequence developed: over-intimate conversations would give way to new bouts of dissension only to be followed by fresh reconciliations. But one day Louis was to remark that when he was with Cinq-Mars he sometimes felt a cold shudder suddenly pass through him.

By seventeenth-century standards Richelieu had reached the summit of social success in February 1641 when his niece Maillé-Brézé had married the Prince of Condé, a fact which led many of his contemporaries to fear that he might try to seize power for himself after the King's death, which was generally felt to be close at hand. But then Richelieu himself suffered a total collapse in Narbonne and was no longer able to follow the King's triumphal procession.

From May 9th onwards Louis XIII was in the army camp at Perpignan. Mazarin had arrived there at the head of an Italian regiment, whose equipment was greatly admired. Louis gave the Italian tokens of special distinction. He discussed the political situation with him and occasionally even asked his advice. Mazarin gave intelligent but carefully considered replies and always referred admiringly to Richelieu. He knew how to hold his peace and he knew how to wait; he observed the French sovereign and realized that a new period of rule was imminent. The King was barely able to hold himself erect; time and again he succumbed to serious attacks of fever. Unfavourable news then arrived from the northern front. The Spanish had retaken La Bassée (near Lens) and checked the French advance. But in the south-west rapid progress was still being maintained. The new Marshal de La Mothe-Houdancourt had pressed forward from Catalonia into Valencia, where he had employed the fearful scorched-earth policy, thus making quite certain that the enemy army was denied food. Sorties from the garrison of Perpignan were driven back. These successes had an exhilarating effect on Louis; as soon as he felt a little better he went hunting again.

Then there was a natural disaster: the heavens opened and torrential rain fell for days on end so that the rivers overflowed their banks. It was not until May 31st that the sun came and the waters receded. Meanwhile disease had broken out in the

French ranks. The throng of courtiers surrounding the King grew and there were as many Catalan nobles in his entourage at Perpignan as French.

At the beginning of that year Richelieu's nephew, the Marquis of Brézé, an Admiral of the fleet, told his uncle in confidence that he had happened to overhear a conversation in which the King and Cinq-Mars had called Richelieu "the devil". This brief statement confirmed the secret reports sent in by the Cardinal's police. One of his top agents had already discovered the relationship between Orléans and Cinq-Mars, and in Fontainebleau it had been established that the favourite possessed a key to the Palais Luxembourg in Paris, where the two conspirators met. Richelieu was sufficiently carried away by this news to exclaim: "This ungrateful creature will destroy himself"; but from then onwards he treated "Monsieur le Grand" with the greatest courtesy and even advised the King to entrust him with the governorship of Touraine. This would have removed the young man from Louis' entourage and, although the monarch found the idea intolerable, he mastered his feelings and agreed. It was during his five-day stay in Fontainebleau that Louis offered Cinq-Mars this new token of his favour. But at that point, when he was so completely engrossed in his sinister plot, Henri d'Effiat could not possibly leave his master's side; and so he answered, as if inspired by the wise Gonzaga, that great rewards should be reserved for those who had acquired great merit in the field and that the Count d'Harcourt had a greater right to this gift than he himself. The King was deeply moved and intensely relieved, for now his friend would not leave him. Richelieu, on the other hand, who had seen through his former protégé's cheap stratagem immediately, tried to force him to accept. But Cinq-Mars remained adamant and exulted to see the mighty man forced to use gentle persuasion on him. Richelieu then suddenly decided to risk everything by appealing to the King in person; he was playing for maximum stakes, and for the first time ever he compiled a complete dossier of the incriminating evidence which he had collected on "Monsieur le Grand". This desperate attempt was mounted on February 2nd under auspices which, it need hardly be added, were extremely unfavourable. The King raised his voice to his First Minister and rebuked him severely; Gassion, who happened to meet him as he was leaving the King's chamber, was shocked to see his deathly pallor; the Cardinal looked years older and utterly dejected. The Court heard of this new incident at once and a late wave of fervour carried the favourite still higher. A regular Cinq-Mars party was formed, in which the ladies played a particularly prominent part. Many noblemen offered to support him with force of arms while outside of France the *émigrés*, active as always, were jubilant at the news.

From the moment the King had set out at the head of a splendid and constantly growing retinue on a journey which carried him through devastated districts, past deserted villages and hamlets Cinq-Mars had spoken ceaselessly of the unbelievable privations imposed by the war, of the misery and death, of the never-ending and completely senseless battles, which remained inconclusive. The only way to save the situation, he argued, was to start peace negotiations, and this could not be done as long as the Cardinal was still there, for Richelieu needed the war in order to make himself indispensable.

Secret peace feelers of a semi-official nature had been going on all the time and the King was loth to believe that his Minister had simply been using these for his own ends and deceiving him in the process. Eventually the "Grand Ecuyer" went so far as to suggest to Louis that he should send a confidential observer to Spain to report on the progress of the secret discussions without the knowledge of either the Cardinal or the Ministry. The King is then said to have asked who could be entrusted with such a mission, whereupon the favourite proposed the man who had thought out the scheme, his friend François de Thou. The King agreed to this proposal. De Thou, a jurist, asked for written instructions and the King issued two documents, one for use in Madrid, the other in Rome. For the first time ever, Louis himself was preparing to lay a trap for the great man who stood at his side.

In point of fact nothing was to come of this project, for events moved far too quickly. But for the time being it seemed that the Cardinal's enemies were still making headway in their attempts to influence the vacillating King. Louis had meanwhile taken up quarters half a mile from Perpignan in the spacious country house of a certain Jean Pauques; from there he was able to supervise all the operations of the siege army.

One day, when he was feeling particularly aggressive towards the Cardinal, Louis spoke of the slavery in which he was living, to which Cinq-Mars impatiently replied: "Well, why don't you get rid of him?" He then went further and for the first time openly suggested that the King should have the Cardinal murdered when he next appeared, that Louis should in fact do the very thing for which he himself lacked the courage.

According to Montglas this proposal shocked the King; it sobered him at once and after a long silence he said in an extremely serious tone: "He is a Cardinal and a priest, I would be excommunicated." At this Tréville, one of Cinq-Mars' followers, is said to have volunteered to travel to Rome to obtain absolution and to have assured the King that it would be received.

On May 6th, Richelieu, who was still in Narbonne, wrote to De Noyers, who had not left the King and who had been instructed to keep a special watch on Cinq-Mars:

"A new abscess on my arm and the old incision . . . have reopened and released a great deal of pus. They try to comfort me by suggesting a further operation; I find it difficult to decide for I lack the necessary drive and courage. I pray to God that He will grant me both and so make it possible for me to do His will."

On May 8th he wrote again to the Secretary of State:

"I spent this past night in terrible pain. They have decided

433

to perform a further operation on my elbow but there is a risk that they may sever the vein; I am in God's hands. I would have dearly liked to have completed my will but I cannot do that without you and you cannot get away until Perpignan has fallen."

While the Cardinal was slowly sinking Cinq-Mars continued to incite the King against him but, without the Princess to guide him, he had again grown presumptuous. Surrounded by partisans and flatterers, he behaved in a vainglorious and arrogant manner and interfered in matters which did not concern him.

On one such occasion, when M. de Fabert, the Commander of a Guards battalion, was with the King the favourite held forth at great length on fortification technique and siege methods. Louis grew angry and interrupted him: "Monsieur le Grand", he said, "you have no right to try to teach an experienced man his business, for you have seen nothing of such things." Cinq-Mars left the room in a rage after first saying to Louis: "Your Majesty might have spared me that." Once the King was alone with Fabert he confided in him:

"For six months now I have been sick of him. . . . I know of nobody who is so given over to vice and so ungracious. He is the most ungrateful creature in the world. He has often kept me waiting in my carriage for hours on end while he went his rascally ways. A kingdom could not pay for his extravagance. At this moment . . . he possesses three hundred pairs of shoes."

The favourite, as unrestrained as ever, complained to De Noyers: "For three days on end nothing but spleen from His Majesty!" And only two days later, on May 16th, the Secretary of State wrote to the Cardinal:

"The King has treated Cinq-Mars with coolness for the past days; his former warmth has not returned. If we can so arrange matters that the King remains in Fontainebleau for the next three months, there is nothing Your Eminence could not achieve . . . but if Cinq-Mars has room to manoeuvre and agitate he will destroy in a week all that we have built up in an hour's discussion."

Richelieu knew perfectly well that he was close to death but still he fought back, for his intellectual faculties were not only unimpaired but actually sharpened by the extraordinary circumstances in which he found himself. He recalled the Day of the Dupes and said to De Noyers and Chavigny: "On that occasion God made use of an unlocked door in order that I might defend myself when my opponents were on the point of destroying me."

As often as possible Richelieu presented his respects to the King through De Noyers, enquired with concern as to the state of his health, offered medical advice and assured His Majesty that every ill which afflicted him caused him more pain than his own maladies. Louis for his part advised Richelieu to leave Narbonne and try a change of air. But the Cardinal, who knew the risks attendant on every journey, tried to inform the King of the true state of affairs and to impress on him just how menacing the news then was: he drew his attention to the newssheets from Brussels, the letters from the Prince of Orange, the Queen-Mother's preparations, the reports from the Italian Courts, to "Monsieur's" refusal to come to the camp at Perpignan and his obvious intention of waiting in the wings, while the enemy prepared on all fronts, until the storm, which was then threatening, finally erupted. He warned the King time and again; he insisted that M. de Thou must be removed and also Chavagnac, Cinq-Mars' dangerous shadow. He urged De Noyers and shortly afterwards Chavigny, who was given special duties in this connection, to impress on the King that "If God had called the Cardinal to Him His Majesty would have realized what he had lost. But it would be far more serious if the Cardinal were to be lost as a result of the King's own actions, for this would sap general confidence in the monarch."

On May 27th the Cardinal finally left Narbonne after first

having made his will, which was signed for him since the condition of his arm prevented him from signing it himself. In the small town of Agde, which lies on the road to Arles, he received a letter from Louis XIII, in which the King told him: "Contrary to all the false rumours which are being put about I love you more than ever; we have been together far too long for us ever to be separated."

Were these really words of comfort? Scarcely!

But on June 11th Richelieu sent De Noyers an unexpected and triumphant message from Arles: "The reason for M. de Chavigny's journey will surprise you. God sustains the King through strange disclosures." Chavigny brought this message to the army camp in person together with a document which altered the entire situation.

What had happened?

The Marquis of Fontrailles had carried out his mission in Madrid. The various accounts of his journey are contradictory on certain points and so far it has not been possible to establish the full facts. But it is quite certain that the hunchback reached his destination. He first travelled via Limoges (where he is supposed to have had a further meeting with the extremely optimistic Duke of Bouillon) to his native province of Languedoc. There was nothing in this to attract attention, for he was simply returning to his estate. His friend Aubijoux was already waiting for him at his castle, and the two men then discussed all the practical aspects of the undertaking, especially the question of an itinerary. Fontrailles is said to have chosen the route via the valley of the Aspe which would have taken him across the pass of Canfranc. In his memoirs Rochefort claims to have accompanied him as far as Bayonne disguised as a postillion. Be that as it may, the emissary succeeded in crossing the Pyrenees with the help of a local guide without being halted. It is also said that the authorities in Saragossa were unco-operative and refused to allow his servant to accompany him any further. What is quite certain is that, after being made to wait for some considerable time, he was finally received by Olivares in Madrid. We are told that initially Fontrailles tried to avoid mentioning either Bouillon or Cinq-Mars but that Olivares responded unfavourably to this, declaring that Spain had been deceived too often in the past and that without firm guarantees he could not and would not participate in any further projects. When Fontrailles still persisted in his refusal to give detailed assurances Olivares is said to have had the passes made out for his return journey. At this, we are told, Fontrailles gave in and Olivares was pleasantly surprised to discover the extent of the conspiracy. He then spent four whole days going through the treaty draft article by article until eventually the Frenchman impatiently exclaimed: "Your Excellency is wasting time on trifling details; the important thing is to save Perpignan, for if this fortress falls, you will lose the whole of Catalonia for ever." The fact of the matter is that the treaty was signed on March 13, 1642, and the Marquis then immediately set off on his return journey, taking with him both the treaty itself and a letter from Philip IV, who had granted him a brief audience, to Gaston d'Orléans. This letter reads as follows:

"My dear brother,
"I have noted with great satisfaction the proposals which were made to me on Your Royal Highness' behalf for the peace and prosperity of Christendom and the conclusion of a lasting peace. . . . It is important that all aspects of this undertaking should be well co-ordinated and put into effect with care and that your own firmness and good intentions in the service of God and the common weal should at last be rewarded."

In Huesca Fontrailles met the same Béarnese guide who had led him across the mountains into Spain. This guide told him that he had been kept under observation ever since and that they would have to take a different route on their way back. Fontrailles agreed and eventually reached his castle without having been molested. There he again joined Aubijoux and

437

together they set off without delay for Narbonne in order to report to Cinq-Mars. Fontrailles was still convinced that he was being shadowed and made no secret of his fears when he met Cinq-Mars. And so their former roles were reversed; on this occasion the "Grand Ecuyer" had to calm and encourage Fontrailles. A certain M. de Montmort was then asked to contact Orléans, whose residence alternated between Blois and Chambord, and put him in the picture. It was left to Aubijoux to hand the actual treaty to the King's brother as soon as "the way was clear". Meanwhile the astute Fontrailles requested permission to seek refuge abroad but was refused.

The probable reason why Richelieu did not strike while Fontrailles was on his way back from Spain was that his relationship to the King was far too unstable. He had to be absolutely sure of himself for at that time he could no longer afford to take authoritarian measures if there was the slightest risk of his being proved wrong.

The crucial question as to who delivered the text of the Spanish treaty into Richelieu's hands has never been answered. Hanotaux evades the issue with a cursory "n'importe", but the question nevertheless remains crucial.

This writer believes that it was the Queen who betrayed the secret and handed over the text of the treasonable document. Madame de Motteville, one of the most reliable chroniclers of the times, said that many people had received copies of the treaty. But the reason that leads us to suppose it was Anne of Austria who was Richelieu's informant and who handed him the "corpus delicti", which she had received from Gaston d'Orléans, is that if she had been incriminated yet again her two small sons would have been taken from her, irrevocably. On April 30th she had written to Richelieu: "The threat of separation from my children, when they are at such a tender age, causes me such pain that I no longer have the strength to resist." Richelieu did not reply, whereupon the Queen asked Brassac, ostensibly her confidant but in fact Richelieu's spy: "Can it be that the Cardinal is now deserting me?"

Although she had already assured Chavigny that she would support the Cardinal in every way and was convinced that he for his part would never abandon her, she instructed her secretary Le Gras, who had acted for her once before in connection with the letters she had written in the convent of Val de Grâce, to inform the Cardinal again in still more explicit terms. This was on June 7th.

On June 9th she wrote to the Cardinal in her own hand and on June 15th she at last received his comforting reply: Richelieu sent her a warm and reassuring letter, in which he told her that the King wished her to remain in Saint-Germain with her children. She breathed a sigh of relief and Brassac reported that nothing could now induce her to turn away from the Cardinal or his cause.

It has also been suggested—and the suggestion appears highly probable—that Mazarin was already advising the Queen at that time. At all events it is striking to note the consistency with which this woman kept her sights set on the regency and turned away from Spanish interests once she had sons of her own, who would inherit the Crown of France; it is also perfectly evident that she was quite determined to preclude any possibility of having to share the regency with Orléans. It was therefore also in her interests that her brother-in-law should be utterly compromised.

Orléans appears to have underestimated Anne of Austria; time and again he blindly placed his confidence in her. While he had been waiting for Fontrailles to return with Philip IV's reply he had been subject to considerable psychological strain; he had also been waiting anxiously for news from Bouillon, which would assure him and Cinq-Mars of asylum in Sedan. During this period he held court in great splendour in Blois and Chambord. But Du Boulay, a nobleman and secret agent of Richelieu's, who had visited him on April 19th, reported that he did not look at all well; the ebullient Orléans, the eternal youth, appeared listless, ill-kempt and shabby.

Shortly after Du Boulay Fontrailles also appeared at Chambord, having previously met Cinq-Mars in Perpignan. He had been astute enough to realize that the Grand Ecuyer's days of high favour were a thing of the past; they were then petering out and would never again reach their former peak.

After advising his monarch, first through De Noyers and then in a personal letter, to try a change of air himself Richelieu set out for Arles and during the whole of his journey there, when his future prospects, if indeed it was possible to speak of future prospects in his case, were at their lowest ebb, he continued to conduct a rearguard action of immense difficulty. The precision of his tactical moves is reminiscent of Napoleon I's French campaign of 1814.

On May 26th Guiche had been defeated at Honnecour on the Scheldt by the Cardinal-Infante's successor, Francisco de Melo. Once again the northern frontier had been breached, once again Paris was threatened, and as always in such circumstances the inhabitants of the capital became extremely agitated; rumours spread like wildfire, and among this welter of alarming news reports of the Cardinal's pending fall from favour cropped up time and again. Both he himself and the members of his entourage, especially his niece the Duchess of Aiguillon, lived in constant fear of assault and assassination. The Duchess received threatening letters. Richelieu had first shifted his quarters to Tarascon because the walls of that city were particularly strong, but had subsequently moved on so as to be nearer to the papal territory of Avignon. It was when he reached Arles that the turning point came. All those who saw the Cardinal at that time mentioned the complete transformation he underwent once he possessed absolute proof against Cinq-Mars, the first man ever to come close to destroying the relationship between the monarch and his First Minister. From then onwards the Cardinal continued the struggle at the low level of intrigue; he used methods for which he had a heartfelt loathing but which he had learnt to employ with absolute mastery; and he did not miss a single opportunity: he brought his influence to bear through middlemen, spies, creatures who paid him blind allegiance because they were entirely dependent on his favour, he wrote letters in order to press his case and even to arouse sympathy; he left no avenue unexplored. In Arles, as so often in the past—in Lyons, for example, when the King's abscess yielded to treatment, in the Palais de Luxembourg on the Day of the Dupes, on the two occasions when he received news first of Gustavus Adolphus' death in battle and subsequently of Wallenstein's assassination —an unexpected event suddenly raised him up from the depths of despair. In the last month of his life he spoke and wrote frequently of God, of God's help, of God's understanding for the French cause, for his own cause. Previously he had used this term only on rare occasions and in a purely conventional manner to denote the one thing for which he had always waited so ardently, *fortuna*. All those in his entourage who saw him in Arles on the day on which he finally received absolute proof of Cinq-Mars' guilt were astounded by the jubilation which erupted from him and by the tremendous amount of work he encompassed; he issued instructions until he was near collapse, working out every conceivable development, instructing his agents in minute detail and leaving nothing to chance. Almost as if willed to do so by the Cardinal, Chavigny then appeared in Narbonne on June 12th.

The first thing Chavigny did was to compare his instructions with those issued to Des Noyers and to agree with him on a joint course of action. The two Secretaries of State attended the monarch's *lever*, where Chavigny joined in the general conversation and approached the sovereign. At a certain point he tugged gently at Louis' coat-tail. This was a prearranged signal to let the King know that he had extremely important news for him. Louis immediately went into the adjoining room. Cinq-Mars was about to follow him but Chavigny was now in a position to bar his way. "I have an important communication for His Majesty", he said and the Grand Ecuyer, who was unaccustomed to such treatment, was left dumbfounded. Seized with anxiety, he called for Fontrailles and the two men waited, their throats parched with fear, for Chavigny to emerge. Meanwhile De Noyers had joined his companion to lend him support. But the favourite was not called in and Fontrailles knew immediately what that meant. "All is lost", he said. "There is only one thing we can do now: make for Sedan at once." Cinq-Mars rejected the proposal, whereupon the hunchback at last gave vent to his pent-up anger. "As far as you are concerned", he said, "you will still be big enough when they have cut off your head, but I am too small already." And then, overcome with emotion, he added: "I will never see you again." With this he ran from the chamber and, donning the same Capuchin cowl which he had worn on his journey to Spain, disappeared.

Meanwhile the two Secretaries of State were having a hard time of it. Although the King's feelings for the seductive youth had long been wounded, they were by no means dead. Once again they overpowered him. Quite beside himself, Louis cried out that the whole affair had been trumped up by Richelieu and that he was not going to fall for it. But Richelieu had warned his two followers to expect this initial reaction and accordingly they suggested that "Monsieur le Grand" should be interrogated, for then it would soon become apparent where the truth lay and it would surely be easy enough to reward M. de Cinq-Mars if the charge should prove false. Once the enemy had established himself in Champagne it would be difficult to unravel the whole train of events and discover the guilty parties in retrospect. At this Louis sullenly accepted the proffered document and after a moment's hesitation, as if he were about to throw it away again, began to peruse it:

". . . it is agreed that both parties to the treaty will negotiate with the French Crown only on a joint basis . . . At the end of the war France must restore all strongholds, provinces and kingdoms which have been or will have been conquered by His Most Christian Majesty. . . ."

After reading these sentences again and again Louis' private feelings receded into the background. Pulling himself together, he signed a warrant as King of France for the arrest of Cinq-Mars, de Thou, Chavagnac and Haussonville, one of Bouillon's followers, and ordered M. de Castellane to set out for Casale at once to apprehend the Duke of Bouillon in the midst of his army.

Richelieu received a victory communiqué.

These events were kept strictly secret; throughout the whole of that day no news leaked out and in the evening Cinq-Mars accompanied M. de Beaumont, the Governor of Saint-Germain, to dine at an inn famous for its cuisine as if nothing untoward had happened. As they sat at table a servant appeared to announce that the King was about to retire and, since etiquette required that the Grand Ecuyer should assist at the monarch's "*coucher*", Henri hurried off to the Archbishop's palace where the King was then in residence. But before he entered the building a stranger approached him and thrust a note into his hand. "What is that?" Cinq-Mars asked. "Read it," the man replied and disappeared round the corner of a nearby house. Henri read the words: "Your life is at stake." Was this a warning sent by the King himself? This has been assumed.

Cinq-Mars thought for a moment, then ran to the nearest city gate, which he found closed. His gamekeeper had followed him. There are various versions of the events which then followed; according to some, Cinq-Mars found refuge with a *bourgeoise*, a certain Madame Siousac, who had once been his mistress and had always hoped he would return to her. During that night his followers and employees were interrogated and his papers examined but all that was found were letters from women. While this was going on Henri is said to have told his gamekeeper to see if any of the other city gates were open, only to be told that they were all closed. In fact this was not the case, for one gate had been kept open for the arrival of an army regiment.

We do not really know in whose house Cinq-Mars was arrested; the different accounts are contradictory on this point.

Henri d'Effiat was conducted to the prison of Montpellier by a powerful escort of the Scots guards, whose commander was Jean Ceton. When he was led across the drawbridge and into the fortress he said: "Must a man die at twenty-two? Must a man conspire against his mother country when he is so young?" He was completely disenchanted and also knew that he would never see the Princess again. At that time he was still treated with every consideration; he was allowed two valets, a cup-bearer and his three assistants, a shoe-maker and a *lavandier* (the servant in charge of his linen). Monsieur le Grand was permitted to take exercise three times a day within the ramparts. He was visited by the chaplain of the castle, who brought him historical or devotional books to read.

Tréville, Chavagnac and Ruvigny stood by the deposed favourite. Ruvigny told La Meilleraye: "I belong to him."

Meanwhile de Thou and Chavagnac had been brought to the castle of Tarascon, having been conducted there from Narbonne behind the King's train. Once there, the hardships began, for the two prisoners were separated. During the journey de Thou had managed to write a letter to his friend Dupuy.

On July 4th Richelieu gave instructions that the prisoners should be interrogated as quickly as possible. "We need commissaries and men who can keep silent," he wrote, and he went on to say: "There is a rumour afoot that, if Cinq-Mars was plotting against the Cardinal, he was doing so with the King's full knowledge." In the light of this assertion Richelieu decided that the judges must not only be discreet but also "adroit." He himself set up the special court and among those whom he selected to serve were M. de Chazé, the intendant of the Dauphiné and "Maître des Requêtes," and also Louis Frère, the First President of the parlement of Grenoble. "Time is pressing, delays are harmful", he told the Secretaries of State. He went in constant fear lest the King should change his mind. Moreover, moves were already afoot to rescue the prisoners; François de Chavagnac, de Thou's brother, who was seen near Tarascon with a force of thirty horsemen, was considered particularly suspect. The

Bishop of Toulon, a close relative of Cinq-Mars, had come to beg for mercy. He too was regarded as a potential source of danger and Richelieu sent him straight back to his bishopric. François Chavagnac and his thirty mounted men were pursued by the Cardinal's personal guards as far as the papal territory of Avignon. A group of young nobles was arrested. They all claimed that their only intention had been to plead for clemency for Cinq-Mars and to bring him money for his personal needs. They were all detained in the castle of Tarascon. It was also being said of course that the "Grand Ecuyer's" numerous servants, his master cobbler, his baker and their accomplices were doing their utmost to help him escape. Certainly they smuggled letters out of the citadel, and it was thanks to them that the prisoner received many comforting messages: "We are thinking of you, we will rescue you," and so on. The Cardinal was also told that Orléans had requested La Rivière to ask the King to exercise clemency and forgiveness.

It is not surprising that Cinq-Mars should have charmed some of his guards, and as a result further arrests were made. Richelieu trusted no one, not even Jean Ceton, the Commander of the Scots guards: "He is undoubtedly loyal", he wrote, "but far too unsuspecting and too benevolent even to consider the possibility that a soldier of the guards could be bought. He thinks that, because a few of his men sleep in 'Monsieur le Grand's' room, there is no need for him or his deputy to do so." And he prevailed upon Louis XIII to send the following letter to Ceton which he himself had drafted: "M. Ceton, just a few lines to inform you that, since I had 'Monsieur le Grand' arrested, I have discovered more felonies and crimes than ever before and from now onwards I expect you to treat him as an enemy of mine and a traitor to the State."

Chazé interrogated de Thou on July 6th and his friend Josué de Chavagnac two days later. Both resolutely denied all charges, even those which had long since been fully substantiated. Subsequently, when Cinq-Mars was questioned by Chazé and the President of the parlement of Grenoble, he too

445

denied everything and even maintained that he had had no contact whatsoever with the Duke of Bouillon.

An important incident then occurred: Mazarin was asked to come to Montpellier and take part in the preliminary investigations in order to discover whether the prisoners had ever spoken a careless word to anyone. An informer immediately advised him of the following statement made by Cinq-Mars: "Although Cardinal Mazarin had assured me of his friendship on numerous occasions, I did not trust him, and if I had remained in the King's favour I would have 'annihilated him'."

The tribunal was then required to adopt a formal and as far as possible an intimidating attitude. The weeks had passed by and a great deal of time had been lost, even though Richelieu had been working at fever pitch. The Cardinal's working day during his stay in Montpellier, when he was seriously ill, is described for us in a letter written by Henri Arnauld.

"He works and dictates his letters between seven and eight A.M. Between eight and nine his wounds are dressed, between nine and ten he has discussions and between ten and eleven he works alone. He then hears mass, takes lunch and talks with Cardinal Mazarin and various others until two P.M. Between two and four he again works on his own, after which he holds his audiences."

On one such working day Richelieu decided that the trial must take place in Lyons and he then determined the final composition of the court. Chancellor Séguier, who was entirely devoted to him, was to preside and would be assisted by four *maîtres de l'hôtel des requêtes*, i.e. four Councillors of State, all of them men on whom the Cardinal could rely and one of them an official whom we already know and whose name has become a synonym for a corrupt judge. "He is a real Laubardemont", is still a common expression. Jean Martin, M. de Laubardemont, was the full name of this deputy; we have seen him at work in the trial that led to the condemnation of Urbain Grandier. The other persons taking part in the proceedings were Dyel de

Miromesnil, François Bochart de Champigny, Henri de la Guette, Chazé, Pierre de Marca, the President of the parlement of Navarre, Louis Frère, Claude de Simiane de la Coste and six Councillors from various parlements.

The first task which the Cardinal assigned to the court was the interrogation of Gaston d'Orléans in Annecy. As for the Duke of Bouillon, he had been arrested in Casale in the midst of his army.

The King's brother, whose rank, as always, raised him above the sphere in which other men were judged, posed the most difficult problem. In order to prevent him from escaping across the border, as he had done on so many previous occasions, the King, acting on Richelieu's advice, appointed him Commander in Chief of the army in Champagne, the province in which the enemy invasion was to have been mounted. At first they had conceived the malicious idea of banishing him to Venice on a monthly pension of ten thousand écus, which had prompted the Cardinal to remark: "He will have to make do with the money which the King of Spain should have paid him under the terms of their treaty." But then they decided in favour of Annecy, which would make it easier for him to reach Lyons for the opening of the trial. Originally Richelieu had intended to confront Orléans with his accomplices but, since the Duke had sworn a personal oath of secrecy to each and every one of them and was now proposing to break his oath, he was violently opposed to such a confrontation and declared that he was on no account prepared to play the part of prosecutor. In deciding his case recourse was had to precedents involving other royal Princes, especially that concerning the Duke of Alençon. In the end he was simply asked to make a deposition before the Commission.

"He suggests," Richelieu wrote, "that he should be asked to reaffirm his statements in the presence of the Chancellor and all other persons appointed to this enquiry so that he may be reminded of any omissions in his evidence and can then rectify them." And so Orléans told everything, thus fatally incriminating his followers and accomplices. Like everybody else, he spared the Queen, Anne of Austria, but that was in keeping with the Cardinal's wishes.

Cinq-Mars was brought from Montpellier to Lyons by coach with a cavalry escort. The day before his transfer he might have succeeded in escaping, if he had had the courage to jump from a six-foot wall which he had managed to reach. But his nerve appears to have snapped. For some time he had been suffering from insomnia caused by his having been obliged to share his room; he did not feel at all well. After his arrival in Lyons several new arrests were made; apart from de Terlon and Robert, the two nobles who had been allowed to stay with the "Grand Ecuyer", his shoe-maker André Glatard, his *lavandier*, Samuel Saurry, and two of his guards, Rodes and Carpentier, were imprisoned.

The confrontation between Cinq-Mars and the Duke of Bouillon took place on September 6th. The statements made by the Duke and also the recorded deposition made by Gaston d'Orléans were read out. Reacting quite spontaneously, Cinq-Mars turned to Bouillon and indignantly exclaimed:

"I would never have expected such behaviour from you for I had always heard that you were an honourable and courageous man. I would have died under torture rather than betray a friend after making so many promises and swearing so many oaths; but since you have shown so little constancy I will not pursue what can only be a vain attempt to save my life."

With this the principal defendant had in fact confessed, but he immediately went on to deny everything, doubtless in order to save François de Thou; he claimed that, in trying to win Bouillon's friendship, he had never intended to harm His Majesty; as for the Duke of Orléans' statement, it was false on every count.

On the following day, when Bouillon and de Thou faced one another, the young Councillor of State maintained a perfect defence and the Duke was forced to concede that he had never discussed any project with him.

Of the two principal defendants it was de Thou and not the "Grand Ecuyer" whom the Cardinal really wished to have executed. This is significant: he considered de Thou to be more capable and consequently more dangerous; he was the perfect embodiment of a type who was completely alien to Richelieu, an idealist highly skilled in legal argument but quite indifferent to political reality. Even when he was questioned by Richelieu himself this young man gave absolutely nothing away. He did not contradict his co-defendants on a single point. He could also claim with complete justice that he had not consented to join in an attempt on the Cardinal's life and that none of the other defendants had ever told him anything about the Spanish treaty. In fact he owed his knowledge of the agreement to the one person whom nobody dared arraign.

But de Thou had to die, for he had attacked official policy far more vehemently and far more fundamentally than any of the others. "It will be difficult to convict him", the Chancellor had said to Richelieu. Nonetheless, de Thou was the most important of the chosen victims, for he was able to bring arguments to bear.

Meanwhile Séguier was doing all he could to persuade Cinq-Mars to talk. In the days of the favourite's former glory he had always behaved towards him as a sincere friend and so he adopted a similar approach now: "Let us speak as friends", he said, "for I am not your judge at this moment; nothing that you say will be used against you; the King is prepared to be merciful if you will openly confess everything, especially if you tell us about the circumstances of the assassination plot; this can save you." But he was unsuccessful.

Then Laubardemont was sent to Cinq-Mars. At first he too appeared in the guise of a solicitous councillor but subsequently he told him: "In your situation the only thing that can save you is a full confession. What you don't know is that M. de Thou has already confessed everything for fear of torture. He did not even spare you." This finally worked. The twenty-two-year-old youth broke down and poured out the whole story, although he too said nothing of the part played by the Queen. Laubardemont took his statement down on the spot. From that moment de Thou was doomed.

On September 12th the court convened at 7 A.M. The two young friends were to be interrogated for the last time. Cinq-Mars was called first; the time was 8 A.M. The session had scarcely begun when the defendant rose to his feet and to the surprise of all his judges save Laubardemont and Séguier, who had been initiated into the secret by his colleague, he spoke of his collusion with the Duke of Bouillon and of the part he had played in drawing up the Spanish treaty; finally he declared that de Thou had been informed of everything and had known all about the Spanish treaty. The only thing which Cinq-Mars denied was his complicity in the plot to assassinate Richelieu.

De Thou was then called. As coolly and calmly as ever he denied every one of the charges. "Very well", the President said, "let us recall Cinq-Mars." When he appeared the statement which he had just made was read out to his friend. With a failing voice de Thou asked: "Did you really say all that?"

"Please give me time to explain", his friend called out. But de Thou did not wait for explanations; he admitted that he had known the contents of the treaty, not at first but later; he impressed on the court that he had tried to dissuade the Grand Ecuyer from venturing on this ill-fated enterprise and had told him that he intended to go to Rome so as not to have to take part in it. He then added, however, that he would now gladly sacrifice his life for his friend.

The Chancellor turned to the prosecuting council and asked whether in his opinion there was sufficient evidence against de Thou. "Yes", he replied. "Then pass judgement; the rest is my affair."

Richelieu had said that de Thou must die. Now the time had come.

Cinq-Mars was condemned to death unanimously, his friend

by twelve votes to two (those of Miromesnil and Sautereau). They were to die on the block.

After sentence had been passed Richelieu gave instructions for Cinq-Mars to be conducted to the torture chamber and threatened with torture in the first and second degree in order to force him to reveal the part played by the King in the assassination plot. Cinq-Mars set off on this visit without any sign of fear. When he reached the place of torment all he said was: "What an abominable smell!" He was placed on the rack but was not tortured. This was also in accordance with Richelieu's instructions. Louis XIII's lively imagination must not be overburdened. Richelieu has hinted at the disclosures which were made on that occasion, and we shall be referring to them again.

The way in which the dying Cardinal destroyed these young lives after first subjecting them to mental torment has been attributed to a desire for personal revenge. But there is also another way of looking at it: here was a man who, throughout his life, had used his great gifts and whatever physical strength he possessed to execute a vast design, only to find shortly before its completion, shortly before his death, that everything he had ever achieved had been put in jeopardy by a palace intrigue, by the frivolity and whims of incompetent people. Here was a man not even allowed to die in peace, a man who had lived under constant threat of assassination and who still had much to accomplish in a short space of time. What had really galled him was the imbalance between what he was, what he was striving for, what he had achieved and was still achieving, and these immature stratagems. On the one hand the King's weaknesses, the monarch on whom he depended and who could cast him off at any time, and on the other the sense of his own responsibility, his knowledge, his vision.

Once again he had strained every nerve to eliminate enemies of the State. But in the end this powerful State, which he had so passionately desired, was to turn against him and treat him with terrifying indifference.

Despite the great advances made in modern communications

we possess more eyewitness accounts of the execution of these enemies of the State than of many of the sensational events of our own day. The statements made by the defendants have furnished the material for a wide range of historical literature and for works of the imagination which reveal the sympathy felt by successive generations for the fate of these two young friends of such widely different character. Both died honourably in accordance with the dictates of their age and of their rank, Cinq-Mars in the awareness that he was being watched by a large audience both near and far, which included his beloved Princess. We possess extremely detailed accounts of his dress, his behaviour and his final words. De Thou also spoke nobly and eloquently before he died.

A revealing light is thrown on this tragic event in the life of the Court and the nation by a letter which the King wrote to Chancellor Séguier. Among other things, Louis said that he had come to recognize Cinq-Mars as a great charlatan and slanderer. He also admitted that in his conversations with the favourite he had occasionally expressed his dissatisfaction with his "Cousin", the Cardinal, because the latter had tried to prevent him from taking part in the siege of Perpignan on the grounds that it would be injurious to his health. On such occasions, the King said, Cinq-Mars had tried his utmost to incite him against Richelieu.

The parts played by the various exalted personages—the King, the Queen, the Duke of Orléans and the Duke of Bouillon—were far from edifying.

One small incident may serve by way of an epilogue to the "Cinq-Mars conspiracy", as this episode came to be called: the Princess of Gonzaga applied both personally and through the agency of the Duchess of Aiguillon to the Cardinal; she did not ask him to spare Cinq-Mars' life, but she did ask him to return her letters, which formed part of the favourite's confiscated papers. She had good reason to feel concerned. Richelieu granted her request with great courtesy but not without letting her know that it had been no easy matter to sort out her epistles from the great pile of female correspondence which they had found.

After the Conspiracy

By August 28th Perpignan, which the French with their lace collars and their chivalrous ceremonies had subjected to such a long siege, was finally starved into submission. When the French forces marched into the town on September 9th they found enough war materials and ammunition to equip twenty thousand men. The fortress of Salces fell on September 15th. The Lyons execution took place in the interval between these two great successes. On September 12th, the day of the execution, Richelieu issued the following communiqué:

"Perpignan is in the King's hands. Monsieur le Grand and M. de Thou are in the other world. These are two proofs that God is well disposed towards our State and towards our King, who are one and the same." One and the same!

Cardinal Mazarin was asked to deal with the Duke of Bouillon. The Duke was quite shattered by the fate of the two youths, and the Neapolitan exploited this fact by offering him a full pardon in return for his principality. Bouillon accepted.

And so Sedan passed to France. On September 29th the Duchess of Bouillon left the town and the King's troops marched in. Orders were then given for Bouillon's immediate release. Subsequently, on March 10, 1651, although he did not restore Sedan to him, Mazarin did bestow the County of Evreux and the Duchies of Château-Thierry and Albret on Bouillon in compensation for his loss.

As for Orléans, he had already accepted the conditions laid down in the following declaration in August:

"We, Gaston, a son of France, having furnished the King with detailed information regarding the crime in which M. Cinq-Mars, Grand Ecuyer de France, persuaded us to participate by his persistent and skilful advocacy and having thrown ourselves on the King's mercy, declare that we will consider ourselves to have been well treated and consequently under an obligation to His Majesty if he should deign to permit us to live within his kingdom as a private individual without a governorship, without a company of gendarmes of Chevau-légers and without accepting offices or administrative functions of any kind, irrespective of the circumstances in which these may be offered to us."

This final provision was incorporated by Richelieu and Mazarin as a safeguard in case there should be a regency.

As early as August 15th Gaston informed his sister, the Duchess of Savoy, that the King had been pleased to permit him to return to France and to enjoy all previous privileges including his appanage. This he owed to the monarch's magnanimity and to the influence exercised on his behalf by the Cardinal.

Shortly before his own death Louis XIII was to rescind all the restrictions embodied in the declaration. The "sacred blood" was still inviolable.

CHAPTER XVII

RICHELIEU'S DEATH

Richelieu had gained little or nothing from the rigour with which he had proceeded against the conspirators. His fear of falling out of favour with the King never left him and the understanding which had once existed between him and the monarch was never really re-established. Following his beheading, the favourite's hold on the King was evidently stronger than ever.

On October 17, 1642, after a nine-day journey down the Seine, Richelieu landed in Paris in the harbour of St Paul and took up residence in his *palais*. He was obsessed with the idea that Cinq-Mars' friends, Madame Tilladet, Des Essarts and La Salle, a number of Captains of the Guards and also a Lieutenant of the Musketeers, a certain Tréville, had remained in close contact with the King and were still influencing him. No, on this occasion the King had not forgiven his First Minister. Somewhere in the labyrinth of Louis' psyche the Cardinal had touched on a spot which was not accessible to rational argument, while the King for his part had both transcended himself and transgressed against himself by this action, which he had undertaken for reasons of State; for the sake of the Crown he had mercilessly prosecuted the man whom he had loved and still loved. And he was unable to explain, even to himself, the secret motivations which had prompted him to do so. He never really freed himself from this youth even though, at the time fixed for the execution, he had said in an attempt to assert his authority and give an appearance of unconcern: "I would like to see the kind of face the 'Grand Ecuyer' is making now."

And so, not in words and not in deeds but silently, he released the Cardinal, released him as it were from the inner bond that had united them for so long.

Richelieu made it difficult for the King, especially in the closing months of his life, to come to more easy terms with him. He subjected Louis to an avalanche of requests which were all directed against the surviving members of Cinq-Mars' circle. The dead man's aged mother was driven from her castle, which was then destroyed; its towers were razed and its forests, which had once belonged to the loyal Marshal d'Effiat, were cut down to the height of a man's hip or, in the popular parlance of the day, to the "height of infamy". Richelieu also insisted that Abbé d'Effiat, Henri's brother, an abbot, be deprived of his benefices and the above-mentioned young men of the Cinq-Mars party be driven from the Court. The Cardinal threatened —this was for the last time—to resign unless the following conditions were met: the King must have no favourite save the State, he must instantly punish all slanderers, pass no resolution without first consulting his ministers and banish all political agitators and detractors. These requirements were followed by the sentence: "Great powers must occasionally reveal a stern countenance and set harsh examples."

Richelieu also brought pressure to bear on his master by letting him know that he was in possession of certain secrets which Cinq-Mars had revealed out of fear of torture and of which no use had as yet been made. Louis was told that special measures had had to be taken to prevent the condemned man from shouting these secrets to the crowd from the scaffold, for Cinq-Mars had threatened to spare no one if he was tortured.

Chavigny had the extremely unpleasant task of informing his sovereign of all this and then of advising the Cardinal of Louis' reaction. The Secretary of State pressed his suit in an unseemly manner, with the inevitable result that the King lost patience with him. Louis knew that every step he took, every word he spoke, every expression on his face was relayed back to the Cardinal, and when Chavigny began to insist that certain persons must be instantly dismissed from his entourage he retorted: "Is it fitting that the Cardinal should take a greater interest in those people who are close to me than I take in his intimates?"

To this Chavigny replied: "If His Eminence were to find within his circle any person with whom Your Majesty was displeased he would no longer look at him."

Louis then exploded angrily.

"In that case he would no longer look at you, for I find you intolerable," he said and turned his back. Chavigny was utterly deflated.

Following such vexations the King would often set off on a hunting trip from which he usually returned refreshed.

But what was the real issue here? Quite apart from the many imponderables arising out of a spent relationship between two human beings there was the fact that the King himself was tired of war and now inclined towards peace; the burden of his deeds was beginning to tell.

On November 5th or 6th Richelieu had written to Chavigny:

"Without knowing the exact circumstances certain people are beginning to suspect that I am on bad terms with the King. Not only could there be nothing less likely to restore me to health than the impression produced by such suspicions but this rumour is also prejudicial to the interests of the King (i.e. the State)."

On November 13th, by which time the monarch had still not replied to the detailed memorandum of October 27th, Richelieu decided to make a conciliatory move. He wrote:

"His Majesty is humbly requested to note his wishes in the margin of this memorandum. We implore him to inform us of the conditions under which he would be prepared to make peace. If the Spanish were then foolish enough to reject these conditions and the war were to continue, this would be enough to show that the injustice of their cause is the real obstacle to peace and not the attitude adopted by the Cardinal, who will always religiously observe His Majesty's wishes."

About November 20th the King added his comments to the *aide-mémoire*.

After assuring the Cardinal of his friendship and refusing to accept his resignation, he agreed that the State itself should be his only favourite and undertook to purge the Court of undesirable elements from time to time. He then outlined his conditions for a peace settlement:

"As far as peace is concerned, I would be exposing myself to the ridicule of the whole world and enabling my enemies to embroil me in wars whenever they saw fit if I failed to exact from them the cost of the campaign which they have forced me to conduct. There can be no question of our restoring Lorraine or of giving up Arras, Hesdin, Bapaume, Perpigan, Roussillon, Breisach and the strongholds in Alsace.... The acquisition of Pinerolo was entirely legitimate and I would never consider ceding it. The restitution of my nephew, the Duke of Savoy, is such an obviously just measure that I would never accept a peace settlement until it had been effected.

"Provided these conditions are fulfilled I will gladly authorize you to employ all your resources in bringing about a general peace, which, however, must not be allowed to separate me from my allies."

What more could Richelieu have asked for? These were the ideas he himself had always held.

The King also fulfilled his promise in Saint-Germain by ordering Tréville, Tilladet, La Salle and Des Essarts to leave the Court. Although he thanked them for their services and guaranteed them their pensions, by banishing them he again "trod his own inclinations underfoot."

We have already seen that, following his return from Lyons, Richelieu had taken up residence in his Paris *palais*. On October 26th he travelled to Rueil and was visited there by the Queen on October 30th. On November 4th he returned to the *palais* to put his house in order before making his "final move". On November 28th he suffered a severe attack of fever and complained of violent pains in the side. These soon became intolerable. Marshals Brézé and de la Meilleraye and the Duchess of Aiguillon spent the night with the dying man. It was then Monday, December 2nd. Blood-letting afforded temporary relief but it was not long before Richelieu had an attack of asphyxia and began to cough up blood. The only remedy known to Bouvard and his colleagues was phlebotomy.

At two in the afternoon the King arrived from Saint-Germain accompanied by the Captain of his Guards.

"Sire," said Richelieu, "this is my last farewell; in taking leave of Your Majesty I draw comfort from the fact that the kingdom has reached a peak of glory and renown such as it has never known before; your enemies have all been dispersed and humbled. The only thing I would request from Your Majesty in return for my endeavours and services is that you should continue to extend your goodwill to my nephews and other kin. I for my part shall give my blessing to my relatives only on condition that they undertake never to fail in the loyalty and allegiance which they have sworn and will always owe to Your Majesty."

The King promised all that was asked of him. Then everybody was required to leave the room and Louis spoke alone with his First Servant. Richelieu is said to have advised him to retain the Secretaries of State (including Chavigny) and especially De Noyers. He then designated Cardinal Mazarin as the man most worthy to succeed him. The King agreed. Before leaving he fed the exhausted Cardinal with two egg yolks. While making his way from the *palais* Louis, who had been joined by the Duke of Montbazon, the Count d'Harcourt, Henri de Lorraine, and Marshals de la Force, Brézé and la Meilleraye, was seen looking at pictures and laughing out loud. He did not return to Saint-Germain but went to the Louvre to wait for the Cardinal's illness to take its course.

When Louis had left him Richelieu sent for his doctors and asked: "How long?" When told "Within twenty-four hours you will either be cured or be dead" he replied: "Well spoken."

At one in the morning he confessed and received extreme unction. The statements which he is alleged to have made on that occasion have been repeated time and again. None of them has been authenticated.

On Wednesday, December 3rd, the King again appeared at the Cardinal's deathbed. He spent a whole hour alone with him and this time, when he left him, he appeared more disturbed than the members of his retinue.

At ten in the morning of December 4th the Cardinal received a courtesy visit from La Rivière, who called on Orléans' behalf. He was then alone for a moment with the person who had been closest to him, his niece the Duchess of Aiguillon. He said to her: "Remember that I loved you more than all the others; you have a good heart. It would not be right for you to have to see me die; I must ask you to leave now."

She withdrew and Father Léon granted him absolution once again. Richelieu's waxen hands began to tug at the sheets, suddenly his eyes grew glassy, he sighed, a burning taper was held before his lips but did not flicker.

EPILOGUE

Richelieu always tried to base his foreign-policy aims on arguments drawn from international law. The many jurists and historical researchers who worked for him provided endless material with which to justify his claims. The allegation that this was primarily a question of "salving his conscience" is altogether too subjective an interpretation. The crucial factor was his realization that positions which are acquired by force can only be maintained if they are based on an arguable and enduring legal premise and both the foreign-policy aim and its legal justification are in accord with the principle of moderation, which alone can ensure that new international orders established by the conclusion of peace treaties are afforded some degree of durability.

Nowhere was the Cardinal's flexibility seen to better advantage than in the great variety of projects which he evolved for purposes of instituting general negotiations in order to end the war and establish a new balance of power in Europe, one which would guarantee French security and authority. Richelieu's plans for the future territorial division of Europe were worked out down to the smallest detail. In drafting his "general instructions" his political insight and experience prompted him to urge moderation. Punishment, that dire element in the justice of the conqueror, which he used throughout his life in his dealings with individuals, disappeared from his armoury when he found himself confronted—in a sphere which transcended good and evil—with collectives and the elements which fused them into a whole, i.e. the State. This held good despite all the rhetorical effects produced in his public statements by the use of such concepts as "prestige", "affront" and "atonement."

Richelieu always remained the great pragmatist, open to every opportunity. This statesman, with his phenomenal will-power and his stupendous achievements, was neither the ice-cold representative of a doctrine based exclusively on "reasons of State" and belonging more properly to the domain of scholars than to the world of action, nor was he the executor of a rigid program of annexation. We must not try to identify him with any of the political theories which were evolved in his time; when he did advance theorems in his aphoristic manner he always had some immediate practical purpose in view. He was a very great judge not only of political reality but also of human beings and their propensity for automatism. His intellectual roots were in the sixteenth century and its theological categories; time and again he had recourse to the old concept of the *corpus christianum*, even if he did exploit its dissensions and, like Francis I before him, called non-European powers into the European theatre of war. Until the very end of his life the security of France remained Richelieu's principal concern. The assertion that in his role of "conqueror" he himself jeopardized this security by what his contemporaries decried as "the boundlessness" of his enterprises loses much of its validity when we consider that ever since the wars of religion France had been in any case ceaselessly threatened by both internal and external enemies. It was only in the early 1640s that this immediate threat began to recede.

The Cardinal's system of alliances was never entirely stable; there were always unreliable elements and time and again he was obliged to forge new bonds with every one of his allies. The most difficult problem of all was posed by the relationship with the Swedes, who had been regarded as the protectors of the German Protestants ever since 1631. This relationship was gravely threatened when Richelieu concluded his treaty with the members of the Heilbronn League. Oxenstierna was then on the verge of breaking with France. In 1635 the tension was relieved to some extent by the conclusion of the Treaty of Compiègne, which may be regarded as a more or less personal agreement between the Swedish Chancellor and Richelieu. But by then it was too late to establish a relationship based on mutual trust. The reservations which the Swedes always had *vis-à-vis* Paris are clearly expressed in Grotius' reports. In the mid-1630s, after the French declaration of war, Oxenstierna was especially irritated when Richelieu tried to keep the Franco–Spanish war within set limits and to defer open hostilities with the Emperor for as long as possible, which meant of course that the main burden of the German campaigns fell on the Swedes. It was only after 1637, when Ferdinand II had died and was succeeded by his son Ferdinand III, that this situation began to change. But even in the following year it proved impossible to reach a binding agreement in Wismar. The French demanded ratification of their proposals and refused to pay the subsidies until they received it; the Swedes, on the other hand, pressed for French intervention against the Emperor. But the talks were never completely broken off and eventually an interim agreement was concluded (primarily to prevent the enemy from realizing that no treaty existed between the two irresolute partners) whereby Sweden undertook to make no peace with Ferdinand for a period of six months while France agreed to advance part of the subsidies.

It was thanks to the French diplomat d'Avaux that Paris and Stockholm finally reached a settlement, whose terms are already known to us and which lost Sweden a lot of confidence among the Protestants.

The first part of the Thirty Years War, the period between the Battle of the White Hill and the Battle of Nördlingen, was of great consequence for the future development of international affairs; the conditions which arose between 1618 and 1634 determined the course of events right down to the late eighteenth century but above all they determined the outcome of the Peace of Westphalia which, although it did not concern itself with either Spain or Eastern Europe, cast the central core of the European continent in a mould which was to remain intact until shortly before our own time. It was Cardinal Richelieu who, beyond the grave, fashioned this peace. Despite France's Protestant alliances, Calvinism, which had taken root in so many political systems, was halted everywhere by the Thirty Years War with the single exception of Holland; as for the Liberties of the Estates, they were crushed in large areas of Europe by the concentrated power of absolutism; Spain affords the clearest example of this process. Those territories in which the ancient Liberties were preserved promptly disintegrated into countless numbers of principalities, and in every one of these independent petty States the contemporary trend of absolutism then proceeded to assert itself despite repeated appeals on the part of the Estates to their prescriptive rights. A circumstance which has been singled out for attention time and again, especially by nineteenth-century historians, is the fact that, irrespective of whether it was to their advantage to do so, the German Princes all joined in censuring their Hapsburg Emperor in Vienna for maintaining close ties with Spain. Faced with a similar situation, the French "politicians" would have considered such a constellation a piece of good fortune, a strategic advantage. As it happens, however, in the Thirty Years War it was the German Emperor who was able to force his adversary to fight a war on two fronts or, to be more precise, who occupied all the initial positions which would have enabled him to encircle the French, who were then his principal adversary. In the subsequent course of her history Germany herself was to be defeated twice as a result of having to fight a war on two fronts.

It was due primarily to the statesmanship of the French, to their skilful manipulation of German discord, that from the sixteenth to the early nineteenth century the Germans were quite unable to move towards a confederacy or even to establish a Pan-German internal policy.

From 1640–1 onwards Ferdinand III was prepared to negotiate with both Sweden and France simultaneously at a universal peace congress. Lützow, the Imperial representative in Hamburg, was authorized to agree to a venue for the congress with his Swedish counterpart, Salvius. The French plenipotentiary, however, insisted that the Spanish must also be represented. But despite both French and Imperial resistance a preliminary agreement was concluded in Hamburg between December 15 and 25, 1641, which appeared to have opened the way for universal negotiations. Denmark again offered her services as mediator. Of the belligerent nations it was Sweden who pressed most actively for the conclusion of the preliminary agreement.

Richelieu did not live to see the peace; it was concluded in Münster and Osnabrück six years after his death. But it was from the Cardinal that it derived its whole import; the event which finally took place in Westphalia, bringing relief to Germans, Swedes and Italians alike and creating in Central Europe an empire of many capitals, a richly orchestrated culture, owed many of its essential qualities to Richelieu's thinking and planning, although it was actually put into effect by his successor, Jules Mazarin.

Richelieu had first encountered Mazarin—Giulio Mazarini, as he then was —in Lyons at the time of the War of the Mantuan Succession, when the young papal delegate was engaged on a mission to bring peace to Piedmont and Savoy. Richelieu said very little; he let the Italian do the talking and observed him closely. Even at this first meeting he realized that he was dealing with a quite remarkable negotiator. As for Mazarin, he was immediately won over by the Cardinal's personality and remained so from that day on. It was Richelieu who discovered and promoted Mazarin; this was one of the rare instances of a person in power being able to look beyond himself and seek and find a successor, win his services for his nation's cause, initiate him in good time into the essential affairs of the State and convince the King of his suitability.

Mazarin, who had been trained by the Jesuits, concluded the Turin agreement between France and Savoy in 1632. He was then appointed papal legate to Avignon and from 1634 to 1636 papal nuncio to France. When he realized that with French help he could receive his Cardinal's hat (he did so in 1641) he entered Louis XIII's service and acquired French nationality in 1639. In 1640, it will be remembered, Richelieu again employed him in Savoy, where he acted as peace-maker between the regent Christine and her two brothers-in-law.

Mazarin always regarded himself as Richelieu's executor. One portion of this inheritance, which set in immediately after the death of Louis XIII, that is, during Louis XIV's minority and Anne of Austria's regency, was the struggle against the great nobles, which erupted into open opposition for the last time in the Fronde, when the nobles turned against the Crown, refusing to recognize Louis XIII's will and threatening to destroy all that Richelieu had achieved. Mazarin was forced to flee the country for a time. Eventually, however, the monarchic principle, which had been greatly strengthened in the course of the preceding decades, carried the day.

Where foreign policy was concerned Mazarin implemented Richelieu's plans with dexterity and assurance. If we consider Richelieu's *Political Testament* in the light of his instructions for a general peace, which he constantly reworked and in which he made allowance for every conceivable exigency, then it seems clear that this fragmentary and much disputed but highly perceptive work was in fact his masterpiece, a compendium of the art of politics, typically French in its approach, which will always remain a significant and exemplary book.

Three years after the Cardinal's death a decisive battle was finally fought, the battle of Rocroi, where the "Great Condé", Richelieu's nephew and Commander of the French army, was victorious. Spain never recovered from this defeat, although hostilities were constantly renewed over a considerable period; in fact, between 1648 and 1815 they seldom ceased. Towards the end of his life Louis XIV, in whom French absolutism came to its apogee, had to contend with a number of extremely grave crises. For a long time to come the principal enemy for the French in these never-ending wars on the Continent of Europe were the English, who have so often emerged from periods weakness to achieve their greatest successes and, even in times of defeat, have always stood firm on certain fixed points of foreign policy. It was a long time before England was superseded by Germany as France's principal enemy.

BIBLIOGRAPHY

CHAPTER I: LORRAINE

Batiffol, Louis: *La duchesse de Chevreuse*, Paris, 1913.

Bernard, Jacques: *Recueil des traitez de paix, de trêve, de neutralité, de suspension d'armes, de confédération, d'alliance de commerce, de garantie et d'autres actes publics etc.*, Amsterdam, 1700.

Goulas, Nicolas: *Mémoires de Nicolas Goulas, gentilhomme ordinaire de la chambre du Duc d'Orléans*, edited by Charles Constant, Paris, 1879.

Laugel, Auguste: *Henry de Rohan, son rôle politique et militaire sous Louis XIII (1579–1638)*, Paris, 1889.

Rohan: *Mémoires du Duc de Rohan sur les choses advenues en France depuis la mort de Henry le Grand, jusques à la paix faite avec les Réformez au mois de juin 1629*, no place, 1646.

Stählin, Karl: *Geschichte Elsass-Lothringens*, Munich–Berlin, 1920.

Wandruszka, Adam: *Das Haus Habsburg*, Stuttgart, 1956.

CHAPTER II: BEFORE THE DECLARATION OF WAR

d'Aumale, Duc: *Histoire des Princes de Condé*, Paris, 1886.

Droysen (Jun.), Gustav: *Bernhard von Weimar*, Leipzig, 1885.

——— *Gustav Adolf*, Leipzig, 1869–70.

Feuquières: *Lettres et négociations du Marquis de Feuquières*, Amsterdam, 1753.

Oxenstierna: *Rikskanslern Axel Oxenstiernas Skrifter och Brevväxling*.

Röse, Bernhard: *Herzog Bernhard der Grosse von Sachsen-Weimar*, 2 vols., Weimar, 1828–9.

Saint-Évremond: *Oeuvres mêlées de Mr. de Saint-Évremond*, Vol. 2: "Dissertation sur le mot, 'vaste'," Cologne, 1708.

CHAPTER III: FRANCE'S ENTRY INTO THE WAR

Acta Pacis Westphalicae, Series I Instruktionen, Vol. 1: "Frankreich–Schweden–Kaiser", adapted by F. Dickmann, K. Goronzy, E. Schieche, H. Wagner and E. M. Wermter, Münster (Westf.), 1962.

Capefigue, M.: *Richelieu, Mazarin, la Fronde et le régne de Louis XIV*, 6 vols., Paris, 1835.

"Succinte Narration", in: *Testament politique du Cardinal de Richelieu*, edited by Louis André, Paris, 1947.

Wandruszka, Adam: *Reichspatriotismus und Reichspolitik zur Zeit des Prager Friedens von 1635*, Graz, Cologne, 1955.

CHAPTER IV: SPAIN

Anonymous: *L'Espagne aux temps de Philippe II*, Paris, 1966

Ballesteros y Beretta, Antonio: *Síntesis de Historia de España*, Madrid, 1950.

Balzac: *Les lettres diverses de Monsieur de Balzac*, Paris, 1663.

Bataillon, Marcel: *Erasme en Espagne*, Paris, 1937.

Behn, Irene: *Spanische Mystik*, Düsseldorf, 1957.

Berber, F.: "Das Problem des gerechten Krieges im Völkerrecht", in: *Studien zur Auslandskunde (Politische Wissenschaft*, Vol. 1, Issue II), Berlin, undated.

Brenan, Gerald: *The Literature of the Spanish People*, Cambridge, 1951.

Burckhardt, C. J.: "Karl V.", zum 400. Todestag des letzten europäischen Kaisers", *Neue Zürcher Zeitung*, 21.9.1958.

Castro, Americo: *Spanien, Vision und Wirklichkeit*, Cologne, 1957.

Coleccion de documentos inéditos para la historia de España, Madrid, 1842–5.

Curtius, Ernst Robert: *George, Hofmannsthal und Calderón. Kritische Essays zur europäischen Literatur*, Bern, 1954.

Defourneaux, Marcellin: *La vie quotidienne en Espagne au siècle d'or*, Paris, 1965.

Diez del Corral, Luis: *Der Raub der Europa*, Munich, 1959

Essen, Léon van der: *Alexandre Farnese. Prince de Parme, Gouverneur Général des Pays-Bas (1545–92)*, Brussels, 1933–7.

Essen, Alfred van der: *Le Cardinal-Infant et la politique européenne de l'Espagne (1609–41)*, Brussels, 1944.

Gracián, Baltasar: *The Art of Worldly Wisdom.*

Guiraud, Jean: *Histoire de l'inquisition au moyen-âge*, 2 vols, Paris, 1935–8.

Hartlaub, F.: *Don Juan d'Austria und die Schlacht bei Lepanto*, Berlin, 1940.

Henrard, Paul: *Marie de Médicis dans les Pays-Bas, 1631–8*, Brussels, 1876.

Huizinga, Jan: *Erasmus*, London, 1924.

Kamem, Henri: *Histoire de l'Inquisition espagnole*, Paris, 1965.

Konetzke, Richard: *Die Entstehung des spanischen Weltreiches*, Munich, 1943.

Lucas-Dubreton, J.: *Philippe II*, Paris, 1965.

Marañón, Gregorio: *Antonio Pérez*, 2 vols, Madrid, 1944.

—— *Olivares*, Munich, 1949, Preface by Ludwig Pfandl.

Mattingly, Garrett: *The Defeat of the Spanish Armada*, London, 1959.

Menéndez y Pelayo, Marcelino: *Los heterodoxos españoles*, 3 vols, Madrid, 1880–1.

Mignet: *Antonio Pérez et Philippe II*, Paris, 1865.

Pfandl, Ludwig: *Geschichte der spanischen Nationalliteratur in ihrer Blütezeit*, Freiburg i. Br., 1929.

—— *Karl II. Das Ende der spanischen Machtstellung in Europa*, Munich, 1940.

—— *Philipp II*, Munich, 1938.

Pidal, Marquis de: *Philippe II, Antonio Pérez et le royaume d'Aragon*, 2 vols., trans. from the Spanish, Paris, 1867.

Sainte-Beuve, Charles-Augustin: *Histoire de Port-Royal*, Paris, 1908.

"Succinte Narration", in: *Testament politique du Cardinal de Richelieu*, edited by Louis André, Paris, 1947.

Toerne, P. O.: *Don Juan d'Austria et les projets de conquête de l'Angleterre, 1568–78*, 2 vols., Helsingfors-Abö, 1915–28.

Tyler, Royall: *The Emperor Charles the Fifth*, London, 1956.

Vossler, Karl: *Calderón*, Munich, Berlin, 1940.

—— *Lope de Vega und sein Zeitalter*, Munich, 1932.

Williamson, J. A.: *The Age of Drake*, London, 1938.

CHAPTER V: DECLARATION OF WAR ON SPAIN

d'Avenel, Vicomte G.: *Richelieu et la monarchie absolue depuis les origines jusqu'à la Révolution*, Paris, 1887.

Baraude, Henri: "López", in *Revue Mondiale*, Paris, 1933.

Barthélemy de Bainville, Charles: *Les vérités françaises opposées aux calomnies espagnoles*, no place or date.

Clamageran, J.-J.: *Histoire de l'impôt en France*, 3 vols., Paris, 1867–76.

Groulart, Claude: "Mémoires de Claude Groulart ou voyages par lui faits en cour 1588–1606", in: *Nouvelle collection des mémoires . . .*, par Michaud et Poujoulat, Paris, 1836–9.

Hanotaux, Gabriel et le Duc de La Force: *Histoire du Cardinal de Richelieu*, 6 vols., Paris, 1893–1947.

Hauser, Henri: *La pensée et l'action économique du Cardinal de Richelieu*, Paris, 1944.

La Force, Jacques Nompar de Caumont, duc de: *Mémoires authentiques de Jacques Nompar de Caumont, duc de La Force*, Paris, 1843.

Mariéjol, J. H.: "Henri IV et Louis XIII", in Ernest Lavisse: *Histoire de France depuis les origines jusqu'à la Révolution*, Vol. 6, Part 2. Paris, 1903–1911.

Mercure François, Vol. XX.

Pagès, Georges G.: *La monarchie d'ancien régime en France*, Paris, 1932.

Ranum, Orest A.: *Richelieu and the councillors of Louis XIII*, Oxford, 1937.

Relations de ce qui s'est passé en l'Assemblée du Thiers État de France en 1576, published 1576.

Sully: *Mémoires des Sages et royalles Oeconomies d'Estat, domestiques, politiques et militaires de Henry le Grand . . .*, Amsterdam, 1638.

Thou, J. A. de: *Histoire universelle depuis 1543 jusqu'en 1607*, London (Paris), 1734.

CHAPTER VI: FOLLOWING THE DECLARATION OF WAR

Blet, Henri: *La Colonisation française*, Paris, 1946.

Boiteux, L. A.: *Richelieu—grand-maître de la navigation et du commerce de France*, Paris, 1955.

Bonnassieux, Pierre: *Les Grandes Compagnies de Commerce*, Paris, 1892.

BIBLIOGRAPHY

Graham, Gerald S: *Empire of the North Atlantic. The maritime struggle for North America*, Toronto, 1950.
Guicciardini, Francesco: *Storia d'Italia*, 20 vols., Venice, 1567; Basel, 1574.
Hardy, Georges: *Histoire de la Colonisation française*, Paris, 1938.
Montchrestien, Antoine de: *Traité de l'oeconomie politique, dédié au roy et à la reyne-mère du roy*, Rouen, 1615.

CHAPTER VII: FRANCE GAINS BERNHARD OF
SAXE-WEIMAR

Aubéry, Antoine: *Mémoires pour servir à l'histoire du Cardinal Duc de Richelieu*, Paris, 1660.
Bernard, Jacques: *Recueil des traitez de paix, de trêve, de neutralité, de suspension d'armes, de confédération, d'alliance de commerce, de garantie et d'autres actes publics etc.*, Amsterdam, 1700.
Duval, François, marquis de Fontenay-Mareuil: *Mémoires 1609–47*, Paris, 1886.
Feuquières: *Lettres et négociations du marquis de Feuquières*, Amsterdam, 1753.
Goulas, Nicolas: *Mémoires de Nicolas Goulas, gentilhomme ordinaire de la chambre du Duc d'Orléans*, edited by Charles Constant, Paris, 1879.
Griffet, le Père Henri: *Histoire du Règne de Louis XIII, Roi de France et de Navarre*, 3 vols., Paris, 1758.
La Force, Duc de: *Histoire et portraits.—Les Deux Courriers La Casaque Écarlate*, Paris, 1937–9.
La Force: *Mémoires authentiques de Jacques Nompar de Caumont, duc de La Force*, Paris, 1843.
Lehrkamp, Helmut: *Jan von Werth*, Cologne, 1962.
Lepré-Balin: *La vie du Rév. Père Joseph*, unpublished study.
Montglat: *Mémoires de Montglat*, in *Collection des Mémoires relatives à l'histoire de France*, by Petitot, 2nd Series, Vol. XLIX, Paris, 1825.
Montrésor: *Mémoires de Monsieur de Montrésor*, Cologne, 1663–5.
Oxenstierna: *Rikskansleren Axel Oxenstiernas Skrifter och Brevväxling*, Vol. 7, 1888.
Röse, Bernhard: *Herzog Bernhard der Grosse von Sachsen-Weimar*, Weimar, 1828–9.
Tallemant des Réaux, Gédéon: *Les Historiettes*, 8 vols., Paris, 1932–4.
Vaunois, Louis: *Vie de Louis XIII*, Paris, 1944.

CHAPTER VIII: THE ITALIAN FRONT

Feller, Richard: *Geschichte Berns*, Bern, 1953.
Pieth, Friedrich: *Die Feldzüge des Herzogs von Rohan im Veltlin und Graubünden*, Chur, 1935.
Sprecher, J. A.: *Päpstliche Instructionen betreffend Veltlin aus der Zeit Gregors XV*, Zürich, 1858.

CHAPTER IX: THE RHINE FRONT

Acta Pacis Westphalicae, Series I Instruktionen, Vol. I: "Frankreich–Schweden–Kaiser", edited by F. Dickmann *et al*, Münster (Westf.), 1962.

Dickmann, Fritz: *Der Westfälische Friede*, Münster, 1959.

Erlach, Albert: *Mémoires historiques concernant M. le Général d'Erlach*, Yverdon, 1784.

Hauser, Henri: *La Prépondérance Espagnole 1559–1660*, Paris, 1933.

Hugonis Grotii epistolae, No. 1047, Amsterdam, 1687.

Mommsen, Wilhelm: *Richelieu, Elsass und Lothringen*, Berlin, 1922.

Röse, Bernhard: *Herzog Bernhard der Grosse von Sachsen-Weimar*, Weimar, 1828–9.

CHAPTER X: COURT INTRIGUES

Bondois, P.: "L'affaire du Val-de-Grâce en 1637," in *Bibliothèque de l'École de Chartres*, 1922.

Brantôme, Pierre de Bourdeille, Sieur de: *Oeuvres complètes de Pierre de Bourdeille* . . . edited by L. Lalaune., 11 vols. Paris, 1864–82,

Dethan, G.: *Gaston d'Orléans, Conspirateur et Prince charmant*, Paris, 1959.

Griffet, le Père Henri: *Histoire du Règne de Louis XIII, Roi de France et de Navarre*, 3 vols., Paris, 1758.

Huxley, Aldous: *The Devils of London*, London, ——.

Montrésor: *Mémoires de Monsieur de Montrésor*, Cologne, 1663–5.

Motteville, Françoise Bertault, dame de Langlois: *Mémoires pour servir à l'histoire d'Autriche, épouse de Louis XIII, roi de France*, Amsterdam, 1783.

Perrin, F. T.: *Les libertins en France au XVIIᵉ siècle*, Paris, 1899.

CHAPTER XI: POPULAR REVOLTS

Albertini, R. von: *Das politische Denken in Frankreich zur Zeit Richelieus*, Marburg, 1951.

d'Avenel, Vicomte G.: *Histoire économique de la propriété des salaires*, Paris, 1913.

—— *Richelieu et la monarchie absolue*, Paris, 1890.

Bigot de Monville: *Mémoires du Président Bigot de Monville sur la Sédition des Nu-pieds et l'interdiction du parlement de Normandie en 1639*, Rouen, 1876.

Cahiers des États de Normandie sous les règnes de Louis XIII et Louis XIV, collected and annotated by Ch. de Robillard de Beaurepaire, Rouen, 1876–8.

Clamageran, J.-J.: *Histoire de l'impôt en France*, 3 vols. Paris, 1867–76.

Floquet, A.: *Histoire du parlement de Normandie*, Rouen, 1841.

Göhring, Martin: *Die Ämterkäuflichkeit im ancient régime*, Berlin, 1938.

Hugonis Grotii epistolae, Amsterdam, 1687, Nos. 1249, 1264, 1303, 1310, 1328, 1335.

Marion, Marcel: *Histoire financière de la France depuis 1715*, 4 vols., Paris, 1923–5.

Massiou, D.: *Histoire politique, civile et religieuse de la Saintonge et de l'Aunis depuis les premiers temps historiques jusqu'à nos jours*, Paris, 1836–1838.

Mercure François, Vol. XXIII.

Montglat: *Mémoires de Montglat*, Vol. I, in *Collection des Mémoires relatives à l'histoire de France*, by Petitot, 2nd series, Vol. XLIX, Paris, 1825.

Mousnier, Roland: *Lettres et mémoires adressés au Chancelier Séguier (1633–49)*, collected and published by Roland Mousnier, Paris, 1964.

Porchnev, Boris: *Les Soulèvements populaires en France de 1623 à 1648*, Paris, 1963.

Rambaud, B.: *La question des fermiers généraux en France et à l'étranger*, Paris, 1913.

Séguier: *Diaire ou journal de voyage du chancelier Séguier en Normandie, après la sédition des Nu-pieds (1639–40)*, edited by A. Floquet, Rouen, 1842.

Tallemant des Réaux, Gédéon: *Les Historiettes*, 8 vols., Paris, 1932–34.

CHAPTER XII: THE GENERAL SITUATION

Barrès, Maurice: *Les Bastions de l'Est*, Paris, 1909.

Beauchamp, Comte de: *Louis XIII d'après sa correspondance avec le Cardinal de Richelieu*, Paris, 1902.

Dufour, Auguste and François Rabut: *Le Père Monod et le Cardinal de Richelieu*, Chambéry, 1878.

Lalevée, Victor: "La Lorraine héroique: La Mothe, ville martyre", in *Le Pays Lorrain—Journal de la Société d'archéologie lorraine*, 46th year, No. 2, Nancy, 1965.

Particelle (Particelli), Sieur d'Émery: *Diverses relations*, no origin, 1632.

CHAPTER XIII: OPPOSITION AT COURT

d'Astarac Fontrailles, Louis: *Mémoires*, Cologne, 1663.

Aubéry, Antoine: *Mémoires pour servir à l'histoire du Cardinal Duc de Richelieu*, Paris, 1660.

Campion, Alexandre de: *Recueil de lettres, qui peuvent servir à l'histoire, et diverses poésies*, Rouen, 1657.

Carras, le Père Ch. Nisard: *Mémoires du Père Carras Ch. Nisard*, Paris, 1861.

Erlander, Philippe: *Cinq-Mars ou la passion et la fatalité*, Paris, 1962.

Fouqueray, le Père Henri (S.J.): *Histoire de la Compagnie de Jésus en France*, Paris, 1910–13.

Gachard, Louis-Prosper: *Histoire politique et diplomatique de P. P. Rubens*, Brussels, 1877.

Griffet, le Père Henri: *Histoire du Règne de Louis XIII, Roi de France et de Navarre*, 3 vols., Paris, 1758.

Pure, Abbé de: *Vie du Maréchal de Gassion*, Paris, 1673.

Rubens, P. P.: *Die Briefe des P. P. Rubens*, translated into German by Otto Zoff, Vienna, 1918.
Turenne: *Mémoires du Vte de Turenne, depuis duc de Bouillon, 1565–86*, Paris, 1901.
Weygand, Maxime: *Turenne*, Munich, 1937.

CHAPTER XIV: CULTURAL ASPECTS

Adam, Antoine: *Histoire de la littérature française au XVIIe siècle*, Paris, 1948.
Batiffol, Louis: *Autour de Richelieu*, Vol. I, Paris, 1937.
Blunt, Anthony: "Art and architecture in France. 1500–1700", in *The Pelican History of Art*, London, 1953.
Boislisle, Arthur Michel de: *Les collections de sculptures du cardinal de Richelieu*, Nogent-le-Rotrou, 1882.
Bonnaffé, Édouard: *Recherches sur les collections de Richelieu*, Paris, 1883.
Bossebœuf, L. A.: *Histoire de Richelieu et des environs*, Tours, 1890.
Bray, René: *La formation de la doctrine classique en France*, Paris, 1927.
Breuil, Jacques du: *Le Théâtre des antiquitez de Paris*, Paris, 1639.
Champier, Victor and G.-Roger Sandoz: *Le Palais Royal (1629–1900)*, Paris, 1900.
Corneille: *Oeuvres complètes de Corneille*, edited by Marty-Lauveaux, Paris, 1862.
Cramail, Alfred: *Le Château de Ruel et ses jardins sous le cardinal de Richelieu et sous la duchesse d'Aiguillon*, Fontainebleau, 1888.
Deloche, Maximin: *La Maison du Cardinal de Richelieu*, Paris, 1912.
Desmarets, J.: *Les Promenades de Richelieu ou les Vertus chrétiennes*, Paris, 1653.
Faret, Nicolas (Ed.): *Recueil de lettres nouvelles*, Paris, 1627.
Franklin, Alfred: *La Sorbonne, ses origines . . .*, Paris, 1875.
Hanotaux, Gabriel and le Duc de La Force: *Histoire du Cardinal de Richelieu*, Vol. VI, Paris, 1947.
Hautecœur, Louis: *Histoire de l'architecture classique en France*, Vol. I, Paris, 1943.
———— *La peinture au Musée du Louvre, Écoles italiennes*, Paris, 1929.
Herland, Louis: *Corneille*, Paris, 1956.
Jamot, Paul: *Les Le Nain*, Paris, 1929.
Lambeau, Lucien: *La place Royale*, Paris, 1906.
Léris, A. de: *Dictionnaire portatif historique et littéraire des Théâtres contenant l'origine des différents théâtres de Paris*, 2nd Ed., Paris, 1763.
Pevsner, Nikolaus: *European Architecture*, London, 1947.
Segrais, Jean Regnault de: *Mémoires*, Amsterdam, 1723.
Simson, Otto von: *La Galerie Médicis de Rubens et les dessins politiques de Richelieu*, Paris, undated.
Valabrègue, Antony, in *Les frères Le Nain*, Paris, 1904.
Vallery-Radot, Jean: *Le dessin français au XVIIe siècle*, Lausanne, 1953.

BIBLIOGRAPHY

Vulson, Sieur de La Colombière: *Les portraits des hommes illustres françois qui sont peints dans la Galerie du Palais Cardinal de Richelieu*, Paris, 1668.
Weisbach, Werner: *Französische Malerei des XVII. Jahrh.*, Berlin, 1932.
―――― "Philippe de Champaigne und Port-Royal", in *Deutsch-Französische Rundschau*, Vol. III, Part 2.
Wissenschaft und Unterricht, Baden, 1951.

CHAPTER XV: FINAL STRESSES

Dahl, Folke, et al.: *Les débuts de la presse française—nouveaux aperçus*, Paris, 1951.
Morgues, Mathieu de: *Lettres de Monsieur le Cardinal de Lyon à Monsieur le Cardinal son frère*, Antwerp, 1643.

CHAPTER XVI: CATALONIA

Assarino, Luca: *Delle revoluzioni di Catalogna*, Bologna, 1645
Capefigue, M.: *Richelieu, Mazarin, la Fronde et le règne de Louis XIV*, 6 vols, Paris, 1835.
Chavagnac: *Mémoires de Gaspard comte de Chavagnac, maréchal de camp*, Amsterdam, 1700.
Du Plessis-Besançon: *Mémoires de Du Plessis-Besançon*, edited by H. Beaucaire, Paris, 1892.
Elliott, John Huxtable: *The Revolt of the Catalans. A study in the Decline of Spain, 1598–1640*, Cambridge, 1963.
Hauser, Henri: *La Prépondérance Espagnole 1559–1660*, Paris, 1933.
Lalevée, Victor: *La Mothe, ville martyre*, in *Le Pays Lorrain—Journal de la Société d'archéologie lorraine*, Nancy, 1965.
La Mothe-Houdancourt: *Défense de Philippe*, Paris, 1649.
Motteville, Françoise Bertault, dame de Langlois: *Mémoires pour servir à l'histoire d'Anne d'Autriche, épouse de Louis XIII, roi de France*, Amsterdam, 1783.
Sourdis, Henri de: *Correspondance de Henri de Sourdis*, edited by Eugène Sue, Paris, 1899.
Vassal-Reig, Charles: *La guerre en Roussillon sous Louis XIII—1635–39*, Paris, 1934.

CHAPTER XVII: RICHELIEU'S DEATH

Griffet, le Père Henri: *Histoire du Règne de Louis XIII, Roi de France et de Navarre*, 3 vols., Paris, 1758.
Montglat: *Mémoires de Montglat*, Vol. I, in *Collection des Mémoires relatives à l'histoire de France*, by Petitot, 2nd series, Vol. I, Paris, 1825.

EPILOGUE

Dickmann, Fritz: *Der Westfälische Friede*, Münster, 1959.

475

INDEX

476

Soler, José, 425
Sötern, Philipp Christoph von, Elector of Treves, 26 f., 70, 310
Soubise, François, Duke of, 35, 343, 367
Sourdis, Henri d'Escoubleau de, Cardinal, Admiral, 266, 268, 280, 312 f., 413, 416 ff.
Spínola, Ambrosio, Marqués de, 101 f., 149
Spínola, Bartolomé, Marqués de, 401
Spínola, Felipe, Marqués de, 412
Streiff, Philipp, 52
Sully, Maximilien I de Béthune, Duke of, 37, 72, 85, 129 ff., 159, 258, 335, 388

Tallemant des Réaux, 259, 301, 328
Talleyrand-Périgord, Charles Maurice de, 388
Tasso, Torquato, 328
Taupadel, Georg Christof von, 59, 199, 217
Tavannes, Gaspard de Saulx, Seigneur de, 120
Terlon, de, 444, 448
Thibault, Jacques de, 265
Thou, Christophe de, 335
Thou, François Auguste de, 332, 335, 356 f., 359, 427, 432, 435, 433 ff., 448 ff., 452 f.
Tilladet, Madame, 455, 458
Tilly, Johann Tserclaes, Count of, 47
Toiras, Jean de Saint-Bonnet de, 102
Toledo, Antonio de, 73
Toledo, García de, 78
Torstensson, Lennart, 235, 351
Trajan, Roman Emperor, 72
Tranquille, Father, 269
Treves, Elector of. See Sötern
Tréville, 433, 444, 455, 458
Tromp, Maarten Harpertszoon, 314
Truchsess, Count of, 201 f., 216
Turenne, Henri de la Tour d'Auvergne, Vicomte de, Duke of

Bouillon, 46, 121, 199, 202, 339, 429

Urban VIII, Pope, 236 ff., 309, 321, 366

Valdés, Fernando, 76
Valemani, Papal Chamberlain, 428
Vallerant le Comte, 373
Valois, Charles of, Duke of Angoulême, 312
Valois, Louis-Emmanuel of, Duke of Angoulême, 114
Vanini, Vanino, 262
Vasconcellos, Miguel de, 423
Vassor, 335
Vaudémont, François de (Francis II of Lorraine), 27
Vaudémont, François-Nicolas, Prince of Lorraine, 28, 30 f.
Vaudémont, Marguerite de. See Orléans
Vaugelas, Claude, 376 f.
Vauvenargues, Luc de Clapiers, Marquis de, 248
Velásquez, Diego de, 95
Vendôme, Alexandre, Duke of, Grand Prior of France, 256, 336
Vendôme, César, Duke of, 336
Verthamont, Intendant of the Treasury, 287 f., 291
Viau, Théophile de, 260 f., 269
Vignerot, Françoise, née Du Plessis-Richelieu, 336
Vignerot, Marie-Madeleine. See Combalet
Vignerot, René de, Sieur de Pont-de-Courlay, 336
Vignolles, 170
Villafranca, Marqués de, Duke of Fernandina, 404, 419
Villanueva, Jerónimo de, Protonotario, 400
Villaplana, Francisca, 414
Vincent de Paul, St, 368

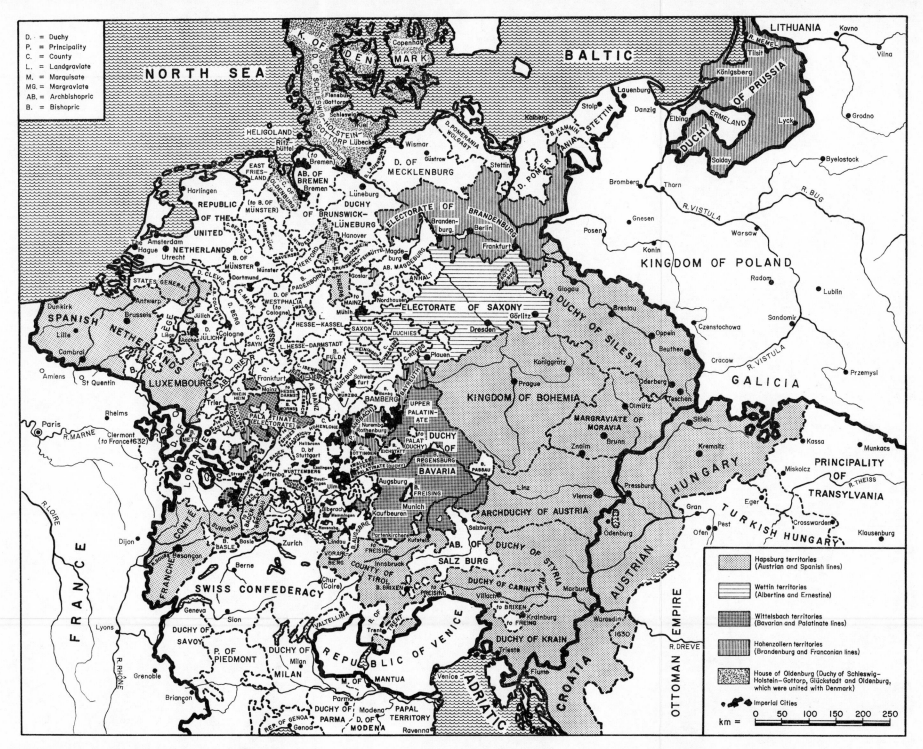

Germany in the seventeenth century (*Note:* Trier = Treves; Spires = Speyer)